BW

D1001245

WITHDRAWN

BRITISH LABOUR, EUROPEAN SOCIALISM
AND THE STRUGGLE FOR PEACE

324.1
N482b

BRITISH LABOUR, EUROPEAN SOCIALISM

AND THE

STRUGGLE FOR PEACE
1889–1914

DOUGLAS J. NEWTON

CLARENDON PRESS · OXFORD

1985

Oxford University Press, Walton Street, Oxford OX2 6DP

Oxford New York Toronto
Delhi Bombay Calcutta Madras Karachi
Kuala Lumpur Singapore Hong Kong Tokyo
Nairobi Dar es Salaam Cape Town
Melbourne Auckland

and associated companies in
Beirut Berlin Ibadan Nicosia

Oxford is a trade mark of Oxford University Press

Published in the United States
by Oxford University Press, New York

© Douglas J. Newton 1985

All rights reserved. No part of this publication may be reproduced,
stored in a retrieval system, or transmitted, in any form or by any means,
electronic, mechanical, photocopying, recording, or otherwise, without
the prior permission of Oxford University Press

British Library Cataloguing in Publication Data
Newton, Douglas J.
British labour, European socialism, and the
struggle for peace, 1889—1914.
1. Labor and laboring classes—Great Britain
—History—19th century   2. Labor and
laboring classes—Great Britain—History—
20th century   3. Great Britain—Foreign
relations—1837—1901   4. Great Britain—
Foreign relations—20th century
I. Title
327.41   DA560
ISBN 0-19-822766-3

Library of Congress Cataloging in Publication Data
Newton, Douglas J.
British labour, European socialism, and the
struggle for peace, 1889—1914.
Bibliography: p.
Includes index.
1. War and socialism—Great Britain—History.
2. War and socialism—Europe—History.   3. Labour
Party (Great Britain)—History.   4. International
Socialist Congress—History.   5. World War, 1914—
1918—Causes.   I. Title.
HX545.N48 1985 324'.1   84-20767
ISBN 0-19-822766-3

Printed in Great Britain by
the Alden Press, Oxford

For David Keir
and his generation

85-3499

Acknowledgements

FEW of us, with any degree of honesty, can ever claim to be 'self-made'. I certainly have a number of major debts which I must acknowledge at the outset. First of all, I must thank my late father and my mother for the gift of education, and for the incentive which their interest and encouragement always provided. Secondly, I must thank the working people of Australia whose taxes paid for my tertiary education and made possible my postgraduate study. Thirdly, I must thank all my teachers at Macquarie University, North Ryde, from whose teaching and research I have profited. Fourthly, I must acknowledge my debt to those historians who have previously written on the history of Europe and European socialism before 1914.

I would like to thank the staff and special collections librarians at a number of institutions for their assistance to me during my research in Britain, including Richard Storey at the Modern Records Centre, University of Warwick, Judith Woods at Transport House, Angela Raspen at the British Library of Political and Economic Science, and the staff of the International Institute for Social History, Amsterdam. I would also like to thank Professor James Joll and Dr Ross McKibbin who kindly found the time to offer me some guidance and encouragement during my stay in Britain. Professor Joll, Professor Alan McBriar, and Dr Kenneth O. Morgan also examined this work as a thesis and made many valuable suggestions that were of assistance to me in transforming it into a book. I am especially grateful to my original thesis supervisor and friend Dr Joy Melhuish who first introduced me to the subject of international socialism and war, watched over the production of two theses on the subject, and provided constant and most generous assistance, both with the research in Britain and with the final writing here in Australia. She has encouraged me at each stage and has always been a quiet inspiration to this whole enterprise. Special thanks are also due to my two typists, Margaret Chedra, who typed this work as a thesis and then as a revised manuscript with great patience and care, and Audrey Jaques who typed the final manuscript with great skill and kept to a demanding timetable.

Finally, I would like to thank my wife Julie who has lived with the anxieties produced by this book for four years, complicated by the arrival of our son, without complaining. My most sincere thanks to her for all her assistance, from vigilant proof-reading to simple encouragement.

'Glendallo'   DOUGLAS J. NEWTON
31 July 1983

Contents

Abbreviations

ASE	Amalgamated Society of Engineers
ASRS	Amalgamated Society of Railway Servants
BNC	British National Committee (British Section of the Second International)
BSP	British Socialist Party
CIOS	Congrès International Ouvrier Socialiste
CIS	Commission Interparlementaire Socialiste
DWRGL	Dock, Wharf, Riverside and General Labourers' Union
GFTU	General Federation of Trade Unions
IFTU	International Federation of Trade Unions
IISG	Internationaal Instituut voor Sociale Geschiedenis (International Institute for Social History), Amsterdam
ILP	Independent Labour Party
IMF	International Miners' Federation
ISB	International Socialist Bureau
ISC	International Socialist Congress
ITF	International Transport Federation
LL	*Labour Leader*
LPGC	Labour Party General Correspondence
LP INT.	Labour Party letter files, international correspondence
LRC	Labour Representation Committee
MFGB	Miners' Federation of Great Britain
Mins.	Minutes
MRC	Modern Records Centre, University of Warwick
NAC	National Administrative Council of the Independent Labour Party
NEC	National Executive Committee of the Labour Party
NUB and SO	National Union of Boot and Shoe Operatives
NUDL	National Union of Dock Labourers
NUT	National Union of Teachers
PRO	Public Record Office, London
Proc.	Proceedings

SDF	Social Democratic Federation
SDAP	Social Democratic Workers' Party (Holland)
SDP	Social Democratic Party
SFIO	Section Française de l'Internationale Ouvrière
SPD	Sozialdemokratische Partei Deutschlands
TC	Trades Council
TUC	Trades Union Congress
TUC PC	Trades Union Congress, Parliamentary Committee

Introduction

SOMETIME during 1940, George Orwell began one of his most famous essays with these words:

As I write, highly civilised human beings are flying overhead, trying to kill me.

They do not feel any enmity against me as an individual, nor I against them. They are 'only doing their duty', as the saying goes. Most of them, I have no doubt, are kind-hearted law-abiding men who would never dream of committing murder in private life. On the other hand, if one of them succeeds in blowing me to pieces with a well-placed bomb, he will never sleep any worse for it. He is serving his country, which has the power to absolve from evil.[1]

Orwell's reflections on his situation capture something of the emotion that has always been at the heart of the socialist view of war: the sense of horror that working men could be flung, through their loyalty to national policies and carefully cultivated 'patriotic' ideals, into situations where they faced men of their own class and yet felt compelled to kill or be killed. It was this same realization of the awesome absurdity of war, of the utter irrationality of combat between working people, that appalled the socialists of the Second International and underlay their peace campaign in the twenty-five-year period prior to the outbreak of the Great War. Indeed, the socialists' increasing fear that war was very likely to arise from the militarist and imperialist tendencies at work within the existing capitalist societies led them to make the attack on war a fundamental part of their attack on capitalism itself. As early as 1898, Jean Jaurès, the leading French socialist, predicted that:

if war breaks out it will be vast and terrible. For the first time, it will be universal, sucking in all continents. Capitalism has widened the field of battle, and the entire planet will turn red with the blood of countless

---

[1] George Orwell, *The Lion and the Unicorn: Socialism and the English Genius* (first published February 1941, reprinted London, 1962), p. 9.

men. No more terrible accusation can be made against this social system.[2]

There is something both daunting and fascinating in the idea that the socialists of the International may have had the power to save Europe from its first massive tragedy of this century. It is not surprising, therefore, to find that several historians have already been attracted to the history of the Second International. James Joll and Julius Braunthal have completed major studies of the Second International and Georges Haupt, in his *Socialism and the Great War*, has examined in detail the International's policies with regard to war and peace.[3] These studies have naturally tended to concentrate upon the German and French socialists, as they were undoubtedly the leading forces within the International. Considering the importance of the enmity between Germany and France in pre-1914 Europe, it is clear that this emphasis on the activities of the German and French socialists is crucial to an understanding of the International's peace efforts. The British contribution to the International has not as yet seemed to merit any close inspection by the historians of international socialism. After all, it was, at first glance, a rather modest one. The small British socialist societies, who commanded such little influence at home, were not likely to be acknowledged as a major force within the International. The new Labour Representation Committee created in 1900, to be renamed the Labour Party in 1906, had a more significant following among the people, but the new party was regarded with some suspicion by Continental socialists because of its moderate trade union basis. Thus, British socialists were never in a position to challenge the ideological leadership of the German and French socialists in the International.

Conversely, historians of the British labour movement have given small attention to the British connection with the International. The British trade unions had little time for

---

[2] *La Petite République*, 17 November 1898, quoted in Harvey Goldberg, *The Life of Jean Jaurès* (Madison, Wisc., 1968), p. 245.

[3] James Joll, *The Second International* (New York, 1966; 2nd ed., London, 1974); Julius Braunthal, *History of the International, Vol. 1: 1864–1914* (London, 1977); Georges Haupt, *Socialism and the Great War: The Collapse of the Second International* (Oxford, 1972).

internationalism, and so, understandably, historians of British trade unionism have not felt the need to explore the international connections.[4] Historians of the Labour Party have also noted the insularity of outlook on the part of most members, and so they have not given very great attention to the occasional contacts with the International and the Continental socialist parties prior to 1914.[5] The connections with the International were largely the business of a select group of socialists in the Labour Party itself and in the two leading socialist bodies, the Independent Labour Party (ILP) and the Social Democratic Federation (SDF). Most work on the British labour movement's links with the Continent and its contribution to the peace campaigns of the International has been done by those historians who have focused upon the ideas and activities of leading socialists. Kenneth O. Morgan, in *Keir Hardie: Radical and Socialist*, includes a good deal of material on Hardie's internationalism and the peace campaigns of the ILP. This can be supplemented by information in Laurence Thompson's gossipy biographies of the Glasiers and Robert Blatchford.[6] Chushichi Tsuzuki, in *H.M. Hyndman and British Socialism*, and Walter Kendall, in *The Revolutionary Movement in Britain 1900—1921*, also provide information on the quarrels over the issues of war and peace within the SDF.[7] The reaction of the labour movement to the war itself from 1914 to 1918 has attracted some attention; but only brief backward glances have been given to the attitude of the labour movement to war in the pre-1914 period.[8]

[4] There are only a few references in the major study for this period, H.A. Clegg, Alan Fox, and A.F. Thompson, *A History of British Trade Unions Since 1889, Vol. 1: 1889—1910* (Oxford, 1964), pp. 87 and 301—2.

[5] See Henry Pelling, *The Origins of the Labour Party* (Oxford, 1974), pp. 86—7, 193—4; Henry Pelling, *A Short History of the Labour Party* (London, 1974), pp. 28—9.

[6] Kenneth O. Morgan, *Keir Hardie: Radical and Socialist* (London, 1975); Laurence Thompson, *The Enthusiasts: A Biography of John and Katharine Bruce Glasier* (London, 1971); Laurence Thompson, *Robert Blatchford: Portrait of an Englishman* (London, 1951).

[7] Chushichi Tsuzuki, *H.M. Hyndman and British Socialism* (Oxford, 1961); Walter Kendall, *The Revolutionary Movement in Britain, 1900—1921* (London, 1969).

[8] For example, see Peter Stansky (ed.), *The Left and War: The British Labour Party and World War I* (Oxford, 1969); and J.M. Winter, *Socialism and the*

Therefore, the story of the British labour movement's campaign against militarism and war in the pre-war years has never been told in its own right. Even so, it is an aspect of the history of pre-war socialist and labour internationalism that is not without special interest. In the first place, it was the British socialist and labour movement that faced the trauma of a major national imperialist war, the war in South Africa, during the pre-1914 period. Second, in the persons of Hyndman and Blatchford, the British socialist movement had its share of supposed 'social chauvinists'. Third, because the reformist trend was triumphant in British socialism, Britain still provides something of a test case for the view that reformism lies at the root of the powerlessness of the socialist movement when it came to resisting war. Fourthly, it was Keir Hardie, the leading British socialist, who was to be associated with the proposal for an anti-war strike during the years 1910 to 1914. A consideration of the British labour movement's contribution to the International's struggle for peace should therefore help to fill a gap in the history of this struggle and may also allow some fresh judgements on some controversial aspects of it. Thus, the aim of this study is to review the policies and activities of the British labour movement in relation to the issues of peace and war during the years 1889 to 1914, that is, during the lifetime of the Second International. The term 'labour movement' has been used to include the broad spectrum of industrial and political working-class organizations, including the trade union movement, the Labour Party, the ILP, and the SDF. Robert Blatchford, the influential socialist journalist and editor of the *Clarion* newspaper for much of the period under study, has also been included because of his influence in the labour movement and his special concern with military issues. For reasons of economy, the Fabian Society has been excluded from consideration. Of the three major socialist organizations,

Challenge of War: Ideas and Politics in Britain, 1912—18 (London, 1974). There are also some glimpses of the labour movement's concern for peace in the pre-war period in two general studies of Labour foreign policy; see Kenneth E. Miller, *Socialism and Foreign Policy: Theory and Practice in Britain to 1931* (The Hague, 1967) and William Percy Maddox, *Foreign Relations in British Labour Politics: A Study of the Formation of Party Attitudes on Foreign Affairs, 1900—1924* (London, 1934).

the Fabian Society seemed the least necessary to be considered: first, because its membership[9] was so much smaller than that of the ILP and the SDF; and, second, because detailed research into the Fabian Society and its attitudes to imperialism has already been completed.[10] Also, no attempt has been made to include the two small splinter groups from the old SDF, the Socialist Labour Party and the Socialist Party of Great Britain, because neither party attracted any significant support in the pre-war years.[11]

It is now generally accepted that genuine 'labour history' must do a great deal more than simply describe the activities of the small group of leaders who attended congresses, made speeches, and proposed resolutions. In this study it has been difficult to abandon a certain degree of concentration upon the leaders of the British labour movement precisely because only a select group of leading socialists took a lively interest in the peace campaign and in the business of internationalism. However, these same socialists were well aware that the effectiveness of their struggle against militarism depended upon a genuine mass mobilization of the labour movement in the cause of peace. The campaign cannot be understood, therefore, even in its own terms, if it is considered in isolation from the broad labour movement. For this reason I have sought to probe beyond the level of the socialist and trade union leadership chiefly by exploring the attitudes of trade unionists represented at the local trades council level. At first it would appear that there is little internationalist activity to be discovered at that level. However, certain issues did attract the concern of the councils, and the very selectivity of the trades councils in this regard, and much of their normal business too, reveals a good deal about the priorities and

[9] See A.M. McBriar, *Fabian Socialism and English Politics, 1884—1918* (Cambridge, 1962), p. 166, showing that membership of the London Fabian Society never exceeded 3,000 in the period under study. See Pelling, *Origins of the Labour Party*, Appendix A for a comparison of the membership figures of the SDF, ILP, and Fabian Society from 1884 to 1901.

[10] See McBriar, *Fabian Socialism and English Politics*, ch. V, and Bernard Semmel, *Imperialism and Social Reform: English Social-Imperial Thought, 1895—1914* (London, 1960), ch. III and VI.

[11] On these splinter groups see Kendall, *The Revolutionary Movement in Britain*, ch. 4, and Raymond Challinor, *The Origins of British Bolshevism* (London, 1977).

patriotic assumptions of the trade union movement. In this way it is possible to gain an insight into the underlying convictions of the rank-and-file members of the labour movement, convictions which governed their attitude to the controversial issues of foreign policy and defence.

1

The British Labour Movement
at the Turn of the Century:
Some Ideological Perspectives

A powerful political Labour movement apart from trades unionism
is an impossibility.

Keir Hardie, *Labour Leader*, 27 December 1902

DURING the twenty-five years prior to the outbreak of the
Great War, the idea of a single and united labour movement
for the working people of Britain remained a dream. To begin
with, by no means were the working people as a whole committed to the organized labour movement in either the industrial or the political sense of the term. A majority of the
wage-earning class still worked without any allegiance to
trade unionism, and most still divided their votes between the
two traditional parties, Liberal and Conservative. The formation of the Labour Representation Committee (LRC) in
1900 arising from a Trades Union Congress (TUC) resolution
of the previous year, and its evolution into the new Labour
Party in 1906 were certainly signs of progress. However, it is
important to stress at the outset that the creation of a new
indepedent labour grouping in parliament did not involve any
genuine unification of the various forces that composed the
British labour movement. Rather, from the very beginning,
the LRC was described by its supporters as representing a
'federation' or a 'labour alliance'. Within this alliance the
socialist societies and the trade union movement agreed to
a measure of co-operation in order to promote a carefully
defined and limited object, namely, increased independent
labour representation in the House of Commons. Neither the
socialist societies nor the trade unions surrendered their
separate identities. Indeed, many trade unionists remained
deeply suspicious of all attempts to make politics the first
business of the trade unions. The socialists, for their part,

were also divided over fundamental ideological questions. The two principal socialist organizations, the idealist Independent Labour Party (ILP) and the marxist Social Democratic Federation (SDF, and from 1906 the Social Democratic Party or SDP) were engaged in a war of words in which each sought to justify its own brand of socialism and magnify the faults of the other.

While these differences in outlook persisted it was scarcely surprising that the new Labour Party, the child of socialist hope and trade union pragmatism, experienced difficulties in fashioning coherent policies on foreign affairs and defence matters. Too often the impression was created of a vast gap between the soaring internationalism of the socialist leaders and the moderate assurances of commitment to peace given by union leaders, whose ardour seemed tempered by the knowledge that many of their members were indifferent to these issues. To understand these different responses one must begin a study of this kind with a brief survey of the ideological assumptions or 'habits of mind' which held sway within the various elements of the British labour movement at about the turn of the century.

1. 'Labourism': the Trade Unions and the Labour Party

The starting-point of any examination of the British labour movement must be the trade unions, for very clearly the overwhelming majority of those people who counted themselves members of the labour movement owed their first allegiance to the trade unions. In the Labour Party itself, the unions provided the great bulk of the formal membership as well as most of the funds.[1] In fact, the massive numerical dominance of the unions over the various socialist societies increased during the Edwardian years and this was acknowledged right through to the highest levels of the Labour Party. On the original LRC executive, for instance, the trade unions were accorded just seven of the twelve positions,[2] but by 1910 they controlled eleven of the sixteen positions on

---

[1] Henry Pelling, *A Short History of the Labour Party* (London, 1974), Appendix A: Party Membership, pp. 156–7.
[2] *Report of the Conference on Labour Representation, 27 February 1900*, resolution 3, p. 14.

the Labour Party's National Executive Committee (NEC).[3] Thus the Labour Party belonged to the trade unions, in spite of the fact that many of its better-known leaders, men such as Keir Hardie and Ramsay MacDonald, came from the socialist wing of the party.

It is important to emphasize at the outset the essentially moderate perspective of most British trade unions. The creation of the LRC itself had only been accomplished after many years of agitation by the socialists amongst the trade unionists in favour of independent working-class political representation. The struggle to detach the trade unionists from the idea of political neutrality had not been easy and had provoked some intense opposition.[4] The creation of the LRC certainly signalled that a majority of union leaders were willing to give the idea of independent labour politics a trial. But the old conception of trade unionism did not collapse overnight. Many trade unionists still clung to the view that a trade union's first and only concern should be 'trade matters'. Many bitterly resented the new course being undertaken by the LRC and distrusted the socialist agitators who were seen to be the real proponents of this dangerous experiment in political trade unionism. There were many signs of this resentment. The most spectacular came in 1902 when an attempt was made at the Trades Union Congress to have the TUC Parliamentary Committee call its own conference on labour representation, a clear move to side-step the new LRC.[5] Feelings were still running high two years later when there was a lively quarrel within the TUC Parliamentary Committee over whether or not to accept an invitation to send delegates to the LRC Conference of that year.[6] Clearly the 'labour alliance' had not forged an absolute unity.

The very tone of the Trade Union Congresses contrasted with the socialists' gatherings. The delegates often seemed willing to use the occasions to demonstrate how their

[3] *Ross McKibbin, The Evolution of the Labour Party 1910—1924* (Oxford, 1974), p. 2.
[4] For example, see the events at the TUC of 1895 described in Henry Pelling, *The Origins of the Labour Party* (Oxford, 1965), pp. 192—3.
[5] See the report in *ILP News*, September 1902.
[6] TUC Parliamentary Committee *mins.*, 20 January and 1 February 1904; hereafter abbreviated to TUC PC.

achievement of high office within the trade union sphere had bestowed a new social eminence which made it possible for them to mix with the governing élites. In 1902, for example, the TUC officials accepted an invitation to dinner from Horatio Bottomley, the ultra-patriotic proprietor of the *Sun* newspaper.[7] During the Congress at Bath in 1907 the TUC officials were entertained by the Lord Mayor and several Liberal MPs at a garden party and tea in the Pump Room.[8] In this way the trade union leaders exhibited their own desires to seek a better place in the established order for the working man rather than to challenge that order.

Some indication of the priorities of trade unions at this time can also be found in the annual reports and journals issued by the unions. In most cases these publications show that union officers were absorbed in ensuring the correct and just administration of the various benefit schemes operated by the trade unions. It is also evident that the threat of unemployment loomed largest in the minds of unionists, for these same reports and journals often devoted much space to a careful analysis of the state of trade, region by region. The typical trade union secretary's annual report of the period made an assessment of the financial health of the union, its membership and benefit schemes, and either rejoiced over boom conditions or lamented the poor state of trade. Political subjects were rarely included.[9]

The old commitment to the political neutrality of the trade unions is well illustrated in an editorial comment in the *Postmen's Gazette* (organ of the Postmen's Federation). In January 1900, under the heading 'Our Parliamentary Policy', it was noted that:

In seeking the assistance of Members of Parliament we do not stop to enquire as to their political views, we simply ask their support for what we consider a just and righteous cause. They may be Liberal, Con-

---

[7] *ILP News*, September 1902.

[8] *Labour Leader* (hereafter abbreviated to *LL*), 6 September 1907.

[9] The most complete collections of trade union journals and annual reports for the period under study can be found in the Modern Records Centre at Warwick University and at the British Library of Political and Economic Science in the London School of Economics.

servative, Socialist, Labour Representative or Home Ruler; it is all the same to us from a Federation point of view.[10]

Certainly this idea was fading, and the Postmen's Federation itself was to join the LRC in 1901—2; but even after a union had thrown its support behind the Labour Party, the belief often lingered that the union's political activity was definitely of secondary importance.[11] Indeed, the formal list of objectives of some trades councils confined their activities to 'trades matters' only, a limitation which could be used to prevent political discussion.[12] Occasionally the trade unionists' claim to be apolitical could be most useful in defending the trades councils. For instance, in 1909 the Nottingham Trades Council was warned by the Mayor that if it persisted in using the local Exchange Hall for 'political purposes' he would prevent the council from meeting there. The council's minutes record that:

The Executive were of the opinion that the Trades Council was not a political association (Hear! Hear!). Whenever they discussed politics it was in relation to their own particular industries and interests. They, therefore, did not propose to deviate from their usual course. They were a trades union organisation, and only discussed politics as other non-political bodies in the city did.[13]

Notwithstanding the growing acceptance of the idea of political involvement, some trade unionists clearly resisted the assumption that their political loyalties lay necessarily with the Labour Party, and in particular that they lay with the socialists within it. Some trade unionists displayed great sensitivity on this point. In January 1910, for instance, the London Trades Council passed a resolution requesting all 'friends of labour' to vote for the 'Labour candidate:' but an amendment to add the words 'and socialist' was lost by

[10] *Postmen's Gazette*, 13 January 1900.
[11] See the comments of a new union organizer reported in Friendly Society of Operative Stonemasons, *Journal*, 16 October 1912.
[12] For example, the Leeds Trade Council operated under a standing order which stipulated that the agreement of a two-thirds majority of the council delegates was necessary 'to allow discussion on a political question'; see Leeds Trade Council *mins.*, 29 November 1899. (Hereafter, Trades Council is abbreviated to TC.)
[13] Nottingham TC *mins.*, 15 September 1909.

thirty votes to twenty-nine.[14] Of course, the whole problem
of how political the trade unions should be was brought on
to the national stage by the notorious Osborne Judgement
of 1909, which made illegal the channelling of trade union
funds to the Labour Party. Following that decision the trade
unions called ballots on the question of using union funds for
political purposes, and the results showed that there was
still a good deal of opposition to the concept.[15] The reluctance of many trade unionists to become absorbed in the
political struggle in this period was also shown in the continued existence side by side of trades councils and local
LRCs in many regions,[16] and in the persistent failure of the
various efforts that were made in these years to organize a
fusion between the TUC and the Labour Party.[17] If the
'labour alliance' was to hold firm, the socialists would need
to tread carefully. As Keir Hardie counselled his ILP followers in 1902, 'the march of an army must be regulated to
suit the pace of the slowest'.[18]

The nature of the 'labour alliance' and the moderation of
the trade unions is well illustrated in the debates on the
socialist objectives within the LRC and subsequently in the
Labour Party. From the first the marxists of the SDF attempted to give the new LRC a socialist objective and urged
that only socialists be accepted as candidates. The ILP always
rejected any such binding commitment, arguing that the
sensitivities of the moderate majority of trade unionists on
the matter of socialism must be respected. Thus, at the 1900
and 1901 LRC Conferences the SDF's socialist resolutions
were rejected with the aid of ILP delegates' votes.[19] In order

---

[14] London TC *mins.*, 13 January 1910.
[15] Max Beer, *A History of British Socialism* (London, 1940), pp. 343—4.
Beer records that, up to may 1914, sixty-three unions had taken ballots, with
the result that 678,063 members voted for political contributions and 407,356
against.
[16] McKibbin, *The Evolution of the Labour Party*, pp. 33—4.
[17] In June 1910 the Labour Party National Executive Committee (NEC)
concluded that a proposal for fusion which had come from the 1910 Labour
Party Conference was 'not within the range of practical politics': NEC *mins.*,
30 June 1910. See also TUC, *Annual Report*, 1910, pp. 118—21 and TUC PC
mins., 25 April 1911.
[18] *LL*, 27 December 1902.
[19] *Report on the Conference on Labour Representation*, 1900, pp. 11—12;
LRC, *Annual Conference*, 1901, p. 21.

to ensure the continuation of the trade unionists' support for the new and fragile 'labour alliance', even Keir Hardie seemed ready to play down his socialism. He told the 1903 LRC Conference that the LRC must 'have done with Liberalism and Toryism and every other "ism" that was not Labourism'.[20] This policy of seeming to hide one's socialism under a bushel naturally irritated some of the more fervent brethren of the ILP, and as early as 1903 there were the first rumblings of discontent within the party over the compromises and equivocations that seemed to be needed to sustain the 'labour alliance'.[21]

In spite of periodic pangs of conscience among the ILP leaders and some continuing discontent among the ILP rank and file, the governing majority of the ILP steadfastly maintained the view that the socialists must not force their own ideological faith upon the trade unionists within the Labour Party.[22] And, certainly, there were continuing signs of reciprocal goodwill on the part of the trade unionists toward their socialist colleagues. In 1903 both the LRC and the TUC rejected moves designed to exclude the socialists from their ranks.[23] In addition, the Trade Union Congress of 1904 and the LRC Conference of 1905 passed resolutions expressing general support for the nationalization of the means of production, distribution, and exchange.[24] The ILP weekly *Labour Leader* was realistic enough to note that these generalized resolutions did not signify the victory of socialists in either body, and that the LRC's formal parliamentary object remained unaltered.[25] Yet, these 'socialist' resolutions were undoubtedly most gratifying for those who believed in the slow permeation of socialist ideals. Fortified by such signs of

[20] LRC, *Annual Conference*, 1903, p. 31. The version of the speech given in the *Labour Leader* is even more extreme: 'This new party must be a Labour Party, knowing neither Socialist, nor Tory, nor Liberal'; *LL*, 28 February 1903.

[21] See, for example, a squabble in the letters column of the *LL*, 28 February, 7, 14, 21, and 28 March 1903, and Hardie's reply to the critics within the ILP in *LL*, 4 April 1903.

[22] See Hardie's speech at the ILP Conference in York, *LL*, 18 April 1903.

[23] LRC, *Annual Conference*, 1903, pp. 26–7; *LL*, 19 September 1903.

[24] *LL*, 16 September 1904; RTC, *Annual Conference*, 1905, p. 52. The LRC simply declared that its 'ultimate object' was the overthrow of capitalism.

[25] See the comments on the 1904 TUC resolution in *LL*, 16 September 1904 and on the 1905 LRC resolution in *LL*, 3 February 1905.

socialist insight among the trade unionists, the leaders of the ILP seemed content to accept the hard realities of political compromises, such as the stipulation of the LRC in 1903 that its candidates appear before the electorate 'under the title of Labour candidates only'.[26] In fact, Hardie and his companions denied that there was any serious equivocation on the matter of socialism; for, under the 'Labour Candidate' title, the socialist was still perfectly free to preach socialism and to present to the electors an avowedly socialist election address. In the last analysis, according to Hardie, the creation of an independent working-class party was of the highest priority, for its creation was more than half the battle in building a socialist party. As he explained it in 1907:

To unite the working class in a party of its own is the first and most important task for those who wish to hasten the advent of socialism, and that is what is being done. Everything else will follow in good time.[27]

Therefore, in the continuing quarrels within the Labour Party over the socialist objective and over the SDF's reforming proposal that candidates describe themselves as 'Labour and Socialist', the socialists of the ILP always sided with the trade unionists in rejecting any change. At the Labour Party Conference in 1907, Keir Hardie, Bruce Glasier, and Pete Curran were prominent in a debate that saw the defeat of an SDF motion to alter clause II of the party constitution so as to give the Labour Party a socialist objective. Curran argued that:

The carrying of this resolution would be the destruction of the movement as it existed today. The trade unions, who made up the bulk of the movement and contributed the funds of the movement, would not pledge themselves to this class consciousness.[28]

It was obvious that this spirit of co-operation between socialists and trade unionists rested largely upon the self-effacement of the socialists. The 'labour alliance' survived because the ILP socialists were realistic enough to recognize the limited influence they possessed in the trade unions, and

---

[26] LRC, *Annual Conference*, 1903, p. 32.
[27] *LL*, 4 January 1907.
[28] LRC, *Annual Conference*, 1907, p. 52.

because they agreed to hasten slowly in deference to the moderate outlook of most trade unionists. The leading socialist personalities within the Labour Party were certainly under no illusions concerning the weakness of socialism in most trade unions. In July 1907 Ramsay MacDonald set out to reply to an International Socialist Bureau (ISB) request for information on British trade unions. In the original draft of his reply he wrote, 'In many cases socialist propaganda is conducted by the trade unions, many of them embracing the socialist basis in their rules.' He then struck out the word 'many' in both instances and inserted the words 'some' and 'several'. On this occasion his second thoughts were both honest and accurate.[29] Similarly, in his address as chairman of the 1910 Conference of the Labour Party, Keir Hardie stressed that the distance between the trade unionists and the socialists and the imperative need to build unity in spite of that distance had been the leading themes of his work during the Labour Party's first decade. He recalled that

Ten years ago we were timidly venturing upon a doubtful and venturesome experiment. Trade unionist and socialist were still eyeing each other askance, and it remained to be seen how far these two sections of one movement could be made to harmonise.[30]

As for the prospects for socialism, after ten years Hardie still looked to some future date for the conversion of the party:

The Labour Party is not avowedly a socialist party in its political profession, but the feeling grows that, so long as land and industrial capital are privately owned and controlled, the mass of the people are bound to be in bondage to circumstances over which they have no control.[31]

Under the 'labour alliance', therefore, the idea of socialism assumed a shadowy existence. The Labour Party clearly sympathized with the socialist movement, yet refrained from any outright adoption of a socialist objective. The vision of socialism lived chiefly in the imaginations of the ILP minority who clung to their belief that the Labour Party would move irresistibly toward the socialists' ideals as reform followed

---

[29] J.R. MacDonald to C. Huysmans, 11 July 1907; Labour Party General Correspondence (LPGC)/17/358. The corrections are in MacDonald's handwriting.

[30] Labour Party, *Annual Conference*, 1910, p. 55.

[31] Ibid., p. 57.

upon reform. Socialism existed somewhere in the ideal near-future, in the dream of the new age to come which inspired the enthusiasts of the ILP. For convinced socialists like Keir Hardie and Robert Smillie, the new humanitarian socialist society was only a few years away anyhow.[32] The vividness of their dreams perhaps sustained their faith and made the plain fact of the absence of socialism from both the Labour Party's constitution and its objective a little easier to bear.[33]

The moderation of the trade unionists and of the majority of Labour Party members was also evident in their approach to the question of the British monarchy. On this particular question the ideological gap between the socialists and the trade unionists was apparent to all. On the one hand, the ILP and the SDF were frankly republican, and their publications were always critical of the lavish expenditure, the 'sycophancy', and the militarist displays which surrounded the royal occasions of the period.[34] The more outspoken socialists, such as Keir Hardie, made their feelings known even in the House of Commons. During the 1901 session Hardie proposed an amendment to the Address in Reply in favour of abolishing the monarchy, and another to reject the entire civil list. He declaimed against the militarism which dominated the funeral ceremony for Queen Victoria, and he caused a sensation when he went so far as to assert that the Government had sought to use the dead queen's body as a 'recruiting sergeant'.[35] Most members of the Labour Party and the trade unions, on the other hand, shied away from anything that smacked of disloyalty to the throne. In their acceptance of royal ceremonies, their attendance at royal

---

[32] See Robert Smillie's recollection in his *My Life for Labour* (London, 1924), p. 100.

[33] Resolutions in favour of socialism were passed by the Labour Party Conference again in 1908 and 1909, by 514,000 to 469,000 votes in 1908 and by 362,000 to 313,000 in 1909. However, in neither case did the resolution embody an alteration of the party objective as had been contemplated in 1907; see Labour Party, *Annual Conference*, 1908, p. 76 and *Annual Conference*, 1909, p. 73.

[34] See, for example, the SDF attitude to Queen Victoria's death; *Justice*, 26 January, 2 and 9 February 1901. For the ILP attitude to Queen Victoria's passing see editorial, *LL*, 26 January 1901 and 'Is Britain Ruled by Chance?' and 'The Queen's Funeral: A Protest' in *LL*, 2 February 1901.

[35] *LL*, 23 February, 2 and 30 March, and 18 May 1901; *Hansard*, IV: 90: 1188, 1190, 1197 and IV: 93: 1230, 1251, 1254.

functions, and in their insistence that the people admired and loved the throne, the majority of Labour Party members and trade unionists demonstrated their own recognition of the monarchy as a legitimate symbol of national unity, as propounded by press, Parliament, and pulpit. When the Labour Party proposed several amendments to the civil list in the Commons in July 1910, the speeches of several Labour MPs were chiefly distinguished by disavowals of any intention to attack the throne itself and assurances that Labour members fully appreciated the 'deep affection' of the people for the monarchy.[36] On the occasion of a special Labour Party dinner in 1911 for Andrew Fisher, the Labour Prime Minister of Australia, toasts were drunk to 'The King', 'Our Guest', and 'The Labour Movement'. Hardie's attempt to have the loyal toast deleted from the toast list was defeated in the National Executive by six votes to five.[37]

Similar patriotic gestures were commonplace amongst the trade unionists. The TUC Parliamentary Committee dutifully dispatched appropriate messages on the coronations, illnesses, and deaths of the various monarchs, and some individual unions made similar declarations of loyalty on royal occasions.[38] On a local level too, amongst the trades councils, it was evident that most trade unionists accepted the monarchy. Many trades councils and individual trade unions sent messages of loyalty to the throne on royal occasions, and sometimes delegates were sent to London to attend coronations or funerals.[39] Although these loyal gestures were sometimes challenged in the councils, the challenges were seldom successful. For instance, in 1910 four delegates from the Nottingham Trades Council were appointed on the Mayor's invitation to attend a memorial service for the late Edward VII, and the Trades Council executive also agreed to send letters of sympathy to Queen Alexandra and King George V. When one delegate later objected to the sending of condolences the

[36] See the speeches of J.A. Seddon and G.H. Roberts on 14 April, 22 and 26 July 1910, in *Hansard*, V: 16: 1460–1461 and V: 19: 1681–1682, 2069–2070.

[37] Labour Party, NEC *mins.*, 9 March and 26 April 1911.

[38] For example, see the TUC PC *mins.*, 18 May 1910 and 24 May 1911.

[39] For example, London TC *mins.*, 31 January 1901; Nottingham TC *mins.*, 31 July 1901; Aberdeen TC *mins.*, 12 July 1906; Liverpool TC *mins.*, 11 May 1910.

council endorsed the executive's action with only four dissenting votes cast from the 107 delegates present.[40] The patriotic sentiment of most trade unionists was not to be violated with impunity.

2. *The Socialists*

Those who carried the banner of socialism in Britain in this period can hardly be described as a united band of brothers. Differences of ideology, personality, and political style cut deeply, and so socialists were divided into several competing groups, each of which fiercely proclaimed the worth of its own particular vision of socialism. The case for socialism in Britain emanated from four major organizations. First in importance was the idealist Independent Labour Party (ILP), founded in 1893 and controlled by such figures as Keir Hardie, Ramsay MacDonald, J. Bruce Glasier, and Philip Snowden, all of whom wrote constantly for the party's weekly paper the *Labour Leader*. The ILP's sternest critic was the Social Democratic Federation (SDF), founded in 1881 and dominated by the leading British marxist Henry M. Hyndman and his loyal companion Harry Quelch. Together both men kept a firm grip on the party weekly *Justice*. Much smaller than either the ILP or the SDF was the Fabian Society, which, for the reasons already given, is not included in this study. Finally, there was the *Clarion* newspaper, founded in 1891 and controlled by the vivacious and eccentric veteran socialist journalist Robert Blatchford, author of the highly successful propaganda book *Merrie England* (1894).

To the devoted followers of the ILP the socialism which inspired their party was much more than an ideology—it was a ruling passion. Early in the new century Fred Brocklehurst, a prominent ILP member, wrote confidently that the future historian of the ILP could not fail to be struck by the 'wealth of feeling and enthusiasm' which pervades the party. 'He will come across the record of the missionary lives of numberless

---

[40] Nottingham TC *mins.*, 15 and 25 May 1910. For a similar incident see also London TC *mins.*, 12, 25 May, 9, 30 June, and 28 July 1910.

[41] Two exceptions should be noted. In 1910, the Huddersfield TC and the Glasgow TC rejected invitations to attend Edward VII's funeral; see Glasgow TC *mins.*, 18 May 1910 and Huddersfield TC *mins.*, 19 May 1910.

men and women who travelled literally from John o'Groats to Land's End in their burning zeal', Brocklehurst predicted.[42] His words well describe the almost religious quality of the devotion to the vision of socialism within the ILP. Even the language which was used in ILP circles indicated the 'gospel fervour' which burned within the heart of the committed ILP socialist. The party conducted 'missions' rather than propaganda;[43] the socialist movement was the 'new Messiah' and Hardie was an 'inspired prophet';[44] socialism was 'the cause of Humanity, the cause of God';[45] socialists were 'apostles'; many ILP members spoke of their 'conversion' to socialism;[46] and it was commonplace to speak of 'the religion of socialism'.[47] Many of the leading members of the ILP freely admitted to a religious inspiration at the core of their socialism.[48]

The socialism of the ILP was of that idealistic and compassionate brand calculated to inspire the loftiest emotions in the loyal party worker. The dream of a new order, as presented in the fervent prose of Hardie and Glasier, was rooted in their faith in human fellowship. Socialism for the ILP meant the reordering of society so as to cease doing violence to the principles of egalitarianism and human fellowship. The need for socialism followed on from the profound goodness of the ethics of selflessness, kindness, and mutual aid. The evil of capitalism was clear from its disregard of these moral values. The ILP leaders did not apologise for the moralistic tone of their rhetoric. Rather, they regarded their own ability to tap both the truly Christian and the secular humanitarian traditions as the source of their strength. Glasier told the ILP Conference in 1901 that the ILP's

[42] *LL*, 25 October 1902.

[43] See, for example, William Stewart to J. Penny, 3 July 1901, ILP Archives 1901; 30 c.

[44] Katharine Glasier's speech, ILP Conference 1914, *LL*, 16 April 1914.

[45] From Hardie's election address, *LL*, 13 October 1900.

[46] See the examples collected by Stephen Yeo 'A New Life: the Religion of Socialism', *History Workshop*, 4 (Autumn 1977), pp. 10—13.

[47] For some examples of this type of discussion in the *LL*, see 3 June 1904, 30 March 1906, 18 January 1907, 10 July 1908, 24 February 1911, 28 April 1911, and 30 April 1914.

[48] For some useful insights into the religious motivation of many of the ILP leaders see the 'How I Became a Socialist' series in the *LL*, May—August 1912.

conception of socialism was akin to the belief that 'God . . . is an unutterable sigh at the bottom of the human heart.' He added:

> That, I believe, is the conception of socialism which inspires the great bulk of the membership of the ILP, and it is because of the religion of that conception that the ILP, with all its imperfections of men and methods, has attained to the position of being the great conquering socialist movement in Britain.[49]

The ILP leaders, therefore, were unashamedly idealist and non-marxist. The leading personalities of the party were constantly at pains to distinguish their own evolutionary, humane, and non-violent socialism from the marxism of the SDF which they considered quite inappropriate to British conditions. The idealism of the party leaders and their rejection of the materialist dogmas of marxism sprang in some cases from their romantic, poetic, and even spiritualistic habits of mind. Hardie's column in the *Labour Leader* always began with a specially chosen poem, usually moralistic or religious in theme. On one occasion, Glasier observed that Hardie's half-belief in palmistry and horoscopes was 'in his blood'.[50] Russell Smart was repeating a commonplace observation when he noted that for the ILP socialists 'there was little question about the arithmetic or proof of socialism—it was enough to them that socialism had become once for all the desire of their lives.'[51]

It should be noted that a commitment to internationalism was from the early days a characteristic of the ILP, blending easily with the guiding emotions of fraternity and brotherhood emphasized by the party. Opposition to war and imperialism was a constant theme in the pages of the *Labour Leader* during the 1890s. For Keir Hardie in particular the achievement of internationalism and peace became central to

[49] *LL*, 13 April 1901.
[50] Glasier to Lizzie Glasier, 23 October 1903, Glasier Papers, I. 1. 1903/13. See also Hardie's comment at the 1914 ILP Conference: 'I am not guided so much by a consideration of policy or by thinking out a long sequence of events as by intuition and inspiration. I know what I believe to be the right thing, and I go and do it'; *LL*, 23 April 1914.
[51] *ILP News*, October 1899.

his socialism. In 1907 he chose the following lines to serve
as an introduction to his book *From Serfdom to Socialism*:

> ... to fight
> Not in red coats against our brother man,
> The pawns of empire, or a despot's will,
> But in grey lines of sober brotherhood
> Against the flaunting evils of the world,
> The cruelty that fastens on men's lives,
> The dread brutality that hedges earth.[52]

Increasingly for Hardie and the ILP, militarism and war became the ultimate enemies, designed to distract the people
from the true struggle for socialism.

On the basis of this ideology the ILP sought to convert
the British people to socialism. The main organ of propaganda was always the *Labour Leader* owned and edited by
Keir Hardie from its foundation in the late 1880s until it was
bought by the ILP in April 1904.[53] Glasier then held the
editorship from 1905 until he was succeeded by J.F. Mills in
1909. Mills in turn was replaced by Fenner Brockway in
1913. Circulation was not large, rising from 13,000 in 1904
to about 40,000 in 1909.[54] Sales were limited, in the main
to the party's own branches; so much so that in 1898 Hardie
admitted his surprise when

For the first time I saw a workman—evidently an engineer by his
garb—reading the paper. It was at Preston station, and I don't think he
was an ILP'er as he didn't recognise me, although I passed and re-
passed half a dozen times.[55]

Similarly, the strength of the party membership was not
impressive. Taking the year 1909 as a representative one in
the period under study, party membership stood at only
30,000.[56] Nevertheless, the enthusiasm of its members and

---

[52] Hardie, *From Serfdom to Socialism.*
[53] See the final negotiations in ILP NAC *mins.*, 15—6 January 1904.
[54] Circulation figures are given in Glasier 'Why I Resign the Editorship', *LL*,
7 May 1909. William Stewart, *J. Keir Hardie* (London, 1925), p. 298 says circulation climbed to 40,000 under Glasier's editorship.
[55] Hardie to D. Lowe, (?) January 1898, ILP Archives, 1898/8. See also
Robert William's opinion that the *Leader* was not read by the trade unionists;
Williams to MacDonald, 6 August 1914, MacDonald Papers, PRO 5/98.
[56] ILP NAC *Report*, 1909—10.

the stature of its leaders ensured that the ILP exerted considerable influence within the Labour Party. In the 1906 elections, at least seventeen of the twenty-nine successful LRC candidates were ILP members.[57] In the elections of January 1910, there were twenty-six ILP members amongst the forty Labour Party candidates.[58] The election of Hardie as chairman of the Parliamentary Labour Party in 1906 was a clear indication of the respect commanded by the ILP amongst the Labour Party MPs. Thus, in spite of the small membership of the ILP itself, the party's success within the Labour Party structure made it easily the most important socialist force in Edwardian Britain.

The second major socialist group in Britain at this time was the defiantly marxist Social Democratic Federation (SDF). The Federation was the older of the two bodies, having been founded in 1881 (as the Democratic Federation) by its dedicated leader Henry M. Hyndman, who continued to exercise great personal command within the SDF throughout the period under study. The membership of the SDF remained small, rising from about 9,000 in 1900 to about 15,000 in 1914.[59] In terms of ideology, the SDF proudly maintained an undeviating loyalty to marxist precepts and considered itself undefiled either by making compromises with 'labourism' or succumbing to the temptation of anarchism. The party's strict ideological outlook tended to be attractive to the uncomprising dogmatists or, in the words of one critic, the 'roaring lions' of the socialist movement.[60]

The SDF policy toward the Labour Representation Committee in the early years of its existence demonstrates the more inflexible marxist outlook of the SDF, and at the same time illustrates the central issue of tactics which divided the SDF and the ILP. At first, the SDF welcomed the new moves in the late 1890s to promote the cause of working-class representation and agreed to attend the historic Memorial Hall conference in London in February 1900. From the outset, however, the SDF maintained that the formation of a new

[57]   *LL*, 2 February 1906.
[58]   *LL*, 10 June 1910.
[59]   Tsuzuki, *Hyndman*, Appendix B.
[60]   *LL*, 2 May 1903.

independent working-class party was an acknowledgement of class antagonism between workers and owners, and so the SDF delegates argued that the party should logically be constituted on a socialist basis.[61] As we have seen, the SDF's proposal that the new LRC should be 'based upon the recognition of the class war' and have a socialist objective was voted down with the aid of ILP votes at the Memorial Hall conference.[62] The ILP's opposition was bitterly resented, and *Justice* railed against this 'display of treachery to which we have, unfortunately, by this time become accustomed'.[63] This editorial splutter was too much for the ILP. Its Administrative Council enquired of the SDF executive whether this insult reflected the official view. When they were curtly informed that it did, they declared that the ILP would formally sunder all relations with the SDF 'until all such imputations had been withdrawn'.[64] This particular quarrel was typical, based as it was on a mixture of ideological differences and personal antipathies. At the next LRC conference in 1901 the squabble was reopened. This time it was the ILP who offered a resolution in favour of the setting-up of a 'co-operative commonwealth'. But, as ILP speakers explained, their resolution did not seek to impose a 'socialist test' on LRC candidates, but would merely serve as an expression of conference opinion. At that point Quelch, for the SDF, sought to strengthen the motion by urging that the LRC should indeed refuse to support any candidate who was not committed to the socialist objective. Quelch argued that the LRC must stop 'floundering', should adopt a definite policy, and accept 'the class war' as 'an article of faith' as was the case with the Continental working-class parties. The conference, however, was unmoved and neither the ILP motion nor the SDF amendment was accepted.[65] *Justice* concluded that the result was a disappointment for all those wanting to establish 'a real independent fighting working class party'.[66]

The SDF's dissatisfaction over the lack of socialist

---

[61] *Justice*, editorial, 24 February 1900.
[62] *Report of the Conference on Labour Representation*, 1900, pp. 11–12.
[63] *Justice*, editorial, 3 March 1900.
[64] *LL*, 21 April 1900.
[65] LRC *Annual Conference* 1901, pp. 20–21.
[66] *Justice*, 9 February 1901.

commitment within the 'labour alliance' climaxed in August 1901 with the decision of the 'Coming of Age' Conference of the SDF to withdraw formally from the LRC. Reflecting on the decision in *Justice*, Quelch stressed that the SDF was 'not prepared to sacrifice any principle for a temporary advantage' and noted that the party's paramount aim would continue to be 'the formation of a class-conscious working class party for the realisation of social democracy'.[67] The LRC was not that party, at least in the opinion of the SDF. The alliance with trade unionists was believed to involve too great a departure from strict class-consciousness and the stress on ultimate socialist objectives that distinguished the party.[68]

The SDF's attitude to the LRC at this time well illustrates the party's insistence that it must remain ideologically immaculate and absolutely faithful to what was called the 'recognition of the class war' in its policies and rhetoric. This ideological inflexibility was attractive to some socialists no doubt, but other sympathetic observers were repelled by what they suggested was a tendency toward an unrealistic dogmatism in a party dominated by self-opinionated and rather prickly personalities. On the reported retirement of H.M. Hyndman from the SDF executive in 1901 (which in reality proved to be short-lived), Keir Hardie voiced the feelings of many when he commented that Hyndman's career had shown

that the most brilliant talents, even when combined with unsullied honesty, can never take the place of that touch of human sympathy in which he has shown himself strangely deficient. He never understood the working class, nor could he get into touch with their point of view. It thus happened that he often antagonised when he was making his greatest efforts to propitiate.[69]

In the ideological squabbles of the time it was the SDF's fidelity to the concept of 'class war' which proved to be most irritating to the non-marxist sections of the labour movement,

---

[67] *Justice*, 10 August 1901.

[68] For example, see Rothstein to Kautsky, 15 September 1901, 11SG, Kautsky Archive, D XIX 578.

[69] *LL*, 17 August 1901. For a similar verdict from Max Beer, the London correspondent of the German Socialist paper *Vorwärts*, see Beer to Kautsky, 28 July 1902, 11SG, Kautsky Archive, D IV 47.

and so the SDF's use of the term requires some explanation. The term 'class war' cast something of a spell over the SDF. It marked the party off from 'the trimmers' and gave the SDF members a certain revolutionary mystique and notoriety. Hence their dedication to the offending term seemed to become more heartfelt the more their critics attacked it. By the time of the 1906 general election Hyndman was urging the LRC to make a final decision between 'Liberal-Labour trade unionism' and the SDF's socialism by then specifically described as 'out-and-out Class-War Socialism'.[70] The description frightened and appalled the SDF's critics because it linked hatred and violence with socialism and implied that these were acceptable and even necessary methods. In response the SDF proudly refused to deny that such methods might be necessary. George Lansbury recalled that Quelch and other SDF members actually drilled for the coming revolution and proclaimed their belief in the use of any means, 'bomb, bullet, or ballot box'.[71] In a typical statement in 1901 *Justice* declared that the SDF was committed to both electioneering and revolutionary action. 'We want both our hands free to fight with. Our object is the Social Revolution. Peaceable if possible, forcible if necessary.'[72] These rousing statements no doubt helped establish the SDF's reputation for intransigence. However, it should be stressed that the SDF's dedication to the 'class war' concept did not arise principally from any real belief that street-fighting and barricade-building were imminent. Rather, the term 'class war' reflected the party's conviction that the relation between the worker who sold his labour power and the owner of the means of production was always one of exploitation. 'Class war' described the *situation* of the class of workers relative to the owners in the capitalist order—it did not necessarily mean a commitment to violence as a *method*. Those who used the term were defiantly affirming crucial marxist economic concepts such as the theory of surplus value and immiseration. To deny the term meant to deny their view of

[70] Quoted in C. Tsuzuki, *H.M. Hyndman and British Socialism* (Oxford, 1961), p. 156.
[71] George Lansbury, *My Life* (London, 1928), p. 80.
[72] *Justice*, 24 August 1901.

the grossly unjust workings of the capitalist system. Thus the
SDF would argue that recognition of the 'class war', that is,
acknowledgement of the inevitable 'robbery' of the working
class under capitalism, was the sole guarantee of rock-solid
commitment to socialism.[73]

The ideological differences between the SDF and the ILP
were enough to undermine the many attempts that were
made during this period to achieve socialist unity in Britain.
In addition, the irreconcilable personal temperaments of the
leaders added to the friction between the two socialist bodies.
The rationalists of the SDF leadership had always scoffed, in
Hyndman's words, at the 'queer jumble of Asiatic mysticism
and supernatural juggling which we call Christianity',[74] to
be found in the ILP. For their part, Hardie and Glasier set
their teeth against any fusion proposal. In 1899, for instance,
Hardie claimed that the men and methods of the SDF would
soon transform any new unified party into 'a small dogmatic
sect, without influence or power'.[75] In Glasier's words, the
SDF 'had no kindness for anyone who differed from them in
the slightest'.[76] The leaders of the two rival socialist bodies
were jealous guardians of their own positions. There was
much truth in Quelch's remark to Bruno Karpeles in 1898:
'I think Hardie is for one party, but it must be Keir Hardie's
party, that's all, or else he won't play.'[77] Yet it is equally
obvious that neither Hyndman nor Quelch, for their part,
could have easily defered to Hardie's leadership in any united
socialist party.

Finally, the flamboyant Robert Blatchford and his newspaper the *Clarion* must be taken into account as a significant
force in the socialist movement. Blatchford himself had no
formal connection with any socialist or labour organization
by the turn of the century, and similarly the Clarion Fellowship and the Clarion Scouts were not political bodies but
primarily recreational clubs for socialists from both the ILP

---

[73] For example, see Tattler's criticisms of Hardie, *Justice*, 17 August 1901.

[74] Quoted in Tsuzuki, *Hyndman*, p. 100.

[75] *LL*, 25 February 1899.

[76] *LL*, 8 April 1899. See also Glasier's speech opposing fusion with the SDF
at ILP, *Annual Conference*, 1891, p. 27; and see his letter to Blatchford on this
same issue, Glasier to Blatchford, 19 October 1901, Blatchford Papers.

[77] Quelch to Karpeles, 31 December 1898, 11SG, Karpeles Archive.

and the SDF. The *Clarion* itself, however, had a real influence among socialists and was the most popular organ of the socialist press, achieving sales of 60,000 per week in 1914.[78] Blatchford's socialism was colourful, colloquial, and difficult to fit into an ideological category. He spurned both the marxism of Hyndman's SDF and the 'puritanism' of the ILP and of Hardie in particular; 'the only man I have ever tried to like and failed'.[79] As Blatchford explained to his sub-editor Alec Thompson in 1906: 'See here Thompson, it is not argument we want: it is passion. The dullest and the most intellectual catch alight at the sound of a drum.'[80] Blatchford's ideological haziness naturally offended the SDF, while his cavalier style and withering attacks upon religion got him into trouble with the ILP.[81] His consequent aloofness from the socialist parties and from the Labour Party tended to re-inforce his own disregard of ideology. He advocated instead the paramount importance of 'making socialists'; 'convince the people and never mind the parties', he advised Thompson constantly.[82] In 1910 he broke away completely from the organized socialist movement and retired to his cottage in Norfolk; but he continued to write for the *Clarion* from his retreat.[83]

In spite of the difficulties of classifying Blatchford's ideological position, it is important to stress several aspects of his early socialist writings which bear upon this study. First, Blatchford's most successful books, *Merrie England* and *Britain for the British* were not imbued with the same internationalist spirit which could be found in the marxist tradition and in the idealist approaches of the ILP. Issues of peace and war were in the main ignored. However, one of Blatchford's most important arguments against industrial capitalism in Britain was that it had led to the decimation of

---

[78]   Robert Blatchford, *My Eighty Years* (London, 1931), p. ix.

[79]   Blatchford to Glasier, 19 October 1901, Blatchford Papers; and see another equally vindictive opinion on Hardie in Blatchford to Glasier, (?) December 1901, Blatchford Papers.

[80]   Blatchford to A. Thompson, 14 May 1906, Blatchford Papers.

[81]   Especially Blatchford's *God and my Neighbour*; see Laurence Thompson, *Robert Blatchford: Portrait of an Englishman* (London, 1951), p. 183.

[82]   Blatchford, *My Eighty years*, p. xiii.

[83]   Ibid., p. 230.

British agriculture, which in turn had left Britain vulnerable
to blockade and thus endangered 'the safety and honour of
the Empire'.[84] Blatchford also attacked such important
figures in the Liberal anti-war tradition as John Bright, on
account of Bright's faith in free trade under capitalism.
Second, Blatchford's writings were never as anti-militarist
as those of his rival socialist comrades. Blatchford's own
period in the Army proved to be the most decisive period of
his life. He constantly referred to his military experiences
in his writings, and it was clear that he retained a deep respect for British military institutions.[85] It was perhaps symptomatic of Blatchford's more tolerant outlook toward all
things military that the Clarion Sports of 1904 could include
a special fireworks display at dusk entitled 'Siege of Port
Arthur: Japs versus Russians'.[86] Such panderings to the
popular interest in war would never have been tolerated in
the ILP or the SDF.

[84] Robert Blatchford, *Britain for the British* (London, 1902), p. 117. See also
Robert Blatchford, *Merrie England* (London, 1895), ch. IV.

[85] On Blatchford's military background and writings see the early chapters of
Thompson, *Portrait of an Englishman*.

[86] *LL*, 1 July 1904.

2

'Our Continental Comrades':
The Second International
and the British Connection

If only our Social Democratic German friends were a little more social and a little more democratic!

> J. Bruce Glasier, after attending a meeting of the International Socialist Bureau, *Labour Leader*, 21 June 1907

1. *The Second International*

It is a curious fact that the birth of the Second International, the 'Socialist Parliament of the World' so revered by pre-war European socialists, can be traced back, however indirectly, to a body which had little time for either socialism or internationalism, that is, the British Trade Union Congress. The decision of the TUC of 1887 to support an international conference on the eight-hour day, and the TUC Parliamentary Committee's readiness to enlist the aid of various French 'Possibilists' in furthering this proposal, eventually resulted in the calling of the famous 1889 'Possibilist' International Congress in Paris.[1] This congress, in company with the rival marxist congress held simultaneously in Paris at the Salle Petrelle, marked the formal birth of the Second Socialist International.

What was the Second International? During the 1890s the only real signs of the existence of the International were the periodic congresses held in different European cities (Brussels in 1891, Zurich in 1893, London in 1896). These congresses, variously entitled International 'Socialist', 'Socialist and Labour', or even 'Workmen's' congresses, according to the varying degrees of ideological tolerance on the part of the organizers, attracted delegates whose ideological positions ranged from anarchism to mildly reformist liberalism. The invitations to these early congresses were sufficiently all-

[1] James Joll, *The Second International* (New York, 1966), pp. 28–30.

embracing to allow trade unionists as well as socialists to gain admission.[2] For instance, the invitation to the Brussels Congress of 1891 announced (in rather imperfect English) that 'All workmen's or Socialist Parties, all working men's Associations, all groups of working man indistinctly are invited'.[3] By the time of the Paris Congress of 1900, however, the rules of admission were becoming more restrictive. One stipulation, that delegates must acknowledge 'the necessity of political action', had been inserted in order to exclude the anarchists who had proved so troublesome at the London Congress in 1896. In addition, the Paris Congress laid down that only bodies acknowledging the principle of the 'class war' were eligible for membership of the International[4]—a rather belated and imprecise formulation designed to achieve socialist purity in the ranks of the International. For one other reason also, the Paris Congress marked something of a turning-point in the history of the International. It was decided at Paris to establish a permanent central committee for the International, to be known as the International Socialist Bureau (ISB). The Bureau was to be composed of representatives from the various national sections and would meet at least once a year. In between meetings, a small Bureau executive with a full-time secretary, would watch over the affairs of the International from the Maison du Peuple in Brussels.[5]

By these decisions the International achieved some semblance of visible permanence which added to its stature. Yet the powers of the ISB must not be misunderstood. By definition, the delegates who assembled in the periodic international congresses still held ultimate power to express the

---

[2] See the specific summons to trade unions for the 1893 Zurich Congress, 'The Organisation Committee to the Workers of all Countries', in *Congrès International Ouvrier Socialiste, Zurich 1893* (reprinted, Geneva 1977), p. 27, hereafter cited as *CIOS, Zurich 1893*.

[3] 'International Workmen's Congress 1891: To the Workmen's Associations, of all countries, from the Belgian Workmen's Party, 15 December, 1890', in *Congrès International Ouvrier Socialiste*, Bruxelles 1891 (reprinted Geneva 1977), p. 23, hereafter cited as *CIOS, Bruxelles 1891*.

[4] *Regulations of the Congress and of the Bureau* (Brussels, 1912), p. 23; LP/INT/11/1/427.

[5] The idea of an International Bureau had also been suggested in 1896; see the discussion in the ILP, *Annual Conference*, 1896, p. 19.

policy of the International. There could be no escape from the fact that the International was still a federation of autonomous national sections, representing in turn autonomous parties. Moreover, neither the ISB nor the International Congress claimed the powers of a party executive or party congress, where the majority could vote policy into existence with the minority accepting its defeat. The International had no such coercive authority in this sense. Resolutions and manifestos, therefore, usually expressed a consensus acceptable to a clear majority. The aim was to find common ground rather than to create policy against the will of dissenting parties.[6] If serious dissent was encountered in the halls of the International, the troublesome issues were likely to be referred back for further study,[7] or a way out would be found by declaring that member parties were of course free to decide on the exact means of implementing the International's policy according to their own circumstances.[8] Naturally this quest for consensus involved some resort to vague generalizations, and some critics attacked the International's lack of centralized authority which they correctly identified as the cause of the occasionally ambiguous 'phrase-mongering'.[9] The ISB always ran the risk of declining into a mere 'letter box for the socialist world'.[10] One small example from the 1907 Stuttgart Congress may serve to underline this point. At Stuttgart the ISB reported its decision to reject an Italian request for a special International identity card, noting that the Italian idea 'presupposes a centralised international organisation which does not exist'.[11] In the words of Friedrich

[6] Georges Haupt, *Socialism and the Great War* (Oxford, 1972), pp. 15–16. A contemporary, Richard Fischer of the SPD, made the same analysis at the Magdeburg Congress of his party in 1910, see Wilhelm Schroeder (ed.), *Handbuch der Sozial Demokratischen Parteitage von 1863 bis 1909*, Vol. 2, p. 2.

[7] As occurred in the case of the Keir Hardie–Vaillant amendment on a general strike in case of war at Copenhagen in *1910, Huitème Congrès Socialiste International, Copenhague 1910, Compte Rendu Analytique* (Gand, 1911), p. 475, hereafter *ISC Proceedings 1910.*

[8] See the 'Resolution sur l'exécution des Resolutions Internationales', in *ISC Proceedings 1910*, p. 475.

[9] See for example the memoirs of Henri de Man, *The Remaking of a Mind* (New York, 1919), pp. 27–31.

[10] Haupt, *Socialism and the Great War*, p. 16.

[11] *Proposals and Drafts of Resolutions with Explanatory Reports submitted to the International Socialist Congress of Stuttgart, 1907* (Brussels, 1908), p. 400.

Adler, a leading Austrian socialist, 'The new International is not an independent organisation, it has no sphere of activity which can be separated from that of its sections.'[12]

Therefore, if the history of the International itself is to be followed, it is the fortunes of the various national sections that must be understood, and in particular the fortunes of the German and French socialist parties, the Sozialdemo-kratische Partei Deutschlands (SPD) and the Section Française de l'Internationale Ouvrière (SFIO) as the French socialist party was known after unity was achieved in 1905.

During the twenty-five years of the pre-war International, the SPD was both the pride of European socialists and, at the same time, increasingly the focus of their profound suspicions. There was no questioning the fact that the party founded by August Bebel and Wilhelm Liebknecht in 1875, the party which had survived Bismarck's persecutions and later counted among its hierarchy such respected marxists as Karl Kautsky and the controversial Rosa Luxemburg and Karl Liebknecht, was indeed a great party. In terms of electoral success the SPD towered above other socialist parties, gaining over three million votes in the 1903 elections, the figure rising to four and a quarter million, or one-third of the popular vote, in 1912.[13] Yet, as so many recent studies have shown, during the pre-war decade the party seemed to be steadily retreating from its marxist creed and from its tradition of standing in proud isolation, separate from and supremely critical of the dominant power élite and the in-stitutions of Imperial Germany.[14] Under the influence of Bernstein's revisionist ideas the party tended to be increasingly equivocal regarding time-honoured 'revolutionary' socialist principles. Critics of the SPD could point to the power of the trade unions over the party. The union movement was for-mally separate from the party, but was recognized as the

[12]   Friedrich Adler, July 1914, quoted in Haupt, p. 16.
[13]   Carl E. Schorske, *German Social Democracy, 1905–1917* (New York, 1972), pp. 7, 13, 228, and 233.
[14]   The most useful studies on this theme are Schorske, *German Social Democracy*; Peter Gay, *The Dilemma of Democratic Socialism* (New York, 1970); G. Rother, *The Social-Democrats in Imperial Germany* (Totowa, NJ, 1963); and J.P. Nettl, 'The German Social Democratic Party 1890–1914 as a Political Model', *Past and Present*, 30 (1965).

party's obvious ally and most powerful external pressure group, with over two and a half million trade union members listed in 1912.[15] The trade unions certainly exercised a moderating influence over the party, a moderation well represented in the person of Karl Legien, the leader of the trade union movement. This influence was perhaps most spectacularly revealed in 1906 when the party was forced to reconsider and qualify its support of the proposal for a political mass strike following determined protests against the idea from the trade unions.[16] This is not the place to discuss the extent to which the SPD may have retreated from the socialist-internationalist tradition, but it will suffice to say that by 1914 prominent critics at home and abroad believed the process had proceeded so far as to cast significant doubt on the party's otherwise enviable reputation in the International.

The SPD was by no means the only party within which the more dogmatic marxist factions vied for supremacy with a less revolutionary section variously labelled 'idealist', 're-visionist', or 'reformist'. These same divisions, amongst others, plagued French socialism and were particularly bitter in the long quarrel over the so-called 'cas Millerand'. This was a major ideological squabble provoked by the entry of Alexandre Millerand, a moderate socialist, into a 'bourgeois' cabinet of republican defence formed in 1899 at the height of the Dreyfus upheavals.[17] The marxist faction, led by Jules Guesde, condemned the move, while the moderate idealist faction around Jean Jaurès gave guarded approval. An eventual settlement of the quarrel was made easier by Millerand's steady retreat from his socialist convictions resulting in his exit from the party, and by Jaurès's determination to create unity in French Socialism in spite of the strong tone of the re-affirmation of marxism made by the Amsterdam International

---

[15] Schorske, pp. 12–13.

[16] Schorske, ch. 2. British and American socialists were certainly aware of the power of the moderate German unions; see for example W.E. Walling, 'The New Revisionism in Germany' *Social Democrat*, October 1909, p. 465.

[17] The most useful sources on this dispute are Aaron Noland, *The Founding of the French Socialist Party, 1893–1905* (New York, 1970); and Harvey Goldberg, *The Life of Jean Jaurès* (Madison, Wisc., 1962), ch. 11.

Congress in 1904.[18] By 1905 a new mood of tolerance prevailed between the two factions, and, heeding the call for unity also made by the Amsterdam Congress, they combined to form the new SFIO. This new party was never more than a determined minority party on the French political scene, but its strength did increase steadily at the polls, rising from 877,000 votes in 1906, passing the one million mark in 1910, and achieving a poll of 1,398,771 votes in 1914, equal to about one-sixth of the popular vote. Similarly in the 600-strong Chamber of Deputies, the number of SFIO deputies rose from fifty-four to seventy-six and then 101 in the same years.[19] The party's major newspaper *L'Humanité* probably achieved sales of around 100,000 a day throughout the period 1904 to 1914.[20] So, although not as large a party as the SPD, the SFIO was respected as the standard bearer of the important French socialist and revolutionary heritage. Jean Jaurès, the party leader, was widely acknowledged as a particularly gifted orator in the passionate, idealist tradition.

Whereas German unionists were considered to be moderate in their outlook, their French counterparts, the members of the Confédération Générale du Travail (CGT) in particular, were often more radical than the party men, spurning 'parliamentarism' and flirting instead with syndicalism.[21] This was particularly the case under the secretaryship of Victor Griffuelhes from 1902 to 1909, although his successor, Léon Jouhaux, did exercise some moderating influence. The CGT's *Charte d'Amiens* of 1906, in which the trade unions affirmed their absolute independence from all political parties, including the new SFIO, remained its settled policy in the prewar years. However, while the CGT's robust independence and radical ideology may have suggested strength, the actual

    [18] Joll, *Second International*, pp. 100–6; Goldberg, pp. 322–30.

    [19] Noland, pp. 204–5.

    [20] Various claims were made as to sales figures. The *Labour Leader*, 16 July 1914, claimed the total was 110,000 a day. See also Goldberg, p. 320 where he notes initial sales of 130,000 but continuing financial problems and lagging sales thereafter.

    [21] See Peter N. Stearns, *Revolutionary Syndicalism and French Labor: A Cause Without Rebels* (New Brunswick, 1971); and F.F. Ridley, *Revolutionary Syndicalism in France* (Cambridge, 1970).

numbers mustered under the CGT banner told a very different story. The number of workers in trade unions affiliated to the CGT rose from about 100,000 in 1902 to about 600,000 in 1914; but this last figure represented only one-half of all unionized workers in France; and less than 10 per cent of all wage-earners in the total work-force.[22] Compared with German and British trade unions, the finances of the CGT were also in a remarkably parlous condition.[23]

The French and German socialist parties certainly represented the strength of the Second International. However, it is important to stress that neither of the two parties, nor their comrades in the trade unions for that matter, could claim to represent the working class as a whole in their respective countries. Indeed, in no European country did a member party of the International possess influence over a majority of the working people. The socialists of the International claimed to speak 'on behalf' of the working class, but in no real sense did they speak with the mandate of the people. Throughout the period under study the International remained a federation of small, opposition parties who were still competing for the support of the mass of the people.

2. British Connections with the International: the Trade Unions

Perhaps the most important feature which emerges from the history of British connections with the Second International is the steadily declining interest shown by the trade unions in the affairs of the International as it became more and more clearly identified with dogmatic socialism and with German marxism in particular. After some promising early contacts, the British trade unionists progressively abandoned the International to the socialist societies and the Continental marxists. As was noted above, the TUC had been somewhat indirectly involved in the birth of the International with the summoning

[22] See the complete chart of membership of the CGT in Milorad M. Drachkovitch, *Les Socialismes Français et Allemand et la Problème de la Guerre, 1870–1914* (Genève, 1953), pp. 150–1; Stearns, *Syndicalism*, p. 22.

[23] Drachkovitch, p. 151. See also the low circulation figures of syndicalist newspapers given in Jacques Julliard, 'La CGT devant la Guerre (1900–1914)', *Le Mouvement Social*, 49 (October–December 1964), p. 54.

of the Possibilist Congress in Paris in 1889. The representatives of fifteen trade unions were included among the thirty-nine British delegates to that Congress.[24] Further, when a letter of invitation to the next International Congress was read to the Liverpool TUC in 1890, 'amidst much cheering', it was unanimously accepted.[25] Consequently, at Brussels in 1891, at least a dozen trade unionists sat amongst the socialists in the British delegation which this time numbered twenty-eight.[26] Following this pattern the organizing committee for the Zurich Congress of 1893 dispatched an invitation to the Glasgow TUC of September 1892. However, the summons met with a rather cool reception, for the TUC was already considering a major national conference of its own on the eight-hour day. At first, an attempt was made to withhold the invitation from the delegates. Then, when it was eventually read, the Congress voted to persevere with the TUC's own plan to call a conference on the eight-hour-day issue and rejected an amendment urging trade unionists to attend the coming Zurich Congress.[27] The organizing committee, 'astonished and pained' by this 'discourteous rebuff',[28] drafted another pleading summons specially addressed to British trade unionists and this extra effort seems to have had the desired effect; sixty-eight British delegates eventually arrived in Zurich, forty of whom were listed as representing trade unions or councils, including four members of the TUC Parliamentary Committee.[29] Notwithstanding this quite respectable record of attendance at these early congresses, there were some signs that the official British trade union movement was not really at home in the International. For instance, soon after the Paris Congresses of 1889, the TUC

[24] Tsuzuki, *Hyndman*, p. 117; Pelling, *Origins of the Labour Party*, p. 86.

[25] Reported in the invitation to the Zurich Congress, 1893, 'To the Trades Unions, Trades Councils and Labour Organisations of Gt Britain and Ireland', in *CIOS, Zurich 1893*, p. 34.

[26] 'List des Délégués', CIOS, *Bruxelles 1891*, pp. 274–5.

[27] As above, n. 25.

[28] Ibid.

[29] 'List of Delegates', *CIOS, Zurich 1893*, pp. 192–4. The TUC Parliamentary Committee found it 'impracticable' to summon the British Conference and had decided instead to be represented at Zurich. This is explained in the British Report to the Congress, in *CIOS, Zurich 1893*, p. 397. See also TUP PC *mins.*, 30 January 1893.

Parliamentary Committee proclaimed only guarded support for the new International in a policy motion which bound the committee to promote such gatherings 'provided that they were composed of bona-fide trade unionists and that trade questions alone were to be discussed at their meetings'.[30] The Parliamentary Committee seems to have played down its role on the International quite deliberately. The committee chose not to send any representatives to a preparatory conference prior to the Zurich Congress in 1893,[31] and it also seems to have abandoned the task of writing a formal national report for the 1891 and 1893 Congresses and left this to a small team of enthusiasts from the Gasworkers' Union, the SDF, and some smaller socialist societies who always attended the International in good numbers.[32]

The International Congress in London in 1896 proved to be something of a turning-point in this regard. The cautious attitude of the British union leadership was revealed even in the preparations for the congress when a determined bid was made within the Parliamentary Committee to give the words 'trade unionist' precedence over the words 'socialist workers' in the formal title of the congress. The attempt was narrowly defeated and the compromise title 'International Socialist Workers' and Trade Union Congress' was adopted.[33] When the gathering eventually opened, naturally British trade unionists and socialists attended in force, providing a delegation some 190 strong.[34] The congress was chiefly marked by the expulsion of the anarchist group which provoked several noisy demonstrations.[35] Apparently the British trade union leadership was not impressed by this encounter with the Second International at close quarters, for the TUC Parliamentary Committee reported to the next TUC its serious doubts as to the prudence of identifying the trade

[30] TUC PC *mins.*, 6 November 1889.
[31] Ibid., 10 March 1893.
[32] *CIOS, Bruxelles 1891*, p. 475 and *CIOS, Zurich 1893*, pp. 388 and 395.
[33] TUC PC *mins.*, 4 February, 1895.
[34] Clegg, Fox and Thompson, *British Trade Unions*, p. 301.
[35] Joll, *Second International*, p. 74. According to Hardie's recollection, one delegate had several ribs broken when thrown from the platform during 'wild scenes' on the opening day of the congress; *LL*, 19 August 1904.

unions with congresses of that character in the future.[36] After 1896 most British trade union office-holders appear to have come to regard the International as a forum for theoretical debates between cantankerous Continental marxists and their British socialist colleagues. The last time the TUC seems to have entertained an invitation to an International Congress was in 1903.[37] The very important decision by the TUC Parliamentary Committee in 1905 to have nothing to do with the new British National Committee,[38] the formal link between the 'British Section' and the International, exemplified the determination of the trade unionists to keep the Continental socialists and their International at a safe distance. The socialists in turn were forced to take account of the trade unionists' coolness toward the International. Thus, in 1906, Hyndman advised a committee organizing an appeal for the oppressed in Russia not to mention the ISB by name in their leaflets if they wished to raise more money.[39] Only a small minority of trade union leaders, in the main those with connections in the SDF or ILP, retained any interest in the International after 1900.

For a great many rank-and-file trade unionists the International remained virtually unknown. Bruce Glasier admitted as much to his readers in the *Labour Leader* as late as 1912, when, writing his report on an ISB meeting in Brussels, he acknowledged that 'the great majority of the readers of the *Labour Leader* and socialists generally have at best only a very vague notion of what the International Bureau really is'.[40] What was true for the socialists of the ILP was certainly true for the trade unionists. Very few of the surviving trades council minute-books or trade union journals of the period make any mention of the International.[41] By far the largest number of international contacts by British unionists were

---

[36] Clegg, Fox and Thompson, *British Trade Unions*, p. 302; Pelling, *History of British Trade Unionism*, p. 119.

[37] *TUC Proceedings, 1903*, 10 September 1903. The TUC's reply made no commitment to delegates and simply wished the International Congress success.

[38] TUC PC *mins.*, 28 July 1905.

[39] J.F. Green to Hardie, 9 August 1906, ILP Archives 1906/296.

[40] *LL*, 31 October 1912.

[41] To take a major union as an example, the annual reports of the Amalgamated Society of Railway Servants (ASRS) show no references at all to the

made under the auspices of international trade union bodies rather than through the International. Reference to the correspondence of the International Transport Federation (ITF) will perhaps serve to illustrate the priorities of British trade unionists in this regard. In June 1907, James Sexton, secretary of the National Union of Dock Labourers, had just succeeded in persuading his union to join the ITF and looked forward to the ITF's conference which, he expected, would be held in Stuttgart, for the convenience of all, directly after the forthcoming International Socialist Congress in Stuttgart. When Sexton learned from Hermann Jochade, the ITF secretary, that the ITF would not in fact be meeting until 1908 in Vienna, he replied to Jochade that unless some kind of ITF meeting could be organized at Stuttgart 'we shall not be justified in going' to the International Congress. He added:

I trust you will be able to arrange this, even an informal conference will do, on one day previous to the International. Otherwise I am afraid we shall not be able to go. Try and manage this if you can so that we may justify our journey.[42]

The incident affords an insight into the low priority accorded a Second International Congress in comparison with an international trade union gathering. By 1914 only the Gasworkers', Steel Smelters', and Textile Workers' unions were listed as intending to send delegates to the proposed Vienna International Congress.[43]

Second International apart from a decision by the executive on 14 March 1904 *not* to send any delegates to the Amsterdam Congress (ASRS *Report*, 1904). In the Amalgamated Society of Engineers (ASE) *Journal* there is one brief reference to the 1907 Stuttgart Congress but no details are given (September 1907). Of the very few references to the International in trades council minutes, most are concerned with invitations to the Paris Congress. On most occasions the councils took no action in response to the invitations; see the London TC *mins.*, 28 June 1900, Nottingham TC *mins.*, 18 July 1900, and Glasgow TC *mins.*, 4 July 1900. There are no references to the International's activities at all in the TUC PC *mins.* after 1903.

[42] See Sexton to Jochade 10 June 1907, Jochade to Sexton 14 June 1907, and Sexton to Jochade 20 June 1907; in ITF Correspondence, National Union of Dock Labourers' file, MRC.

[43] *LL*, 2 July 1914.

The British trade unions' neglect of the International naturally caused some concern among the leadership of the ILP for whom the principle of close co-operation between socialists and trade unionists had become sacrosanct. Just as the party fought to preserve the policy of the 'labour alliance' in Britain, the ILP now attempted to build a new sense of tolerance within the International toward their moderate trade union comrades. This effort amounted to an attempt to break down the mood of socialist exclusiveness which had developed within the International as a result of the German-directed campaign against revisionism at Paris in 1900 and Amsterdam in 1904.[44] The ILP strategy was evident in some small ways. For instance, at a meeting of the Interparliamentary Socialist Commission held in London in July 1906, a body created by the Second International, Hardie piloted through a Labour Party motion which inserted the words 'and Labour' into the title of the Commission.[45] But the main effort came in the period just prior to the Stuttgart Congress of 1907. First of all, at a meeting of the ISB in November 1906, Hardie suggested straight out that the invitations to Stuttgart should be unambiguously addressed to the trade unions. Hyndman, ever vigilant against any attempt to water down the marxist character of the International, immediately objected, explaining that he opposed any invitations to trade unions which had not accepted the class struggle. Eventually, Anseele, the Belgian ISB chairman, smoothed over the clash by explaining that the rules of admission were quite clear, and that all trade unions accepting the principle of the class struggle were already welcome.[46] After this preliminary skirmish it was evident that, to achieve their purpose, the ILP leaders would have to secure a change

[44] See Glasier's comments on this ILP effort, and particularly his comment that about 1904 trade unionists at the International had been made to feel 'outsiders', in *LL*, 9 April 1914. See also Hardie's comment in 1904 that 'the borders of an International Congress ought to be wide enough to cover every phase of anti-capitalistic thought', in *LL*, 19 August 1904.

[45] 'Compte-rendu de la première session plénière de la Commission Interparliamentaire Socialiste et de Travail (CIS), Londres, 17–19 juillet 1906', in Haupt (ed.), *Bureau Socialiste International: Comptes Rendus des Réunions Manifestes et Circulaires*, Vol. 1, 1900–1907 (Paris, 1969), p. 220.

[46] 'Compte-rendu de la huitième réunion plénière du BSI, Bruxelles, 10 novembre 1906', ibid., p. 252; *LL*, 16 November 1906.

in the rules of admission.[47] Therefore, at the next meeting of the Bureau in June 1907, Glasier presented an ILP motion quite openly tailored to suit the needs of the British unions. It read:

That the standing orders of the International Socialist Congress be amended so as to make clear that a bona fide trade union or combination of unions is entitled to membership in the congress, with all the rights and privileges thereof, as a section of the international working class movement, provided that union or combination has declared in favour of political action in alliance with socialist parties.[48]

In support of this proposition Glasier argued that the insistence on 'class war' in the prevailing rules was a barrier to the British unions as the phrase was 'foreign and ambiguous to the British ear'. He appealed to the Bureau to make it clear in the invitations and rules that the British unions were 'warmly invited'. The International, Glasier explained, could hardly be regarded as representative of militant democracy in Europe if 'on account of any technical barriers it excluded or admitted only on sufferance the vast body of workmen'. In the ensuing discussion Glasier found himself 'obstructed by the orators' who felt bound to resist any weakening of the rules of admission and claimed that 'yellow unions' would take advantage of any alteration. 'Again and again I attempted to get in my English tongue edgeways', complained Glasier. When the vote was taken only Glasier's hand was raised in support.[49]

Thus the efforts of the ILP to build a more tolerant attitude within the International toward the trade unions, and to encourage trade union interest by a clear invitation of welcome, had failed. Technically, the British unions might have been eligible to attend through their affiliation to the Labour Party; but, in practice, the trade unionists continued to feel alienated from the International, and so no meaningful

---

[47] Thus see the decision of the NAC of the ILP to instruct MacDonald, Hardie, and Snowden to frame an amendment to clause 2 of the rules of admission, NAC ILP *mins.*, 15–16 February 1907.

[48] *LL*, 21 June 1907, gives Glasier's English text.

[49] 'Compte-rendu de la neuvième réunion plénière du BSI, Bruxelles, le 9 juin 1907' in Haupt (ed.), *Bureau Socialiste International*, pp. 276–7 and p. 285; *LL*, 21 June 1907; ISB Circular no. 6, June 1907 (LPGC 20/47).

links between the central British trade union organizations and the International were ever established.

3. *British Connections with the International: the Socialists and the Labour Party*

The history of the relations between British socialists and the ISB illustrates very well how the continuing rivalry between the ILP and the SDF and the quarrel over the possibilities of socialism in the 'labour alliance' were extended into the international socialist arena. Both the ILP and the SDF competed with each other for the goodwill of the Continental socialist parties, and both sought to cultivate their connections with Continental socialists with a view to securing international endorsement of their own particular ideological stance. Hyndman, a frequent visitor to the Continent and a man with some command of the languages, clearly enjoyed a head start over the ILP officials in the quest for Continental friendship. It was typical that, during Jaures's visit to London in 1899, Hardie was summoned to Hyndman's home to meet Jaurès and found the French socialist chatting in his native tongue with Hyndman, while Hardie needed an interpreter.[50] Hardie suspected that Hyndman was using his influence with the Continental leaders to undermine the standing of the ILP and he complained bitterly and frequently of the SDF's 'Continental campaign of slander and abuse' against the ILP.[51] Hardie's sensitivity on this point was of long-standing. In 1896 he quarrelled bitterly with Victor Adler, the Austrian socialist leader, after hearing that Adler, whilst attending the International Congress in London, had been spreading the tale that Hardie was a Tory agent.[52] For their part the Continental socialist leaders tried to steer a neutral course between the rival British socialist groups. For instance, when Liebknecht visited Britain in May 1896 he declined Hardie's personal invitation to his home on the ground that he wished 'to avoid

[50] *LL*, 18 March 1899.

[51] Hardie to Lady Warwick, 28 December 1904, ILP Archives, 1904/67.

[52] Hardie to Adler, 18 December 1896, ILP Archives, 1896/70 (i); Adler to Hardie, 23 December 1896, ILP Archives, 1896/89 (ii).

all suspicion of partiality with regard to the internal divisions which unhappily exist still in England'.[53]

Hardie was determined to improve the ILP's contacts with the Continental socialist parties. He was quite candid about his motives in this respect. At the July 1900 meeting of the ILP Administrative Council he

> urged on the council the importance of the cultivation of closer relations with the Continental socialists in order to counteract the damaging statements that were frequently made with regard to the position and standing of the ILP. With the approval of the council he undertook to work up the international correspondence of the party.[54]

It appears that in 1902 Hardie undertook a visit to the Continent with the specific aim in mind 'to establish personal relations' with the Continental socialist leaders.[55] Within a few years the ILP leaders had certainly improved their personal contacts with the Continental socialists, especially with the more moderate and revisionist figures. However, the struggle for full Continental recognition of the ILP and the Labour Party was to be long and difficult.

Hardie was certainly not mistaken in his assessment in 1900 that the enemies of the ILP held greater sway than its friends at the international level at that time. Events at the Paris International Socialist Congress in September 1900 seem to have confirmed his fears. Here the SDF delegates used their majority to secure for their own leaders, Hyndman and Quelch, the only two seats allocated to Britain on the new ISB. This provoked a long and bitter quarrel, for the ILP refused to negotiate with the SDF and even withheld its dues from the ISB in an attempt to gain separate affiliation.[56] The dispute was still unresolved by the time of the Amsterdam

---

[53] W. Liebknecht to Hardie, 15 May 1896, ILP Archives, 1896/46.

[54] ILP NAC *mins.*, 28 July 1900.

[55] Hardie to Glasier, 8 November 1902, Glasier Papers, I. 1. 1902/50; 'H.M.H. comes here regularly and at first the coldness of some of our folks here could be felt. They have not only thawed now but are positively beaming.'

[56] ILP NAC *mins.*, 29 October 1900, 17–18 June 1901, 16–17 September 1901; V. Serwy to J. Penny, 2 November 1901, Glasier Papers I, 1, 01/37; ILP NAC *mins.*, 22–3 November 1901; Glasier to J. Penny, 5 November 1901, Glasier Papers I, 1, 01/38; H.W. Lee to J. Penny, 7 November 1901, Glasier Papers I, 1, 01/39; and see also *Justice*, 4 January 1902; ILP NAC *mins.*, 28 February 1903.

Congress in 1904,[57] a testament to obstructionism based on personal animosities and ideological conflict. Needless to say the more fundamental problem of the affiliation of the LRC to the International had not been settled either.

The Amsterdam Congress is usually remembered for the fierce and closely contested ideological struggle between Jaurès, the spokesman of the reformist 'Left Bloc' tactic in France, and the German-dominated marxist factions. In the final outcome the slender victory gained by the Germans' Dresden resolution meant the defeat of Jaurès and the re-affirmation of marxism as the fundamental faith of the Second International. It was not, therefore, a very favourable occasion for the moderate ILP and LRC leaders to press on with their challenge to the marxist SDF's dominance of British representation at the International. Indeed, the ILP and LRC leaders were repelled by much of the dogmatism and oratorical pyrotechnics they encountered at Amsterdam. Glasier's comments are most revealing in this respect. Of the open-air demonstration in a public park in Amsterdam prior to the opening of the congress, Glasier wrote:

I was disappointed with the speaking and the size of the crowds. All the speakers with the exception of Bebel seemed to rant away at the phantom enemy 'capitalisme' and I less than ever felt drawn to the typical 'continental' socialist. Hardie was not asked to take part—Hyndman and Quelch as usual did the British serio-comic turn—nay I am wroth when I think of the ineptitude of it all.[58]

The favours enjoyed by the SDF at the International are perfectly captured in this scene; for, while Hyndman and Quelch enjoyed the limelight of the platform, Glasier discovered Hardie, MacDonald, Sexton, Shackleton, and Hodge 'sitting peacefully, smoking their pipes on a bank outside the stir of the crowd', apparently quite unrecognized.[59]

As discussions got under way in the British section it was soon apparent that the SDF delegates were much more familiar than the ILP group with the ideological issues before

---

[57] See Glasier's editorial urging ILP members to come to Amsterdam in large numbers so that the SDF's seizure of the two ISB seats at Paris could be challenged; *LL*, 6 May 1904.

[58] J.B. Glasier to Katharine B. Glasier, 14 August 1904, Glasier Papers I, 1. 04/22.

[59] *LL*, 19 August 1904.

the International Congress. In Hardie's words, many of the ILP people found themselves 'out of touch with those currents and cross-currents which are always at work in the great ocean of Continental Socialism'.[60] At the second meeting of the British section the divisions between the ILP and the SDF on the old 'class war' issue were opened up once more with a speech from Glasier against the terms of the Dresden resolution. 'We had a lively scene', wrote Glasier. 'I fell foul of the class war: and lo Hyndman, Quelch raving and the wolves were on me.' Quelch is reported to have cried out, 'And think of it, he was chairman of the ILP for three years!' When the crucial vote on the issue of socialist tactics came up in the congress hall, the SDF cast its votes for the Dresden resolution and the ILP opposed it.[61] The victory of the Dresden resolution was, therefore, an apparent victory also for the SDF's uncompromising marxist viewpoint on parliamentary and electoral tactics in Britain.

In some ways, however, the ILP and their trade union allies were quite pleased with the results of the Amsterdam Congress. There had been one important victory; the section had convincingly elected Hardie along with Hyndman as the delegates on the ISB, thus ending the long haggle with the SDF over the 'seizure' of the two seats at Paris in 1900.[62] Informally, the ILP and LRC leadership had also established and renewed some valuable personal friendships with Continental socialists.[63] Even the size of the 'labour alliance' delegation this time *vis-à-vis* the SDF group was felt to be quite gratifying. Glasier reported that 'for the first time the Continental movement begins to realise the real position of

---

[60] *LL*, 26 August 1904.

[61] See *LL*, 26 August 1904, and *Justice*, 20 August 1904; J.B. Glasier to Katharine B. Glasier, 15 August 1904, Glasier Papers, I, 1. 04/23; *Justice*, 27 August 1904.

[62] *LL*, 26 August 1904.

[63] For instance, Glasier noted concerning his service in the Commission on Colonial Policy, 'Bernstein is on the Commission with me and we have become friends' (Glasier to Katharine B. Glasier, 16 August 1904, Glasier Papers, I, 1. 04/24). Of Bebel, Glasier wrote, 'I like the man: though I recognise that his environment has made him somewhat hard and metallic' (Glasier to Katharine B. Glasier, 19 August 1904, Glasier Papers, I, 1. 04/27). See also Hardie's claim that the ILP policy had now 'the support of nearly every Continental leader of note', editorial, *LL*, 26 August 1904.

the labour socialist movement in this country'.[64] Quite un-
expectedly then, in view of the hardening of commitment
to marxism at Amsterdam as shown in the Dresden resolution,
this congress appears to have marked a turning-point in favour
of the 'labour alliance' group in the competition between the
two British factions for influence among Continental socialists. Hardie rejoiced that the SDF's position of domination
had at last been 'remedied'; still he found it 'unforgivable'
that Hyndman and his companions had 'systematically
stuffed' the Continental socialists with false information
about the ILP in the past.[65]

Another of the major decisions of the Amsterdam Congress
had been an historic call for socialist unity to be achieved in
all lands. On the face of it the British delegation seemed
amongst the least likely to heed this well-intentioned call to
bury differences and let bygones be bygones. And yet, behind the public disputes on matters of principle at the
congress, several normally antagonistic participants had
noted that, in informal gatherings between congress sessions,
personal relations between the SDF and ILP had been wholly
amicable.[66] Mrs Hyndman had even been seen to kiss two
ILP women delegates when the call for unity was passed.[67] It
was in this spirit of reconciliation that the formal British
connection with the International was at last clarified early
in 1905. After several preliminary conferences of all the
British organizations represented at the Amsterdam Congress,
it was eventually agreed in July 1905 that a special committee
should be established, to be known as the British National
Committee (BNC) for the purpose of managing the British
connection with the Second International.[68] The BNC was
to have seven members, four representing the trade unions
and three the socialist societies. Although this formula ap-

[64] Glasier to Katharine B. Glasier, 17 August 1904, Glasier Papers, I, 1. 04/15.
[65] *LL*, 30 December 1904.
[66] See Hardie's comment that Quelch 'shone' in his search for common
ground, *LL*, 26 August 1904; and Glasier's comment that both Hyndman and
Quelch 'seemed eagerly disposed to be friendly and even went out of their way
to be agreeable to us', Glasier to Katharine B. Glasier, 20 August 1904, Glasier
Papers, I, 1. 04/28.
[67] Glasier to Katharine B. Glasier, 20 August 1904, Glasier Papers, I, 1.
04/28.
[68] British National Committee (BNC) *mins.*, 14 April 1905 and 27 July 1905.

peared to give control to the trade unions, it was soon clear that the real power still lay with the socialists. In the first place, the TUC Parliamentary Committee decided almost immediately that the business of the BNC was outside the legitimate interests of trade unionism, and so, as was noted previously, it refused any connection with the BNC.[69] Thus the four trade unionists who were elected to the BNC, Henderson (LRC), Hodge (Steel Smelters), Thorne (Gasworkers), and Tillett (Dockers) did not represent the trade union movement as a whole, but rather had found their way on to the BNC by invitation simply because of their personal interest in internationalism. Moreover, Tillett and Thorne were well known as prominent socialists, and so only Henderson and Hodge could be said to be truly representative of the moderate trade union viewpoint. Finally, the decision to add Hyndman and Hardie, the two ISB representatives, to the original committee of seven further strengthened the socialist majority on the BNC. From the very beginning, therefore, the BNC gave the unfortunate impression of being yet another socialist forum in which several trade unionists were represented merely for appearances' sake.

Indeed, the continuing inclusion of the trade unionists on the BNC caused persistent difficulties from the outset. At the July 1905 meeting Hyndman's coolness to the trade unionists gave some offence, and later the LRC executive moved the deletion of his comments from their record of the meeting.[70] The LRC executive also refused to bow to the BNC's polite suggestion that, as the BNC was the new international committee, it should perhaps take over the LRC's current invitation to the leading French socialist, Jean Jaurès, to visit Britain.[71] The trade union representation on the BNC did not increase in the years to come and there was never any formal connection with the TUC. Even the select few trade unions who were affiliated with the BNC began to have second thoughts about the worth of this rather

[69] TUC PC *mins.*, 28 July 1905. It was resolved 'That the Committee take no part in the International Committee proposed by Messrs. Keir Hardie and J. Frederick Green on behalf of the International Socialist and Trade Union Congress.'

[70] LRC NEC *mins.*, 5 October 1905.

[71] Ibid., and see BNC *mins.*, 27 July 1905.

expensive relationship. In July 1909, for example, the Steel Smelters wrote to the BNC proclaiming that it was 'impossible to pay more fees on the present scale'.[72] The Dockers resigned from the BNC in 1909 but reaffiliated in 1910.[73] The 1910 Executive Report of the Labour Party included a plea for increased trade union involvement in the BNC and in the work of the Second International, but the appeal had no effect. The BNC financial accounts show that by 1912 the separate trade union affiliations had finally ceased.[74] Thus, it is clear that the formation of the BNC in 1905 did not herald the creation of a truly representative body capable of rallying the interest of the British labour movement as a whole in international questions, or even of speaking for the movement on issues of peace and war with any degree of authority or credibility.

The relationship between the Labour Party and the International also remained confused during these years. For its part, the International seems to have accepted from the first that the LRC would be a valuable addition to its ranks, and had therefore invited the LRC to attend the 1904 International Congress. David Shackleton, the LRC chairman, and Ramsay MacDonald, had formed the official deputation.[75] Whilst in Amsterdam, Shackleton and Hardie had attended the initial meeting of the Interparliamentary Socialist Commission, a new body created by the Amsterdam Congress, and later Hardie had done his best to persuade the executive of the LRC to join this new body and so secure the International relationship.[76] The 1905 conference of the LRC decided to follow Hardie's advice and joined the Interparliamentary Commission of the 'International Socialist and Trade Union Congress', as the NEC Report tactfully described it. This was achieved over the objections of Quelch who protested that the LRC, as a group which had refused to adopt a socialist programme at home, had no right to pose

---

[72] BNC *mins.*, 9 July 1909.
[73] BNC *mins.*, 10 June 1910.
[74] LP/INT/11/1/202 and 217; also BNC *mins.*, for 1913.
[75] LRC *Annual Conference 1905*, p. 41; LRC NEC *mins.*, 12 May 1904.
[76] LRC NEC *mins.*, 27 September 1904. A proposal at this meeting to affiliate immediately was defeated in favour of a proposal to ask instructions from the LRC Conference of 1905.

as a socialist organization abroad.[77] Thus, by 1905 the LRC could be said to have 'joined' the International in that it had a member on the new BNC and had affiliated to the International's new Interparliamentary Commission. So matters stood on paper.

As a result of these arrangements, according to the poetically optimistic columns of the socialist press and the inspiring rhetoric of socialist speakers in city halls and Parliament itself, the masses of British cloth-capped workers and their families now stood in close and cordial contact with their working-class brothers and sisters of the Continent as fellow members of the Second International. But such rhetoric as this, proclaimed by enthusiasts who were seeking to plant the seed of internationalism in the British labour movement does not by its exaggeration prove any naïvety. Everyone involved in the tiny BNC could not but fully realize the fragility and almost token nature of the connection with the International in these years. The reality was plain: a small group of socialists had managed to register their ideologically eclectic fledgling, the LRC, as a formal member of a Continental socialist forum which met infrequently and had, as yet, little real power. Most trade unionists were undoubtedly quite unaware that, through their affiliation to the LRC, they had become enrolled in something called the Second International. And so, it must be conceded, the early connection between the British labour movement and the Second International was far more a matter of symbolism than substance. Yet, beginnings must be made somewhere and somehow as best they can.

[77] LRC *Annual Conference 1905*, p. 41 and see the Executive Report, p. 27.

3

The Issues Emerge: The International, The British Labour Movement, and the Problems of Imperialism and War during the 1890s

This Council calls attention of the workers of the nation to the serious outlook at home and abroad which may result in a disastrous war, and further points out that these troubles have their origins in the desire of each nation to acquire land for the exploitation of the workers, and also that short of socialism, there is no possibility of the workers of the world living together on terms of amity.

> National Administrative Council of the ILP, January 1896, at its first meeting following the Jameson Raid, ILP, *Report of the Annual Conference*, 1896, p. 13.

At the time of the birth of the Second International the socialists of Europe held a proud and tenacious commitment to internationalism and peace, although there was a good deal of room for debate on the issues of national defence, foreign policy, and on the best means of preventing war. These issues had been discussed by liberal, radical, socialist, and marxist thinkers at intervals since the early nineteenth century and in the First International, but never so fully or so systematically as the leaders of the Second International were to do from 1891 onwards.

1. *The Early Congresses of the Second International*

The debates on militarism and war at the early congresses of the Second International soon revealed how difficult it was for socialists to organize, from a position of numerical weakness in each nation, a credible plan of action to prevent war, especially as almost all socialists admitted it was their duty to defend their nation against a neighbouring state's aggression. The debates at the International Socialist Congress at Brussels in 1891 revealed deep divisions amongst social-

ists on these very questions.[1] At that congress, Wilhelm
Liebknecht and Edouard Vaillant reported for the Congress's
Commission on Militarism and presented a resolution condemning war as a fatal product of capitalism, declaring that
lasting peace would come only with the creation of a socialist
order, and calling upon the working class to mount an incessant agitation against militarism and war. This agitation
was 'the only means capable of warding off the catastrophe
of a general war',[2] proclaimed the resolution.

After listening to the supporting speeches of Liebknecht
and Vaillant the delegates seemed willing to close the discussion; but Domela Nieuwenhuis, the leading Dutch delegate, rose and demanded the right to present and defend the
Dutch delegation's resolution on war. This resolution denounced war as never being in the interests of the workers;
and, pointing out that every government pleaded that it was
defending itself against provocation, the resolution insisted
that socialists must condemn *all* wars as capitalists' wars.
The resolution ended with a call to 'the socialists of all
countries to reply to the proposition of a war with a call
to the people to proclaim a general strike'.[3] Speaking in
support of the Dutch resolution, Nieuwenhuis complained
that the Liebknecht—Vaillant resolution was far too vague.
Nieuwenhuis's main point was that if socialists were to have
any real hope of preventing war they must 'renounce all
chauvinism and all distinction between offensive and defensive wars'.[4]

In making their replies Vaillant and Liebknecht no doubt
were confident that the weight of socialist opinion on the
matter of defensive war was behind them. Vaillant defended
the lack of specific instructions in the original resolution,
pointing out that this vagueness was necessary in deference
to socialists from certain countries who ran the risk of persecution on their return home if more radical commitments

---

[1] All the quotations from the Brussels Congress are taken from the official
Report, republished in Vol. 8 of the series *Histoire de la IIe Internationale,* under
the title *Congrès International Ouvrier Socialiste, Bruxelles 1891* (*CIOS*). I have
adopted the pagination of the new volume.

[2] *CIOS, Bruxelles*, pp. 98—9.

[3] Ibid., pp. 99—100.

[4] Ibid., p. 101.

were made.[5] Liebknecht was more spirited in his reply. He rejected the charge that his resolution was a 'tissue of phrases' and condemned the general strike proposal as the real example of utopian 'phraseology'.[6] The proposal was quite impractical, Liebknecht argued, because any working-class leader who dared to call for such a strike against war would be quickly seized and shot by the state authorities. A compromise British amendment, that simply 'recommended' the general strike to the workers as an anti-war weapon, was added to the Dutch proposal; but even that failed to sway the congress.[7] The Dutch resolution was defeated, with only the British, French, and Dutch delegates supporting it. The original Liebknecht–Vaillant resolution was then agreed to, with the Dutch entering a quite protest by abstaining.[8]

Nieuwenhuis had been decisively defeated. Yet the debate provoked by his intervention had in fact done much to vindicate his argument that, if socialists accepted defensive wars, it would be virtually impossible to plan for specific action against war. Vaillant's observation that unanimity on this question could only be achieved through vague generalizations was an acknowledgement of Nieuwenhuis's logic. Similarly, Liebknecht's insistence during the debate, that only the French and German socialists truly understood the difficulty of planning to resist war,[9] merely reinforced the point that it was virtually impossible for socialists on either side of a tense frontier to present a convincing and solid front against war-mongering once they had conceded their duty to defend their nation. Having rejected the 'anti-patriotic' position, the congress majority really had no choice but to admit that specific anti-war plans were impossible. Thus not surprisingly, the congress placed all its faith in 'incessant agitation' against war. No more specific a commitment was logically possible. Of course, another problem hovered behind all these considerations, namely, that of the

[5] Ibid., p. 103.
[6] Ibid., p. 104.
[7] Ibid., p. 108. The British resolution also attempted to commit the Congress to international arbitration and invited members of the various parliaments to press for arms reduction.
[8] Ibid., p. 111.
[9] Ibid., p. 106.

still largely unchallenged patriotic assumptions of the ordinary working people. As Hyndman noted on his return from Brussels:

It was all very well that Liebknecht and Vaillant had both denounced the growth of militarism in Europe and had taken care not to mention the question of Alsace-Lorraine; nevertheless, it is not the few well organised and thoughtful socialists of France or of Germany that govern in these questions, but the mass which is still stirred when the patriotic chord is touched.[10]

At the next congress of the International, held in Zurich in 1893, the same issues were debated between the same protagonists, although the arguments had become a little more sophisticated.[11] The resolution on this problem, presented this time by the Russian socialist Plekhanov, seemed to subordinate the struggle against war to the wider struggle for socialism.[12] The resolution called upon all socialists to combat chauvinism and uphold international solidarity, and it noted that the response of the working class to war had been defined 'in a precise fashion' by the Brussels Congress. This last claim must have been particularly irritating to Nieuwenhuis and his supporters who had always insisted that the chief weakness of the International on this question was its reluctance to give any specific instructions. Nieuwenhuis immediately brought forward a new Dutch counter-proposal, namely, that socialists everywhere should hold themselves ready 'to reply immediately to any declaration of war on the part of any governments, by means of a general strike and wherever the workers can exercise influence upon the war, in the countries affected, by a military strike'.[13] In the course of his speech the controversial Dutchman also repeated allegations of chauvinism against the SPD which he had first raised at Brussels in 1891. He chided Bebel for having

---

[10] *Justice*, 5 September 1891, quoted to Tsuzuki, *Hyndman*, p. 120.

[11] According to Michel Winock, the official proceedings of the Zurich Congress and, in particular, the records of the debate on militarism, are incomplete and inaccurate. Therefore I have chosen to use the speeches of Nieuwenhuis and Plekhanov which appeared in the socialist press after the congress. These are found in the appendix of the reprint *CIOS, Zurich 1893*, pp. 535–46. See Winock's comments in his introduction to this volume, ibid., p. 14.

[12] Ibid., p. 227.

[13] Agenda Paper, ibid., p. 69.

professed his eagerness to defend Germany against Russian barbarism 'as if Germany were the country of sweet kindness and excellent civilisation'.[14]

Once again, however, Nieuwenhuis's arguments and criticisms of the Germans were not sufficient to sway most of his hearers, who held to their conviction that a just war of defence must be allowed for and, therefore, refused to bind their hands in advance to a fixed response to war. In his speech in reply, Plekhanov focused attention on the Russian threat, and argued that the general strike against war would simply deliver up western and central Europe to the Cossacks. He defended Bebel's emphasis on the Russian menace, and appealed to the Polish delegates present to confirm the fearful nature of a tsarist regime of occupation.[15] Liebknecht, Adler, and others rose to support Plekhanov's points, stressing the threat from Russia and the futility of 'puerile barrack insurrections'.[16] In the view of the majority, the International could only commit itself to action which was demonstrably within its power, namely, tireless propaganda and mass demonstrations against war as part of general socialist campaigning. This time the British delegation was persuaded by the case put forward against the general strike, and Edward Aveling announced that Britain too would support the motion presented by Plekhanov. The English, he proclaimed, were united in their determination to combat war, but they also did not believe the workers were strong enough yet to organize a military strike; if they had the strength they would not just prevent war, but press forward 'to push capitalism to heaven or hell'.[17] Once again the 'German' viewpoint carried the day by winning the votes of fourteen nations, while only three nations (including the French majority socialists) supported the Dutch in their proposal.[18]

These debates at Zurich in 1893 appeared at first to be no more than a simple repetition of the clashes at Brussels. In relation to later events, however, it is clear that the 1893

---

[14] Ibid., p. 537.
[15] Ibid. pp. 541–6.
[16] Ibid., pp. 231–3.
[17] Ibid., p. 234.
[18] Ibid., p. 237.

debates were important in confirming certain prejudices in the minds of many socialists with regard to the question of the proper socialist attitude to war. First, the dominant role played by Nieuwenhuis in the discussion tended to confirm the view that the proposal to prevent war by means of a general strike was something of an anarchistic idea, attractive only to woolly-minded, impractical visionaries. Second, the debates tended to raise some suspicions that perhaps the Germans were reluctant, at least a little more reluctant than the French, to confront militarism at home. At Zurich the German socialists had again been cast in the role of moderates on this issue. They had once more been seen to oppose the French on the matter of the general strike, and they had again been accused by their critics of harbouring chauvinistic sympathies. The scepticism regarding the German's inter-nationalism, which may be said to have first gained a foot-hold in socialist circles at these two congresses, proved diffi-cult to extirpate, and in the years ahead was seriously to undermine attempts to present a public face of mutual trust between the socialist parties of Germany, France, and Britain. Third, the debates confirmed the assumption in the minds of almost all observers that the general strike against war was a plan that necessarily came into effect *in reply* to a declaration of war. The wording of the Dutch proposal and all the speeches on the matter assumed that the strike would begin only upon the outbreak of war. This assumption was to make it all the more difficult for Keir Hardie and others in the years after 1907 to revive interest in the general strike as an anti-war weapon for use in a crisis situation *prior to* any declaration of war.

Officially, the Zurich Congress recorded the International's continuing faith in the prevention of war by means of propa-ganda and peace demonstrations. But it should be noted that one additional commitment had been made. As a result of a Belgian amendment to the Plekhanov resolution, the socialist parties were now obliged to vote against their government's war budgets in each country on every occasion, and to cam-paign for general disarmament.[19] This commitment was

[19] Ibid., p. 235.

accepted by all. The German socialists willingly agreed, for their famous rallying cry of 'Not a man nor a penny for this system' seemed to have been elevated to the level of dogma within the International by the Belgians' move. Yet the consensus masked an obvious contradiction. How could those who believed in defensive war undertake to oppose military spending on *every* occasion? If socialists were ever to gain decisive numbers in any parliament such a blanket policy might deprive the nation of the means of maintaining its defence capability relative to potential aggressors, that is, its capacity to wage a defensive war. It was exactly this contradiction which, in future years, would haunt the SPD as its fears of Russia grew, and which, in turn, would haunt some French and British socialists whose disquiet over German militarism could not be suppressed indefinitely.

The next two International Socialist Congresses, in London in 1896 and in Paris in 1900, did little to alter the International's policy on war. The official view on war and its causes remained unchanged. But several aspects of the debates at London and Paris are noteworthy. Firstly the International remained firmly committed to the long-standing radical notion that the abolition of standing armies and their replacement by national citizens' militias was vital to peace. On the Continent the International's policy on this issue hardly mattered at all, for clearly there was no prospect that the governments of Russia, Germany, or France would agree to convert their massive standing armies into tame, democratically run citizens' militias. But in Britain, the possibility of some kind of citizens' force to add strength to the small British army was on the political agenda, and, indeed, the creation of the Territorial Army in 1907—8 was on the model of a citizens' military force. Thus, it should be noted that opinion on this matter in Britain was always divided. At the London Congress, notwithstanding the almost unanimous views of Continental socialists, the ILP announced it would never accept the citizen army policy because, in its view, short-term universal military training would give a fillip to militarism.[20] Second, the London Congress was notable in

---

[20] *International Socialist Workers' and Trade Union Congress, London 1896: Report of Proceedings* (London, 1896), p. 42.

that the concept of international arbitration gained official endorsement, in spite of the exclamation of one delegate that the idea was all 'middle-class molasses'. Finally, that most controversial of proposals, the general strike against war, fared no better, either at London or Paris. At London the French delegates were content to declare their own private support for the idea. When at Paris they pressed for the inclusion of the anti-war strike in the official resolution, they were defeated.[21]

At the turn of the century, therefore, the International's policy was of the utmost simplicity. Peace would come with socialism. In the meantime, socialists were dedicated to persuading their fellow citizens to detest war and, by means of mass demonstrations, to deter their governments from waging war.

2. *The British Labour Movement, War, and Imperialism in the 1890s*

Only very gradually did British labour leaders absorb the intensely critical attitudes toward militarism, imperialism, and war that were commonplace among Continental delegates at the early congresses of the Second International. It was not until the mid 1890s that criticisms of the military system and imperialist wars began to be voiced with determination in British labour circles, and even then the small socialist societies were the ones who were seen to be making the running on these issues. The Lib-Lab parliamentarians of the 1880s and 1890s, who normally upheld the trade union view that domestic and industrial issues were the sole concerns of a labour representative, had been silent on the great issues of Empire.[22] With few exceptions, the Lib-Lab MPs and organized labour generally ignored or acquiesced in the annexations

---

[21] Joll, *Second International*, p. 134.
[22] For a more lengthy review of the reasons why labour neglected foreign affairs in this period see Tingfu F. Tsiang, *Labor and Empire: A Study of the Reaction of British Labor to British Imperialism Since 1880* (New York, 1923), p. 218, and Bernard Porter, *Critics of Empire: British Radical Attitudes to Colonialism in Africa, 1895–1914* (New York, 1968), pp. 105–6 and 137.

of territory in Africa in these years, and paid scant regard to the activities of the Chartered Companies.[23]

In the pages of the British socialist press, however, anti-imperialist and anti-war themes began to be given greater prominence from the early 1890s onward. Hardie's articles in the *Labour Leader* show him moving from sporadic criticisms of the more brutal incidents in the story of the Empire to a determined anti-militaristic position during the years when imperialist policies seemed to be giving rise to more frequent conflicts and increased tensions. In 1895 he attacked the Liberal Government over the fighting in Chitral and Nicaragua, noting that these were wars 'to protect the traders' accounts'. In a comment that seemed to leave open the possibility of support for Empire Hardie wrote, 'We are not "little Englanders", but we indignantly protest against all this pitiful devilment being carried out in the name of Great Britain. Bullets will not carry England's message to the world.'[24] At this point imperial issues must still have been of minor importance to the ILP, for the party manifesto for the 1895 elections made no mention of foreign or imperial affairs.[25] But with the return of a Conservative Government in 1895, the *Labour Leader* seemed to find many more imperialist excursions about which to protest, especially in southern Africa.[26] The Ashanti War in late 1895 brought forth some bitter editorial onslaughts from Hardie and others, and even a condemnation of the Duke of Connaught who, while attending a farewell for the Ashanti expedition, had indiscreetly expressed the hope that the soldiers would soon have a chance to use their carbines.[27] The Venezuelan crisis in December 1895 also

[23] Tsiang, *Labor and Empire*, pp. 60–70, reviews the years 1880 to 1890. See also his review of the awakening interest in the years 1891 to 1895, ibid., pp. 60–5. Tsiang concluded that 'the predominant characteristic of the reaction of British Labor to British Imperialism in Africa from 1880 to the 1920s is acquiescence', ibid., p. 95.

[24] *LL*, 4 May 1895; see also Hardie's comments *LL*, 20 April 1895.

[25] See 'To the Electors', *LL*, 6 July 1895.

[26] See article on Rhodes, 'The African Colossus', *LL*, 14 September 1895, and on the colour bar in South Africa, *LL*, 9 November 1895; also small articles on the Congo (19 October 1895) and on Bechuanaland (14 September 1895).

[27] On the Ashanti War see article by Isabella Mayo, *LL*, 30 November 1895; on the Duke of Connaught see *LL*, 14 December 1895; and also see *LL*, 4 January 1896, 1 and 8 February 1896.

attracted Hardie's scathing editorial pen. In Hardie's opinion, US President Cleveland was drumming up a crisis for the coming election and for the purpose of securing a major increase in defence spending.[28] This interpretation of 'scares' manufactured for internal consumption remained central to Hardie's analysis of foreign affairs for years to come.

The Jameson Raid in December 1895 at once breathed new life into the issues of imperialism and war, and the socialist press as a whole now sought to discredit the Salisbury Government on the basis of its imperialist entanglements. From this time onward the pages of Hardie's *Labour Leader* reflect the depth of his personal revulsion of war. His comments on the Jameson incident are particularly worthy of attention for here can be seen the germination of an idea which was later to obsess him. This was the formulation of a plan to prevent war, even to the point of bluffing the warmakers. He wrote in passionate terms:

If peace is to be maintained at this juncture it is to the forces of organised labour we must look for help. The workers of the world have everything to lose by war. They supply the soldiers to be shot and the money for the conflict ... None of the glory can by any possibility filter down to them. Their sons who die on the field of battle will be shovelled into nameless trenches, whilst those who survive will be left to die uncared for and unhonoured in our workhouses ... If our comrades of Germany, France, Belgium and the Continent generally would let it be known in unequivocal fashion what their sentiments are on this war question they would do good service to the cause and to humanity. The socialist movement by reason of its strength has now responsibilities which did not belong to it in the struggling days of adversity. The socialists of the world can prevent war ... If it were known that not only would socialists take no part in war, but that they would use at all hazards the opportunity which a world-wide conflagration would provide to give effect to their principles, then there would be no war. A word to the wise is sufficient.[29]

Hardie was not alone in seeing the Jameson raid as a turning-point in the socialists' approach to foreign and imperial affairs. He carried the ILP with him. At its first meeting in 1896 the ILP Administrative Council called the attention of the workers to 'the serious outlook at home and

[28] *LL*, 28 December 1895.
[29] *LL*, 11 January 1896.

abroad which may result in a disastrous war'.[30] In the wake
of the raid all the *Leader's* writers maintained a steady stream
of articles critical of Joseph Chamberlain, Rhodes the 'African
Colossus', and all manifestations of imperialism.[31] *Justice*
and the *Clarion* also now focused their propaganda upon imperialism and the menace of war.[32] The International Congress
in London in the summer of 1896 also reinforced the tendency within Britain for a more thoroughgoing socialist
critique of imperialism.[33] The demonstration in Hyde Park,
organized by the congress, was dedicated to peace and a
resolution was presented to the crowds condemning war as
the product of the ruling classes' rivalry for markets.[34]

The militaristic displays associated with the Queen's
Diamond Jubilee in 1897 also alerted British socialists to the
dangers inherent in the imperialist revival. The socialists
searched for effective counter-propaganda. For instance, the
ILP News remarked that there was 'dry rot in the imperial
fabric'; for while London celebrated, the Jameson raiders
were officially white-washed and the Queen's Indian subjects
endured terrible famine.[35] Even Robert Blatchford's Clarion
Press was moved to attack the Jubilee. A.M. Thompson,
Blatchford's closest companion, wrote a militantly anti-
imperialist pamphlet entitled *Toward Conscription—Jubilee
Patriotism: Its Meaning, Cause and Effects*, in which he
ridiculed the Jubilee celebrations as an 'organised conspiracy

[30]   NAC Report, ILP, *Report of the Annual Conference, 1896*, p. 13.

[31]   See cartoons *LL*, 29 February and 11 April 1896; 'Marxian's comments,
LL, 2 and 9 May 1896; cartoon against the Chartered Companies *LL*, 23 May
1896; full-page illustration 'Peace or War' in the May Day issue, *LL*, 2 May 1896;
'Marxian' again on Rhodes, 2 and 9 January, 27 February, and 27 March 1897.

[32]   See Tsuzuki's review of the SDF response in *Hyndman*, pp. 125—6; and
B. Porter's review of *Justice* and the *Clarion* in *Critics of Empire*, pp. 99—100 and
103—4.

[33]   See the article by Prince Kropotkin 'War and Peace', *LL*, 25 July 1896, and
the editorial by Isabella Mayo in *LL*, 1 August 1896. It is interesting to note that
also in contrast to the silence of the 1895 ILP election manifesto on foreign
affairs, in the East Bradford by-election Hardie attacked the imperialist policies
of the British Government and the military system of Europe as a whole; see
K.O. Morgan, *Keir Hardie*, p. 92.

[34]   *LL*, 25 July 1896.

[35]   *ILP News*, July and August 1897.

of patriotic brag, bounce and bluster'.[36] Meanwhile, *Justice*, reflecting Hyndman's special interests, concentrated its attacks upon the inequities of British imperialism in India.[37]

The British campaign in the Sudan from 1896 to 1898 also provoked the anger of the socialists.[38] In October 1896 the ILP made a formal protest to the Government comparing the 'wholesale massacres' in the Sudan at that time with the Armenian massacres of the same year.[39] 'Pious bible-reading England', predicted the *Labour Leader* bitterly, 'is preparing to close the century perhaps in an orgy of blood.'[40] Ramsay MacDonald certainly agreed in sensing the dangerous mood of the nation's rulers. In January 1898 he urged socialists to modify their preoccupation with the domestic scene and give closer attention to the issues of foreign and imperial policy.[41] Similarly, in February 1898, Hardie and David Lowe, the editor of the *Labour Leader*, made plans to upgrade the foreign affairs coverage of the paper.[42] When the victory in the Sudan finally came with the Omdurman battle late in 1898 the socialist press reacted with hostility. Hardie was full of contempt for Kitchener, who, he claimed, had violated the ethics of a slaughterhouse in littering two square miles of desert with Dervish corpses.[43] *Justice* denounced in particular the alleged slaughter of the Dervish wounded and the desecration of the grave of the Mahdi as 'an eternal blotch' on the reputation of England.[44]

Colonial conflicts and threats of other conflicts seemed to be multiplying during 1898. Not only were there Britain's own wars in the Sudan and in Matabeleland, but also there was growing friction with both France and the Boer Republics.

---

[36] Alexander M. Thompson, *Towards Conscription* (Clarion Pamphlet, no. 21, London, 1898), p. 3.

[37] Tsuzuki, *Hyndman*, pp. 125–6.

[38] On the Sudan see comments by Marxian, 21 and 28 March 1896, Hardie's editorial, 11 April 1896, the cartoon of 13 June 1896, and Hardie's editorials, 26 September and 31 October 1896, all in *LL*.

[39] *LL*, 17 October 1896; NAC Report, *ILP Conference 1897*, p. 13.

[40] *LL*, 11 April, 1896.

[41] *ILP News*, January 1898.

[42] Hardie to David Lowe, 3 February 1898; ILP Archives 1898/11.

[43] *LL*, 10 December 1898.

[44] *Justice*, 12 November 1898.

The tensions between Japan and Russia and between Spain and the USA caused concern too in the socialist press. The proposals for German naval expansion announced early in 1898 and the unfolding Dreyfus affair in France were other unsettling events which seemed to show that militarism was becoming a 'fetish' on the Continent.[45] All the more worrying was the fact that the militaristic and imperialist spirit seemed to have gained a hold on the working people. As the *Labour Leader* reflected gloomily in 1898, 'No doubt the mass of men everywhere are quite ready in the name of patriotism to hate their fellow creatures as enemies at the word of their capitalist rulers.'[46] British socialists were under no illusions as to their weakness in the face of a threatened war. It was in this context that the ILP Conference in April 1898, in a move anticipating the formation of the ISB two years later, urged the creation of a permanent 'International Socialist Committee' to build up international solidarity and co-ordinate a common policy for socialists in the event of war. At the 1898 Conference Hardie also delivered a major attack on imperialism and the growth of the 'war spirit'.[47] For good measure the conference declared its opposition to conscription, its introduction having been rumoured for several months.[48]

The seriousness of the threat to European peace posed by competitive imperialism was brought home to British socialists during the Fashoda crisis in the latter months of 1898 when France and Britain seemed suddenly to be close to actual war over their rival ambitions in Africa. The protracted war scare over Fashoda was also the real test of the internationalism professed by British socialists. To their credit they correctly appreciated their lack of power and so limited their actions to strong words and pleas for wider protests.[49] After hurriedly

---

[45] *ILP News*, April and February 1898.

[46] Editorial by Ruddifarne, *LL*, 26 March 1898. For other admissions of the patriotic assumptions of the British people see Hardie's comments *LL*, 7 May 1898 and Marxian's comments, *LL*, 7 May and 15 October 1898.

[47] *ILP Annual Conference 1898*, p. 24.

[48] Ibid., p. 47.

[49] On Fashoda see Marxian's comments, 17 September, 8 and 15 October, and editorials 29 October, 5 and 12 November 1898. On Hyndman's attitude see Tsuzuki, *Hyndman*, p. 126.

gaining the agreement of other ILP leaders, Hardie dispatched a petition to Lord Salisbury calling upon the Government to submit the dispute to international arbitration.[50] At the height of the crisis Hardie called upon every trade council, trade union, co-operative society, ILP and SDF branch to forward similar petitions. In so doing he revealed much of his own personal conviction that the voice of labour could prove decisive in such crises. 'Let organised labour speak out here and in France', he wrote, because 'no government would dare declare war if national feeling be opposed.'[51] *Justice*, which had long predicted trouble between Britain and France over Africa, also campaigned for peace during the crisis and gave prominence to the anti-imperialist stand of the French socialists. However, *Justice*, characteristically, found greater fault with England's rival. France had 'traded continuously on our desire for peace' and, bad as the British press may have been, the French papers were 'foul-mouthed gutter sheets'.[52] None the less, *Justice* stood firm against the 'English war fever' and denounced any war with France as a 'crime'.[53] Fortunately the crisis was eventually resolved without war, but the mood of jingoism within the nation had been starkly revealed, and socialists in the ILP and the SDF frankly confessed their deep concern over this aggressive spirit.[54]

A wholly unexpected event at this time, the promulgation of the Tsar's Rescript of August 1898 in which a call was made for a peace conference to consider arms limitation, was also important in assisting the socialists to clarify their own approach to the problems of war and peace. The markedly different responses of the trade unions, the ILP, and the SDF to the Tsar's initiative and the 'Peace Crusade' which followed also served to underline the importance of ideology in the determination of policies on militarism and war. The TUC, meeting in Bristol in September 1898, hailed the Tsar's

[50] See the telegrams and letters on this in the ILP Archives, FJ 1898/117–24. The resolution was also sent to the press.
[51] *LL*, 29 October 1898.
[52] *Justice*, 5 and 12 November 1898.
[53] Ibid., 15 and 29 October 1898.
[54] *Justice*, editorial 14 January 1899 and NAC report to ILP *Annual Conference*, 1899, p. 4.

proposal and urged the British Government to give its full co-operation.[55] This expression of support provoked the attention of the bourgeois peace movement. For example, the famous German peace campaigner and novelist Bertha von Suttner lavished praise on the British trade unionists for their far-sightedness.[56] At first, the ILP seemed equally enthusiastic about the Tsar's Rescript. Indeed it was an ILP member, Pete Curran, who had introduced the motion welcoming the Russian proposal at the Bristol TUC. Russell Smart, editor of the *ILP News*, rejected the cynical interpretation quickly afoot in some quarters that the Tsar was merely seeking to advantage Russia:

His motives are to us of no moment. If the result be to avert, or even postpone war, and to decrease the burdens of the armed peace that are crushing the workmen of Europe by their exactions of blood and treasure, socialists may be indifferent as to which country will reap the greatest economic or diplomatic advantage.[57]

Hardie also believed that, irrespective of the Tsar's motives, the holding of a peace conference (soon organized for The Hague) would provide good anti-war propaganda and ought to be supported.[58] A discordant note, however, was sounded by the *Labour Leader* when G.H.A. Samuel ('Marxian') whose articles were often decidedly more militant than Hardie's,[59] denounced the Tsar's initiative from the outset. In Samuel's opinion it was vital that the people realized that militarism and war were inherent in capitalism. 'No strokes of the pen can separate capitalism and bloodshed', Samuel proclaimed.[60] The ILP Administrative Council in its official resolution refrained from praising the Tsar, but expressed hearty sympathy with the proposal for arms limitation.[61] The controversy within the ILP bubbled along for some time

[55] Tsiang, p. 169.
[56] Caroline E. Playne, *Bertha von Suttner and the Struggle to Avert the World War* (London, 1936), p. 104.
[57] *ILP News*, September 1898.
[58] *LL*, 31 December 1898.
[59] In fact Samuel and Hardie had quarrelled in 1896 over Hardie's 'tampering' with Samuel's copy for the *Labour Leader*; see Samuel's letters to Hardie in the ILP Archives, FJ/1896/13, 15, 17, 20, and 22.
[60] *LL*, 3 and 10 September 1898. See also Felix Moscheles's letter complaining about Samuel's negative attitude in *LL*, 31 December 1898.
[61] NAC Report, *ILP Annual Conference*, 1899, p. 20.

and was eventually settled at the party conference in April 1899. In a closely contested struggle the conference rejected a resolution congratulating the Tsar, rejected another welcoming 'every endeavour' to achieve peace, and finally passed by a margin of fifty-three votes to fifty-two an uncompromising resolution which ignored the Tsar's initiative and simply reaffirmed that only socialism could bring peace.[62] It was hardly a decisive victory for the Samuel viewpoint.

In any case the ILP leaders had already given valuable assistance to the major public propaganda associated with the Hague Peace Conference, the 'Peace Crusade' organized by the irrepressible journalist W.T. Stead. In December 1898 Stead had launched the idea of a pilgrimage of peace to all the European capitals to drum up support for the coming Hague Peace Conference. Two of the ILP's leaders, MacDonald and Sam Hobson, joined a number of other socialists on the Peace Crusade Committee which sought to organize meetings in favour of the Hague Conference. The trade unionists also provided valuable support for Stead. A special Labour Committee was formed and the 'old unionists', including Thomas Burt, Henry Broadhurst, W.R. Cremer, and Sam Woods, joined such 'new unionists' as George Barnes and Will Crooks on that committee. The committee drew up a special address to the working class which was duly signed by all members of the ILP Administrative Council.[63] Keir Hardie, however, showed only guarded support for Stead and declined his invitation to join the pilgrimage to the European capitals because too many of the 'pilgrims' were self-confessed enemies of the labour movement.[64]

The SDF, by contrast, was sceptical of the Tsar's Rescript and the proposed Peace Conference from the very beginning. Hyndman, who had so often declared that Russia was the arch-enemy of human progress,[65] was not about to change

[62] Ibid., p. 44.

[63] *ILP News*, February 1899.

[64] F.T. Whyte, *The Life of W.T. Stead* (London, 1925), vol. 2, p. 289. See Hardie's support for the Crusade, editorial *LL*, 25 February 1899, and his guarded criticism, *LL*, 18 March 1899.

[65] For example, see Hyndman to Bebel, 14 February 1896, 11SG Bebel Archive, 110/1: 'The real danger to Europe is Russia ... She does threaten all freedom.'

his attitude to the Russian potentate on this issue. He poured scorn on the 'Russian disarmament dodge',[66] and *Justice*, in the main, supported the Hyndman line.[67] Similarly, *Justice* attacked the 'saintly Stead' and his 'peace professing humbugs' who had joined the Crusade.[68] *Justice*, much in the style of G.H. Samuel, hammered away at the theme that capitalism and war were inextricably linked, and that 'bourgeois' pacifists were therefore guilty of utterly transparent hypocrisy. There were some dissenters from this viewpoint within the SDF. Herbert Burrows and J. Frederick Green did join the Peace Crusade Committee, and five members of the SDF executive signed the Committee's address to the working class.[69] Overall, however, Hyndman's viewpoint was dominant, especially in the pages of *Justice*.

Hyndman's position also received the endorsement of the Continental socialist leaders when in March 1899 Jaurès, Emile Vandervelde, and Wilhelm Liebknecht attended an SDF-sponsored internationalist demonstration at St. James's Hall.[70] Here Jaurès proclaimed that it was 'absurd to imagine that capitalism and capitalist governments will ever bring about peace'. Vandervelde, too, expressed his scepticism that the Tsar's Rescript would achieve anything, and Liebknecht denounced the Tsar's peace agitation as a 'swindle and a snare'. Hyndman and Quelch echoed these ideas, and even the ILP speakers present, Pete Curran and Fred Brocklehurst, stressed that socialism alone could achieve lasting peace and they refrained from any favourable references to the Hague initiative. This tone of outright opposition to the Hague experiment obviously disturbed Hardie, and he complained in a speech at a dinner for the visiting foreigners that there was no united voice on this matter.[71] However, Hardie's reservations on these matters only served to highlight the distance

---

[66]   See Hyndman's letters, *Justice*, 10 September 1898.

[67]   *Justice*, 17 September and 24 December 1898.

[68]   *Justice*, 21 January, 4 and 11 February 1899; see also Hyndman, *Further Reminiscences*, pp. 305–7, 309–10.

[69]   *ILP News*, February 1899 and letter of F. Davey, *Justice*, 18 February 1899.

[70]   For the proceedings see *Justice*, 11 March 1899. See also Liebknecht's editorial, *Justice*, 25 March 1899. *Justice* also contains reports of members of the SDF disturbing Stead's Peace Crusade meetings; see *Justice* 1 and 15 April 1899.

[71]   *LL*, 18 March 1899.

that still remained between his own viewpoint and the un-compromisingly hostile attitudes held by most Continental socialists toward 'bourgeois pacifism'. A convincing demonstration of this hostility was soon to follow. At the International Socialist Congress in Paris in 1900, the official resolution on militarism condemned outright peace conferences such as that held at The Hague in 1899.[72]

To sum up, the years from 1895 to 1899 had not been without profitable lessons for British socialists. In response to the many conflicts and tensions of these years they had evolved increasingly critical analyses of imperialism and militarism, and they had made a beginning in pressing the importance of these matters upon the rest of the labour movement. The socialist critique of imperialism, first presented by Belfort Bax in *Justice* in 1894,[73] depicted the push for empire as a result of the workings of an under-consumptionist capitalist home economy. The class of owners, having restricted purchasing power at home, chose to embark upon an endless quest for new markets to absorb surplus production and for new fields of investment for accumulated profits. According to this view, the propertied classes sought to direct the foreign policies of the state in their own interests, and they would use the state's own military forces to secure the commercial monopolies that lay at the heart of imperial conquests. The civilizing mission, national glory, and religious zeal were mere pretexts to mask sordid commercial greed. This critique was adopted by Hardie and G.H. Samuel and presented repeatedly in the *Labour Leader*.[74] Quite apart from their analysis of the process of imperialism, all socialist factions agreed that the popular press, in whipping up enthusiasm for adventures abroad, was a sinister new factor in this dangerous situation. The American press had shown its power over public opinion at the time of the war with Spain, and the British and French press had similarly competed in sensationalism and war-

---

[72] Haupt (ed.), *Bureau Socialiste Internationale*, p. 27.

[73] Porter, *Critics of Empire*, pp. 99–100, and see also Bax's article in *Justice*, 1 May 1898. The idea can also be seen in William Morris, *News from Nowhere* (first published 1891, reprinted London, 1933), p. 110–11.

[74] See Marxian on imperialism, *LL*, 18 April 1896 and 27 February 1897, and Hardie's editorial, *LL*, 4 January 1896.

mongering during the Fashoda crisis.[75] By the turn of the century, therefore, British socialism was moving toward a strongly anti-imperialist outlook. While the socialist parties' evolution toward this position may have been gratifying to those whose long-term hope was to build resistance to war, there were few signs that the wider labour movement, the instrument of any future resistance to war, yet shared this outlook. For many years previously the socialists themselves had frequently dismissed foreign affairs and defence matters as distractions; in the words of Grant Allen, an ILP activist, writing in 1896, 'Militarism exists in order to be dragged as a red herring at every turn across the path of domestic progress.'[76] The moderate trade union men and women, absorbed as they were in the day-to-day business of protecting working conditions, could be forgiven in persisting in the view that they had nothing to fear from the 'red herring' of militarism and need give it only passing attention.

[75] *ILP News*, May, July, and November 1898.
[76] *LL*, 25 July 1896.

4

The Limits of Commitment:
Internationalism and the
British Trade Union Movement

We are here in the endeavour to break down racial animosities
nourished by politicians and capitalists, and so help on the
brotherhood of man. We demonstrate by meeting together, no
matter to which nation we belong, our desire to know one another
better, to make plain that in each country we suffer from the
same economic evils. International brotherhood has been making
great progress, and we realise more and more, day by day, that
you do not want to slit our throats, nor we yours. Wars are made
by politicians, not by peoples, and such congresses will further
the time when wars will become impossible.

> John Hodge, President's Address, *Proceedings of the
> International Metal Workers' Federation Congress, Brussels,
> 1907* (Birmingham, 1915), p. 369.

1. *Indifference towards Foreign Affairs among British Trade
Unions*

At the turn of the century, as we have seen, it was still common within British trade unions for many of the more
traditional members to insist that trade matters were the
only legitimate concern of their union and to resent the trend
toward open political involvement.[1] It is not surprising,
therefore, to find that many trade unionists also maintained
that their movement had no business in passing judgement on
foreign affairs or in seeking to influence the foreign and defence policies of the government. Thus, there was little
direction from the leadership as to the formulation of distinctive trade union responses to such issues among the rank and
file. Important trade union journals such as the Amalgamated
Society of Railway Servants' *Railway Review*,[2] or the Dock,
Wharf, Riverside and General Labourers' *Dockers' Record*,[3]

---

[1] See Chapter 1.
[2] Copies of *Railway Review*, Unity House, Euston Road, London.
[3] Copies of *Dockers' Record*, 1901—14 and also the union's *Annual Report*
at MRC, MSS 126.

almost entirely ignored the various international crises of the period under study. The surviving executive records and annual reports of such important unions as the Railway Servants,[4] the influential and long-established London Society of Compositors,[5] or the new and militant Workers' Union,[6] show virtually no interest in foreign affairs. Apart from an intensely patriotic reaction to the Boer War, the various postal unions also maintained a virtual silence on such matters as foreign policy and national defence.[7] The executive of the Miners' Federation, one of the most powerful unions in the land, also allowed every important international crisis of the period under study to pass without comment, and seemed to leave the rhetoric of internationalism to the small number of its delegates who attended meetings of the International Miners' Federation.[8] Similarly, the records of smaller craft unions, such as the Operative Stonemason's Society,[9] Operative Bricklayers' Society,[10] Carpenters' and Joiners',[11] and the Friendly Society of Iron Founders,[12]

[4] See ASRS, *Reports and Proceedings*, 1876–1913, and *Executive Committee Decisions*, 1896–8, 1902–5, 1911–19, at MRC, MSS 127.

[5] See London Society of Compositors, *Annual Reports*, 1886–1914, at MRC, MSS 28. It is important to note that this union was not totally insular. For instance, the *Annual Report* for 1914 reveals a long list of donations to assist foreign trade union causes in the printing industry. However, the records of the Compositors' political committee reveal that the committee neither received reports from, nor recommended any action to its parliamentary member, C.W. Bowerman, upon any of the more general issues of war and peace. The union's internationalism, therefore, seems to have been limited to trade union causes; see London Society of Compositors, *Political Committee, Section Minutes*, 1909–14, MSS 28.

[6] See the Workers' Union, *Annual Reports*, 1905–14, MRC, MSS 126.

[7] See the bound volumes of *The Post*, *Postmen's Gazette*, and *Postal Clerks' Herald* for this period at UPW House, Clapham, London. On the postal unions' response to the Boer War, see below, Chapter 5.

[8] See the annual volumes of *Proceedings*, which incorporate the MFGB Executive *mins.*, and International Miners' Federation Congress Reports, at the national office of the National Union of Mineworkers, St. James's House, Sheffield.

[9] Operative Stonemasons' Society, *Journal*, 1911–14, MRC, MSS 78.

[10] Operative Bricklayers' Society, *Minutes of the Annual Moveable General Council and Monthly Reports*, 1905–14, MRC, MSS 78.

[11] Amalgamated Society of Carpenters and Joiners, *General Council Minutes*, 1871–1910, MRC, MSS 78.

[12] Friendly Society of Iron Founders, *Annual Report*, 1900–19, MRC MSS 41.

give no indication that the union executives ever discussed international relations or that any serious attempt was made to educate the rank and file in a trade union approach to the problems of peace and war. Even the National Union of Teachers, a union which presumably could have played a crucial role in combating chauvinism amongst the young, had very little to say on the subject.[13] Not until 1911 did the NUT Conference declare that its members should inculcate in the schoolchildren of the nation a concern for international peace and goodwill.[14]

At the highest level of the trade union movement, at the Trade Union Congress itself, internationalism seemed to attract little interest. Even that least painful method of honouring the idea of international solidarity, the exchange of fraternal delegates, was not popular. An invitation from the SPD to send a delegate to its 1899 Congress was politely turned down, and although the TUC Parliamentary Committee did issue a return invitation to the Germans in that same year, no tradition of mutual exchanges developed.[15] Only the Americans sent a regular deputation to the TUC, beginning in 1894. It was not until the 1913 Congress, the last before the war, that delegates from France and Germany were invited to mingle with their British trade union brothers.[16]

The records of the TUC Parliamentary Committee reveal that here too there was a certain unwillingness to join in the broader campaign for peace and international working-class solidarity. A clue to the reasoning behind the Parliamentary Committee's attitude can be found in the periodic negotiations between the trade union bodies and the Labour Party over the question of defining the legitimate areas of concern for each body so as to guard against 'overlapping'. In the notional 'carving up' of trade union and Labour Party spheres of interest both sides appear to have been quite willing to

[13] See the bound volumes of *The Schoolmaster* and NUT, *Annual Reports*, at Hamilton House in London.

[14] NUT, *Annual Report*, 1911, also reported in *The Schoolmaster*, 22 April 1911.

[15] TUC PC *mins.*, 10 May 1899, and see Pelling, *History of British Trade Unionism*, p. 118.

[16] TUC PC, *17th Quarterly Report*, p. 13; see also TUC PC *mins.*, 15 January 1913.

assign all responsibility for the campaign for peace to the Labour Party, thereby ignoring the fact that the party could hardly make valid statements or commitments on behalf of the British working class if the trade unions were not taking part in the peace campaign and were doing so little to educate their members in its principles. For example, in 1905, at the first meeting of the Joint Board (the LRC, GFTU, and TUC Parliamentary Committee), a suggestion from the LRC that all three bodies should join forces in sending a delegation to the colonies 'with a view to solidifying the international labour movement', was turned down by the trade unionists. The TUC delegates stated that they were unable to give assistance and they recommended that the matter be left entirely to the LRC.[17]

It is not surprising, therefore, to find that the TUC Parliamentary Committee sought to limit its internationalist activities, and dragged its feet in identifying itself with the wider peace campaign. This tendency can be seen in the first place in some quite minor decisions. For instance, until 1913 the Parliamentary Committee declined year after year the National Peace Council's invitations to send a delegate to its annual congress, although an exception was made in 1908 when London hosted the more prestigious Universal Peace Congress.[18] Similarly, the committee rejected several suggestions that it should join in fraternal visits to Germany.[19] But, it should not be thought that the committee's reluctance to confront militarism was merely a matter of declining to make formal internationalist gestures. The TUC Parliamentary Committee, the supreme trade union committee in Britain, also neglected to give any lead to the trade union movement on major defence and foreign policy issues. The committee remained silent at all the great moments of international tension in the period 1899 to 1914. For example, the committee had no comment to make at the time of the first Moroccan crisis in 1905, but it proceeded to dis-

---

[17] TUC PC *mins.*, 29 November 1905.
[18] See, for example, ibid., 16 May 1906, 19 June 1907, 16 June and 28 July 1909, and 16 March 1910. On the 1908 decision see 14 April and 12 May 1908.
[19] See the rejection of the Printers' Assistants' plans, ibid., 14 February 1912, and the rejection of the London Trades Council's invitation, 23 July 1913.

cuss plans for demonstrations on unemployment.[20] In July 1909 the committee resolved to take no action on a Labour Party request for a speaker to address the Trafalgar Square rally against the Tsar's visit; but, at the very same meeting, the committee decided to accept a social invitation from Lady Warwick to spend an afternoon with her just prior to the opening of the next congress.[21] The committee had not a word to say on such major military and diplomatic events as the naval scare of 1909, the Agadir crisis of 1911, or the outbreak of war in the Balkans in 1912.[22]

This record of apparent indifference reveals the extent to which the trade union movement accepted a traditional view of the formulation of the nation's foreign and defence policies. According to this view, there was little room for controversy and no real need for vigilance on foreign and defence policies. It was believed that these matters were subject to a degree of consensus above party disputes, and that they could be safely entrusted to diplomatic and military experts who were, after all, right-thinking British patriots who could be relied upon to act with the nation's best interests at heart. To the more critical socialists, the apparent endorsement of this view by their trade union comrades involved a clear abrogation of duty. To the trade unionists, however, their reluctance to enter into speculative debates on the issues of peace and war followed quite naturally from their long-standing belief in the limited aims and duties of the trade union movement.

2. *Patriotic Assumptions within British Trade Unions*

But that is not the complete explanation. One additional factor needs to be taken into account, namely the strength of what might be called 'patriotic assumptions' among the

[20] Ibid., 20–1 June 1905. The committee did, however, submit a resolution calling for friendship with Germany to the TUC in September 1905; *Justice*, 9 September 1905.

[21] TUC PC *mins.*, 7 July 1909. Lady Warwick was, of course, well known for her interest in social questions and the socialist movement.

[22] During the Agadir crisis the TUC PC attended a Fair Wages Conference in London; see ibid., 18–19 July 1911. During the Balkan Wars the TUC PC was busily organizing demonstrations on the eight-hour-day issue; see ibid., 19 June and 9 August 1912 where plans for demonstrations are discussed.

trade unions. In this regard, the contrast with the prevailing ideas in the socialist camp can be noted immediately. The socialists, of course, believed that patriotic fervour should be regarded with some scepticism, and they always distinguished between true and false patriotism. Similarly, in the sceptical eyes of the socialists, speculations about invasion were merely newspaper scares and politicians' bogies designed to win mass support for the armaments competition. Imperialism also was a discredited policy, according to the socialists, and so too the institutions of the Empire were to be regarded with deep suspicion. The trade unionists' views on these same matters were seldom as critical.

The degree to which the leaders of British trade unionism were integrated into the prevailing value system of Queen and Empire can be gauged from the links that were established in the 1890s between the TUC Parliamentary Committee and the Imperial Institute. The establishment of an Imperial Institute to promote the cause of Empire had been suggested by the Prince of Wales in 1886, and Queen Victoria was to open its impressive buildings in 1893. In 1890 the new Institute approached the Parliamentary Committee to appoint a representative to its board, and in June 1891 the members agreed unanimously that their president, Edward Harford of the ASRS, should be appointed to fill the post. In 1899 the Parliamentary Committee appointed its chairman, W.J. Davis of the Amalgamated Brassworkers, as 'life-member' of the Imperial Institute. That the trade union movement should be offered a position on the Board of Governors of the Imperial Institute was obviously regarded as a tremendous honour by the union leadership. When in April 1902 the Prince of Wales attended a meeting of the Institute and happened to congratulate W.J. Davis on a speech he delivered there, a newspaper cutting reporting the incident entitled 'A Compliment for Mr W.J. Davis—Received by the Prince of Wales' was pasted into the Parliamentary Committee's minute book with the agreement of all members. It is the only newspaper cutting to appear in the minute book from the time of the founding of the Parliamentary Committee until 1914.[23]

[23] TUC PC *mins.*, 28 August 1890, 1 June 1891, 8 February 1892, 18 July 1899, and 1 May 1902.

The Parliamentary Committee's early contacts with the Imperial Institute do not, of course, prove that the leaders of British trade unionism were all enthusiastic promoters of Empire. Perhaps the Empire was simply accepted as a fact of life. It is difficult to determine which of these emotions was at work here, but whatever emotion it was, most trade unionists were simply reluctant to identify themselves with outspoken criticism of either the Empire itself or the military services of the Empire. They certainly saw no need to campaign publicly against imperial institutions. In 1913, when the British Socialist Party approached the TUC Parliamentary Committee and several major trades councils with the suggestion that trade unionists should withdraw their children from school on Empire Day as a protest against imperialism, the party received either polite explanations that there was insufficient time to arrange such a protest, or, in the case of the Parliamentary Committee, a blunt refusal even to consider the idea.[24] Similarly, it is indicative of the various trade councils' concern over defence that so few were moved to protest over the creation of the Territorial Force in 1907, while some councils even agreed to nominate representatives to serve on the County Associations that managed the new Force.[25] The trade unionists obviously did not regard the Empire and the armed forces with the same hostility as did most socialists.

Quite to the contrary, some trade unionists exhibited a fervent concern for the issues of national defence during the Edwardian years. This can be illustrated by noting the significant number of anguished resolutions concerning Britain's food supply in time of war which were passed through many trades councils in 1902 and for several years

[24] Leeds TC *mins.*, 26 March 1913; London TC *mins.*, 27 March and 10 April 1913; Edinburgh TC *mins.*, 1 April 1913; TUC PC *mins.*, 18 March 1913. Only the London TC entertained a motion to advise the withdrawal of children from schools; but this was lost in favour of a motion simply protesting against the use of schools in Empire Day celebrations. Contrast this with *LL*, 28 May 1909.

[25] Edinburgh TC *mins.*, 21 January 1908, show that it was left to the TC president's 'own discretion whether he should become a member of the City of Edinburgh County Association under the new Territorial Army Scheme'. The *mins.*, of 5 May 1908 show that the president did join, and the *mins.*, of 21 January 1913 show that the TC also appointed a new delegate to the County Association on the retirement of the former president.

following that date.[26] The idea that British agriculture had
been sacrificed on the altar of the Manchester school was
common-place among critics of Cobdenism in the late nineteenth century, and so too was the argument that this decimation of Britain's own food-growing capacity would create
a situation of grave peril in time of war.

Perhaps it was this anxiety over the adequacy of the
nation's defences that lay behind the sympathetic attitude
shown by some trades councils in their dealings with the
National Service League, a body which was anathema to the
socialists. The records of the Edinburgh Trades Council
throw some light on this point. On 12 November 1912
the council was informed by its secretary that the National
Service League had asked him to supply a list of trade union
secretaries in order to assist the League in its propaganda.
Apparently no protest was made when the secretary reported
that he had provided the list. Then, two weeks later, when
the secretary notified the council that he had refused an
offer from the League to discuss the citizen army issue, the
meeting promptly displayed its disagreement with the secretary's action by requesting him to take up the matter with
the council executive. On Christmas eve 1912, a League
deputation did indeed visit the council, and it was unanimously agreed to hear the visitors, although it is recorded
that 'the deputation received a lively heckling'. Subsequent
events reveal that the heckling could not have arisen from
all the council benches. For, on 4 March 1913, the council
first of all decided, by forty votes to ten, against accepting
an invitation from the League for supper and discussion, and
then immediately undercut this decision by voting 'by a
large majority to accept the invitation to discuss but not to
supper'. On 1 April 1913 the Edinburgh Trades Council
decided once more 'by a large majority' to hold another
discussion with the League on the question: 'Is it the duty

---

[26] For examples of trades council resolutions on this issue see Aberdeen TC
mins., 22 June 1898; London TC *mins.*, 13 February and 13 March 1902; and
Huddersfield TC *mins.*, 23 April 1902; Aberdeen TC *mins.*, 16 April and 1 October
1902; Ashton-under-Lyne TC, *Annual Report 1903*; Huddersfield TC *mins.*,
23 April, 14 October, and 31 December 1902; Leeds TC *mins.*, 7 November 1902;
York TC *Annual Report*, 1902; Aberdeen TC *mins.*, 7 April and 19 December
1909; Scottish TUC PC *mins.*, 3 July and 25 September 1909.

of the British working class to organize for the defence of their country?' Then came an invitation to the council to send a delegate to be on the platform with Lord Roberts at a Glasgow rally; but in that instance the council voted to let the letter lie on the table. Finally, on 29 April, the council agreed by forty-six votes to four 'that we do not approve of the National Service League and that we do not meet them again'. In the end, therefore, the council decisively rejected the League. However, it had been a long flirtation, with the council members displaying a strong desire to hear the League's viewpoint. Perhaps the explanation for this lies in the coincidence of the Balkan War which had been raging throughout these same months and probably heightened the concern felt by the trades council delegates over defence issues. The persistency of the League's approaches to the council certainly suggests that the League was aware of a certain receptivity to its ideas amongst the trades councillors at this time. Possibly the League had gained some supporters upon the council executive, for, in a curious sequel, the council executive was censured at a full meeting of delegates late in 1913 for accepting a National Service League advertisement for publication in the council's Annual Report.[27]

The Edinburgh Trades Council was not alone in showing some sympathy toward those who proclaimed the case for stronger armaments, national service, and imperialism. The Glasgow Trades Council provides a further example. In January 1914 the Glasgow council decided 'by a large majority' to hear a speaker from the National Service League. A Major Robertson addressed the council in February, and his request to be heard a second time was rejected a fortnight later by the less than decisive margin of forty-six votes to thirty-two. On 11 March the Glasgow council considered a further request from the League for co-operation in convening a special national service meeting. The request was rejected by forty-eight votes to forty, a margin which again indicated

---

[27] Edinburgh TC *mins.*, 12, 26 November, and 24 December 1912, 7 January, 4 March, 1, 14, 29 April, 28 October, and 11 November 1913. The spate of National Service League activity is explained by the fact that the League executive decided in January 1913 to begin a drive for the support of the labouring classes; see David P. James, *Lord Roberts* (London, 1954), p. 459.

the strength of the substantial minority that favoured the project. In April when Major Robertson donated '250 books on war' to the council, no member appears to have protested against receiving them. While the council seemed rather tolerant of the National Service League, it was, by contrast, somewhat impatient with the peace movement; for in 1910 and 1911 the council declined invitations to send delegates to the National Peace Congress.[28]

Another rather striking example of the strength of patriotic assumptions amongst trade unions is to be found in the records of the Bristol Trades Council for 1908.[29] In that year, the council was forced to choose between its fidelity to that most powerful of patriotic symbols, the monarchy, and its solidarity with that most favoured working-class internationalist ideal, the cause of Russian freedom. It had been announced to the nation early in 1908 that in June Edward VII would visit the Tsar at Reval. Coming within a year of the Anglo-Russian diplomatic agreement, the visit was naturally interpreted as a means of tightening the new accord with Russia. In the House of Commons the Labour MPs, who had always condemned the tsarist regime as the most brutal imaginable, protested against this latest indication that the Government intended to build an alliance with Russia.[30] As part of the campaign against the Reval visit, Keir Hardie had spoken out at a number of public meetings, including one at Bristol in late May.[31] It so happened that shortly after his return from Russia, Edward VII was scheduled to visit Bristol to open the new Corporation Dock at Avonmouth. Troubles began for the Bristol Trades Council when, in preparation for the royal visitor, the Mayor of Bristol appointed a reception committee and invited one member

---

[28] Glasgow TC *mins.*, 11 May 1910, 7 June 1911, 21 January, 18 and 25 February, 11 March, and 1 April 1914. The issues could become even more confused when trade unionists were confronted by a war hero such as Lord Roberts. For example, in 1913 the solidly anti-conscriptionist Aberdeen Trades Council refused to mount a counter-demonstration against Roberts when he visited their town; see Aberdeen TC executive *mins.*, 2 July 1913 and *mins.*, 9 July and 12 November 1913.

[29] The details of this incident are given in *LL*, 10 and 17 July 1908.

[30] See Chapter 6.

[31] Hardie spoke at Bristol on 24 May; see *LL*, 29 May 1908.

from the trades council to join in. At first, responding perhaps to Keir Hardie's recent speech in Bristol, the trades
council stood firm and passed the following motion of
protest, albeit by a slim margin of twenty-nine votes to
twenty-four:

As a protest against the action of the advisers of the King in recommending that a state visit be paid to the Tsar of Russia, which visit
can only be regarded by the Russian people as a condonation of the
tyrannical repression of the political freedom for which they are
rightly struggling, this trades council take no official part in the reception of His Majesty on the occasion of his forthcoming visit to
Bristol.[32]

It is noteworthy that even this motion of protest singled
out 'the advisers of the King' rather than Edward VII himself for criticism. The trade unions affiliated to the council
were now caught in an uncomfortable dilemma. Their basic
patriotic yearnings, so flattered by the impending royal visit,
were caught in conflict with the instinctive desire to be
loyal to the labour movement's record of antagonism to
tsarism. It was soon clear that the patriotic impulse was the
stronger. In the wake of the protest resolution seven local
trade unions had their normal weekly meetings and it was
decided to demand a special council meeting to rescind the
resolution, on the grounds that insufficient notice had been
given and that a significant number of delegates had been
absent from the original council meeting. The special meeting
was duly convened, and new arguments raised against any
protest. It was contended that the King's visit 'found work',
that it was 'good for trade', that a disloyal stand by the
council might prejudice the traditional alms distribution to
Bristol's poor, and that 'as the Labour Party had made their
protest in Parliament against the Reval meeting there was no
necessity for local action'. The original protest resolution was
then rescinded by forty-eight votes to twenty-nine, and the
Bristol TC was officially represented at the Royal reception.[33]
    It should not be thought that this was an isolated display
of exaggerated patriotism on the part of one local trades
council. The TUC Parliamentary Committee itself made no

---

[32] *LL*, 10 July 1908.
[33] *LL*, 17 July 1908.

effort to give a stronger lead on this matter. When Keir Hardie's name, amongst some others, was struck off the list of invitations to the King's Garden Party in July 1908 in an obvious gesture of disapproval of Hardie's criticism of the Reval visit, the Parliamentary Committee turned down a Labour Party request that it issue a protest.[34] Internationalism, and even solidarity with Russian liberation, had its limitations.

It is plain that the sense of loyalty felt by many trade unionists toward the Crown, the Empire, its heroes, and its institutions, prevented many of them from entering wholeheartedly into the internationalist campaigns of the British socialists. The trade unionists were quite willing to profess solidarity with the cause of freedom abroad and to pass resolutions declaring for peace and international understanding; but they shrank from these same ideals if they were thereby identified with those agitators who were so vehemently critical of the Empire's military might, of Britain's foreign policy, and even of the Crown.

3. *The Priorities of the Trade Unions with regard to Internationalism*

Given the strength of these patriotic assumptions within the British trade union movement, it is not surprising to discover that certain internationalist causes had greater priority than others in the estimation of the trade unions. The issues likely to attract the attention of the unions included such matters as the violation of the rights of trade unionists abroad, the use of the military or the police against strikers at home or abroad, and, of course, the cause of Russian freedom. By contrast, the wider campaign against chauvinism, imperialism, and the menace of war was generally neglected. This dichotomy in the international interests of the trade union movement is again shown quite clearly in the records of the TUC Parliamentary Committee and the various trades councils.

Of all the international or imperial issues causing concern in the pre-war decade, it was the issue of indentured 'Chinese labour' in South Africa in 1904 to which the TUC Parliamen-

---

[34] TUC PC *mins.*, 16 July 1908.

tary Committee devoted more attention than any other.[35] The committee organized a monster demonstration in Hyde Park in March 1904 complete with actors masquerading as Chinese; and the committee also wrote to every union and trades council in England informing them of the Hyde Park protest and asking them to hold local demonstrations. Significantly enough, the resolution drawn up by the Parliamentary Committee for use at the demonstrations denouncing the 'conditions of slavery' also called on the Government 'to protect ... the Empire from degradation'.[36] Such wording was hardly anti-imperialist in tone. The next most important international issue in the eyes of the committee was Russian liberation. Especially after the 1905 revolution the committee was quite energetic on the matter, organizing fund-raising efforts, co-operating in demonstrations, and sponsoring resolutions.[37] No comparable activity was forthcoming from the committee in the cause of arms limitation, opposition to the alliance system, secret diplomacy, or even in response to international crises.

The committee was not averse, however, to general declarations of its internationalist convictions and its devotion to peace. For instance, in 1904 the committee took a stand against conscription and in the same year, and again in 1905, it proclaimed its support for peace through international arbitration.[38] The committee also took some interest in the problem of Anglo-German relations. In 1908 its chairman and vice-chairman accompanied a delegation from the International Arbitration League to Berlin, and in the following year four members joined a Labour Party delegation on a goodwill visit to Germany.[39] In another important step,

[35] See the TUC PC *mins.*, February—March 1904.

[36] Ibid., 18 March 1904.

[37] For example, see TUC PC *mins.*, 13 February, and 15 November 1905, 26 April, 30 August 1906, and 8 September 1906.

[38] Ibid., 1 June and 17 November 1904, and 30 August 1905. Two of these proclamations show the committee merely congratulating world leaders on their work for peace; in November 1904 the committee endorsed references to peace in one of Edward VII's speeches, and in August 1905 the committee sent its personal congratulations to President Roosevelt for his efforts in connection with ending the Russo-Japanese war. This was indeed the pursuit of peace through 'respectable' channels.

[39] Ibid., 18 June and 18 November 1908.

during the December 1909 election campaign, the committee issued a press statement regretting the rash of sensationalist articles (chiefly those of Robert Blatchford) drawing attention to the so-called 'German menace'. The committee decried this newspaper scare as a distraction 'calculated to turn the thoughts of the workers from the great issue now before the country', namely, the Lords' resistance to the Lloyd George budget.[40] However, the wording of the committee's protest on this occasion seemed to reinforce the impression that such matters as foreign policy and defence were mere distractions that normally lay outside the trade unionists' sphere of concern. Moreover, no matter how strongly worded were the Parliamentary Committee's rather infrequent resolutions on such issues, it never translated its professed anxiety into action, in marked contrast to its efforts to mobilize trade union opinion on the issues of 'Chinese slavery' and unemployment.

Some insight into the priorities of the Parliamentary Committee can also be gained by noting the issues which deputations from the committee usually raised in their traditional private interviews with government ministers. Among the issues raised most frequently at the War Office and the Admiralty were the Musicians' Union's claims regarding unfair competition from military bands. As one would expect there was also the matter of War Office and Admiralty contracts which the committee was determined to see allotted only to those firms offering fair wages and conditions.[41] The use of the police and the military against strikers was another issue raised.[42] Only once in the pre-war decade, in February 1914, did the Parliamentary Committee's deputation to the Prime Minister raise the wider problems of the 'armaments burden' and the alleged nefarious activities of the 'armaments ring'.[43]

---

[40] Ibid., 15 December 1909.

[41] On the military bands issue see for example ibid., 20 January 1909, 9 April and 22 May 1913. On War Office, Admiralty, and India Office contracts see for example ibid., first half of 1906, 17 November 1909, and 22 February 1910.

[42] Ibid., 16 and 17 August 1911.

[43] For a record of the interview see TUC PC *Quarterly Report*, no. 17, May 1914, pp. 13–20.

The surviving records of the trades councils tend to confirm this picture. Where a trades council was persuaded to make a statement or take action on foreign or military matters, it was almost always in cases where traditional 'labour' interests were seen to be involved, or else the trades council lifted its voice to protest over the brutalities of Russian autocracy. The issue which aroused more vociferous protests from the trades councils than any other foreign policy matter in the pre-war decade was, as in the case of the TUC Parliamentary Committee, 'Chinese slavery' in South Africa.[44] The next most popular international cause espoused by the trades councils was, of course, the liberation of the Russian people from tsardom. Trades council minute books are littered with denunciations of tsarism, and it is true to say that for many councils, their excursions into the area of foreign policy began and ended with criticism of the Russian autocracy and the British connections with it.[45]

The other minor international causes which attracted the attention of the trades councils were, in most cases, similarly bound up with either international 'labour' issues or the cause of Russian liberation. In 1907 there was some concern over the actions of British blacklegs during the Hamburg dock strike and resolutions were passed decrying the black-

---

[44] Public demonstrations or resolutions on this issue are noted in London TC *mins.*, 11 and 25 February 1904; Huddersfield TC *mins.*, 23 March 1904; Leeds TC *mins.*, 27 January and 26 February 1904; Stockton TC *Annual Report* 1904; Blackburn TC *Annual Report* 1905; Glasgow TC *Annual Report* 1903–4; Warrington TC *Annual Report* 1905; South Western District TC *Annual Report* 1904; Accrington TC *Annual Report* 1905; Sunderland TC *Annual Report* 1904; *History of the Plymouth and District TC 1892–1952* (Plymouth, 1952), p. 14; E. and R. Frow, *To Make That Future Now: A History of the Manchester and Salford Trades Council* (Manchester, 1976), p. 66; Mary Ashraf, *Bradford Trades Council, 100 Years, 1872–1972* (Bradford, 1972), p. 79.

[45] For examples of the trades councils' concern with Russia, see Liverpool TC *mins.*, 14 July 1909; Aberdeen TC *mins.*, 7 July 1909; Glasgow TC *mins.*, 21 October 1913; Edinburgh TC *mins.*, 2 June 1908, 29 June and 13 July 1909; London TC *mins.*, 28 May 1903, 26 January and 9 February 1905, no day given July 1909, 25 May 1910, 13 July 1911, and 13 June 1912; Sheffield TC *mins.*, 21 May 1912; Nottingham TC *mins.*, 10 May 1912; Birmingham TC *mins.*, 13 June 1908; Birkenhead TC *Annual Report* 1909; Bermondsey TC *Annual Report* 1905–6; Southampton TC *Annual Report* 1907; Frow, *History of the Manchester TC*, p. 67: Ashraf, *Bradford TC*, p. 89; Peterborough TC, *Diamond Jubilee 1899–1959*, Leicester TC *Annual Report* 1910 and *Year Book* 1913.

legging.[46] Several trades councils objected to Tom Mann's arrest in 1912 over his *Don't Shoot* pamphlet;[47] and in 1913 there were many resolutions deploring the arrest of the Russian trade unionist Adamovitch by Russian agents in Egypt.[48] In 1913 also many trades councils passed resolutions against the action of the police during labour disputes in Dublin[49] or else condemned the use of troops against strikers in South Africa.[50] In 1914 another *cause célèbre* was found in the deportation of certain trade union leaders from South Africa. A great many councils passed resolutions denouncing the deportations in the strongest terms, and some councils were sufficiently concerned to mount demonstrations.[51] Again, resolutions condemning the deportations sometimes made mention of the fact that Britons had fought for freedom in South Africa and pleas were made that their sacrifice should not be defiled by such tyranny.

Whenever the trades councils turned their attentions to the general issues of imperialism, peace, and war, more often than not this arose from the proddings of some outside body. In 1905, after a visit from the Indian Nationalist G.K. Gokhale, the Manchester Trades Council passed a resolution urging the British Raj to grant to the Indian people 'a fair share in the management of their own affairs'.[52] It would be difficult

[46] For example, see the Southampton TLC resolution sent to the International Transport Federation, in National Amalgamated Union of Labour file of ITF correspondence, MSS 159, MRC.

[47] Bristol TC sent a circular on this issue to several councils: see for example, Aberdeen TC *mins.*, 3 April and 8 May 1912, and London TC *mins.*, 14 and 28 March, 25 April, 9 May, and 13 June 1912.

[48] See Glasgow TC *mins.*, 21 May 1913; Huddersfield TC *mins.*, 28 May 1913; Leeds TC *mins.*, 28 May 1913; Scottish TUC Parliamentary Committee *mins.*, 27 May 1913; and London TC *mins.*, 29 May 1913.

[49] Leeds TC *mins.*, 9 and 24 September, show a protest meeting with James Larkin; Glasgow TC *mins.*, 3 September and 5 November 1913; Sheffield TLC *mins.*, 23 September 1913; Leicester TC, *Year Book*, 1914.

[50] Leeds TC *mins.*, 23 July 1913; Jacobs, *London Trades Council*, p. 99; Huddersfield TC, *Annual Report*, 1913.

[51] Leeds TC *mins.*, 11 February 1914, show a protest meeting; London TC *mins.*, 12 February and 27 March 1914; Liverpool LRC *mins.*, 18 February 1914, show that a protest meeting was held; Aberdeen TC *mins.*, 4 February and 1 April 1914 show that a demonstration was organized in co-operation with the Aberdeen Labour Party. See also Glasgow TC *mins.*, 18 March 1914; Nottingham TC *mins.*, 28 January 1914; Leicester TC, *Year Book*, 1914; and Birmingham TC *mins.*, 7 February 1914 for resolutions on this question.

[52] Frow, *History of the Manchester TC*, p. 67.

to discover another single reference to Indian affairs in existing trades council records. Similarly, it was in response to a visit from a National Peace Council activist in 1908 that the Liverpool Trades Council considered the formation of a local peace committee.[53] In December 1911 the Huddersfield Trades Council condemned imperialism and 'war-like agitation' and called for democratic control of foreign policy, but this was done only after a letter from the National Peace Council on Anglo-German understanding had been read to the council.[54] The trades councils at Blackpool and Plymouth also responded to calls from the National Peace Council in late 1911 for resolutions favouring reconciliation with Germany.[55] Earlier in 1911 a number of trades councils also agreed to sign a general declaration against war, the declaration being circulated by the General Federation of Trades Unions.[56]

Of course, the passing of resolutions was an inexpensive form of protest. The full range of resources available to the trades councils for exerting pressure on a chosen issue, even the simple device of organizing deputations to local MPs, was not employed in the campaign against chauvinism, armaments expenditure, and war. The financial resources of the trades councils were carefully husbanded for the domestic struggle. The minutes of the Nottingham Trades Council are revealing in this regard. In 1911 and 1913 the Nottingham Trades Council responded to approaches from the National Peace Council and the Anti-Conscription Committee by proclaiming its support for the objectives of the two organizations; but on both occasions the council stipulated that it could not accept any financial obligations.[57] These were characteristic responses. The threat of some future war was a problem quite

[53] Liverpool TC *mins.*, 9 September, 11 November, and 9 December 1908.

[54] Huddersfield TC *mins.*, 20 December 1911.

[55] Blackpool TC, *Diamond Jubilee*, p. 23. It is interesting to note that the National Peace Council resolution calling for Anglo-German reconciliation was passed by the Blackpool TC by fifteen votes to five against; *History of the Plymouth and District TC, 1892–1952*, p. 14. Note also that Aberdeen TC voted twelve to nine to take no action on a National Peace Council letter in December 1911; see *mins.*, 13 December 1911.

[56] Aberdeen TC *mins.*, 19 April 1911; Blackpool TC, *Diamond Jubilee*, p. 23; London TC *mins.*, 27 April 1913.

[57] Nottingham TC *mins.*, 6 December 1911 and 2 July 1913.

naturally relegated to second place behind the actual present-day problems of safeguarding wages and conditions.

It is not surprising, therefore, to find that almost no trades council saw fit to discuss the proper trade union response to the various international crises of the period, even though council meetings sometimes coincided with the most critical days of international tension.[58] The trades councils reserved the greatest efforts in these years for propaganda work on such issues as the fiscal question, the Education Bill, the problem of unemployment, the eight-hour-day question, the Osborne Judgement, old-age pensions, and the Insurance Act. It was upon these issues that the councils arranged conferences, demonstrations, and deputations; and it was these issues that were raised when councils framed their lists of questions for parliamentary candidates prior to elections.[59]

4. *International Trade Unionism*

In the eyes of most British trade union leaders their obligations to the spirit of internationalism could normally be met within the confines of the trade union movement, perhaps even within the confines of their own particular trades. 'Internationalism' as understood by the trade unionists during the two pre-war decades came to mean, first and foremost, a simple concern for those workers abroad who laboured in the same trade, and, perhaps, occasional fellowship with them. Beyond this, there was also a vague sense of comradeship with all those workers who made up the world-wide trade union fraternity. When internationalism was interpreted in this way, it can be readily seen that the growth in British

[58] Several examples could be given from the Moroccan crisis of 1911. The Liverpool TC *mins.*, 12 July 1911, show that Tom Mann spoke to the council but did not mention foreign affairs. Leeds TC *mins.* show meetings on 12, 20, and 21 July, but the council discussed only trade matters. Nottingham TC *mins.* show meetings on 5 and 19 July and 2 August, where the council considered national insurance, held its annual elections, and prepared its annual report, no mention of the Agadir crisis being made.

[59] For example, Huddersfield TC *mins.*, 23 November 1910, show that the opinions of candidates would be sought on six matters only: the reversal of the Osborne decision, the right to work, state maintenance of schoolchildren, free education, state insurance, and a proposed reduction in the qualifying age for aged pensions.

trade union affiliations with international trade union bodies did not necessarily mean that the socialist understanding of internationalism was coming to be accepted by the trade unionists. Indeed, an examination of the contacts between British trade unions and the largely German-based international trade union bodies tends to show how limited was the sense of working-class solidarity among the trade unionists who engaged in this type of activity.

In terms of the numbers of workers for whom international connections had been organized, the cause of international trade unionism certainly seemed to have progressed handsomely in the two decades prior to the Great War. By 1913 there were twenty-nine international unions in all, the five largest being the International Miners' Federation (claiming a membership of 1,178,000), the International Metal Workers' Federation (970,000), the International Transport Federation (824,000), the International Textile Workers' Federation (423,000), and the International Building Trades' Federation (418,000). Twenty-four of these international unions maintained central offices in Germany, marking a degree of concentration that provoked some resentment from other national sections. Of the major unions only the miners and textile workers had central offices in Britain.[60]

By 1914 a significant number of British unions, including most of the largest unions, had at least sought some contact with workers in the same trades abroad, and many unions had chosen to affiliate with the appropriate international body. The most important of these included the Miners' Federation,[61] the various British metal workers' unions[62] and

---

[60] TUC PC, *15th Quarterly Report*, June 1913, p. 31; F.S. Lyons, *Internationalism in Europe, 1815–1914* (Leyden, 1963), p. 157 gives slightly different figures.

[61] The British Miners' Federation had been instrumental in the creation of the International Miners' Federation; Clegg, Fox and Thompson, *British Trade Unions*, vol. 1, p. 302.

[62] The British metal workers' unions had hosted the first conference of the International Metal Workers' Federation in London in 1896; Charles Hobson (ed.), *International Metal Workers' Federation: Part II: The Origin and Development of Internationalism* (Birmingham, 1915). In addition, from 1908 onwards the British steel smelters and the German metal workers had exchanged fraternal delegates at their annual conferences; Arthur Pugh, *Men of Steel* (London, 1951), p. 167.

the British textile workers' unions[63] who were all affiliated with their respective international trade unions during the 1890s. The various British transport workers' unions, including the railway unions and the dockers' unions were affiliated with the International Transport Federation (ITF) from about 1907 onwards,[64] and the National Transport Workers' Federation joined as well soon after its formation in 1912.[65] Some smaller unions, including the postal unions,[66] the Boot and Shoe Operatives,[67] the Shop Assistants' Union,[68] the National Union of Teachers,[69] and the printing unions[70] also either joined their international trade unions or established their own contacts with foreign trade unions by 1914. Overall, the British unions' record of affiliation with international trade union bodies during this period was quite respectable. However, affiliation did not oblige the British unions to do anything more than send a delegate abroad to the occasional conference, receive in return the occasional fraternal delegate at their own conference, and pay dues, however reluctantly, to the international body. There was very little progress toward that most practical form of international trade unionism, international aid for workers on strike.[71]

[63]   Clegg, Fox and Thompson, *British Trade Unions,* vol. 1, p. 301.

[64]   See below for an analysis of this, pp. 92–4.

[65]   National Transport Workers' Federation, *Annual General Meeting,* 4–7 June, 1912, MRC.

[66]   The Postmen's Federation agreed to invite fraternal delegates from abroad to all its future conferences in 1906, and in 1910 an International Federation of Postal, Telegraphic and Telephonic Employees was launched with a secretariat in Berne; see Postmen's Federation, *Agenda Papers, 1906 Conference* and *Postmen's Gazette,* 23 June 1906, and see *Postal Clerks' Herald,* 20 April 1912.

[67]   National Union of Boot and Shoe Operatives, *Monthly Report,* May 1912, pp. 34–5, 55 and June 1912, pp. 435–8 for descriptions of fraternal exchanges with Germany and the decision to join the International Shoe and Leather Workers' Union (founded in Stuttgart, 1907).

[68]   The International Shop Assistants' Union had been founded in Paris in 1900. See the description of the 1906 Conference in London in *LL,* 27 April 1906.

[69]   The NUT arranged fraternal visits with its Continental counterparts; see *The Schoolmaster,* 29 March 1913.

[70]   R.B. Suthers, *The Story of NATSOPA* (London, 1929), p. 46.

[71]   For example, the metal workers were on the eve of launching a scheme in July 1914; see ASE, executive council proceedings in ASE *Journal,* July 1914. F.S. Lyons, *Internationalism in Europe,* pp. 161–2 has details of the financial outlays of the International Federation of Trade Unions for the purpose of strike assistance.

Indeed, it is a very difficult task to assess the extent to which international trade unionism indicated the coming of a real internationalist consciousness within organized labour. On the one hand, it is clear that those socialists and trade unionists who were interested in the broader peace campaign occasionally used the conferences of the international unions as platforms from which to attack the evils of 'armed peace', and in particular to dispute the assumption that the people of Europe were divided by some irresistible sense of enmity. John Hodge, the leader of the British Steel Smelters' Union, presented this message in a very typical way in his president's address to the International Metal Workers' Federation Conference meeting at Brussels in 1907 which was quoted at the beginning of this chapter. More militant attacks on chauvinism and the evils of war were also made occasionally at such conferences. When Joseph Simon, the president of the German Shoe Operatives' Union and secretary of the international shoe workers' union, visited the Norwich Conference of the British Boot and Shoe Operatives in 1912, he was reported to have declared that:

The German workers, like those in England, were labouring under the capitalist system which at present they could not control. He believed the German workers, rather than take arms in the hand, would be better pleased to take arms against the German capitalist ... The German workman did not regard the English workman as an enemy, but looked upon it as a fact that he had no enemy but capital.[72]

This simple but profound message was certainly not uncommon at such gatherings. Socialists like Wilhelm Liebknecht, who addressed the International Textile Workers in London in 1900,[73] or Robert Smillie, president of the International Miners' Federation in 1912–13, and Ben Tillett and Tom Mann, who were leading personalities within the ITF, carried the socialist critique of militarism and war into the most powerful forums of international trade unionism.

On the other hand, few of the international unions ever responded to these ideas with firm actions or solid commitments to resist the evils of the 'warfare state'. The fact that trade unions could gather in international conference was

---

[72] NUB and SO, *Monthly Report*, May 1912, p. 55.
[73] *Justice*, 4 August 1900.

usually considered in itself to be a spectacular affirmation of working-class internationalism. Only very rarely did the concern for peace move beyond the inspiring occasional address and into the international union's policy resolutions. Some exceptions might be noted. In 1904 the ITF called upon all members 'to agitate against the military spirit of the times'.[74] Further, as will be described below, in the last years of peace before 1914, the International Transport Federation and the International Miners' Federation began to explore the idea of a general strike against war.[75] However, most international unions made no attempt to formulate policy with regard to war, its causes, or the correct trade union response to the problem.

Moreover, relations between the various national sections in the international unions were not always marked by exemplary fraternal warmth. The trade unionists seemed not to rise above the ordinary international jealousies, in particular over such matters as the location of the central offices of the international unions. The ITF is a case in point. The Federation, which had been established in a piecemeal fashion during the 1890s, was losing members rapidly until the central offices were transferred to Germany in 1904.[76] However, the transfer was deeply resented by the British transport unions for the Germans had obtained a stranglehold over the executive positions in the Federation as well. In 1905 Ben Tillett withdrew his union of dock and wharf labourers from the ITF, complaining that the move to Berlin was 'undemocratic and calculated to retard and repel British organisations from affiliations'.[77] The union did not rejoin the ITF until 1910. Even then, it was obvious at the 1910 ITF Convention that the British still harboured misgivings and suspected the Germans of attempting to monopolize power. After Müller, the leader of the German delegation, had spoken, Tillett complained that he had used the 'tone of a teacher'. Tillett continued:

[74] *Dockers' Record*, September 1904.
[75] See Chapter 10.
[76] See *The International Transport Federation: A Brief Survey of History and Activities* (n.d.) at TUC; and N. Nathans, *International Transport Federation: Its Character, Its Aims, Its Aspirations* (Amsterdam, 1922), p. 5.
[77] DWRGL, *Annual Report*, 1905.

It had been a good thing that Müller had pointed out that he was international, or else we would have taken him for a German patriot. They needed no dictatory tone, no emperor, and he regretted that such a tone had come up.[78]

Similarly, John Hodge complained that at each conference of the International Metal Workers' Federation 'it became evident that the Germans would never be satisfied until the headquarters were situated in Germany'.[79] The German unionists' constant assertions that the international unions must remain politically neutral, because of the restrictive German laws governing their unions' activities, proved to be another source of tension.[80] The British and also French unionists began to voice their suspicions that the Germans were using this explanation as a convenient device for enforcing their own moderate outlook upon the international unions while shielding themselves from criticism.[81]

For all their doubts concerning the Germans, the British unions themselves did not always display internationalist fervour. The insularity of the British unions was demonstrated, for example, at the very first conference of the International Federation of Postal, Telegraphic and Telephonic Employees held in Paris in 1911. At the conference a set of simple objectives was debated, including one which suggested that the international union should aim 'to promote international solidarity'. This particular objective 'was strenuously opposed by the British delegation as being open to misinterpretations'. At the end of a lively discussion, the conference agreed to the British postal unions' suggestion that the qualifying words 'of the postal and telegraphic employees' should be added to the disputed objective.[82] On this occasion, then, the British unions had deliberately sought to confine the activities of their international federation to trade union matters, and to exclude the possibility of any

[78] *Proceedings of the Seventh International Transport Federation Convention, Copenhagen 23–7 August 1910* (Copenhagen, 1910), p. 50.
[79] John Hodge, *Workman's Cottage to Windsor Castle* (London, 1931), p. 259.
[80] For example, see *Proceedings of the Seventh International Transport Federation Convention* (Copenhagen, 1910), pp. 58–9, and *Report of the Central Council of the International Transport Federation*, 26–30 August 1913, p. 10.
[81] For example, see M. Goniaux's speech, 'International Miners' Federation Conference, July 1913', in *MFGB Proceedings*, 1913, p. 15.
[82] *The Post*, 22 July 1911.

wider involvement in the campaign for peace and international understanding.

Apart from these quarrels, perhaps the most telling indication of the lack of genuine internationalist sentiment among British unionists was the TUC's decision to be represented at the most prestigious international union body, the International Federation of Trade Unions, only by the TUC's much smaller financial arm, the General Federation (GFTU). In the words of the International Federation's official historian, Walter Schevenels, 'The British TUC, in order to avoid too much entanglement in international problems, let the Federation [GFTU] represent the British movement.'[83] This was clear tokenism, for the GFTU could claim the allegiance of only a quarter of British trade unionists.[84] This situation remained unchallenged until 1911, when, at the GFTU conference, Ben Tillett urged a general extension of the British trade unions' international involvement.[85] Finally, in September 1913, Karl Legien, president of the International Federation, formally invited the Parliamentary Committee to send delegates to the Eighth Conference and his invitation was accepted.[86] Only on the eve of the war, therefore, was the British trade union movement properly represented at the supreme international trade union federation. It was late in the day.

On an individual basis, too, the British unions displayed a good deal of reluctance to rub shoulders with their continental brethren, and they seemed especially unwilling to pay international union dues for the privilege of mingling. The ITF, for instance, experienced serious difficulties in attracting and retaining the support of the British transport unionists. From as early as 1900 the Amalgamated Society of Railway Servants (ASRS) declined ITF invitations to affiliate.[87] At a meeting held in June 1905 which happened to coincide with the Moroccan crisis, the ASRS executive reconfirmed its

---

[83] Walter Schevenels, *Forty-Five Years: A Historical Precis of the International Federation of Trade Unions* (n.d.), p. 47.

[84] GFTU membership in 1911 was only 703,000; TUC PC *Quarterly Report*, December 1911.

[85] *LL*, 14 July 1911.

[86] TUC PC *mins.*, 6 September 1913.

[87] ASRS, *Annual Report*, 1900.

decision not to seek affiliation, 'as we are not convinced that any substantial benefit to this society would accrue from such affiliation'.[88] Following this decision, Richard Bell, the ASRS secretary, told Jochade, the ITF secretary, of his surprise at his union's decision and implied that he would work to reverse it.[89] Nevertheless, in May 1906, the ASRS executive again declined an invitation to send delegates to the next ITF convention, and two months later the executive reaffirmed its decision against affiliation. A year later Bell was still assuring Jochade of his personal support for the ITF and promising to maintain pressure on the union executive in favour of affiliation. However, it was not until Jochade came to England to visit the ASRS leaders late in 1907 that the union finally agreed to affiliate.[90] Even then, the union seemed to be half-hearted in its support. Although ASRS delegates attended the 1908 ITF Convention, and were full of praise for the Federation, by 1910 the union was refusing to send delegates to the convention because of the cost involved.[91] In August 1910, Walter Hudson, by then ASRS secretary, informed Jochade that the union had decided against sending delegates; and he observed by way of explanation, 'I notice that the agenda does not contain any material with regard to workers on railways.'[92] The comment was indicative of the tendency within the British unions to see the purpose of international trades unionism in the very narrowest of terms.

The National Union of Dock Labourers was similarly tardy in joining the ITF. When the ITF sought the union's affiliation in December 1905, James Sexton, the union secretary, although favourable to the idea himself, warned Jochade that the union would probably reject the idea. 'We have so many things to subscribe to', Sexton lamented, 'such as our Trade

---

[88] ASRS, *Annual Report*, 1905.

[89] Richard Bell to Jochade, 30 June 1905, ITF Correspondence, ASRS file, MRC.

[90] Bell to Jochade, 21 May and 27 July 1906, 27 July, 26 September, and 19 December 1907, and 8 April 1908, ITF Correspondence, ASRS file, MRC.

[91] ASRS executive, 14–19 September 1908, in ASRS *Annual Report*, 1908; executive, 20–5 June 1910, in ASRS *Annual Report*, 1910.

[92] Walter Hudson to Jochade, 12 August 1910, in ITF Correspondence, ASRS file, MRC; and see Jochade's reply, dated 15 August 1910.

Union Congress, our national Federation, and the Parliamentary Fund, all of which are a strain upon our funds.' In May 1906 the union did indeed reject the idea of affiliation and Sexton was left to explain that financial considerations were the stumbling-block. However, Sexton's constant assurances to Jochade that he was doing his best to press the case for ITF affiliation were not just polite niceties, for indeed in June 1907 the union did join the Federation. Even so, financial difficulties still persisted, and in 1908 Sexton was forced to ask the Federation to be patient on the matter of dues.[93] Smaller unions, such as the Amalgamated Stevedores' Labour Protection League also declined invitations to join the ITF, and shortages of funds possibly accounted for this.[94] In other industries, too, the British unions were slow to seek affiliation to the international unions. At its 1908 Conference the National Union of Boot and Shoe Operatives rejected a proposal to affiliate to the German-based International Shoe and Leather Workers' Union. It was not until Joseph Simon, a representative of the international body, addressed the 1912 Conference that the British footwear union voted to affiliate.[95]

No doubt the costs of affiliation, the expense of sending delegates abroad, and the fear that union funds could be squandered in a foolish foreign strike, were factors that deterred the British unions from seeking international affiliations. A desire to limit affiliation fees may even explain the TUC's decision to let the smaller GFTU stand as the British link with the central International Federation. As the international fees were based on a fixed sum per thousand members, the GFTU's relatively small membership (703,000 in 1911) meant that the British fees were only a quarter of the sum that would have been needed to support full TUC membership.[96] It seems likely, too, that many thrifty union

[93] Jochade to Sexton, 18 December 1905, 4 April and 26 November 1906, 10 June 1907, and 16 March 1908, ITF Correspondence, NUDL file, MRC.

[94] James Anderson to Jochade, 7 April 1908, ITF Correspondence, Amalgamated Stevedores' Labour Protection League file, MRC.

[95] Alan Fox, *A History of the National Union of Boot and Shoe Operatives* (Oxford, 1958), p. 328.

[96] The fee structure is described in F.S. Lyons, *Internationalism in Europe*, p. 160.

members were sceptical of the benefits to be obtained from their leaders undertaking excursions to the Continent. One piece of evidence at least indicates that was the case. In 1910 the Friendly Society of Iron Founders was polled on the question of whether the union executive had acted properly in sending a delegate to Germany to examine trade union life there. The result, 3,802 in favour and 3,063 against, certainly revealed significant opposition.[97]

When resentment against the high costs of international affiliation was combined with a suspicion that German trade unionists were seeking to dominate the international unions, then strife was inevitable. Tillett's criticism of the German's imperious attitude within the ITF has already been noted. An incident in March 1914 involving the ITF and Robert Williams, secretary of the National Transport Workers' Federation, adds further confirmation. Although all the details are not clear from the remaining correspondence, it appears that Williams encountered what he considered to be German high-handedness during an ITF meeting in Germany early in 1914. His letter to Jochade, the ITF secretary, detailing his grievances, captures the spirit of British resentment over high costs and the alleged overbearing attitude of the German unionists and is therefore worth quoting at length. Williams began by noting the £300 affiliation fees to the ITF and went on to warn Jochade that in the union executive meetings there were many 'pointed questions' being asked about the merits of ITF membership. He continued:

> You may take it from me that I should not approve of secession from the International, as a general principle, but in the existing circumstances, I cannot advocate the continuance of our affiliation with any degree of conviction or sincerity. I see no reason to be very enthusiastic over any advantages to be derived from the ITF . . .
>
> Speaking candidly, the money we spend could be far more profitably spent here in improved organisation. If Britain continues to be insular it is largely because little or no tact has been shown by our Continental friends. I am being constantly taunted by questions as to what I think of my German friends after my recent experiences, and I can say very little in reply. I set out with boundless admiration for your country and methods, and you also taunt me with the threat that my opinions will change in the course of time. Well, my dear Jochade, these changes

---

[97] Iron Founders, *Annual Report*, 1910.

are certainly unfavourable towards you and German things in general. I think on considerable reflection that you are as conservative as anything we have in this country. You have been entrusted with great responsibilities and you act oblivious to everything except maintaining the balance of voting power in the hands of Germany, Austria and Switzerland.[98]

This is a remarkable outburst. Not only does Williams expose his resentment over costs and alleged German arrogance, but there is also the admission that British unions are 'insular' and even a touch of chauvinism in his remark deprecating 'German things in general'. Although the other transport union leaders, Gosling and Tillett, hastened to reassure Jochade when they got wind of the squabble,[99] Williams's criticism must have reflected the views of other dissatisfied British trade unionists. Certainly Williams was not bluffing on the matter of costs: at the 1914 conference of the British transport workers, a unilateral attempt was made to lower the unions' affiliation fees to the ITF from £300 to £200.[100] In the event the motion was lost; but the signs of dissatisfaction were there for all to see.

Why were rank-and-file British trade unionists so insular in their outlook, and why were their unions leaders so lukewarm on the matter of creating a genuine solidarity with the union movements of other European nations? Perhaps the German domination of international unionism provides a clue here. The new Germany was by the 1890s a highly successful industrial power beginning to pull ahead of her economic rivals in Europe. The German leadership of the new international unions seems to indicate that internationalist sentiment was most likely to take root where workers were confident in the long-term future of the industries that employed them, and were without fear of foreign competitors. From a position of relative security it was easier to look abroad with a generous heart. British workers, however, from their situation, may have found the sentiment of internationalism a luxury they could not afford. For there

[98]   Williams to Jochade, ITF Correspondence, Tillett file, MRC.

[99]   Tillett to Jochade, 24 March 1914, and Gosling to Jochade, 27 March 1914, ITF Correspondence, Tillett file, MRC.

[100]   National Transport Workers' Federation, *Annual General Meeting*, 10–11 June 1914, MRC.

was by the end of the nineteenth century a growing awareness that Britain was an industrial power under challenge. The sustained propaganda campaign in support of tariff reform from 1903 onwards gave great currency to the idea that Britain's economic future lay in mortal peril from foreign competition. The tariff reform message was understood by many working people as 'a great Anti-Foreign Crusade', according to Robert Tressell.[101] Of course, tariff reform itself was decisively rejected in 1906, with the working people refusing to vote for a policy which was believed to involve an increase in the price of food, their most fundamental concern. Nevertheless, one cannot discount the effectiveness of the message of foreign competition as a threat to employment. Signs of antipathy toward foreign workers because of the threat to British workers' jobs were seen in the debates on aliens in 1905 and again in the concern over immigration at the TUC in 1906, 1907, and 1911.[102] Significantly, the international theme which was most often treated in trade union journals and papers was that of foreign competition against British industry, a theme which complemented the prominence always given to 'the state of trade' and any other matter bearing upon the crucial issue of unemployment. The Steel Smelters' *Monthly Reports*, for instance, kept German and American competition in steel-making under close surveillance for the benefit of its readers.[103] No doubt the prominence given to such themes created fertile ground among trade unionists for pro-imperialist appeals based on the need to safeguard jobs and expand trade through the expansion of the Empire. In this sense the skilful promotion of love of Empire in the late-Victorian and Edwardian period takes on special significance. For this propaganda constantly put forward the message that Britain's imperial possessions, conquered and held by military might, provided food, cheap resources for industry, guaranteed export markets and, most

---

[101] R. Tressell, *The Ragged Trousered Philanthropists* (London, 1965; originally published 1914), pp. 21–2: 'The Foreigner was the enemy, and the cause of poverty and bad trade'.

[102] See Standish Meacham, *A Life Apart: The English Working Class 1890–1914* (London, 1977), pp. 198 and 258.

[103] See the volumes of British Steel Smelters, *Monthly Reports*, 1892–95, 1898–1900, and 1902, MRC, MSS 36.

importantly, jobs at home. The Empire was to be Britain's shield against foreign competition, as much for workers as owners. The propaganda of imperialism, therefore, encouraged the working people to identify their own self-interest with the nation's military supremacy. In the final analysis, Britain's political leaders were able to choose war instead of neutrality in August 1914 only because they were confident that the vast majority of working people identified the 'national cause' with their own. But this is to look far ahead. At the end of the nineteenth century it was southern Africa, not Europe, that was to provide the flashpoint.

5

The War in South Africa, 1899–1902

I begin to feel that nothing but an utterly disastrous defeat to our entire forces and collapse of the campaign will serve to bring the bulk of the people of this country to its senses.

J.B. Glasier to Lizzie Glasier, 19 January 1900, Glasier Papers, I. 1. 00/7

In the autumn of 1899 two events occurred full of significance for British political life. First, in September, the TUC voted narrowly to join with the socialist groups in a special conference on labour representation, an historic decision which led to the formation of the LRC, precursor of the Labour Party. Second, just one month later, in mid-October 1899, the policy of competitive imperialism pursued by Lord Salisbury's Unionist Government finally resulted in the outbreak of war against the Boer Republics in South Africa. The coincidence of these two events serves to underline the fact that the birth of the Labour Party and its first two years of life were indeed overshadowed by one of Britain's most costly and prolonged colonial wars, a war that created bitter public controversy in Britain. The purpose of this chapter is to show how the various elements of the labour movement responded to the conflict in South Africa, and in particular to indicate how the background of war affected the forging of the 'labour alliance'.

Readers of the British socialist press had been well forewarned of the threat to peace in South Africa. Since the Jameson Raid and the more recent Anglo-French confrontation further north at Fashoda, the *Labour Leader* and *Justice* had given prominence to sophisticated anti-imperialist arguments, and both papers had issued urgent warnings about the imminence of conflict over the Transvaal question.[1] The

[1] See Hardie's editorial on imperialism *LL*, 7 January 1899, Marxian's comments on Rhodes, *LL*, 21 January and 15 April 1899, and for warnings re the situation in South Africa see *LL*, 17 June, 9, 23, and 30 September, and 7 October 1899. On imperialism see also *Justice* editorials, 7 and 14 January 1899, and re

Labour Leader in particular showed a good deal of prescience regarding the South African situation. In April 1899 the paper had explored the possibilities of war in the Transvaal, and forecast that in such a war, 'while England must eventually win, the obstinate resistance of 60,000 burghers fighting for their hearths and homes and aided by a thorough knowledge of the country' would ensure a long struggle.[2] On 3 July an anxious ILP Administrative Council agreed to 'endeavour to form a committee of all bodies opposed to war with the Transvaal',[3] thus giving an indication even at this early stage of the inclusive, broad-front tactics that the ILP would follow throughout the crisis. The ILP's activities, however, did not satisfy Russell Smart, editor of the *ILP News*. In August he wrote to ILP secretary John Penny urging the party to begin full-scale agitation at once: 'We are evidently in for a brutal murderous war if we cannot arrange sufficient public opinion to prevent it',[4] Smart predicted gloomily. The SDF had also been warning of the developing crisis over the Transvaal. In July the SDF organized a protest demonstration in Trafalgar Square, and before its annual conference opened in Manchester in August a public meeting on the Transvaal crisis was held.[5] Of course, the socialists were not alone in anticipating a conflict in South Africa. In June 1899, following the apparent failure of the latest round of negotiations between President Paul Kruger and Lord Milner, concerned Liberals had formed the Transvaal Committee, and on 10 July it held its first public meeting in London to protest 'against reckless threats of war with the Transvaal'.[6]

Thus, well before the actual commencement of hostilities in South Africa in October 1899, the broad outlines of the case against the war had already emerged. Throughout 1899 the socialist press steadfastly maintained that the real cause of tension with the Transvaal was the influence exerted over British foreign policy by a clique of mineowners and financiers

the danger of war in South Africa see *Justice*, 6 and 20 May, 17 and 24 June, 26 August, 2, 9, and 30 September 1899.

   [2] *LL*, 22 April 1899.

   [3] ILP NAC *mins.*, 3 July 1899.

   [4] R. Smart to J. Penny, 12 August 1899, ILP Archives 1899/76.

   [5] *SDF Annual Conference Report*, 1899, p. 17; *Justice*, 12 August 1899.

   [6] See 'Transvaal Committee: Report of Six months' Work, 1 February 1900' in Stephen Koss (ed.), *The Pro-Boers* (Chicago, 1973), pp. 4–6.

who had designs upon the resources of the Boer Republics. It was argued that the electoral and fiscal grievances of the Uitlanders were mere pretexts put forward to obscure Britain's aggressive posture. The British press, it was also asserted, was consciously deceiving the people as to the real sources of tension and were whipping up an irrational and belligerent patriotism.[7] One other clear portent of the struggle to come was evident before the outbreak of war, namely, the violence of the opposition to the anti-war forces. For, on 24 September, a peace demonstration in Trafalgar Square organized by the Transvaal Committee and the Bermondsey Labour League was disrupted by violence.[8] It was the first of the wild clashes that were to mar the anti-war campaign in Britain, especially during the early months of the conflict.

1. *The Response of the Trade Union Leadership, and the Formation of the LRC*

While the socialists were predictably appalled by the war when it finally came, the attitude of the trade union leaders was less clear-cut. At the time there was probably an expectation that the trade unionists would instinctively support those Liberals who took a stand against the war policy of a Unionist Government. After all, the trade unions had only recently endorsed W.T. Stead's 'Peace Crusade' and they had welcomed the Hague Peace Conference.[9] Moreover, in the House of Commons in April 1899 the trade unionist Lib-Lab MPs had opposed the Government's moves to strengthen the South African garrisons.[10] Nevertheless, during the first weeks of the war, they seemed to be in two minds. In the first debate on the war on 18 October, almost all the Lib-Lab MPs supported a motion condemning the Government's handling of the negotiations which had resulted in war.[11]

[7] A good example of the combination of all these themes was the ILP resolution condemning the Government's policy toward the Transvaal; see ILP NAC *mins.*, 9 September 1899.

[8] *Justice*, 30 September 1899.

[9] See Chapter 3.

[10] Tingfu Tsiang, *Labour and Empire* (New York, 1923), p. 77.

[11] *Hansard*, IV: 77: 367–8. According to information given in Clegg, Fox and Thompson, *History of British Trade Unions*, pp. 284–5, there were fourteen Lib-Lab MPs in the Parliament in 1899. Of these, ten supported the Stanhope motion, three were absent, and only one voted against it.

However, during the next week, two Lib-Labs, Maddison[12] and Broadhurst,[13] made it clear that, in spite of their criticism of the Government, they still wished to see a swift victory for British arms in the Transvaal.

In the main, the Lib-Lab MPs avoided both the intensely critical approach to the war adopted by the socialists and the simplistic patriotic response of the majority of MPs. There were only two exceptions to this: John Burns,[14] the former socialist agitator and Lib-Lab MP, and J. Havelock Wilson,[15] the anti-socialist leader of the National Sailors' and Firemen's Union. In the Commons on 6 February 1900, Burns delivered a withering attack upon Rhodes, Chamberlain, and all those mineowners whose avarice, he claimed, had led to the war. He made no mention of any desire to see the British forces succeed, remarking instead that the Army was being used as the 'janissary of Jews'.[16] Havelock Wilson dissented immediately. Where British territory, rights, and liberties were under attack, Wilson proclaimed, 'I forget my party and put the support of my country above all things.'[17] It should be stressed that among the parliamentary trade unionists Wilson was alone in professing such a frankly pro-war viewpoint.

The debates on the war at the Trades Union Congresses revealed how close was the contest between the two powerful ideas that were obviously competing for the conscience of the trade union movement: on the one hand, there was the

---

[12] Fred Maddison was a prominent union official with the Amalgamated Society of Railway Servants and was at that time editor of the *Railway Review*. See Maddison's speech explaining his decision to abstain on John Dillon's amendment against sending the Militia Reserve to South Africa, *Hansard*, 20 October 1899, IV: 77: 399.

[13] Henry Broadhurst was a trade union official with the Operative Stonemasons' Society. He had been a prominent member of the TUC Parliamentary Committee from 1874 to 1890 and again from 1893 to 1895, and had been an MP 1880–92 and again from 1894 onwards. For this speech see *Hansard*, 25 October 1899, IV: 77: 671–74.

[14] John Burns had led the demonstrations which resulted in the 'Bloody Sunday' riot of 1887. He had been a member of the TUC Parliamentary Committee in 1890–1 and 1893–5 and a Lib-Lab MP since 1892.

[15] Joseph Havelock Wilson had been president of the National Sailors' and Firemen's Union since 1895, and a member of the TUC Parliamentary Committee in 1889–98. He had been a Lib-Lab MP since 1892.

[16] *Hansard*, IV: 78: 786–97.

[17] *Hansard*, IV: 78: 798–99.

desire not to be disloyal to those ordinary soldiers fighting under the British flag and, on the other, the desire not to support those owners of mines and industry whose influence, it was suspected, lay at the heart of the war. The prevailing mood at the Congresses shifted back and forth. At the Scottish TUC in April 1900, the war was condemned by Thomas Wilson the chairman and resolutions against imperialism and conscription were passed without controversy.[18] In contrast, when the British TUC met in September 1900, with the war almost a year old, the Parliamentary Committee took the safe course of silence and refused even to mention the war in its Annual Report presented to the Congress. However, the Congress president for that year, William Pickles, an ILP member, felt no such diffidence; he denounced the war and scolded those workers who had been caught up in 'the frenzy of war fever'.[19] Perhaps profiting from Pickles's determined address, John Ward,[20] of the small Navvies' Union, then managed to secure a slender majority in favour of his resolution regretting the Parliamentary Committee's timidity concerning the war and protesting against the suppression of the Boer Republic 'at the dictation of the cosmopolitan capitalists'. The Congress proceedings loyally note that in the vote on Ward's motion 'a large number of the delegates remained neutral'.[21] This high rate of abstentions, as well as the studious silence of the TUC Parliamentary Committee's report, robbed Ward's resolution of much of its force. It was obvious that, whilst the trade union leaders refused to celebrate the war, most of them did not believe they had any business in compaigning actively against it but rather preferred to ignore it.

In the light of these differences, it is vital to ask how the South African issue affected the delicate process of the creation of the LRC on the basis of an alliance between the trade unionists and the socialists? The war, coming as it did

[18] *LL*, 5 May 1900.
[19] TUC *Annual Report 1900*, p. 52.
[20] John Ward was the leader of the small Navvies' Union; he had been a member of the SDF in the early 1890s; see Paul Thompson, *Socialists, Liberals and Labour: The Struggle For London 1885–1914* (London, 1967), p. 120. However, he was no longer a socialist; see *Justice's* comments 14 September 1901.
[21] TUC *Annual Report 1900*, pp. 54–5.

on the very eve of this new experiment in labour representation, could not have erupted at a worse moment. It was
obviously a potentially divisive issue, one that threatened to
highlight the great ideological gulf that separated the trade
unionists from the socialists. Thus, as the famous Memorial
Hall Conference of February 1900 approached, the ILP
leaders spared no effort in stressing time and again that the
conference must not be disrupted by any foolish insistence
upon socialist principles. Smart, for one, warned that the ILP
delegates must approach the conference with 'breadth of
mind and charity of heart', and without any 'fine socialist
oration up our sleeve'. All that was needed, Smart advised,
was a determination to arrive at a working alliance with the
trade unionists.[22] Hardie also warned against any attempt to
impose 'extreme views' upon the conference.[23] On the eve of
the gathering, Joseph Burgess advised that the ILP delegates
to the conference

are not such fools as to believe they can convert the Conference to their
way of thinking. They will be satisfied if the Conference formulates
practical proposals for carrying out the policy, not of the ILP, but of
the Trades Congress, and they have no desire nor intention to press the
Conference to affirm its adhesion to abstract principles in the form of
a programme.[24]

Although these stern warnings against socialist orations and
extreme views made no specific mention of the war as the
kind of divisive issue that must be avoided, they do reveal
well enough the determination of the ILP to avoid any potentially disruptive question. In this regard, it is noteworthy that
the ILP delegates to the Edinburgh Conference in January
1900, at which the Scottish Workers' Parliamentary Elections
Committee was formed, made no effort to raise the matter
of the war in South Africa.[25]

When the Memorial Hall Conference finally opened on 27
February 1900 the dominance of the trade unions was obvious. The precise agenda, originally prepared by a 'Joint

[22] 'Towards a United Democracy', *ILP News*, November 1899 and see also
the review of the conference in *ILP News*, March 1900.
[23] *LL*, 24 February 1900.
[24] *ILP News*, February 1900.
[25] *LL*, 13 January 1900.

Committee' which included socialist members,[26] was presented only after further alterations had been made by the
TUC Parliamentary Committee.[27] The conference was opened
by J.T. Chandler, chairman of the Parliamentary Committee,
and the gathering then elected W.C. Steadman, a Lib-Lab
MP, to be chairman of the conference. There were 116
delegates from the trade unions present, against only seven
delegates from the ILP, five from the SDF, and one Fabian.
The Boer War was mentioned only once in the proceedings
when John Burns warned the conference against 'too much
dictation' on controversial matters. He cited the war as one
obviously contentious issue:

The Labour Party were not united on all questions. Look at the war.
They were not united about that, but he [Burns] was glad to say that
eleven out of the twelve Labour members were dead against that.[28]

There were loud cheers at this point; but immediately W.E.
Clery, a delegate from the Fawcett Association, rose on a
point of order to 'protest about Mr Burns introducing this
kind of thing here'.[29] There were cheers for this protest too.
The war was evidently a most sensitive issue amongst the
trade union leadership. The LRC's silence on the war, therefore, followed from the Parliamentary Committee's careful
control over the agenda of this initial conference, and from
the socialists' desire to avoid controversy. Even the SDF
delegates limited their intervention to a resolution seeking a
socialist objective for the new LRC, a resolution which was
within the terms of the proposed agenda. Both the ILP and
the SDF appear to have accepted that the subject of the war
should not be raised at this conference, even though both
parties were at that time thoroughly absorbed in the anti-war
campaign.[30] For the ILP in particular, this decision not to

[26] See ILP NAC *mins.*, 21 October 1899 for the appointment of Hardie and
MacDonald to this preliminary committee.
[27] *Report of the Conference on Labour Representation, 27 February 1900*,
p. 8.
[28] Ibid., p. 13.
[29] Ibid.
[30] Hardie, for example, had delivered public speeches against the war at the
Oxford Union on 22 February and at the Leicester Corn Exchange on 25 February.
See Hardie to David Lowe, 27 February 1900, ILP Archives, 1900/72, and *LL*,
3 March 1900.

draw the LRC into the struggle against the war resulted from the ILP leaders' recognition of the diffidence of the trade unionists, and from their determination to safeguard the fragile 'labour alliance' from any disruption.

It should not be thought that the socialists were absolutely silent on the war as they sat amongst their trade union colleagues at the remaining major conferences of the war years, namely, the LRC Conference and the Trades Union Congresses of 1901 and 1902. Resolutions against the war were indeed raised at these gatherings, and they met with varying degrees of success, as will be shown later. The essential point to stress here is that the socialists did not seek to involve either the LRC executive or the TUC Parliamentary Committee directly in the anti-war campaign, and neither body chose to enter the campaign on its own initiative.

The socialists' tactics can be readily understood in the light of the continuing divisions amongst the trade union leaders on the war issue. No real determination or enthusiasm on the issue was evident at the TUC or LRC gatherings in 1901 or 1902. At the Scottish Workers' Parliamentary Elections Committee Conference (the Scottish LRC) in January 1901, a resolution denouncing imperialism and urging arbitration to end the war in South Africa was carried; but there were strong speeches against the motion, and the large numbers of abstentions in the final vote meant that less than half the delegates had actually agreed to the anti-war resolution.[31] When the LRC Conference met in Manchester a month later, similar resolutions against imperialism and the war were agreed to, but there was no discussion and no formal voting.[32] Then, in May 1901, the Scottish TUC passed, by a margin of forty-two votes to twenty-two, a resolution urging the restoration of self-government for the two Boer Republics.[33] There was a major clash on the issue at the British TUC in September 1901. Here the TUC Parliamentary Committee again ignored the war altogether in its Annual Report. John

[31] *LL*, 12 January 1901. Of the 243 delegates present, 115 supported the resolution, seventy opposed it, and fifty-eight abstained.

[32] *LRC Annual Conference*, 1900, p. 20.

[33] *ILP News*, May 1901. See the resistance to this resolution in Scottish TUC PC *mins.*, 16 November 1901.

Ward attempted to propose a motion, similar to that carried the previous year, regretting the Parliamentary Committee's neglect of the issue. Significantly, this time the motion also praised the 'noble defence' of the Boers and demanded a cessation of hostilities. In a clear rebuff to the anti-war cause the Congress refused by 138 votes to 115 to agree to the suspension of standing orders so as to debate Ward's motion.[34]

Why did this particular anti-war resolution encounter such opposition? The explanation cannot lie in the popularity of either the war or the Government at this time; for the furore over the concentration camps in South Africa had been raging for some months, and the Government was suffering bitter criticism from trade union quarters owing to the Taff Vale judgement handed down by the Lords in June. *Justice* offered an explanation in terms of the 'spinelessness' of the trade unions.[35] The ILP, on the other hand, tended to excuse the incident. Smart claimed that the TUC was simply reluctant to depart from its agenda paper.[36] Hardie insisted that 'three-fifths of the delegates were pro-Boers': but he could not suggest an explanation for the blow to his cause.[37] Judging from the pattern revealed at earlier conferences, the explanation would appear to lie partly in the trade union leaders' belief that foreign affairs were outside their sphere of interest anyway, and partly in their dislike of 'disloyalty'. At the Scottish LRC Conference in January 1901, for instance, one opponent of the anti-war motion had argued that the conference ought to make no reference to the war because 'the majority of people were in favour of it, as shown by the general election'. Another delegate had argued that he had no instructions from his society on the war issue.[38] These comments, combined with the large number of abstentions in votes on resolutions concerning the war, indicate that many

[34] *TUC Annual Report*, 1901, pp. 37 and 51. The margin on the card vote, 724,000 to 330,000 votes, was even wider, showing that the larger mining and textile unions probably opposed the motion.

[35] *Justice*, 14 September 1901. See also Rothstein's letter of 15 September 1901 to Kautsky complaining of the 'servile fear' of the TUC; 11SG, Kautsky Archive, D XIX 578.

[36] *ILP News*, September 1901.

[37] *LL*, 14 September 1901.

[38] *LL*, 12 January 1901.

trade union delegates preferred to make no comment on the
conflict simply because they were aware that their union
members either supported the war or would at least dis-
approve of 'disloyal' motions. It is important to note that in
Ward's motion of September 1901, his praise of the 'noble
defence' of the Boers seemed by implication to be drawing
comfort from British losses and could easily be construed as
disloyal. The trade unionists, therefore, retained a sense of
identity with the ordinary British soldier in the field, and
they did not wish to express support for his enemies. It was
all very well for Hardie and his socialist companions to embrace the epithet 'pro-Boer', but the trade unionists shunned
that position.

Some further weight is given to this particular explanation
of the thinking of the trade union leadership on the war from
a consideration of the LRC and TUC gatherings in 1902. At
the LRC Conference in January, John Penny, the ILP secretary, was prevented from raising a matter connected with the
war, the president ruling that 'only business directly affecting
the Labour Representation Committee should be discussed'.[39]
Then, at the TUC in September, the Parliamentary Committee's report, cautious as ever, simply noted the ending of
the 'most remarkable war in modern history'. This time Ward
proposed a much more moderate motion than he had in 1901,
and suggested that the war should be described as 'unjust'.
This particular motion, which obviously avoided the 'disloyal' wording of the 1901 motion, was passed by 591,000
votes to 314,000.[40] Conversely, this vote revealed that the
representatives of roughly one-third of organized labour were
refusing to acknowledge the injustice of the war, even after
all the anti-war campaigning of the previous two years. It was
a significant dissenting minority.

2. *The Response of the Rank-and-file Trade Unionists*

The reluctance of the socialists to draw the new LRC or the
trade union movement into the anti-war campaign, as well as
the diffidence of the trade union leaders, is easily understood

---

[39] *LRC Annual Conference*, 1902, pp. 26–7.
[40] *LL*, 6 September 1902.

when the response of the rank-and-file trade unionists to the war is considered. The records of the local trades councils and some individual trade unions do provide some insight into the attitudes of the broad mass of trade unionists. Much the same hesitation can be seen. Many trades councils allowed the war to pass by without criticism, and some explained this neglect by arguing that foreign affairs were nothing to do with the trade union movement. On the other hand, some trade unionists openly displayed their solidarity with the British forces, and some were clearly caught up in the enthusiasm for the war. The evidence reveals that only a small minority of trades councils and trade unions attempted to mobilize their membership against the war, and even this minority encountered stiff resistance.

Before the fighting in South Africa began in October 1899, a handful of trades councils and trade unions followed the socialists' lead and urged the British Government to seek a peaceful, negotiated settlement. The trades councils at Huddersfield, Leeds, Aberdeen, and London all protested against the British Government's belligerence, and expressed scepticism over the Uitlanders' grievances.[41] It is noteworthy that in the case of the London Trades Council a significant minority opposed the protest resolution in favour of an amendment which advised against any declaration on the Transvaal issue.[42] In September 1899, one of the most powerful unions, the Railway Servants' Society, also attacked the Government's sabre-rattling over the Transvaal.[43] The response of these very same bodies to the outbreak of the war in October is most revealing. The Leeds and Huddersfield Trades Councils avoided any mention of the war throughout the remainder of 1899 and most of 1900. The Huddersfield Council managed to avoid the issue of the war altogether until November 1900 when a bitter debate erupted over a proposal that the council should join a committee to welcome home local volunteers from the war. This particular

[41] Huddersfield TC *mins.*, 20 and 29 September 1899; Leeds TC *mins.*, 6 and 27 September 1899; K.D. Buckley, *Trades Unionism in Aberdeen 1878–1900* (London, 1955), pp. 187–8; London TC *mins.*, 10 August 1899.

[42] London TC *mins.*, 10 August 1899. Of the seventy-seven delegates present, eighteen supported the amendment.

[43] Executive meeting, 11 September 1899, in *ASRS Annual Report 1899*.

incident typified the dilemma facing the trade unionists. The council's indecision was also typical: at first it was decided not to join the welcoming committee, but then this decision was reversed.[44] The London Trades Council displayed a similar hesitation regarding the war. Not until March 1900 did the council make any statement on the conflict, and even then it was only to advocate state maintenance for war casualties.[45] Of the four trades councils who had protested over British policy toward the Transvaal during the months preceding the war, only one, the Aberdeen Trades Council, continued to protest once hostilities began, and, as is described below, this provoked a bitter internal controversy. As for the Amalgamated Society of Railway Servants, the only major union to have protested during the period of pre-war tension, there was only a flicker of protest once the shooting started. In December 1899 the union executive, now assailed by critics in the union, defended its peace resolution of September and asserted its right to comment 'on any imperial matter'.[46] This determination apparently dissipated quickly, for the minutes of the executive show no further comment on the war throughout its course. Such examples of hesitation, confusion, and silence regarding the war were characteristic of most trades councils and trade unions. The essential point to note is that even those few trades councils and the single trade union which had shown an awareness of the developing crisis in the Transvaal during the last months of peace in 1899 were not confident enough to speak out against the war when the fighting actually began. No doubt the serious reversals faced by the British forces late in 1899, particularly the disasters of 'black week', increased patriotic pressures upon all trade unionists to support their 'kith and kin' in South Africa during the early months of the war.

The extent of the trades councils' timidity on the war issue can be appreciated most clearly when the full range of propagandist devices open to the trades councils is considered.

---

[44] Huddersfield TC *mins.*, 28 November and 19 December 1900.

[45] London TC *mins.*, 8 March 1900.

[46] This was in response to complaints from two union branches against the previous resolution; see executive meeting, 11 December 1899, in *ASRS Annual Report 1899.*

If the trades councils were united on a particular issue, they were quite capable of organizing effectively to bring pressure to bear upon the Government. Some of the methods at their disposal included public meetings and town meetings, conferences organized among several trades councils, the synchronization of protest resolutions which could be dispatched to the Government and local MPs from several trades councils at once, and combined trades councils' deputations to Westminster or to local MPs. During the period of the Boer War the trades councils used these familiar devices to draw public attention to a variety of domestic grievances. On the old-age-pension issue and the housing question scores of trades councils passed earnest resolutions, many of which were dispatched to the Government, and in the cause of mobilizing public opinion on these and other matters the councils held occasional conferences, lectures and public demonstrations.[47] Similarly, during these years many trades councils organized public meetings on the land issue in co-operation with the Land Nationalisation Society.[48] The education controversy also attracted the attention of the trades councils, and again many resolutions were sent to the Government.[49] The subjects given priority by the councils can also be seen in the questions drawn up by some councils for submission to candidates standing at the 1900 election. For instance, the Nottingham Trades Councils framed questions to elicit the candidates' views on pensions, workmen's compensation, the taxation of ground values, municipal control of local services, and pay-rates for government contracts.[50] The candidates' views on the South African War were apparently not sought.

[47] For examples of trades council activity on these two issues see: Glasgow TC *Annual Report*, 1898–9 and 1900–1; Norwich TC *Annual Report*, 1900; Cheshire TC *Annual Report*, 1900; Derby TC *Annual Report*, 1899, 1901, and 1902; Haslington TC *Annual Report*, 1899 and 1900; Hull TC *Annual Report*, 1900; Nottingham TC *mins.*, 4 October 1899; Scottish TUC Parliamentary Committee *mins.*, 20 October 1899, 16 March and 5 October 1901.

[48] For example, see Derby TC *Annual Report* 1901, and Birmingham TC *Annual Report*, 1899 and 1901.

[49] For example, see Nottingham TC *mins.*, 22 May 1901. Bradford TC went so far as to issue 10,000 copies of a circular on the education question; *LL*, 15 September 1901.

[50] Nottingham TC *mins.*, 19 September 1900.

This is not to say that the councils maintained an utter silence on the war. One particular issue connected with the war was debated by many councils, namely, the care of injured soldiers and of widows and orphans left by the war.[51] Another common response to the war crisis among the councils was an insistence upon the retention of all laws protecting the interests of labour after the annexation of the Transvaal and the Orange Free State.[52] Similarly, the trade unions often limited their discussion of the war to making arrangements for special contribution levels and the adoption of special continuity rules for those among their members called to the colours for service in South Africa.[53] Donations were also made to the various relief funds by some trade unions.[54] Clearly the trades councils and unions felt themselves to be on safe ground discussing those aspects of the war crisis which could be seen to involve 'labour interests' directly.

The reluctance to discuss the root issues, such as the justice of the war, can once again be partly explained by the fidelity of many trade unionists to the traditional view of the union as a defensive industrial organization wholly committed to the domestic scene. Thus the secretary of the Manchester Trades Council, reporting the council's views on state maintenance for war casualties in the Annual Report for 1900, was careful to note that 'it is not our intention to express an opinion in respect to the merits of the war, or in any way to raise the question of its being justifiable or otherwise'.[55] In the same way, the editors of trade union journals, if they mentioned the war at all, assured their readers that they would make no judgement upon it. In late October 1899 the editor of *The Post*, for example, observed that 'with the causes of

[51] For example, Liverpool TC *mins.*, 31 January 1900; Nottingham TC *mins.*, 14 February 1900; Glasgow TC *mins.*, 20 February 1901; Edinburgh TC *mins.*, 6 March 1900; Manchester and Salford TC *Annual Report*, 1900.

[52] For example, Newcastle TC *Annual Report*, 1901, and Manchester and Salford TC *Annual Report*, 1900.

[53] For example, executive meeting, 11 December 1899 in ASRS *Annual Report* 1899; Amalgamated Society of Engineers, *Monthly Journal*, January 1900.

[54] For example, the National Union of Teachers donated to the Mansion House Relief Fund; see *The Schoolmaster*, 27 January 1900.

[55] Manchester and Salford TC *Annual Report*, 1900.

the outbreak of hostilities or the policy of the government we have, of course, nothing to do'.[56]

In addition, there is some evidence which shows that trade unionists identified strongly with the British forces because of a perceived duty to be loyal to the ordinary British soldier. Whether this included any belief in the justice of the war is less certain; for, as explained above, the 'politics' of the war were seldom discussed. The trades unions and trades councils simply noted with pride the departure of some of their members to the war and wished them well.[57] In their social life during these war years some trade unions also displayed a more conventional allegiance to the Crown and pride in the armed forces. For instance, at the annual dinner of the Cardiff branch of the Steel Smelters' Union in February 1900, toasts were drunk to the royal family and the Army and Navy, and several military songs were sung including 'The Soldiers' Farewell', 'Comrades in Arms', and 'The Boys of the Old Brigade'.[58] There is also a good deal of evidence of both sympathy and enthusiastic support for the British forces among trade unionists in the arsenal and dockyard towns, among the shop assistants, and among boot and shoe workers.[59] But, in most cases, the evidence points to no more than a sense of loyalty to those engaged in the fighting on the British side, a loyalty usually manifested in expressions of thankfulness at moments of British victory.

However this sense of loyalty to the British soldier did occasionally blossom into a passionate enthusiasm for the

---

[56] *The Post*, 28 October 1899. For another example, see *The Schoolmaster*, 23 December 1899.

[57] Liverpool TC *Annual Report* 1900–1, noted 'the manly spirit' of the workers who had answered 'duty's call without a murmur'. In the London Society of Compositors, *Annual Report*, 1899, C.W. Bowerman, the secretary expressed his hope that the volunteers from his society would 'return safe and sound, with all honours that active military service can confer upon them'. In the British Steel Smelters, *Monthly Report*, October 1899, John Hodge praised the generosity of union members who had undertaken to support the families of those from amongst the union who were 'away fighting their country's battles'.

[58] British Steel Smelters, *Monthly Report*, February 1900, and see another example in H.J. Fryth and Henry Collins, *The Foundry Workers: A Trade Union History* (Manchester, 1959), p. 108.

[59] See the evidence collected by Frank Bealey in his important article 'Les Travaillistes et la guerre des Boers', *Le Mouvement Social*, October–December, 1963; see especially pp. 54–6.

war itself. It is noteworthy that in the case of the Post Office workers this sentiment appears to have been provoked by the direct involvement of some Post Office workers in the war. In November 1899 the Army Post Office Corps received orders to serve in the South African campaign. The union journal, *The Post*, provided a review of the Corps' farewell parade in London which preserves the emotions of envious fellow workers:

We devoured the South African news with avidity while the war fever flushed our brains . . . At midday first one colleague and then another brought in a copy of the 'extra special' and it was passed from hand to hand and from room to room, and we left our minutes half-written to discuss the stop-press news, our hearts beating proudly the while with the thought that soon we were to send off our own little band to join those who are risking their life and limb so bravely and gallantly in their country's cause . . . Our thoughts went off to the lonely veldt and the mountain passes of South Africa for which the little troop were bound, we heard the cries of the newsboys 'British victory', 'heavy losses', and we felt the full force of the contrast from the peaceful stir of the great metropolis, from the daily drudgery at the desk, to the hazard and peril and all the unaccustomed sights and sounds of 7,000 miles away . . . The grand old patriot passion awoke anew, and we cheered and cheered again because we felt that we must have some vent for our feelings . . . And then the rallying cry that touches a chord in the deepest depths of an Englishman's heart, 'three cheers for Her Majesty the Queen!'[60]

This vivid account is worth quoting at length because it gives a real insight into the emotion of the Post Office workers on this occasion. The report reveals not only the ordinary patriotic passions carefully nurtured by the press, but also the writer's envy of the soldiers' supposed escape from 'drudgery' and his transference to the thrilling and exotic places of the Empire. 'And we—we went back to our desks. It seemed almost like bathos', lamented the writer. It is also clear that a sense of empathy with the ordinary soldier in the field was central to the trade unionists' patriotism; 'and now we shall scan the war news with a feeling that we have our part and lot in the fray', *The Post* concluded.[61] The various union journals of the postal workers did indeed reflect and at the same time foster this sense of empathy throughout the

---

[60] *The Post*, 11 November 1899.
[61] Ibid.

war. *The Post* carried articles and photographs of the action in South Africa sent by members of the Army Postal Corps, the *Postal Clerks' Herald* established a column entitled 'Our colleagues at the Front', while the *Postmen's Gazette* featured a regular column headed 'Incidents of the War'.

Very few other trade union journals gave the war anything like this kind of prominence. Most trade union publications, even those of the largest and most politically active unions that were amongst the first to join the LRC, rarely mentioned the war, and those that included reports of local branch activities show that here too the war was almost completely ignored. For instance, the *Monthly Journal* of the Amalgamated Society of Engineers, although edited by the ILP member G.N. Barnes, gave the war only passing attention. In the January 1900 issue of the *Journal*, Barnes made the revealing comment that

The year just closed has been marked generally by events of great and ominous import, although in our little world of trade unionism there has happened little but of a satisfactory character.[62]

There was no real discussion of the war in the Engineers' *Monthly Journal* until it was proposed that a 6 *d*. levy should be imposed on all members to provide for the Society's war casualties and their dependants. Opinion in the letter columns then seemed to be evenly divided.[63]

With the majority of trade unions holding to a hesitant neutrality over the war, it is not surprising to find that, as the conflict developed, only a handful of local trades councils persistently proclaimed their opposition to the war. The Edinburgh Trades Council was one such council, and in this particular case the strong resentment of the minority to the council's anti-war activity was very plain. The council made no public declaration of its attitude during the early months of the war, but contented itself with several lectures on imperialism for the council delegates. In March 1900, however, the council was forced to show its hand when the Edinburgh Stop-the-War Committee invited it to be represented at a public meeting to be addressed by the notorious anti-war

[62]   ASE, *Monthly Journal*, January 1900.
[63]   See 'General Council Report' in ibid., January, March, and April 1900.

activist Cronwright-Schreiner. At its March meeting the council decided to accept the invitation by twenty-five votes to nine.[64] Soon after there came a typical dissenting response. The local branch of the Amalgamated Society of Carpenters and Joiners lodged a protest with the council, insisting that 'political questions should not be introduced by members of this council, but that their whole time ought to be devoted to trade matters'.[65] The following month the council decided to attend another Stop-the-War meeting, a decision that was unsuccessfully challenged by the minority at the next meeting.[66] The council continued to side with the anti-war cause throughout the South African conflict, but a determined minority always opposed this involvement.

The Aberdeen Trades Council was also one of the few councils to speak out against the war and to lend assistance to the anti-war campaign. The council was united against the war in 1899 and actively campaigned against the war during 1900. However, a serious split which developed in the council in 1901, over an attempt to condemn the 'methods of barbarism' adopted by the British Army, testified to the reluctance of trade unionists, even those who opposed the war, to be seen as critics of the conduct of the British soldier in the field. The rupture began in January 1901 when William Diack, a prominent socialist delegate, gave notice of a motion which declared the council's emphatic protest 'against the brutalities now being perpetrated in South Africa in the name of warfare'.[67] After an extensive debate over two meetings of the council, on 6 March 1901 Diack's motion was carried by thirty-eight votes to twenty-five.[68] However, this victory was short-lived, for at the very next meeting of the council on 13 March, the Diack motion was challenged once more by an amendment declaring that the council ought to take 'no action' on the South African war. This time the amendment was carried narrowly by thirty-seven votes to thirty-four.[69]

[64] Edinburgh TC *mins.*, 6 March 1900.
[65] Ibid., 20 March 1900.
[66] Ibid., 10 and 17 April 1900. The decision to attend the second meeting was passed by nine votes to five, and upheld by twelve to six.
[67] Aberdeen TC *mins.*, 23 January 1901.
[68] Aberdeen TC *mins.*, 20 February and 6 March 1901.
[69] Ibid., 13 March 1901.

Clearly, the determined anti-war group led by Diack had offended against the sense of solidarity with the British soldier, 'their own kindred' as one of Diack's opponents on the council expressed it.[70] Thus the council had retreated into neutrality.

Another noteworthy case is that of the London Trades Council, for it typifies the experience of most trades councils in that the anti-war group was too weak to influence the policy of the council. As was explained previously, the London Trades Council was one of the few councils that complained of the sabre-rattling of the Government prior to the outbreak of war, but it remained silent when the fighting began. In March 1900 the council also refused a suggestion that it should take the initiative in organizing an anti-war meeting in London.[71] In April the council protested over the violation of the right of free speech by 'jingo hooligans'; but the council's refusal to be drawn into any public comment on the war was dramatically revealed in the defeat of an amendment insisting 'that the present disastrous war be brought to a speedy conclusion'.[72] At its next meeting, on 10 May 1900, a motion condemning the war and calling for an early peace under which the two Boer Republics would retain their independence was lost, and a similar motion asking the council to call a trade union conference to advocate peace was also narrowly defeated by thirty-eight votes to thirty.[73] In September 1900 a motion asking the council to convene a conference to protest over the brutality of the prosecution of war was side-stepped by means of an immediate motion of adjournment.[74] In fact only one resolution directly relating to South Africa was allowed to pass through the council during the war, and that was a perfectly innocuous motion regretting that the military authorities had granted a monopoly of printing in Bloemfontein to one

[70] Quoted from *Daily Free Press* report in Richard Price, *An Imperial War and the British Working Class* (London 1972), p. 87.
[71] London TC *mins.*, 29 March 1900.
[72] Ibid., 12 April 1900.
[73] Ibid., 10 May 1900.
[74] Ibid., 13 September 1900.

firm, an action which was condemned as being 'inimical to the interests of labour'.[75]

3. *The Issue of Working Class 'Jingoism'*

In an attempt to ascertain the attitudes of the rank-and-file members of the labour movement toward the war it is necessary to examine the evidence on the controversial topic of working-class jingoism. This may assist in determining whether the diffidence of the trade union leaders followed from an instinctive patriotism or resulted in part from the pressure of patriotic opinion from below. At the outset the work of Richard Price must be acknowledged.[76] Briefly summarizing his position, by an examination of the records of working-men's clubs, a survey of evidence relating to jingo hooliganism, and by statistical analyses of the pattern of recruitment and of the 'Khaki' election of 1900, Price has argued that indifference rather than jingoism characterized the working-class response to the war.

It must be emphasized immediately that it is impossible to assess the precise dimensions of support for the war among all working-class people. The exact proportion of supporters of that bundle of ideas called jingoism will never be determined. But one can concede much to Price. He is undoubtedly correct, judging from his own evidence, that the great mass of the working class remained indifferent, and were not swamped in a tide of jingoistic feeling as is commonly supposed. However, we may still ask, given that the working class was largely indifferent to the war, were those who *did* take an interest in the South African conflict chiefly composed of supporters of the war or opponents?

According to the evidence, it would appear that the leaders of the political labour movement, whose task it was to assess and influence working-class opinions, did indeed believe that pro-war feeling was the stronger amongst the people. As the war continued, Keir Hardie, for one, seemed to accept that jingoism had won more supporters among the workers than had the anti-war message. Speaking at the

---

[75]   Ibid., 9 August 1900.
[76]   Richard Price, *An Imperial War.*

Scottish LRC Conference in January 1900, he explained that the mischief-making press had prevented the workers from making a 'wise judgement' about the war.[77] In March, following the disruption of peace meetings, Hardie lamented that the 'war spirit' had made 'easy victims' among the working people.[78] Even in the House of Commons Hardie did not contest the view that the working class supported the war, but simply retorted that, when unemployment followed the peace, 'thousands and tens of thousands of those same working men . . . will then realise what imperialism means'.[79] The leaders of the SDF made similar admissions that the Government had gained significant support for its war policy among the working people. In March 1900 *Justice* conceded that:

We cannot shut our eyes to the fact, unpleasant though it may be, that a very large number if not the majority of wage-earners have supported the plutocrats and murderers . . . and that the mass of those workers who are opposed to the war have, by their cowardly silence, acquiesced in the degradation.[80]

After the refusal of the TUC to accept Ward's anti-war motion in September 1901, *Justice* made another attempt to estimate the dimensions of working-class support for the war:

It must not be forgotten in this connection that the organised members of the working class form but a fourth of the whole, and that amongst those outside the unions the most virulent of the jingoes were to be found. The trade unions, even if they had all been united against the war, would be but a minority . . . Unfortunately, too many among them have been afflicted with the war fever, and although wherever a collective expression has been given it has been adverse to the war, there is little doubt that the unthinking majority of the workers, as well inside as outside the unions, have been supporters of the government.[81]

This is not to contest Price's refutation of the familiar vision of the working class as quite overwhelmed by jingo-

[77] *LL*, 13 January 1900.
[78] *LL*, 17 March 1900.
[79] *Hansard*, 17 July 1901, IV: 97: 759.
[80] *Justice*, 10 March 1900.
[81] *Justice*, 14 September 1901.

ism. For indeed these same contemporary socialist observers agreed that the workers had not been thoroughly captured by the war fever. Hyndman perceived that most workers, rather than being enthusiastic about the war, simply wished to see it through.[82] Both the ILP and the SDF emphasized that working-class audiences were, in the main, quite ready to give their anti-war speakers a fair hearing.[83] *Justice* also reminded its readers that, when all was said and done, it must not be forgotten that not a single working-class organization had declared its support for the war.[84] Thus, the socialists were not suggesting that the whole of the working class had been overcome by the war fever; but they did recognize that pro-war feeling had made greater inroads amongst the working people than had their own anti-war campaign.

The opinions given in the socialist press on the class composition of the jingo crowd are also relevant. Many reports of the disturbances at anti-war meetings do lend support to Price's view that many of the violent jingoes were middle-class youths. As early as October 1899 the London Trades Council referred to the disruptive tactics of 'well-dressed ruffians'.[85] *Justice* also occasionally described the jingo hooligans as 'well-dressed', and specifically mentioned 'medical students', 'stock-exchange rowdies', 'the class to which the city clerk belongs', and the 'snob class' as being responsible for the violence.[86] Just as often though, the reports in *Justice* and the *Labour Leader* either made no assessment of the class of the jingo hooligans or conceded that they included working people. In the reports of the violence at the anti-war meetings in the early months of 1900 in particular no attempt was made to suggest that the

[82] *Justice*, 17 March 1900.

[83] For example, see the reports of Hardie's speeches in South Wales, *ILP News*, July 1900, and in North Scotland, *ILP News*, February 1901.

[84] *Justice*, 17 March 1900.

[85] London TC *mins.*, 12 October 1899.

[86] For example, see *Justice*, 31 March 1900, 15 and 29 June 1901. Hardie also agreed that most of the trouble in Glasgow in early 1900 came from the students of Glasgow University; see Lowe to Hardie, 26 February 1900 and Hardie to Lowe, 27 February 1900, ILP Archives, 1900/70 and 72.

violent jingoes were middle class.[87] Rather, the socialist press
described them as 'the mob', 'bullies and bawds', 'gangs of
ruffians', 'rabble', 'criminals', 'howling yahoos and non-
descripts', 'prostitutes' bullies' and, on one occasion, 'a mob
of jingo hooligans from the slums of Holloway'.[88] The
socialist press would not have hesitated to point out that
these violent jingoes were always middle-class youths if that
had indeed been the case. Evidently, it was not. Thus, the
role of the middle-class groups in jingo rowdyism was certainly acknowledged by the socialist press; but the participation of workers was not denied. In his most famous editorial
on the war, penned in January 1900, Hardie was surely
lamenting the involvement of working people in jingoistic
displays when he wrote:

There is something truly pathetic in the spectacle of poor, degraded,
underfed wretches cheering themselves hoarse over the victories of their
country and then creeping back to their cheerless homes to gain a few
hours pestilential sleep to fit them for the toils of the coming day.[89]

Finally, Price's statistical work on the 'Khaki' election must
be taken into consideration. Price has shown that the Government's imperialist rhetoric by no means carried all before it
in the working-class constituencies, and that strong appeals
to social reform could effectively counter the patriotic drumbeating.[90] The observations of the socialist press and some
labour candidates tend to confirm these findings. The *Labour
Leader*, reviewing the victories of several prominent pro-Boers
and the increased vote for most labour candidates, concluded
that:

[87] For example, see the report of the violence at the public meeting at Mile
End on 12 February 1900 in *Justice*, 17 February 1900. For general assessments
of jingo rowdyism see also *Justice*, 24 February, 10 March, and 21 April 1900,
and *ILP News*, April and June 1900. See also Hardie's comment 'the war is the
most popular war ever waged by England. Mobs of working men nightly invade
and smash up public meetings held in the interests of peace', in *LL*, 31 March
1900. Similarly, in a letter to Kautsky in March 1900, Hardie did not claim that
support for the war was predominantly middle class. He noted that 'the multi-
tude which shouts for the war does so because it is war and for no other reasons';
Hardie to Kautsky, 17 March 1900, 11SG, Kautsky Archive, D XIV 12OA.

[88] *Justice*, 17 March 1900.

[89] 'A Capitalists' War', *LL*, 6 January 1900.

[90] Price, *An Imperial War*, ch. 3.

The general election has gone pretty much as expected, although probably the war party is disappointed at not having swept the boards. So far as one can gather the facts, the war has had comparatively little influence on the final result of the polls ; . . Local affairs and the personnel [sic] of the candidate have told far more than any general feeling of khakiness.[91]

Justice agreed that the overall election results revealed that the Government had by no means 'swept the country'.[92] Again, it is impossible to quantify the specific proportion of working-class voters for whom the war was the decisive issue. However, the reports of the various local labour and socialist campaigns do show that in about half of these campaigns either the candidate or the party workers did acknowledge the importance of the war issue among the electors. Of the fifteen candidatures attempted under the auspices of the LRC, in seven cases jingoism was cited as a contributing factor in the defeat of the candidate.[93] Of the two successful LRC candidates, Hardie and Bell, Hardie gave great prominence to his anti-war position during the campaign in Merthyr;[94] but at Derby, Bell played down the war issue and ignored it completely in his election address.[95] W.C. Steadman, a sitting Lib-Lab MP and a prominent anti-war figure, lost his seat at Stepney in a campaign in which the war issue played a large role according to Steadman himself.[96] The evidence, therefore, does not point only in one direction. The familiar vision of 'khaki-mania' overwhelming the working class is certainly not borne out by the evidence. Yet many of those

---

[91]   *LL*, 13 October 1900.

[92]   *Justice*, 20 October 1900.

[93]   See the comments of the candidate or the election agents in the following contests: F. Brocklehurst, South-west Manchester (*LL*, 20 October 1900); A.E. Fletcher, Camlachie (editorial, *LL*, 13 October 1900); J.R. MacDonald, Leicester (*LL*, 20 October 1900); James Parker, Halifax (*LL*, 17 November 1900); A. Clarke, Rochdale (*LL*, 27 October 1900); W. Thorne, Westham (*Justice*, 6 October 1900 and *LL*, 10 November 1900); J. Johnston, Ashton-under-Lyne (*LL*, 3 November 1900).

[94]   See the opinions of a campaign worker: 'Keir fought his fight primarily upon the war. He elected to stand or fall by his condemnation of the war', *LL*, 20 October 1900.

[95]   Price, *An Imperial War*, p. 119.

[96]   Steadman asserted that 'The contest in Stepney was, from start to finish fought on khaki lines. I was in speech and poster denounced as a pro-Boer', *LL*, 3 November 1900. See also Marxian's comments, *LL*, 13 October 1900.

who fought for the LRC in the election campaign still believed that the war had significant support amongst working-class voters, or at least that the workers were sensitive to criticisms of the war. In spite of the assurances of Hardie, Bell, and Burns that their victories indicated a strengthening of anti-war feeling amongst working people,[97] it is unlikely that the leaders of the labour movement in general were convinced of this. They may have been ready to revise their ideas concerning the real dimensions of violent jingoism among the people. Nevertheless, it seems very likely that most trade unionists continued to perceive some pressure from below against the trade unions taking an active part in the anti-war campaign. It was not to be their task.

4. *The Socialists' Campaign against the War*

For this reason the contribution of the labour movement to the anti-war campaign was chiefly limited to the eager participation of the socialists of the ILP and the SDF. As was noted previously, the leaders of the ILP preferred not to saddle the fledgling LRC with the task of waging an anti-war campaign in the name of the labour movement. The SDF, which was from the outset a reluctant participant in the LRC, understandably did not wish to use the new union-dominated body as the platform for its anti-war campaign. Therefore, both the SDF and the ILP organized their own propaganda and public meetings, and in addition both sought to contribute to the anti-war campaign mounted rather haphazardly by the three anti-war committees: the Transvaal Committee, and the two new committees established in the early months of the war, the South African Conciliation Committee, and the Stop-the-War Committee. Co-operation was the rule, and neither the ILP nor the SDF attempted to capture the leadership of the anti-war movement which was quite naturally in the hands of the traditional radical critics of expansionist foreign

---

[97] See, for example, Burn's speech, *Hansard*, 7 December 1900, IV: 88: 282. Bell claimed that 'the war fever seems to have died out entirely', *LL*, 27 October 1900. Hardie always maintained that his victory at Merthyr resulted from his confident espousal of an anti-war point of view; see *LL*, 13 October 1900 and recollections of the contest in *LL*, 28 February 1903.

policy, ably supported by a small band of religiously motivated pacifists.

The ILP's effort to collaborate with these Radicals and pacifists began in the first weeks of the war. The ILP Administrative Council's initial response to the outbreak of war was to authorize Hardie to visit the Manchester-based Transvaal Committee to see if the ILP could contribute to 'a national agitation'. Similarly, MacDonald was sent to the London division of the Transvaal Committee to obtain a grant to aid the publication of a manifesto.[98] At this stage the *Labour Leader* lavished praise upon any MP who attacked the war, even on the Unionist, Sir Edward Clarke.[99] The ILP leaders also welcomed the creation of the two new anti-war committees in the early months of the conflict. Hardie eventually served on the executive of the South African Conciliation Committee and wrote a pamphlet that was published by the committee.[100] He and MacDonald also joined the more belligerent Stop-the-War Committee,[101] which was founded by the Revd Silas Hocking in January 1900 and was soon chiefly identified with its most prominent activist, the new-style journalist with a reputation for sensation and self-advertisement, W.T. Stead.

However, the ILP's first effort in collaboration with the bourgeois peace enthusiasts, an attempt to mount a joint 'peace candidate' in the York by-election in January 1900, ended in an embarrassing failure. This incident is worth relating also because it shows the belief of some ILP leaders that the people would not tolerate any anti-war agitation at a time of serious military reverses in South Africa. Throughout December 1899, the ILP leaders toyed with the idea of putting forward a peace candidate of their own. Reports from ILP supporters in York were not very encouraging, and some members of the ILP Administrative Council were very pessimistic about the chances of an anti-war candidate.[102]

---

[98]   ILP NAC *mins.*, 21 October 1899.
[99]   *LL*, 28 October 1899.
[100]   J.S. Galbraith, 'The Pamphlet Campaign on the Boer War', *Journal of Modern History*, XXIV (June, 1952), p. 120.
[101]   F.T. Whyte, *The Life of W.T. Stead* (London, 1925), II, 172.
[102]   See, for example, Fred Morley (secretary of the York ILP branch) to John

Glasier warned Hardie that ILP sponsorship of a peace candidate would be disastrous:

We would be overwhelmingly defeated at the polls: we might even emerge from the contest with as high a percentage of personal casualties as Buller at Tugela!—No attention whatever would be paid to the labour or socialist object of our campaign. There would be a universal outcry that we were playing the part of traitors and adding to the task of our poor soldiers abroad . . . Above all we would not be allowed the credit of even acting from sincere conviction or humanitarian principle as John Bright was, but would be vilified as irresponsible humbugs seeking notoriety.[103]

Glasier's reference to the long-standing anti-war tradition of John Bright is most revealing here. Clearly the ILP socialists regarded Radical leadership of an anti-war movement as its best chance of retaining public respect and credibility, for the Radicals could draw on the traditions of Cobden and Bright to shield themselves from the jibes of 'disloyalty'. To have seized leadership for themselves or the new LRC would have inevitably created the impression that anti-war opinions were the property of little-known fringe groups. No doubt the coming LRC foundation conference was in Glasier's mind when he warned Hardie that the proposed peace candidature 'would jeopardise seriously all our other forthcoming parliamentary ventures, and rouse I fear the trade unionists against us'.[104]

In the light of these warnings, the ILP Administrative Council compromised. It decided on 8 January 1900 that 'if the Liberal candidate should be weak in his criticisms of the

Penny, 19 December 1899, ILP Archives 1899/146: 'There is not a very strong feeling in favour of running a candidate at all.' For similar statements see F. Littlewood to Penny (Telegram), ILP Archives, 1899/148; Smart to Penny (Telegram) 1899/150; J. Rowntree to A. Priestman, 20 December 1899, 1899/151; J. Penny to J. Keir Hardie, 23 December 1899, 1899/155; Robert Williams to Penny, 3 January 1900, 1900/5. The only confident supporter of the York candidature was W.T. Stead who gave Hardie the hardly inspiring advice that 'the number of votes that the candidate polls is a matter of absolute insignificance . . . A party that is credited with nothing has everything to gain if it polls only one vote', Stead to Hardie, 6 January 1900, ILP Archives, 1900/14.

[103] Glasier to Hardie, 19 December 1899, Glasier Papers, I, 1, 1899/61.
[104] Ibid.

war' the ILP should try for a 'joint Peace candidate'.[105] On 13 January Hardie attended a conference at York where it was decided to form a 'York By-election Peace Committee', and on the following day he addressed a large anti-war public meeting at the Corn Exchange in York.[106] Soon after, the local Liberal Association chose its candidate, Alexander Murray, the Master of Elibank. The By-election Peace Committee duly interviewed Murray and, finding his views on the war equivocal, requested the London Stop-the-War Committee to supply a peace candidate to stand against both the Conservative and Liberal candidates. However, when the Stop-the-War Committee's representative, Harold Rylett, arrived in York he advised the York committee not to mount a third candidate because, no matter how equivocal Murray's views, 'outside of York' he was seen as the peace candidate and he had a greater chance of achieving a respectable protest vote.[107] After protesting against Rylett's advice, the York Peace Committee eventually agreed to abstain from the contest.[108] In the wake of this disappointment, the anti-war campaign in York faltered;[109] and even the Transvaal Committee took no further interest in the contest.[110] The pessimists had prevailed. In the event, the Conservative candidate was returned with a greatly increased majority.

This was not a very promising start to the ILP's broad-front tactics, but the party persisted on this course none the

---

[105] ILP NAC *mins.*, 8 January 1900.

[106] See Fred. Morley to Hardie, 8 January 1900; S.G. Hobson to Hardie, 10 January 1900; J.F. Green to Hardie, 10 January 1900; W.T. Stead to Hardie, 10 January 1900; Fred. Morley to Hardie, 11 January 1900; Hardie to Stead, 11 January 1900; L.T. Hobhouse to Hardie, 16 January 1900 all in ILP Archives, 1900, numbers 16, 23, 24, 27, 32, and 38. These letters all show that it was Hardie who was chiefly responsible for calling anti-war activists to the conference at York.

[107] See F. Morley to Hardie, 25 January 1900, ILP Archives, 1900/49; and *LL*, 3 February 1900.

[108] *LL*, 10 February 1900.

[109] See the report of a peace meeting that ended in a farce when a local trade unionist spoke in favour of the war, in F. Morley to Hardie, 29 January 1900, ILP Archives, 1900/53. See also the report that the Quakers of York were changing their allegiance to Murray, in A. Priestman to Hardie, 29 January 1900, ILP Archives, 1900/54.

[110] E.W. Nicholson (Transvaal Committee) to Hardie, 30 January 1900, ILP Archives, 1900/157.

less. The *Labour Leader* attacked the Liberal Imperialists un-
mercifully; and it applauded every small flicker of protest
from amongst the Radical minority within the Liberal Party,
singling out John Morley and Leonard Courtney for special
praise.[111] Hardie collaborated quite willingly with the anti-
war Liberals. For instance, he joined Lloyd George and
H.J. Wilson on the platform at a rowdy anti-war meeting in
Glasgow on 6 March 1900;[112] and on one occasion the *Labour
Leader*'s editorial column was granted to J.A. Hobson.[113]
Hardie co-operated with S.C. Cronwright-Schreiner and J.X.
Merriman, the two South African anti-war activists, during
their lecture tours in Britain in 1900 and 1901.[114] Funds
from the Quaker George Cadbury to support the ILP's anti-
war campaign were accepted,[115] and Hardie developed close
and friendly relations with W.T. Stead on the Stop-the-War
Committee.[116]

The high-point of this policy of collaboration came in late
May 1900 when the ILP Administrative Council announced
that the time had come to hold a national convention to press
for peace in South Africa.[117] The timing of this announcement, soon after the relief of Mafeking, probably reflected
the belief of the ILP leaders that the prospects of a successful
anti-war campaign were probably much better now that the
British forces seemed under less strain in South Africa. The
ILP made it clear that invitations for the national convention
it envisaged should be sent 'to all political bodies likely to be
sympathetic with the object of the same, to trades councils
and to trade union and socialist organisations'. In a move
which demonstrated the ILP's belief in a broad-front approach, the Administrative Council decided not to issue the
invitations itself. Instead it recommended to the three anti-

[111] *LL*, 3 February 1900.
[112] *LL*, 10 March 1900.
[113] *LL*, 2 June 1900.
[114] S.C. Cronwright-Schreiner to Hardie, 20 February 1900, ILP Archives,
1900/66A; Hardie to D. Lowe, 18 February 1901, ILP Archives, 1901/3.
[115] George Cadbury to Hardie, 14 and 19 February, and 12 March 1900,
in ILP Archives, 1900/65/66 and 75.
[116] 'There is no man in England for whom I entertain a greater respect than
I do for Mr Stead', wrote Hardie; *LL*, 3 January 1903.
[117] ILP NAC *mins.*, 28 May 1900.

war committees, the Transvaal, Conciliation, and Stop-the-War Committees, that they should take the initiative in summoning the national convention. This act of deference again points to the ILP's conviction that the middle-class peace agitators were in the best position to mobilize dissent within the Liberal camp, thereby forcing the Liberal Party to take a definite stand against the war. However, the hopes of the ILP were soon dashed. Several committee meetings were held with a view to summoning a national convention but no agreement could be reached.[118] Bitterly disappointed, Hardie blamed the Liberal Party officials who 'shirked taking any part in the convening of the convention, well knowing that Liberalism would not be adequately represented'. Even so, Hardie did not lose faith entirely in the 'popular front' tactic. He confessed that

Personally, I refuse to believe that the rank and file of Liberalism is so hopelessly given over to Jingoism as this implies. We all know that the official element is hopeless and only concerned with keeping the party together, but outside officialdom thousands of earnest men and women are opposed to the war and to annexation.[119]

Thus, Hardie continued to urge the leading Radicals to break with the official Liberal Party and lead the anti-war forces. In June 1900 he addressed an open letter to John Morley urging him to take up the leadership of the democratic and anti-war movement.[120] Hardie was now deeply sceptical about the capacity of 'official' Liberalism to respond to the war crisis effectively. When H.W. Massingham, a prominent anti-war publisher, took up the call for a national conference against the war in July 1900, Hardie warned him the idea would fail because most Liberal Party bosses were fearful of being submerged by the socialists at any such conference.[121] In the immediate aftermath of the general election in October 1900, Hardie was even more pessimistic. Speaking at a public meeting in Manchester, he warned that the future of the Liberal Party appeared to lie in the hands of the most strongly committed imperialist group led by Rosebery, Grey, and

---

[118]   *LL*, 16 June 1900.
[119]   Ibid.
[120]   Ibid.
[121]   *LL*, 21 July 1900.

Asquith.[122] Overall, 1900 was a disappointing year for those in the ILP who believed in the viability of the 'popular front' against war.

The SDF, on the other hand, showed less tolerance of Liberal Party timidity. From the very beginning of the war *Justice* asked, 'Where are the Radicals?' and complained that the 'Rosebery–Asquith gang' dominated the party.[123] Rothstein lamented that there was not a single Zola amongst all British radicals.[124] Whereas Hardie and his ILP colleagues tended to scold the Liberals for having abandoned their true anti-imperialist Gladstonian heritage, the SDF argued that the Liberal Party's failure to stand against this latest war followed inevitably from that party's capitalist outlook, and from the Liberals' honest realization that capitalism and imperialism were inextricably linked. In August 1900 *Justice* concluded that 'there can be no anti-imperialist party on the basis of Liberalism'.[125]

In spite of the disappointments of 1900, the ILP began the new year with a reaffirmation of its faith in a broad anti-war front. At its first meeting of 1901 the ILP Administrative Council announced the establishment of a special £1,000 campaign fund to help bring into Parliament reformers who would be pledged 'to fearlessly combat the dangerous military spirit'.[126] The administrative council even agreed that this special anti-militarist propaganda fund 'shall not be used for election purposes or in connection with the ordinary work of the ILP'. Another sign of Hardie's revived commitment to the broad-front tactic came at the ILP Conference in April when he moved a resolution requesting the ILP Administrative Council to call once again a conference

---

[122] *LL*, 3 November 1900. None the less, Hardie continued to associate with the anti-war Liberals. In December 1900 he attended a meeting of the League of Liberals against Aggression and Militarism; see Koss, *Pro-Boers*, p. 177.

[123] *Justice*, 16 December 1899 and 27 January 1900.

[124] *Justice*, 31 March 1900; a reference to Emile Zola's leading role in the defence of Alfred Dreyfus.

[125] *Justice*, 25 August 1900. Local SDF groups still co-operated with the broad campaign. See, for example, the report of an SDF meeting at Battersea Town Hall with Dr G.B. Clark MP and Cronwright-Schreiner; *Justice*, 12 May 1900.

[126] ILP NAC *mins.*, 30–1 January 1901.

'of all men and women known to be opposed to this unjust war in order that a national agitation may be inaugurated'.[127] The Administrative Council agreed to investigate what support existed for such a conference; but again, no progress was made.[128] By July, Fred Jowett and John Penny were advising against the calling of an anti-war conference, and eventually their views prevailed.[129] In September the ILP Administrative Council resolved that 'seeing the difficulty of organising representative conferences against the war', no further attempts should be made.[130] Hardie, however, apparently still held some hope that the Liberal Party might adopt a more determined anti-war position, particularly after Campbell-Bannerman's condemnation of the 'methods of barbarism' being used in South Africa in June 1901.[131] Thus, in the North-east Lanark by-election campaign in September Hardie attempted to make the candidature of Robert Smillie, the Scottish miners' leader and one of his own close friends, the rallying point for an anti-war coalition.[132] Following Smillie's defeat, an unrepentant Hardie began a series of discussions in the *Labour Leader* on the merits of the ILP making an alliance with the Irish and Radical MPs in order to fuse the democratic and anti-war forces.[133] This suggested abandonment of the ILP's traditional independence, hitherto always depicted as sacrosant by Hardie himself, provoked little support in the columns of the *Leader*. Outside the ILP Hardie's suggestion aroused a good deal of suspicion. Blatchford wrote angrily to Glasier:

[127]   *ILP News* April 1901; note that the ILP itself was to undertake the task of calling this national conference. Hardie was still sincerely seeking a 'broad front'; see Hardie to Lowe, 3 April 1901, ILP Archives 1901/11 where Hardie explains his reluctance to present a parliamentary report critical of Burns and Pickard at the ILP Conference.

[128]   ILP NAC *mins.*, 9—10 April 1901.

[129]   Jowett to Hardie, 9 and 23 July 1901, ILP Archives, 1901/30—1. Jowett refers to Penny's opposition.

[130]   ILP NAC *mins.*, 16—17 September 1901.

[131]   'Liberal Leaders and the War', *LL*, 27 June 1901.

[132]   At a public meeting in Glasgow City Hall in September 1901, resolutions supporting Smillie's candidature and denouncing the war were passed, *LL*, 21 September 1901. See also Hardie's comments in 'Between Ourselves', *LL*, 2 September 1901.

[133]   See the discussions under the title 'Wanted: A Stalwart Party in Parliament', in *LL*, 19 October—30 November 1901.

I do not trust Radicals, nor Liberals as such. If they are with us let them come to us . . . To me it seems that Hardie always does the wrong thing. Now he is ready to break the socialist line to form an anti-war party. The war is a detail. Someday it will be over. We are for socialism. I do not trust Hardie. He does not steer straight.[134]

Most of the correspondence in the *Labour Leader* during October and November 1901 seemed to agree with Blatchford's sentiments. Finally, Hardie appeared to have been persuaded by this weight of opinion and he returned to his traditional view and declared himself opposed to any alliance with non-socialists.[135] That could not disguise the fact that throughout 1901 his own personal participation in the anti-war campaign had been in close collaboration with the anti-war Liberals and the middle-class peace agitators.

On further noteworthy feature of the socialists' peace agitation remains to be considered, namely, the leading themes developed by the socialists in their campaign. First, the war tended to strengthen and clarify the socialists' intensely critical attitude toward modern imperialism. The ILP's total opposition to imperialism had never been more clearly formulated than in the four resolutions that were passed at the ILP Conference in Glasgow in April 1900.[136] In the most important of these the ILP accepted a defiantly materialist interpretation of imperialism:

On its economic and industrial side, imperialism is either the product of an attempt of the financier and speculator to exploit the natural wealth of foreign territories, or an idea of the British manufacturer that he needs military intervention in the capture of foreign markets for trade, and is, therefore an excuse for his want of business enterprise. Imperialism, therefore, tends to extend the reign of capitalism, not only by increasing the power of wealth but by neglecting the needs of the home market and leaving the natural resources of our own country undeveloped.[137]

The idea that the war was 'a capitalists' war', suggesting a cunning plot by a group of influential entrepreneurs, was, of

---

[134] R. Blatchford to Glasier, 19 October 1901, Glasier Papers, I, 1, 1901/2/ See Glasier's reply, insisting that war is part and parcel of capitalism; Glasier to Blatchford, 19 October 1901, Glasier Papers, I, 1, 1901/3.
[135] *LL*, 30 November 1901.
[136] *ILP Annual Conference 1900*, pp. 27–8.
[137] Ibid.

course, quite common among critics of the war. However, the ILP's policy and Hardie's writings in particular broadened this critique to emphasize the close connections between capitalism, imperialism, and war. The Boer conflict was not just a case of a capitalist clique influencing a particular government, but rather the war revealed the drive toward imperialism implicit within the workings of modern capitalism.[138] These ideas reveal the growing influence of the writings of Belfort Bax, whose theories of imperialism dominated the pages of *Justice*, and also of the work of J.A. Hobson, whose study *The War in South Africa* was applauded by Hardie on its publication early in 1900.[139]

It is important to add that, in the case of the ILP, this did not involve any lessening of the strongly moralistic tone of the party's anti-war propaganda. In his tirades against the South African conflict, Hardie often stressed his personal revulsion, as a Christian, against war; and he dwelt upon the 'debasing' spectacles of war, 'the grief-stricken homes, the mangled remains, the terrible loss of life'.[140] In the pursuit of this same theme the *Labour Leader* often reproduced blood-chilling descriptions of the horrors of the battlefield in South Africa.[141] Thus, while the ILP and the SDF shared a common analysis of imperialist wars as the product of the capitalist economic system, the tone of the ILP's propaganda was still distinctive in that Christian and pacifist arguments against war were combined with a socialist analysis. This tendency within the ILP made it somewhat easier for the ILP leaders to co-operate with the mixture of discontented Liberals, Radicals, Quakers and other non-conformist Christians who made up the middle-class peace committees.

It is also important to note the extent to which both the ILP and the SDF adopted an extreme 'pro-Boer' position in their propaganda. Of course, all opponents of the war were accused of being 'pro-Boer', but the socialists were distinctive in their apparent eagerness to embrace the epithet. Both

[138]   For example, see 'The War in South Africa', *LL*, 3 March and 21 April 1900. 'The war represents imperialism, which must always be founded on conquest and subjection', *LL*, 12 May 1900.
[140]   *LL*, 21 April 1900.
[141]   For example, see a letter in *LL*, 2 December 1899.

Justice and the *Labour Leader* used the term quite openly
to describe the anti-war position, and indeed it was not an
inaccurate description of their attitude to the conflict. Hardie,
for one, tended to magnify the merits of the Boers, to stress
their courage in action and, in so doing, he appeared to be-
little the efforts of the British forces. No doubt attempting
to balance the vilification of the Boers in the British press,
Hardie presented to his readers most sympathetic accounts
of the history of the South African Dutchmen, praising their
rural life style and 'their methods of production for use',
and even claiming that their relations with the tribal peoples
were 'uniformly good'.[142] Throughout the first six months
of the war, a period in which the British forces suffered
serious reverses, the *Labour Leader* seemed to take heart
from the Boer victories. 'We are being punished for our
wrong-doing',[143] explained the *Leader* in February 1900.
When the tide began to turn in Britain's favour the *Leader*
warned that a British triumph would be 'a calamity to us as
a nation'.[144] *Justice* was more careful in this period to remain
neutral in its comments upon the course of the military contest itself.[145] However, the constant assertions in *Justice*
that reports of British victories were exaggerated and the
specific criticism of the British forces' treatment of Boer
prisoners did convey an impression that *Justice*, too, was
siding with the enemy.[146] The unashamedly 'pro-Boer'
attitudes of the socialists, and of the ILP in particular, did
little to endear the anti-war cause to the labour movement as
a whole. The stigma of disloyalty was easily borne by cru-
sading socialists, who often relished their role as persecuted
and outnumbered guardians of justice; but the mass of the
people and most trade unionists still shunned any appearance
of disloyalty.

[142] *LL*, 21 April 1900.
[143] 'Spion Kop', *LL*, 3 February 1900. See also 'At a Standstill', *LL*, 17
February 1900, and 'General Joubert', *LL*, 7 April 1900.
[144] 'The War', *LL*, 14 April 1900.
[145] See, for example, Tattler's comments, *Justice*, 6, 13, and 20 January and
10 March 1900, and 'British Generals and their British Masters', *Justice*, 2 April
1900.
[146] See, for example, 'A Base, Bloody and Brutal Crime', *Justice*, 24 March
1900, and 'A Nation of Brigands', *Justice*, 14 April 1900. See also editorial
Justice, 13 July 1901 embracing the term 'pro-Boer'.

5. *Strain amongst the Socialists*

From the outbreak of the war in South Africa, the socialists of the ILP and the SDF were very much gratified to find that, with few exceptions, the socialist movement in Britain was standing firm against the war fever. Apart from some friction over the SDF's insistence that the Boers' early successes had shown the value of the citizen army concept,[147] the ILP and the SDF were remarkably united in their approach to the war. In April 1901 *Justice* even conceded that the ILP's attitude on the war had been 'irreproachable'.[148] While the two most important socialist groups in Britain congratulated each other on their steadfast resistance to war, there were, none the less, some disturbing signs of equivocation on the fringes of the main socialist forces.

The attitude of the Fabian Society to the war, and especially the decision in March 1900 to make no official declaration on the war in view of the sharp divisions within the society, bitterly disappointed the socialists of the ILP and the SDF.[149] MacDonald, Barnes, Curran, and a number of other ILP members resigned from the society in March 1900 in protest at its failure to condemn the war in South Africa.[150] The defection of Blatchford and the *Clarion* into the patriotic camp was also a blow for the anti-war cause. Yet Blatchford's response to the war was not altogether surprising, considering ex-sergeant-major Blatchford's well-known high regard for the British Army, and considering, too, the emphasis he had always placed on Britain's military vulnerability.[151] Many

[147] On the citizen army see SDF, *Annual Conference, 1900*, pp. 21–2, and *Justice*, 6 January, 10 February, and 17 March 1900. For criticism of the SDF approach to the citizen army, see *LL*, 5 May 1900.

[148] *Justice*, 13 April 1901. See also *Justice*'s endorsement of Hardie's major editorial on the war (*LL*, 6 January 1900) in *Justice*, 13 January 1900.

[149] *Fabian News*, Vol. X, no. 1, March 1900, p. 1. The Fabian Society's response to imperialism and the war has already been fully explored by a number of historians and so the history of the debate need not be repeated here. See A. McBriar, *Fabian Socialism and English Politics, 1884–1918* (Cambridge, 1966), ch. 5; Bernard Semmel, *Imperialism and Social Reform: English Social-Imperialist Thought 1895–1914* (London, 1960); Bernard Porter, *Critics of Empire: British Attitudes to Colonialism in Africa, 1895–1914* (New York, 1968).

[150] See *LL*, 3 March 1900, and *Justice*, 28 April and 6 October 1900, and *ILP News*, July 1900, and McBriar, *Fabian Socialism*, p. 124.

[151] *Merrie England*, ch. 3–4. On the importance of Blatchford's army experience, see Chapter 1.

years later Blatchford recalled that the Socialists who worked with him on the *Clarion* were 'Britons first and socialists next'.[152] Moreover, during the 1890s Blatchford's personal relations with the leaders of the ILP and SDF had become strained, Blatchford finding himself out of sympathy with both the dour marxism of the Hyndmanites and the windy Christian socialist rhetoric of Hardie.[153] Thus, Blatchford was already learning to row his own boat. When the war began he declared that he could no longer criticize the cause of Britain but must give his entire support to the British forces. Both *Justice* and the *Labour Leader* bemoaned his 'fairweather socialism' and his 'socialist jingoism', and both attacked in particular Blatchford's decision to write on the conflict for the conservative *Morning Leader*.[154] In the eyes of the ILP, Blatchford was never to recover his reputation.

Within the ILP and the SDF the policy of opposition to the war and support for the independence of the Boer Republics was largely uncontested. However, from about the middle of 1901 the SDF leadership appeared to have second thoughts about the merits of the anti-war agitation and the SDF executive suspended the party's campaign. Hyndman seemed to object, in particular, to the stress of many socialists on 'pro-Boer' propaganda. He explained that he saw no reason to continue a campaign in favour of independence for the Boer Republics, considering that 'the country belongs to neither Boer nor Briton' but to 'the splendid native tribes'. Hyndman argued that it was time the SDF resumed its general propaganda for socialism.[155] This immediately provoked a bitter row in the federation. Belfort Bax, and also Theodore Rothstein, who had recently clashed with Hyndman over the latter's alleged anti-semitic views, now accused Hyndman of harbouring chauvinistic feelings;[156] and Hyndman replied by pointing out that his critics were victims of a facile craze for

---

[152] Blatchford, *My Eighty Years*, p. 199.
[153] See Blatchford to A.M. Thompson, September 1894 (?) where he complains of the 'slipperiness' of Hardie and the 'blather and humbug' of Hyndman; Blatchford Papers.
[154] *LL*, 2 October and 4 November 1899 and *Justice*, same dates.
[155] *Justice*, 20 July 1901.
[156] *Justice*, 27 July and 3 August 1901.

anti-patriotism.[157] This was not the last time that Hyndman was to be accused of being a secret chauvinist.

A similar quarrel erupted in October 1901 when, at a meeting of the ISB in Brussels, Hyndman insisted that a manifesto against the British concentration camps in South Africa should also make mention of the cruelties inflicted by other European nations and the United States in their colonial wars.[158] Hyndman complained of the 'strong Continental prejudice against England' which existed at the ISB.[159] Again Bax scolded Hyndman over his patriotic sensitivites, but Hyndman rushed to deny Bax's 'grotesque' imputations against his internationalism.[160] These particular incidents were important in that they gave rise to suspicions that perhaps the fire of patriotism did burn secretly within the heart of the leading British marxist; and these suspicions made it doubly difficult for Hyndman in the future to retain credibility when he began to warn his fellow-socialists against the 'German menace'.

Overall, however, the response of British socialists to the South African War had enhanced their reputations in the eyes of Continental socialists. 'You and the socialists of England have done your duty', Liebknecht informed Hardie in January 1900.[161] The British socialists had also sought to publicize their anti-war stand during the International Socialist Congress at Paris in September 1900. Pete Curran, in his capacity as chairman of the British delegation, informed the assembled socialists that the British working-class movement was standing firm against the jingoism of the Government. A resolution denouncing imperialism was passed by the congress and the British delegation voted solidly in its favour.[162] To all appearances, the bulk of British socialists were steadfastly internationalist, although the shrewd observer would have

---

[157] *Justice*, 10 August 1901. For the continuation of the quarrel see Hyndman's letter, *Justice*, 8 February 1902.

[158] 'Circulaire sur les événements du Transvaal, avec les comptes-rendu de deux séances du comite executif', in Haupt (ed.), *Bureau Socialiste International*, pp. 36–9.

[159] *Justice*, 23 November 1901.

[160] *Justice*, 30 November and 7 December 1901.

[161] W. Liebknecht to Hardie, 15 January 1900, ILP Archives, 1900/37.

[162] *Justice*, 29 September and 6 October 1900.

questioned whether the British delegation at Paris, dominated as it was by the SDF, properly represented the British working class.

In summing up, it must be said that those socialists and trade unionists who opposed the South African War in Britain were a part of a campaign which failed in its principal objective. The failure to mobilize mass opposition to the war probably testifies to the difficulties of converting public opinion without having first persuaded the major opposition party, that is the Liberal Party, to embrace the anti-war cause. The division of the Liberals and the refusal of their party to assume the leadership of the campaign meant that anti-war and anti-imperialist opinions were easily deprecated as the confused outpourings of fringe groups, eccentric Liberals, sentimentalists, and extremists. This was no basis upon which to challenge the patriotic and imperialist beliefs so carefully cultivated among the British people at that time.

Finally, it needs to be emphasized that the war was a potential disaster for the socialists of the ILP and the politically motivated unionists who were the architects of the LRC. Poorly handled, the drawn-out conflict could easily have demolished their plan to raise up a third political force in Britain. Their concern can be easily imagined. At the very moment when they were seeking to build up mutual trust between socialist and unionist, the war came along to demonstrate how wide was the gap between their approaches to this all-absorbing national issue. At the very moment when the socialists' ten-year campaign of debunking Liberalism seemed near its climax and the unions were on the point of detaching themselves from the coat-tails of the Liberal Party, the socialists were forced to acknowledge that only the leadership of the Liberal Party could save an anti-war campaign from oblivion. It was a difficult balancing performance for the socialists to continue attacking Liberalism in the hope of building up the LRC on the one hand, and yet seek collaboration with the anti-war Liberals on the other. It is hardly surprising then that leaders like Hardie seemed to fall on either side of the political high-wire at different times. Socialist supporters of the LRC were only saved from the appearance of hopeless inconsistency in the

eyes of their union colleagues by a careful compartmentalization of their political lives for the duration of the war.
The anti-war campaign was pursued quite separately from the
business of the 'labour alliance'. The unions could assist in
the peace movement if they wished, but there was no pressure
on them to do so. This policy probably saved the LRC from
a fatal split. But the achievement carried with it a significant
cost. For it was exactly this kind of compartmentalization
which, in the traditional outlook of the trade unions, tended
to prevent anything but a nodding interest in international
issues. Therefore, the cost of sustaining the LRC through the
episode of war was a most unfortunate reinforcement of the
trade unionists' view that foreign affairs and defence matters
were no concern of theirs. Paradoxically, then, while the
Labour Party was born in the midst of an imperialist war, no
instinctive hatred of war was fixed in its heart on account of
that.

6

The Scent of Danger: Military Build-up and New Alliances, 1902–1907

Is there no question for us to take up? What about militarism? Is there any danger of that becoming a burning question?

T.D. Benson to J. Keir Hardie, 12 March 1906 (ILP Archives 1906/135)

1. *War in the Far East and the Entente with France, 1904*

In spite of the restoration of peace in South Africa in May 1902, British socialists and labour leaders had little reason to relax their vigilance on the issue of imperialism. Several minor military conflicts at the outposts of the Empire kept the issue alive. In 1903 and 1904 British expeditions in Tibet and Somaliland were engaged in military actions against the local peoples.[1] Then in February 1904 came a far more serious sign of the potential danger to peace posed by the policies of competitive imperialism. Japan and Russia drifted into war to settle their long-standing contest for the control of Manchuria and Korea. The alliance between Britain and Japan, concluded without public fuss in 1902, now assumed ominous significance. The socialist press attacked the alliance as an example of the dangers to which the nation was exposed by the process of secret diplomacy. Through a wholly undemocratic and secretly concluded diplomatic arrangement, the British people were now exposed to the risk of entanglement in war at the whim of the imperialist ambitions of a foreign power.[2] The socialist press also denounced the war itself as an

---

[1] For the response of the Lib-Lab MPs Burns and Broadhurst see *Hansard*, IV: 130: 1033–5 and 1042, and 142: 763–8, and Tsiang, *Labour and Empire*, p. 39. Compare with the bitter criticism of the ILP and SDF in *LL*, 9 and 14 April 1904, *Justice* 21 May 1904, and the ILP Conference reported in *LL*, 9 April 1904.

[2] The socialists had first warned of this when the treaty was concluded in 1902; see Marxian's comments, *LL*, 22 February 1902 and Hyndman's speech at a public meeting, *Justice,* 8 March 1902.

imperialists' war foisted on the people. The *Labour Leader* asked:

And what is it all about? Why should hundreds of thousands of men be let loose upon each other to tear each other like beasts of the field . . . ?

The reason is as usual with all reasons for war, the crime of a few men in power. What does the poor miserable peasant on the Russian soil know about the evacuation of Manchuria, or the control of Korea? What quarrel has the underpaid Russian workmen with the exploited Japanese wage earner?[3]

The *Labour Leader*, of course, always reflected the undercurrent of pacifist sentiment within the ILP; above all, war was morally repellent, 'a barbarous and utterly irrational method of settling international disputes'.[4] Bad as the war in the Far East was, the ILP was not without hope that good might come of it. In company with all European socialists, the ILP looked forward to a Russian defeat and the blossoming of a revolution at home. Thus at the end of the war the *Leader* rejoiced in the Japanese victory, and, in addition, expressed the hope that it would inspire Asia as a whole to turn back the tide of European imperialism.[5]

The SDF's response to the war was very similar, and yet there was one important difference in tone. *Justice* denounced the conflict as an imperialist war, but there was not that same sense of moral revulsion against the horror and inhumanity of war. Indeed, Hyndman insisted that the war was beneficial to the socialists' cause, and he took the opportunity to stress that socialists were not advocates of peace at any price. Like the *Leader*, *Justice* eagerly anticipated a Japanese victory that would undermine the tsarist autocracy and awaken the whole of Asia.[6] But *Justice*'s enthusiasm for these consequences of the war seemed to blot out any sense of moral detestation of war itself. Within weeks of the war's opening Hyndman was warning the SDF against 'overdoing the peace cry'.[7] He appeared to excuse entirely the Japanese resort to war when he wrote:

---

[3] *LL*, 9 January 1904.
[4] *LL*, 13 February 1904.
[5] *LL*, 20 February 1904, and 2 June and 1 September 1905.
[6] *Justice*, 13 February 1904.
[7] 'Overdoing the Peace Cry', *Justice*, 20 February 1904, and 'Social-Democracy for Peace even at the Price of War', *Justice*, 5 March 1904.

Would it benefit mankind or Japan herself that Japan should be brought under the domination of Russia? Certainly not. Then Japan is quite right to make war before Russia can use peace to her detriment ... The horrors of peace are often worse than the horrors of war.[8]

Following in Marx's footsteps, Hyndman was judging war solely from the standpoint of the political advancement of socialism. And, in making this stand Hyndman was already constructing the theoretical basis upon which he would later justify his advocacy of a powerful British navy capable of defending the politically advanced nations from reactionary Germany.

Indeed, it is in Hyndman's writings on the Russo-Japanese war that the 'German menace' theme first emerges. With Russia debilitated, Hyndman began to perceive a new threat to Western Europe from the Kaiser's regiments. In November 1904 Hyndman warned that Britain and France must face the fact that Japan's blows against Russia, France's ally, had seriously weakened French security. 'An attack by Germany on France is quite conceivable', Hyndman warned. Germany's immense power and her deferential people could easily be militarized by a 'ramping self-idolator like the Kaiser'. Hyndman then concluded:

The possibilities of dangerous trouble exist, and I for one would like to see a defensive agreement between England, France and Italy, running athwart the triple alliance, expressly in order to keep the European peace.[9]

At an early date, therefore, Hyndman had shown that he was not opposed to war from the proto-pacifist position of the idealist socialists. There were signs too of his special concern with the threat posed to Europe by Prussian militarism.

The Russo-Japanese War and the general problems of militarism and imperialism were naturally the topics of the hour when the International Socialist Congress met in Amsterdam in August 1904. From the outset it was clear that the International wished to use the occasion as an opportunity to project the ideal of working-class solidarity

---

[8] *Justice*, 20 February 1904. For similar statements see *Justice*, 5 March 1904 and 'Japan and Russia', *Justice*, 29 October 1904.

[9] 'France and Foreign Policy', *Justice*, 12 November 1904.

in defiance of the war raging in the Far East. In the ISB the Russian delegate Plekhanov and the Japanese delegate Katayama were seated together to the applause of the Bureau members.[10] Similarly, when the full congress began, Plekhanov and Katayama were given places on the platform on either side of the Dutch presiding chairman van Kol. When they rose and shook hands warmly the symbol was not lost on the assembled delegates. In the words of one ILP delegate:

The effect was electric. The whole conference rose to its feet as it recognised the fact that socialism unites the workers in all lands and that the Socialist party is the only real and genuine party of peace.[11]

It was a dramatic and inspiring gesture. However, it was soon clear that the International could suggest no more specific means for the struggle against war than such demonstrations. The formal resolution on the Russo-Japanese War gave no precise guidance in this matter, declaring simply that social- ists must oppose 'by all means' any extension of the conflict.

The congress debate on the general strike also gave no en- couragement to those who still favoured the use of this weapon against war. The French motion supporting the general strike as a practical and legitimate means of achieving socialist goals was decisively rejected in favour of the more cautious Roland—Holst resolution. Under its terms the use of the general strike was confined to the most exceptional circumstances.[12] The viability of an international anti-war strike seemed as far away as ever. Officially, the socialists' chief weapon against war remained incessant propaganda.

Just two months after the Amsterdam Congress came a spectacular international incident which made the prospect of Britain being drawn into the Russo-Japanese struggle suddenly very real. On the night of 21 October, the Russian Baltic fleet, en route to the war in the Far East, fired on British fishing trawlers on the Dogger Bank. The British press

---

[10] 'Compte-rendu de la cinquième réunion du BSI, le 15 août 1904', in Haupt (ed.), *Bureau Socialiste International*, vol. 1, pp. 107—10.

[11] *LL*, 19 August 1904.

[12] For the debate on the Roland—Holst motion on the general strike see *Sixième Congrès Socialist International, Amsterdam 1904, Compte-Rendu Analytique (Bruxelles, 1904)*, pp. 44—5.

reacted vociferously, and it was believed that the nation stood on the brink of war. The most significant feature of the labour movement's response to this crisis was the virtual silence of the trade unions and the LRC. Neither of the two senior bodies of the labour movement, the TUC Parliamentary Committee and the LRC executive, offered any statement on the 'North Sea Outrage'. Similarly, the trades councils and the trade unions in general do not seem to have discussed the crisis. The trade union leaders evidently saw no reason to disturb the movement from its usual domestic concerns. For example, on Sunday 30 October a trade union demonstration was held as scheduled in Trafalgar Square; and Tillett, Steadman, and Bondfield addressed the crowd on the current cigar-makers' strike.[13] In any case the relative speed of the settlement of the crisis circumvented any widespread trade union response.

The socialist press, on the other hand, presented the crisis as a matter of major importance to the working class. The *Labour Leader*'s first reaction was to plead that the dispute be submitted to arbitration. The panic-mongering of the British press, 'the shrieking Jingo brotherhood', was the most disturbing element in the crisis according to the ILP organ.[14] The *Leader* also pointed out that the crisis was assisting the political fortunes of the Balfour Government. The Conservatives were said to be 'rubbing their hands in delight because Mr Balfour had a foreign crisis to talk about'.[15] The crisis therefore renewed the lessons the socialists had learned during the Boer War about the power of the modern press and the domestic political uses of a 'war fever'. In fact the ILP leaders seem to have been taken by surprise by the very welcome announcement on 28 October that the dispute was indeed to be submitted to the Hague International Commission. The ILP Administrative Council reacted enthusiastically to this news and promptly dispatched an effusive telegram of congratulations to Balfour which praised both the British and Russian Governments.[16]

---

[13] *LL*, 4 November 1904.
[14] *LL*, 2 October 1904.
[15] *LL*, 11 November 1904.
[16] Francis Johnson to A. Balfour, 17 November 1904, ILP Archive, 1904/51.

In contrast, the response of the SDF to the North Sea crisis seemed positively belligerent. In the pages of *Justice* the remorseless hatred of the tsarist regime seemed to overwhelm any sense of satisfaction that war had been avoided. When the settlement was announced, *Justice* criticized it as a 'cowardly climb-down' and proclaimed the SDF's deep regret at the 'lack of firmness in British statesmen.'[17] This response again testified to the strength of that impulse within British marxism to distinguish its own 'tough-minded' style from the sentimentalism of its opponents. Thus the SDF leaders shunned 'morality-mongering' on the subject of war, and they appeared to undermine the idea of international arbitration with their insistence that war was inevitable under capitalism.

In spite of the Russo-Japanese War and the Dogger Bank incident, the year 1904 was not entirely without inspiration for those interested in securing peace between nations. In April 1904, after lengthy negotiations, the Entente Cordiale between France and Britain was at last announced. Initially, the socialists of both nations hailed the Entente as marking the final dissipation of the ill-feeling between the two nations which had been so evident at the time of the Fashoda crisis and during the Boer War. The French socialists took credit for having encouraged all attempts to reach an understanding with Britain, and they rejoiced that France's reliance on the shameful Russian alliance was now diminished.[18] Very few commentators perceived any implicit threat against Germany in the new-found friendship between Britain and France. In fact Jaurès had specifically denied this in a speech at an Anglo-French parliamentary dinner in November 1903 (by which time a diplomatic agreement was confidently expected). He had declared:

This friendship is not exclusive, nor is it offensive. There is nothing secret about it. It not only does not threaten anyone, but it can annoy no one. The trust that exists between us involves no distrust towards others.[19]

[17] *Justice*, 5 November 1904.
[18] Brynjolf J. Hovde, 'French Socialism and the Triple Entente', *Journal of Political Economy*, XXXIV, no. 4, 1926, pp. 473–4; see also interview with Francis de Pressense in *LL*, 10 March 1905.
[19] Jean Jaurès, *Studies in Socialism* (London, 1906), p. 160.

Similarly, the British socialist press welcomed the Entente.[20]

It was not until the Dogger Bank incident that the Entente came to be seen in a more critical light. In the aftermath of the incident, it was realized that France's special relationships with both Britain and Russia had been an important factor in the preservation of peace between the two powers. The British socialist press began to proclaim its suspicions that, through the Entente with France, Britain was being drawn into a new 'Triple Entente' with an anti-German motivation. In Paris this same concern was apparent. In November 1904 Jaurès pressed upon the French Government the need to proclaim that the Entente with Britain implied 'no hidden seed of hostility' toward any other nation.[21] But when a number of French politicians, including Jaurès, went one step further and suggested that France should use her good offices to bring about a new understanding between Russia and Britain, the British socialist press vehemently opposed the idea. The *Labour Leader* rejected the idea out of hand, proclaiming that alliances with Russia were 'a disgrace to any enlightened country which makes them'. The purpose of the Entente must be to detach France from the 'nightmare' of her Russian alliance, not to seduce Britain into a similar alliance.[22] *Justice* was equally vehement: 'We entirely fail to follow Jaurès at times', the SDF organ remarked.[23] As early as 1904, therefore, British socialists had begun to warn their followers of the prospect of Britain's being drawn into a network of opposing European alliances.

By contrast the trade unions and the LRC were slow to react to these developments. Neither the TUC Parliamentary Committee nor the LRC executive made any comment on the Russo-Japanese War. Only at the end of the war did the Parliamentary Committee address a message of congratulations to President Roosevelt for his work in securing the Peace of Portsmouth.[24] Similarly, when the Entente Cordiale

[20] *LL*, 16 April and 25 November 1904. At the SDF Conference, 1–3 April 1904, A.S. Headingly had read a paper arguing for an alliance between Britain and France; see SDF *Conference Report*, 1904, and *Justice*, 16 April 1904.

[21] Goldberg, *Jaurès*, p. 345.

[22] Editorial, *LL*, 25 November 1904.

[23] *Justice*, 19 November 1904.

[24] TUC PC *mins.*, 30 August 1905.

was announced neither the Parliamentary Committee nor the LRC executive had any formal statement to offer. The fiscal controversy and the Chinese labour agitation seemed to absorb all their attention. It was not until the Moroccan crisis of 1905 that the trade unionists were forced to turn their attention to the problems of the nation's foreign policy.

2. *The Moroccan Crisis of 1905 and the Beginning of the 'German Menace'*

During the major Franco-German quarrel over Morocco in 1905, Britain's support for France revealed quite clearly the anti-German potentialities of the Entente Cordiale. Relations between Britain and Germany were already under some strain because of German naval expansion, so the Entente was now interpreted as a further incitement to antagonism. British foreign policy seemed to be embarking on a new and dangerous course of Continental entanglements. Thus, in September 1905, the TUC Parliamentary Committee made one of its very few declarations on foreign policy. A resolution in the name of the committee was presented to the TUC at Hanley. Characteristically, the resolution began with loyal and gracious references to the work of King Edward in bringing about the Entente Cordiale; but the resolution then hastened to

assure our German comrades that we know they wish the same relations to obtain between them and ourselves which have been so happily established with France, and that we will do our utmost to induce our government to cut down armaments systematically on an agreed basis with all nations. Finally we appeal to our German comrades to work continuously and cordially with us in a united effort to check the growth of Jingo feelings on both sides of the North Sea.[25]

The LRC was a little slower to react. Although the LRC executive met three times during the first stages of the Moroccan crisis, between April and June 1905, no protest or statement of policy was issued.[26] The LRC executive proceeded with its agitation on unemployment and a demonstration on this issue was held on 9 July. But no effort was

---

[25] *Justice*, 9 September 1905.
[26] Labour Party NEC *mins.*, 13 April, 2 June, and 4 October 1905.

made to muster public opinion against a possible British involvement in a war over Morocco. Even an approach from Canon Barnett in October asking that the LRC executive make a pronouncement for peace evoked no immediate response. It was not until January 1906 that the LRC (now the Labour Party) Conference unanimously agreed to an ILP resolution which condemned 'the attempts which have been made to use this good understanding with France [the Entente] as a threat against Germany'.[27] The one organization at the centre of the Labour movement which did declare its position on the Moroccan crisis relatively swiftly was the new British National Committee. At its first business meeting in late July 1905 the BNC accepted a resolution from Hyndman which called for an 'entente cordiale with Germany' and pledged the British labour movement to arms reductions.[28] Thus, by January 1906 the labour movement as a whole was pledged to combat the growing assumption of enmity between Germany and Britain, and to support proposals for arms limitation. In addition, the Moroccan crisis marks the origin of the labour movement's suspicion of the French Entente, and of the procedures of 'secret diplomacy'.

The Moroccan crisis also had two important effects upon the socialists. First, the crisis signalled the beginnings of a bitter debate within British socialism over the question of the 'German menace', that is, whether the Kaiser's Germany posed a special threat to the more politically progressive states of Western Europe. If such a threat did exist, should socialists not warn their people of that threat and perhaps reconsider their opposition to all armaments expenditure? Second, the crisis raised doubts in the minds of some British socialists as to whether their German comrades of the SPD were genuinely eager to join them in a combined campaign against militarism and war.

The 'German menace' theme first appeared in the pages of *Justice* during 1905. Throughout the Moroccan crisis Hyndman and Quelch, writing in *Justice*, sounded an insistent note of warning against German expansionism, and they

[27] *LL*, 23 February 1906.
[28] BNC *mins.*, 27 July 1905.

seemed, by contrast, to find little in the actions of the French to criticize. In late April, one month after the Kaiser's landing at Tangier, *Justice* even criticized the French socialists for their attacks on the French Foreign Minister, Théophile Delcassé. 'We begin to doubt very seriously', *Justice* announced, 'the wisdom of a policy which brings French socialists into such close and friendly accord with a dangerous despot such as Wilhelm II . . . We entirely fail to see . . . where M. Delcassé has gone wrong in this Morocco business.'[29] In stark contrast, *Justice* depicted the Kaiser as a figure of appalling evil.

Naturally there were those in the SDF, such as Belfort Bax and the German correspondent J.B. Askew, who objected to the 'anti-German' attitude of the SDF leaders and their apparent refusal to take account of French imperialism and fanatical French patriotism. Letters appeared in *Justice* pleading for a more even-handed approach.[30] Quelch argued in reply that the German Empire was a politically 'backward' nation with a parliamentary façade. Moreover, he asserted that the German socialists had done very little to break down the effective monopoly of power wielded by the Prussian military élite. German ascendancy in Europe, wrote Quelch, would be 'a misfortune to humanity'.[31] In August 1905 Hyndman summarized his own view of the Moroccan crisis in a more one-sided manner than ever:

We have been on the eve of war between France and Germany in which Great Britain would almost certainly have taken the side of France . . . Our opinion is that the Kaiser and his government were entirely in the wrong, and that they are entirely in the wrong at this moment on the whole business . . . This does not mean that we wish to see French capitalism absorb Morocco. But it does certainly mean that it would be far worse for Europe, for civilisation and for socialism, that the reactionary Kaiser should become the dictator of Europe than that the French Republic, with all its drawbacks, should continue to increase in strength and prosperity and develop along the lines of freedom and progress as it has done for the past twenty years . . . We contend that we should have been a contemptible folk indeed had we failed at the

---

[29] *Justice*, 29 April 1905.
[30] *Justice*, 24 June 1905.
[31] *Justice*, 22 July 1905; on the German socialists' powerlessness, see also *Justice*, 17 June 1905.

critical moment to back the French Republic for all we were worth against the jack-boot bullying of Berlin.[32]

The tone of such remarkable passages as this invited criticism.

Neither Hyndman nor Quelch had the type of personality which allowed revision of a point of view in response to criticism. On the contrary, both men were inclined to harden their positions when under attack. Thus the quarrel over *Justice*'s response to the Moroccan crisis turned out to be only the preliminary skirmish in a long and acrimonious debate. In March 1906, during the Algeciras Conference, an unrepentant Hyndman returned to the fray. Again he chided Jaurès for criticizing the French Government. Hyndman urged Jaurès to read the Kaiser's speeches and the propaganda of the Pan-Germans and Navy Leaguers, so that he too would perceive the reality of the German threat. Hyndman had no qualms about the prospect of war:

My conviction is that, with all our faults and selfishness, we should at once declare war against Germany if her armies crossed the French frontier; not because we wish to cripple Germany, but because we are quite determined she shall not cripple France and threaten the liberties of all Europe. . . .

Let us never forget, also, that the Germany of the Kaiser and his friends has taken the place of Russia as the most reactionary and perturbing power in the world.[33]

In the aftermath of the Moroccan crisis, therefore, the idea of the 'German menace' had become fixed dogma in the political outlook of the most influential of British marxists. No amount of criticism was to shake Hyndman's convictions on this matter.

The ILP's reaction to the Moroccan crisis was much less intense. Neither the Kaiser's landing at Tangier in March nor the resignation of Delcassé in June provoked much comment in the *Labour Leader*.[34] It was not until July 1905 that the *Leader* began to give prominence to the crisis, providing extensive coverage of the peace demonstrations in France and Germany. When the German Government refused to give

[32] *Justice*, 12 August 1905.
[33] *Justice*, 3 March 1906.
[34] The ILP NAC *mins*. of 3 April make no mention of the crisis over the landing at Tangier.

Jaurès permission to speak at the main demonstration in Berlin, the ILP's Administrative Council made its first statement on the crisis and invited both Bebel and Jaurès to Britain to continue their peace campaign, an offer that was politely declined in both cases.[35] The *Labour Leader*'s first concern was to warn against the assumption being drawn from the Moroccan crisis that Britain and France had forged an alliance against Germany. The ILP position was, of course, in direct conflict with the views of Hyndman and Quelch who were ardently promoting the idea of the Entente as a pact to contain German militarism.[36] In its coverage of the Moroccan crisis and the subsequent Algeciras Conference, the *Labour Leader* took pains to be even-handed and to counterbalance the view that Germany was 'bullying' France. In March 1906 the *Leader* warned that some commentators were taking a lopsided view of the Moroccan affair. The *Leader* explained that the French attempt to exclude Germany from discussions on Morocco had been a 'preposterous blunder', and that Delcassé's fall had been achieved by Germany's 'superior diplomacy'. The ILP refused to acknowledge that German imperialism was more aggressive or dangerous than any other form of imperialism.[37]

Throughout 1906 and 1907 *Justice*, now the official organ of the renamed Social Democrat Party or SDP persisted with the Hyndman–Quelch analysis. Germany was cast in the role of a brutal bully led by a 'half-lunatic Kaiser'.[38] Whereas ILP MPs such as Jowett continually sought assurances that Britain was free from obligations to France in case of war,[39] *Justice* demanded assurances that Britain would indeed come to France's aid in war.[40]

The continuation of this 'German menace' line in *Justice*

[35] ILP NAC *mins.*, 7–8 July 1905; Jaurès to Hardie, 26 July 1905, ILP Archives, 1905/111; Bebel to Hardie, 29 July 1905, ILP Archives, 1905/112; *LL*, 7 and 14 July 1905.

[36] For example, contrast the reviews of the visit of the French naval fleet to Portsmouth in August 1905, in 'France, Germany and Ourselves', *LL*, 2 August 1905 and 'Vive La France', *Justice*, 12 August 1905.

[37] *LL*, 2 March 1906.

[38] *Justice*, 14 July 1906.

[39] Brockway, *Socialism Over Sixty Years*, pp. 122–9.

[40] *Justice*, 15 September 1906.

in 1906 and 1907 did not pass unchallenged. In April 1906 Belfort Bax again attacked Hyndman's interpretation of the Moroccan quarrel.[41] The decision to campaign against the Kaiser's visit to Britain in late 1907 was also resented within the SDP.[42] Rothstein insisted that Hyndman's harping on German militarism was 'playing into the hands of the jingoes by fanning still more the embers of prejudice and enmity which exist in this country against Germany and thus preparing the ground for a popular war with Germany'.[43]

In spite of this criticism, Hyndman and Quelch always earnestly denied that their concern with the 'German menace' arose from jingoist sentiments of any kind. They contended that their anxiety over the defence of Britain and France did not involve any lessening of their own commitment to an international class struggle above all else; nor did it mean that they excused British and French imperialism. Their position, they argued, was entirely in accord with the long-recognized duty of socialists to defend their nation against a more reactionary power. Their realization of the German threat, they asserted, was based upon a sober estimation of the changes in the European power balance caused by the disabling of Russia. Moreover, they protested that the members of the SDP had 'never been peace at any price folk'.[44] Faced by the reality of the German threat, they maintained that they had a right to warn against it, to advocate a citizen army, and even to acknowledge that 'under existing conditions a powerful fleet cannot be dispensed with'.[45] The problem for socialist journalists like Hyndman and Quelch, familiar as they were with the use of inflated rhetoric, was that their warnings against German aggression were not always in the tone of cool-headed reckonings of the European power balance. Rather, they tended to mirror the hysterical anti-German

[41] *Justice*, 14 April 1906.
[42] See 'King and Kaiser', *Justice*, 1 August 1906; 'The British Democracy and the Kaiser's Visit', *Justice*, 7 September 1907; 'Shall Londoners Welcome the Kaiser as Their Guest?', *Justice*, 2 November 1907.
[43] *Justice*, 14 September 1907; see Hyndman's reply, *Justice*, 21 September 1907.
[44] 'German Imperialism and the French Republic', *Justice*, 16 February 1907.
[45] Ibid.

rhetoric of the jingoist lobby and the popular press. The claim of the SDP leaders that their views were unsullied by jingoist feelings became more and more precarious in their critics' eyes. It seemed to many that if the socialists' duty was to promote internationalist consciousness then it was no part of the socialists' task to highlight the ambitions of the German ruling class in particular, especially when the popular press was already hard at work raising just such an alarm about Germany's quest for world domination. The 'German menace' theme therefore raised questions of tactics and propaganda as much as it raised questions of fact.

Why then did the Moroccan crisis lead Hyndman and Quelch to single out the threat from Germany as a special concern? One important reason lies in the disillusionment the two SDP veteran agitators experienced in their dealings with the German socialists during the crisis, a disillusionment so profound that both came to doubt the willingness and ability of their German comrades to resist German militarism. The apparent reluctance of the SPD leaders to co-operate fully with their socialist colleagues abroad during this crisis convinced both Hyndman and Quelch that a dangerous malaise, perhaps even a patriotic tendency, had gripped the German party. For Hyndman and Quelch the weakness of the SPD only increased the danger of the 'German menace'.

In early June 1905, at the height of the Moroccan crisis, Hyndman had written to Huysmans suggesting that the ISB should meet immediately. In his letter, Hyndman, perhaps unwisely, included the churlish comment that the German socialists 'had not made the least attempt to influence the policy of their government'.[46] On 21 June, Huysmans dutifully circulated Hyndman's letter to other ISB members. Vaillant replied that the French socialists were equally keen for the ISB to meet.[47] The ISB executive (Huysmans, Vandervelde, and Anseele) was also in favour of some co-ordinated peace demonstration, and on 22 June circulated a proposal for a full-scale socialist peace conference to which

[46] 'Circulaire communiquant une lettre de Hyndman à propos de la crise marocaine ... Bruxelles, le 21 juin', in Haupt (ed.), *Bureau Socialiste International*, Vol. 1, pp. 145–6.

[47] Haupt, *Socialism and the Great War*, p. 34.

as many delegates as possible from the French, German, and British socialist parties would be invited, instead of the wider membership of the ISB.[48] However, Bebel's opposition to any such meeting immediately scotched these plans. On 25 June he wrote to Huysmans disputing that the Moroccan crisis was sufficiently dangerous to warrant any meeting organized by the ISB:

It is our impression that people in England are rather nervous and see the situation as more serious than it is. If we convene a meeting whenever there is a minor diplomatic crisis, and immediately pass resolutions, we shall become discredited in no time.[49]

Bebel added that neither he nor his deputy, Paul Singer, were available on the two tentative dates suggested by the ISB because of commitments to meetings on electoral matters. With impartial efficiency the ISB then announced without comment that there would be no ISB meeting or conference on the Moroccan crisis, because the Germans' presence at any gathering was 'indispensable'.[50]

Justice reacted angrily to this turn of events. First the ISB executive's own suggestion of a socialist peace conference exclusively for the French, British, and Germans was attacked as a device to compartmentalize the peace campaign. The Moroccan crisis was of wider European significance, *Justice* protested.[51] Then, when Bebel's negative response to Hyndman's proposal was circulated by the ISB, *Justice* was flabbergasted. In reply to Bebel's optimistic analysis, Quelch listed all the signs of imminent danger, including the concentration of the British fleet in home waters and the blustering in the press. He argued that at the very least a meeting of the ISB would have shown the world 'that socialists are not drifting back towards semi-nationalism, as our opponents never lose an opportunity of declaring that we are'.[52] Whereas

---

[48] 'Amendment du Comité exécutif à la proposition Hyndman', in Haupt (ed.), *Bureau Socialiste International*, Vol. 1, pp. 150–1.

[49] 'Circulaire transmettant la résponse negative de Bebel à la proposition Hyndman', ibid., Vol. 1, pp. 154–6; and see Haupt, *Socialism and the Great War*, pp. 33–4.

[50] Ibid.

[51] *Justice*, 1 July 1905.

[52] *Justice*, 8 July 1905.

Quelch's own doubts about the Germans were to be read between lines such as these, Hyndman's growing suspicions were soon openly declared. In August Hyndman wrote that Bebel's reply to the calls for ISB action had been 'unworthy' of him, and reflected the German socialists' obsession with 'their connoisseur system of vote collection'. Hyndman went on to complain that

this has been our experience throughout, since the deeply lamented death of Liebknecht. I should not write of the matter now, were it not that our whole international policy is so prejudicially affected by the German refusal to act in accordance with their strength.[53]

The Moroccan experience and the quarrel over the International's response was not forgotten by Hyndman and Quelch. The ISB was not scheduled to meet again until March 1906. With that meeting in view, Hyndman's SDP executive considered a number of 'suggestions' designed to ensure that in future the ISB would play a more determined role at moments of international tension. These suggestions were presented to the BNC in February 1906.[54] The most important proposal was that the ISB should meet as a matter of course every three months. The SDP also suggested peace demonstrations, 'if the Germans will attend', in Paris and London. On the eve of the ISB meeting in March 1906, Hyndman was still mulling over the events of 1905:

That such a gathering of the ISB ought to have been held nearly a year ago nobody now disputes. If the Bureau is to have any permanent influence on international politics it must meet more frequently ... Some arrangement should be possible whereby a considerable minority of the Bureau could call its members together for discussion.[55]

At the Bureau meeting it was Hardie who brought forward the BNC's suggestion that the ISB meet more frequently. As a start Hardie proposed that the next ISB meeting should be held in London 'at an early date'.[56] According to Hyndman the Germans at first opposed this, but they finally agreed as

---

[53] 'Social-Democracy and Foreign Policy', *Justice*, 12 August 1905.
[54] BNC *mins.*, 21 February 1906; J.F. Green to Hardie, 1 March 1906, ILP Archives, 1906/122.
[55] *Justice*, 3 March 1906.
[56] 'Compte-rendu de la septième réunion plénière du BSI', in Haupt (ed.), *Bureau Socialiste International*, p. 207; *Justice*, 10 March 1906.

a compromise that a meeting of the ISB's Interparliamentary Commission, followed by a demonstration, should be held in London in the coming July.[57] It was a partial victory for Hyndman, and for Hardie, who evidently shared Hyndman's disappointment over the lack of a meeting in 1905 and yet had refrained from open criticism of the German's role in this.

Another item of major interest at the March 1906 Bureau meeting needs to be noted here, namely the SFIO's proposition on the prevention of war. The resolution, supported by Vaillant, suggested that the International Bureau must be called together 'as soon as secret or public moves give rise to fear of a conflict between governments and make war possible or probable'.[58] Although the Germans were not specifically criticized in this resolution or in the Bureau debate, it was clear that the terms of this resolution also implied some criticism of the unwillingness the Germans had displayed in June 1905 when confronted with a suggested ISB gathering. It was also well known that the CGT leader Griffuelhes had been most disappointed when, in January 1906, both Bebel and Legien had reacted coolly to his suggestion of joint peace demonstrations.[59] Perhaps unwilling to provoke renewed controversy on this point once more, the Germans did not oppose Vaillant's resolution and it was passed unanimously.[60]

The doubts of the British SDP leadership, concerning the capacity of the German socialists to resist Prussian militarism, were apparently confirmed by the results of the German elections in January 1907. The defeats suffered by the SPD in an election in which the conservative parties had loudly beaten the patriotic drum were most disturbing. The danger to Europe had now increased, Hyndman argued, for the election results would be seen as evidence that the German people supported their Kaiser's 'buccaneering'.[61] Soon after

---

[57] *Justice*, 10 March 1906.

[58] Haupt (ed.), *Bureau Socialiste International*, p. 19.

[59] Jacques Juillard, 'La CGT devant la Guerre (1900–1914)', *Le Mouvement Social*, 49, October–December 1964, p. 50; M. Drachkovitch, *Les Socialismes Français et Allemand et le probl+me de la Guerre*, 1870–1914 (Genève, 1953), p. 146.

[60] Haupt (ed.), *Bureau Socialiste International*, p. 19.

[61] *Justice*, 2 and 9 February 1907.

the elections Hyndman still found space in *Justice* to remind
the German socialists of their failure to act decisively during
the Moroccan crisis.[62] Quelch also renewed his criticism of
Jaurès who, he claimed, had encouraged Prussian militarism
by 'declaring that the German wolf was in the right and the
French lamb in the wrong'.[63] For Hyndman and Quelch the
Moroccan crisis was clear evidence of the power of Prussian
militarism in Germany, a power which the SDP leaders suspected had little to fear from German socialism.

Of course, the importance of this 'German menace' theme
on the left of the British labour movement must be kept in
perspective. The SDP was after all a small dissident organization outside the LRC, and even within the SDP the special
anxiety over Germany was not accepted by all. As far as the
LRC and the TUC were concerned, the Moroccan crisis had
shown that Britain was becoming entangled in the Franco-
German rivalry. As a result, both the TUC and the LRC had
formally declared their determination to support a reconciliation with Germany and a mutual reduction in armaments.
The most important effect of the crisis therefore, was its impact upon the outlook of the trade union leaders. They had
been persuaded to lift their heads from the domestic scene
and for the first time to consider the response of the union
movement to a new issue, Anglo-German relations. That the
trade union movement should declare its position on such an
issue was in itself a new departure—for, not five years previously, war itself could not shatter the polite silence of the
union leadership.

3. *Army Reorganization 1906–7: National Defence or Fillip to Militarism?*

Since the end of the South African War the question of army
reorganization had occupied the attention of two successive
Secretaries for War in the Balfour Government. Their plans
had attracted little interest in the labour movement until
1904 when a Royal Commission on army reform reported
that Britain's security could only be properly safe-guarded by

---

[62] *Justice*, 16 February 1907.
[63] *Justice*, 6 April 1907.

the introduction of some form of compulsory military training. Immediately the issue of conscription began to be debated within the labour movement. In June the TUC Parliamentary Committee expressed its 'indignation' that the idea of conscription should be even suggested.[64] In September the TUC passed an equally vehement resolution against conscription, although it is noteworthy that the mover of the resolution, John Ward, included some loyal and generous references to Edward 'the Peacemaker' in his speech.[65] The ILP and SDF also reacted promptly to the Royal Commission's report, both warning that the Government was testing the air before imposing conscription.[66] The campaign in favour of military training, mounted by the National Service League, also began to cause the ILP some anxiety. In July 1905 Glasier noted that 'the air is loaded with rumours of conscription'.[67] The SDF and *Justice* were equally determined in their criticism of the Royal Commission's report of 1904 and the National Service League's proposals.[68]

Those who may have hoped that the election of the Liberal Government in January 1906 would solidify the anti-military training lobby were swiftly disabused. It was soon embarrassingly clear that the twenty-nine new Labour Party MPs had not yet arrived at a common position on the issue. In February, seven of their number, C. Duncan, A.H. Gill, T.F. Richards, J.W. Taylor, W.T. Wilson, J. Wadsworth, and J. Hodge, signed a manifesto sponsored by the National Service League in support of military training in schools.[69] The seven MPs were all trade unionists, and one, Hodge, was a member of the BNC. Here was stark proof that, in spite of the TUC's firm stand against conscription in 1904, the propaganda in favour of lesser forms of military training had made some headway amongst the trade unionists since 1904. And the volume of such propaganda was now increasing. In March 1906 William Le Queux's novel *The Invasion of 1910*

[64] TUC PC *mins.*, 1 June 1904.
[65] *LL*, 16 September 1904.
[66] 'Conscription', *LL*, 3 June 1904.
[67] 'Socialism and Soldiering', *LL*, 21 July 1905.
[68] 'Notes on Conscription', *Justice*, 4 June 1904.
[69] Letter in *LL*, 23 February 1906.

was launched with full-page advertisements in the major newspapers.[70] In the same week as these appeared, the Commons debated the army estimates, and again the Labour MPs were divided. On a motion to reduce army spending, sixteen Labour MPs voted for reductions while seven, including Shackleton, Snowden, and Crooks, supported the Government.[71] There had been no meeting before the division and the Labour MPs had cast their votes freely. 'Allowances must be made for the newness and lack of united training in the Party', pleaded the *Leader*.[72] Yet it was clearly not just a matter of training. Some of the trade unionist MPs simply did not share the socialists' detestation of militarism. Snowden, the only ILP member who had supported the expenditure, hastened to reassure the *Leader* that his vote had been a formal vote of support for the Government on account of the Prime Minister's past record of military economy. Will Crooks, on the other hand, bluntly declared that his first duty was to his constituents, the Woolwich Arsenal workers.[73] It was Crooks who had announced soon after the election that the Labour MPs should concentrate on labour questions and leave matters of foreign policy to the professional statesmen.[74] He was not to deviate from this viewpoint in the years ahead.

This rather chaotic opening performance on the military issue on the part of the new Labour MPs no doubt heightened the socialists' fears that the new Parliament might not resist any pro-conscriptionist experiment of the Government. About this time both the *Labour Leader* and *Justice* made clear their suspicions of the Liberal Government's evident intention to press on with a programme of army reorganization. Both papers exhibited a particular distrust of Haldane, the Secretary for War. Indeed, Hardie had singled out Haldane and Asquith as 'cold-blooded reactionaires of the most

[70] E.L. Woodward, *Great Britain and the German Navy* (London, 1964), p. 117.
[71] *LL*, 23 March 1906. In the wake of the vote the *Leader* reaffirmed its total opposition to military training; see 'Down with Weapons', *LL*, 30 March 1906.
[72] *LL*, 23 March 1906.
[73] Ibid.
[74] *Justice*, 17 February 1906.

dangerous type' when they were first elevated to the new cabinet in December 1905.[75] Two other factors tended to keep the issue of militarism to the forefront during 1906: the continuing British military action against the Zulus in Natal,[76] and the furore in France over Gustave Hervé's anti-militarist propaganda.[77]

In the autumn of 1906 came a preliminary skirmish with the Government on the militarism issue. In September, it was learned that the Kent Education Committee had requested the Board of Education to consider rifle training for schools. The ILP immediately urged the Labour MPs to resist any such scheme.[78] Then, one month later, the *Labour Leader* discovered that the Birmingham Small Arms Company had made known its intention of supplying miniature rifles to the Government for school use. The *Labour Leader* again called on the Labour MPs to protest against 'the plot which the government is evidently conniving at for the introduction of militarism in school'.[79] Eventually, in the Commons, Hardie, Snowden, and John Ward questioned Augustine Birrell, President of the Board of Education, who explained that rifle-shooting lessons had indeed been introduced in five elementary schools on an experimental basis only.[80] The *Labour Leader* was predictably appalled at this 'violent breach of public faith' by a Government that had 'deserted its principles and promises'.[81]

There were signs that the ILP's anxiety on these matters was to some extent shared by the trade union movement too. In September 1906 the TUC passed a resolution, similar to that endorsed in 1904, condemning conscription and all

[75] *LL*, 22 December 1905.

[76] See, for example, the manifesto on the Natal crisis in J. Ramsay MacDonald to Francis Johnson, 30 April 1906, ILP Archives 1906/171, and the considerable correspondence on the Natal crisis in the ILP Archives for 1906, document numbers 105, 170A, 174A, 176, 183, 184, 186.

[77] See 'Anti-Militarism in France', *LL*, 5 January 1906, and 'Hervéism. Anti-militarism: A Great Movement', *LL*, 9 March 1906. The ILP Conference of April 1906 also denounced compulsory military training; see *LL*, 20 April 1906.

[78] *LL*, September 1906.

[79] 'To Militarise the Children', *LL*, 5 October 1906; 'The Autumn Session', *LL*, 19 October 1906; 'The Militarist Plot to Capture Our School Children', *LL*, 26 October 1906.

[80] *LL*, 2 November 1906.

[81] 'The Rifle-Shooting Plot', ibid.

forms of forced military training. Even so, both *Justice* and
the *Labour Leader* doubted that this indicated any strong
feeling on the matter amongst the unions.[82] Glasier noted
that John Ward, who had again introduced the resolution,
adopted a 'self-conscious and obtrusively opportunist air' and
spoke without conviction.[83] Certainly the unions could be
relied upon to oppose conscription, but it was less certain
that there was any deep revulsion against all forms of military
training. Much the same can be said of the motion denouncing
militarism which was passed at the Labour Party Conference
in January 1907. The resolution, grouped with two others,
was endorsed without any formal presentation to the conference and without discussion on the last day of the proceedings.[84] It was a procedure denoting a 'hardy annual'.
Whilst the trade unions were willing to proclaim their anxiety
over militarism, there was little to suggest that their anxiety
was deep-seated. Certainly, there was no evident intention
to instigate a campaign on this issue.

An indication of the different levels of concern felt within
each section of the labour movement was to come with
Haldane's army reform of 1907. Preliminary announcements
were made during 1906 of a scheme to create a Territorial
Force of young male volunteers who would undertake a
fortnight's training each year for four years. In September
1906 Hardie condemned the scheme as a 'thinly disguised
form of conscription', and he urged the labour movement to
provide 'unflinching opposition' to it.[85] The SDP leaders, as
advocates of a citizen army, were embarrassed to discover
that their chief objection to the scheme was its voluntary
basis. Standing armies must be abolished, *Justice* proclaimed,
but the citizen armies that replaced them must be founded
upon universal short-time training.[86] Even before the Haldane
scheme reached Parliament, therefore, the varied responses
of the labour movement were predictable. The moderate

[82] *Justice*, 15 September 1906; *LL*, 14 September 1906.
[83] *LL*, 14 September 1906.
[84] Labour Party, *Annual Conference Report*, 1907, p. 62.
[85] 'The New Danger: Mr Haldane's Nation in Arms', *LL*, 21 September 1906.
[86] See 'The Citizen Army', *Justice*, 24 February 1906; *Justice*, 17 March,
29 September, and 6 October 1906.

majority of the Labour Party and the trade union movement were never likely to be genuinely distressed, for whatever the rhetoric the socialists hurled against Haldane, his voluntary training scheme hardly amounted to conscription, and only conscription could provoke the bulk of the labour movement to protest.

When the Territorial and Reserve Forces Bill came before Parliament in 1907 it soon became apparent that the ILP's arguments against the bill were designed specifically to appeal to moderate trade union opinion. The central theme of the ILP's campaign was the claim that the actual purpose of the scheme was to prepare public opinion for conscription. The ILP also played up Haldane's self-confessed determination that the Force should be officered only by the British élite, 'young men of the upper and middle classes' supplied from the universities and public school cadet corps. Hardie also stressed that the Force could not be intended for home defence as the Navy was invincible. The Territorials, therefore, were destined for overseas aggression or 'social control' at home. Moreover, the scheme sought to militarize the young. All these themes were canvassed at the ILP Conference in April 1907 which enthusiastically endorsed a resolution rejecting Haldane's scheme in its entirety.[87]

Vital to the ILP's campaign was the conversion of the trade unionist Labour Party MPs. The ILP exercised great influence in the parliamentary group, for Hardie had been elected chairman in 1906 and MacDonald still held the position of secretary. As chairman, Hardie drafted a special report on the Haldane scheme for the Labour Party's consideration, in which he denounced the scheme unequivocally. Hardie's influence prevailed, and the report was accepted by a special Labour Party committee on the scheme. The Labour Party MPs agreed to oppose the bill on the second reading and to submit amendments subsequently.[88]

In the Commons it was chiefly the ILP members who spoke for the Labour Party against the bill. MacDonald condemned

[87]   J. Keir Hardie, 'Mr Haldane's Scheme: Towards Conscription', *LL*, 1 March 1907; 'The Militarist Peril', *LL*, 12 April 1907. See also reports of Hardie's speeches at Hull, *LL*, 8 March 1907, and at West Bromwich, *LL*, 22 March 1907.

[88]   Hardie's report is reproduced in *LL*, 19 April 1907.

the expansion of the strength of the Army and the élitist officer class envisaged in the bill.[89] Hardie concentrated his attack on the 'military spirit' nurtured by the extension of rifle clubs and cadet corps, and he accused the Government of hypocrisy in proceeding to the Hague Peace Conference after having augmented the Army.[90] In June 1907, at the final reading stage of the bill, the non-socialist Labour Party MP Arthur Henderson announced the Labour Party's continuing opposition to the Haldane scheme, and he delivered a speech against the bill which echoed most of the arguments put forward by the ILP.[91] In the end, the Labour MPs obeyed their Whip, and voted solidly against the bill, with the single exception of Will Crooks who supported the Government. This was a heartening result for the ILP. Yet, it was disturbing that at least thirteen of the Lib-Lab MPs, including such trade union leaders as Abraham, Burt, Edwards, Fenwick, Steadman, Vivian, and John Wilson, had voted in favour of the Haldane scheme.[92] It was with some justification then that the *Labour Leader* expressed its disappointment that, notwithstanding the Labour Party's firm stand in the Commons, the labour movement as a whole had not stirred itself to mount a loud protest against the Territorial scheme.[93] Soon afterwards the *Leader* was aghast to discover that three trade unionist Labour MPs, Seddon, Macpherson, and Kelly, were touring Switzerland to enquire into the citizen army system at the invitation and expense of the National Service League.[94]

In spite of the ILP's agitation, the new voluntary military training scheme did not fill the trade union leadership with dread. The spectre of conscription was not really credible. Very few trade unions or trades councils appear to have protested over the creation of the Territorial Force in 1907.[95] The TUC itself, which met in September 1907, passed a

---

[89] *Hansard*, 23 April 1907, IV: 172, 1593–1600.

[90] *Hansard*, 28 February 1907, IV: 172, 311.

[91] *Hansard*, 19 June 1907, IV: 176, 529–32.

[92] The vote is given at *Hansard*, 19 June 1907, IV: 176, 578.

[93] *LL*, 28 June 1907.

[94] *LL*, 6 September 1907.

[95] One of the only unions to protest, through its journal, was the Amalgamated Society of Engineers; see ASE *Journal*, April 1907.

resolution against *compulsory* military training, but the terms of the resolution gave no hint of opposition to Haldane's proposals.[96] The TUC of 1908 ignored the issue. It was not until 1909 that the trade unions began to display a serious interest in the new Territorial Force. This concern was prompted by a well-publicized decision by Lord Rothschild of the Alliance Assurance Company in February 1909 to make enlistment in the Territorials a prerequisite for employment with his firm. When Haldane refused to condemn this action, the controversy over conscription blossomed forth once more.[97] Not only the socialist press but now the trades councils as well denounced Haldane and his scheme.[98] Lord Rothschild's edict was soon withdrawn, but the damage had been done. There was a warm debate at the TUC in September 1909, and tempers flared when Shackleton sought to assure the sceptical delegates that he had Haldane's word of honour that the Territorials could not be used against strikers. Once more the TUC passed a resolution against compulsory military training, but this time there was also an unambiguous declaration concerning the Territorial Force:

it is absolutely inconsistent with the policy of trade unionists for them to enlist in this force, as they are thereby liable to be called out in times of industrial disputes to quell and possibly shoot down their fellow workers.[99]

On the face of it, this marked the victory of the socialist viewpoint within the TUC. However, the terms of the resolution, nominating the possibility that the Territorial Force might be used against strikers as the major objection of the trade union movement to it, once more testified to the differences in tone and spirit between the trade unions and the socialist leaders of the ILP. Moreover, the resolution was not acted upon. Neither the TUC Parliamentary Committee nor the trades

---

[96] *Justice*, 14 September 1907.
[97] 'Conscription by Capitalist Compulsion', *LL*, 12 February 1909; G.H. Perris, 'Territorial Serfs', *LL*, 26 February 1909.
[98] Sheffield TC *mins.*, 12 January 1909; Aberdeen TC *mins.*, 24 February 1909.
[99] See TUC PC *mins.*, 6 September 1909, and TUC *Annual Report*, 1909, p. 134.

councils appear to have actively discouraged enlistment in the Territorials. The 1909 resolution remained as a bold declaration of policy, but a rather isolated one, from an angry moment in the Trade Union Congress.

Finally, an important debate on the fringe of the major controversy over the Haldane scheme needs to be mentioned, that is, the debate on the SDP's alternative citizen army scheme. Loyal to the marxist tradition and the Second International's official policy, Hyndman's SDP steadfastly maintained that a national citizen army, based on universal short-time training, directed by democratically elected officers, and disciplined without the force of military law, was the true solution to the problem of national defence.[100] Unfortunately for the SDP, it strained credibility to attack the Haldane scheme as the thin end of the conscriptionist wedge while arguing for compulsory military training in its place. Moreover, the key reform which was supposed to accompany the creation of a citizen army, that is, the abolition of the standing army, was unthinkable outside of a revolutionary situation. There were those within the SDP who pointed out these problems, notably J.B. Askew,[101] but Quelch thumbed his nose at his critics by unashamedly quoting Lord Robert's recommendation in the advertisements in *Justice* for his pamphlet *Social Democracy and the Armed Nation.*[102]

The SDP's campaign, however, had very little impact on the labour movement. It seemed to cause friction only. *Justice* fell to attacking the Labour Party politicians' denunciations of military training as symptomatic of their attachment to bourgeois, liberal peace sentiment.[103] The ILP found the SDP line immensely irritating because they too believed it was adding to the militarist agitation. There was

[100] See the SDP manifesto 'Down with Militarism: No Conscription', *Justice*, 20 April 1907; SDP Executive Report, SDP *Annual Conference Report*, 1907, p. 14; 'Socialism and Militarism', *Justice*, 23 March 1907. An SDP demonstration against the Haldane proposals was held at Trafalgar Square on 21 April 1907.

[101] See Askew's letter and Quelch's reply, *Justice* 20 Oct./10 Nov. 1906; also another letter from Askew, *Justice*, 17 Nov. 1906, and A. Hickmott, 'Socialism and Militarism', *Social Democrat*, May 1907.

[102] See, for example, *Justice*, 20 July 1907.

[103] *Justice*, 27 April and 4 May, and editorial 'The Labour Party and the Army Bill', 11 May 1907.

also a quarrel when the SDP's only Labour Party MP, Will Thorne, put forward his own amendments to the Territorial Forces Bill in order to introduce compulsory military training on the citizen army plan.[104]

The SDP's persistence on this issue was never rewarded. Trade Union Congresses and Conferences of the Labour Party repeatedly rejected motions sponsored by the SDP in favour of a national citizen army.[105] The idea simply made no headway in the labour movement. Indeed, the failure of this campaign in itself demonstrated the very profound ideological differences between the British labour movement and the socialist and labour movements of the Continent. The idealist and non-marxist modes of thought, exemplified by the ILP, still represented the intellectual basis of the British labour and socialist tradition.

4. *The International Socialist Congress at Stuttgart, 1907*

British socialists were not alone in their anxiety over the problem of militarism and the increase in friction between the great powers in the aftermath of the Moroccan crisis. Tension arising from the Entente, the Anglo-German naval rivalry, and the looming prospect of an Anglo-Russian understanding, were matters of concern for all the leading socialist parties. The French and German socialist parties in particular perceived an increasing risk of war, and both devoted time to a reconsideration of their policies regarding militarism in preparation for the International Socialist Congress which was scheduled to meet in Stuttgart in August 1907.

In France, the socialist parties and the trade unions of the CGT tended to favour vigorous anti-militarism and the use

[104] On this quarrel see *LL*, 7 June 1907, and *Justice*, 8 June 1907.

[105] The TUC rejected resolutions in favour of a citizen army in 1907, 1909, and 1911. At the TUC in 1907 Thorne had to withdraw his citizen army motion on instructions from the Gasworkers' Union; *Justice*, 14 September 1907. See also TUC, *Annual Report*, 1909, pp. 126–8, where the motion was lost by 933,000 votes to 102,000, and TUC, *Annual Report*, 1911, pp. 176–82. See also Labour Party, *Annual Conference Report*, 1909, pp. 89–90, and Labour Party, *Annual Conference Report*, 1910, p. 94 where amendments in favour of the citizen army were defeated.

of the general strike against war.[106] The anti-patriotic agitation of Hervé and the Russian Revolution of 1905 had also given new prominence to the idea of an anti-war strike.[107] The matter was eventually clarified at the National Conventions of the SFIO at Limoges in 1906 and Nancy in 1907.[108] Hervé's insistence that nationality was a delusion and that the worker had nothing to defend was rejected. So too was the marxist Guesde's proposal that anti-militarism should be entirely subordinated to the struggle for socialism. The Vaillant–Jaurès compromise resolution was accepted, and by its terms French socialists declared that, although they would never abandon their right to defend France, their hatred of war was such that they would consider all possible means to prevent it, including a general strike.

The German socialists, on the other hand, regarded any general strike proposal with suspicion. The German trade unions in particular set their teeth against the idea. At their congress in Cologne in 1905 they warned that the suggestion of a general strike would prompt the destruction of the whole labour movement in Germany. At Jena in 1905 the SPD Congress was forced to take account of the unions' intransigence and the general strike was accepted as an emergency measure only.[109] At Mannheim in 1906, the SPD Congress ruled out the use of a general strike against war. Bebel described the idea as 'puerile'.[110]

When the congress opened at Stuttgart in late August 1907, interest naturally centred on the Commission on

---

[106] On the anti-militarism of the CGT see Jacques Juillard, 'La CGT devant la Guerre (1900–1914)', *Le Mouvement Social*, 49, October–December 1964, pp. 49–53. See also the speeches of Allemane and Briand at the Amsterdam Congress in *Sixième Congrès Socialiste International, Amsterdam 1904, Compte Rendu Analytique*, pp. 49–50, 53–5.

[107] On Hervéism see Gustave Hervé's *Leur Patrie*, translated into English by Guy Bowman and published under the title *My Country Right or Wrong* (London, 1911); and Jack D. Ellis 'French Socialist and Syndicalist Approaches to Peace, 1904–1914' (unpublished Ph.D. thesis, Tulane University, 1967), ch. VI.

[108] On the Conventions at Limoges and Nancy see Braunthal, *History of the International*, vol. 1, p. 333; Aaron Noland, *Founding of the French Socialist Party*, p. 196.

[109] Richard Hostetter, 'The SPD and the General Strike as an Anti-War Weapon, 1905–1914', *The Historian* XIII (1950–1), pp. 37–9.

[110] For Bebel's speech see R.C.K. Ensor (ed.), *Modern Socialism*, (London, 1907), p. 195.

Militarism where the conflicting viewpoints of the French and Germans were to be resolved. The contribution of the British delegates was not expected to be crucial, for neither the ILP nor the SDP, whose delegates formed the bulk of the British delegation, had yet established their policies on the means of preventing war. Rather, both were preoccupied with their squabble over the citizen army. The Labour Party and the trade unions, who were hopelessly under-represented at Stuttgart anyway with nine delegates, had no settled policy on the prevention of war either. As MacDonald reflected, it was 'humiliating' to discover at Stuttgart that 'every big country except our own' had already debated the issues.[111] The only certainty was that all sections of the British labour movement supported the concept of national self-defence and thus rejected Hervé's anti-patriotism.[112] The British contribution to the famous Commission on Militarism was limited to the intervention of Russell Smart, the ILP delegate, who secured a minor change in the final resolution so as to allow for the ILP's refusal to accept the concept of a citizen army.[113] Glasier's pressure on the ISB also resulted in both Vandervelde and Adler acknowledging before the congress that the reference to a citizen army in the final resolution did not apply to Britain, America, and other nations fortunate enough to be free of conscription.[114] It was a minor victory for the ILP.

Absorbed in this side issue, the British delegates tended to overlook the vital debate in the Commission on Militarism over what means socialists should use to prevent war. The fifteen Commission members deliberated for three days. 'It was necessary for our reputations', commented Smart, quite underestimating the importance of the issues involved.[115]

---

[111] *LL*, 30 August 1907.

[112] For example, see J.B. Glasier 'Socialism and Nationhood', in *LL*, 26 October 1906 and H. Quelch, 'Social Democracy, Nationalism and Imperialism', *Social Democrat*, July 1907.

[113] H. Russell Smart, 'Among the Socialist Leaders: In the Military Commission at Stuttgart', *LL*, 6 September 1907; *Justice*, 31 August 1907. In the Commission Smart also made clear his rejection of Hervé's plan for a military strike; see *Septième Congrès Socialiste, Stuttgart, 1907: Compte Rendu Analytique* (Bruxelles, 1908), p. 155, cited hereafter as *ISC Proc. 1907*.

[114] *LL*, 30 August 1907.

[115] *LL*, 6 September 1907.

Hervé was soon isolated in the debate, all delegates rejecting his anti-patriotic premise that invasion was of no consequence to the working class. The duty of national defence was accepted by all.[116] Bebel refused to accept any mention of the general strike against war. It would incite the German rulers to crush the SPD, he asserted. Moreover, he argued, a general strike in a situation of war, amidst confusion and mass patriotic emotion, was utterly impractical. 'Upon our first appeal we should be laughed down', he predicted. Only propaganda against war was possible, Bebel concluded. Jaurès tried to sooth the Germans' disquiet on the matter of the general strike by pointing out that the SPD already accepted it as an emergency measure in case of an attack on the suffrage.[117] Was not a war an even more terrible disaster necessitating emergency measures? Finally, Jaurès contended that the SPD's fears of persecution over the general strike policy were quite exaggerated.

But, as Smart observed, the feeling of the Germans and Austrians on this matter was so strong that eventually the Commission members accepted Adler's suggestion that 'instead of saying what they would do, they would state what had been done'.[118] The final compromise resolution, therefore, described the peace demonstrations mounted by the socialists at moments of international tension in the past. It was implied that the International still placed its faith in mass demonstrations to prevent war. There were references too, to parliamentary opposition to arms spending and propaganda work amongst the youth, but no specific commitments were made as to working-class action to prevent war. The general strike was not mentioned; the workers were simply exhorted to 'do everything to prevent the outbreak of war by whatever means seem to them most effective'. Then, in deference to

---

[116] For Hervé's proposed resolution see *ISC Proc. 1907*, p. 111. For Hervé's speech see *ISC Proc. 1907*, pp. 121–3. For criticisms of Hervé, see the speeches of Bebel (pp. 116–19), Troclet (p. 126), Vaillant (p. 129), Jaurès (p. 131), Vollmar (pp. 139–40), Vandervelde (p. 144), and Victor Adler (p. 148).

[117] For the text of the Jaurès–Vaillant resolution, see *Proposals and Drafts of Resolutions ... Stuttgart 1907*, pp. 405–6. For Jaurès's speech in favour of the resolution see *ISC Proc. 1907*, pp. 132–6; for Vaillant's speech see *ISC Proc. 1907*, especially pp. 129–30. For Bebel's reply, see *ISC Proc. 1907*, pp. 159–60.

[118] *LL*, 6 September 1907.

Lenin, Luxemburg, and the left generally, a paragraph was added stating that, should war break out in spite of all, the workers had a duty to use the crisis to 'hasten the abolition of capitalist class rule'.

There can be no doubt that the famous Stuttgart resolution on war represented a victory for the German socialists. The lack of any reference to a strike against war accorded entirely with their wishes. Glasier even suspected underhand tactics on the part of the Germans at Stuttgart. He wondered if it was by design that the Military Commission's deliberations had been delayed so long as to leave the resolution on war to the 'fag end of the proceedings', with no chance of debate and with many members absent. Nevertheless, when the resolution was finally carried by the acclamation of the remnants of the congress, the ebullient Hervé leapt on to his seat cheering and waving. 'Why he did so I do not understand', wrote Glasier, 'and Kautsky, Bebel, and the platform men around me were no less confounded and surprised.'[119] Perhaps it was the same tendency to optimism which led Jaurès on his return to France to proclaim that the Stuttgart resolution was 'in perfect harmony' with the SFIO policy.[120] Both men were putting on a brave front. The Stuttgart resolution was clearly a triumph for the German socialists and marked the formal commitment of the Second International to a moderate anti-war position.

5. The Anglo-Russian Agreement of 1907

Within a week of the return of the British delegates from Stuttgart there came a sharp reminder that Britain was no longer isolated from the rivalries and tensions of the Continent which the socialists had discussed so earnestly. On 31 August 1907 an agreement between Britain and Russia was signed in St Petersburg which liquidated 'misunderstandings' between the two powers regarding Persia, Afghanistan, and Tibet. Both powers, of course, denied that the agreement implied any aggressive intention toward Germany. However, only

---

[119] *LL*, 30 August 1907.

[120] Jaurès 'Après le Congrès de Stuttgart (Speech at Tivoli-Vaux Hall)' in Madeleine Rébérioux (ed.), *Jean Jaurès: Textes Choisis, contre le Guerre et la Politique Coloniale* (Paris, 1959), p. 149.

the most naïve observer could have believed that Germany would simply ignore the obvious outlines of a 'triple entente' against her.

Sir Edward Grey could hardly have expected anything other than anger from the labour movement in response to the Anglo-Russian agreement. From the beginning of the revolution in Russia in 1905 the labour movement had shown heartfelt sympathy for the revolutionaries and unremitting hostility toward the Tsar. The LRC Conference in January 1905 organized an appeal for funds for those left widowed and orphaned by the Bloody Sunday Massacre,[121] and in the Commons in February Hardie asked Balfour to register a protest against the massacre with the Russian Government (which Balfour declined to do).[122] Fund-raising efforts and protests continued during 1905 and 1906, including a resolution of sympathy for the Russian reform movement passed at the TUC in September 1906.[123]

The labour movement had some grounds for hoping that the Liberal Government would eschew any close connection with the tsarist regime, especially after the dramatic incident at the Interparliamentary Union Conference in London in July 1906, when Campbell-Bannerman had cried out 'Vive Le Douma!' at the end of his speech.[124] However, it was clear that Grey favoured an accommodation with Russia, and negotiations at St Petersburg actually began in May 1906.[125] The first obvious sign of Grey's intention was the announcement in June that a British naval contingent would make a goodwill visit to Kronstadt during a forthcoming Baltic cruise. The Labour MPs immediately re-kindled the torch of protest on this issue. In the Commons on 18 June Hardie and Thorne asked Grey whether the visit should proceed in

---

[121] LRC, *Annual Conference Report*, 1905, p. 40; *LL*, 3 February 1905.

[122] *LL*, 24 February 1905.

[123] 'Warsaw', *LL*, 5 May 1905; BNC *mins.*, 29 November 1905; *LL*, 2 February 1906 describes a demonstration held in Manchester. The proposal for a TUC resolution was first made in the BNC; see BNC *mins.*, 2 August 1906. The BNC also launched a further appeal for funds; see *LL*, 17 August 1906.

[124] Morris, *Radicalism Against War*, p. 62.

[125] Luigi Albertini, *The Origins of the War of 1914*, vol. 1 (Oxford, 1952), pp. 187–8; Morris, *Radicalism Against War*, p. 52–9; Sir Edward Grey, *Twenty Five Years* (London, 1925), Vol. 1, pp. 152–4.

the light of Jewish pogroms and other massacres, but Grey refused to see that Russia's internal affairs were at all relevant.[126] On 28 June Thorne asked whether Grey was aware of the massacres in the Baltic area and if, in view of the facts, the Government would cancel the visit to Kronstadt. Quite unmoved, Grey replied that the answer to all Thorne's questions was in the negative.[127] A week later Grey dismissed a similar question from Hardie.[128] However, in a dramatic turnabout, the Russian Government then announced the cancellation of the visit.[129] Thorne and Hardie were at once the toast of the socialist press.[130] The incident, small as it may seem, was important in confirming the socialists' personal detestation of Grey, who was now seen as a dangerous Germanophobe, willing even to sup with the devil in order to encircle Germany. Throughout the remainder of 1906 and the first half of 1907, the socialist press and the leading Labour Party MPs remained vigilant on the issue of Russia. Hardie's first act in the new parliamentary session of 1907 was to appeal to the Government to protest over new reports of massacres in Russia.[131] The socialist press also hailed the revolutionary events in Persia and warned against Russia and Britain conniving at intervention.[132] Rumours of a coming Anglo-Russian agreement were very strong. In June a memorial against any such agreement was prepared and signed by Radical and Labour MPs.[133] In July the Labour Party and the socialist societies gave their official support to a Friends of Russian Freedom demonstration which ended in scuffles with the police outside the Foreign Office.[134] From June to August, MacDonald and T.F. Richards, another ILP member, asked repeatedly in the Commons whether an agreement with

[126] *Hansard*, VI: 159: 1365–6.

[127] *Hansard*, IV: 159: 1132.

[128] *Hansard*, 5 July 1906, IV: 160: 228, 298–300.

[129] Grey, *Twenty Five Years*, vol. 1, p. 156.

[130] See *Justice*, 23, 30 June and 7 July 1906; 'An International Triumph', *LL*, 20 July 1906.

[131] *LL*, 15 February 1907; see also another BNC manifesto on Russia and appeals for funds, in *Justice*, 19 January 1907.

[132] For example, *LL*, 15 February and 1 March 1907.

[133] *Justice*, 5 June 1907.

[134] *Justice*, 6 July 1907; for a report on the violence see *Justice*, 20 July 1907.

Russia was contemplated.[135] Each time Runciman, answering for Grey, took refuge in the old insistence on the need for secrecy, noting on one occasion that it would be 'unusual and most undesirable to make statements as to the special reason for the movements of any ambassador'.[136] When the agreement was finally announced in early September 1907, Parliament had only just risen.[137]

The news of the Anglo-Russian agreement and the publication of its terms appalled the socialist press. It was criticized as a pact between predators who had come to terms over their 'respective areas of spoliation'.[138] The agreement was also attacked on the ground that it demonstrated secret diplomacy at its worst. Guy Bowman pointed out that just three men, Lansdowne, Delcassé, and now Grey, had achieved a triple entente against Germany 'without the consent or the knowledge of the 150 millions of people whom it most vitally concerns'.[139]

The response of the more moderate elements of the labour movement, the trade unions and trades councils, contrasts with the intense and immediate reaction of the socialists. The trade unionists were at first not unduly perturbed by the news of the Anglo-Russian agreement, which seemed to be nothing more than a sensible division of spheres of interest in some sensitive territories. Thus, in spite of the concern shown by trade unionists over events in Russia in 1905 and 1906, the TUC of September 1907, which met only days after the announcement of the new agreement, made no protest. The news from St Petersburg also evoked no response from the trades councils in 1907. Similarly, by the time Parliament reassembled in late January 1908, the Labour MPs appear to have accepted Grey's *fait accompli* of the previous September.

---

[135] MacDonald asked questions on 5 and 13 June, 29 July, and Richards asked a further question on 7 August 1907; see *LL*, 2 and 16 August 1907.

[136] *Hansard*, IV: 179: 481.

[137] Grey assured his critics that this was quite by chance; see Grey, *Twenty Five Years*, Vol. 1, p. 166.

[138] *Justice*, 7 September 1907.

[139] Guy Bowman, 'Secret Diplomacy', *Social Democrat*, September 1907, p. 534. The SDP also pointed out that the agreement would isolate Germany and increase hostility toward Britain in Germany; Editorial, *Social Democrat*, October 1907, pp. 579–80.

Although the Speech from the Throne made mention of the Anglo-Russian agreement, the Labour Party's new chairman, trade unionist MP Arthur Henderson, made no reference to it in his speech on the Address in Reply. Instead, the Labour Party proceeded with an amendment to the Address stressing the need for unemployment relief.[140] When the Government allowed a brief debate on the agreement on 17 February, the Labour MPs took no part in the debate.[141] The Labour Party's response might well have been different had Hardie still held the chairmanship of the party; but he had been taken ill in mid-1907 and was still abroad on his recuperative world tour when the 1908 parliamentary session began. In any case, the mood of the trade union movement, and therefore of most Labour MPs, appeared to be one of resignation in the face of the new Russian agreement. The ILP Conference of 1908 might rail against the agreement,[142] but it was clear that the moderate majority of the labour movement would not be stirred to protest over the Russian connection until it was shown that the government was indeed intent upon elevating its new friendship with Russia to the level of an alliance.[143]

Signs of such an intention were not long in coming. In May 1908 it was announced that in the following month King Edward would visit the Tsar at Reval. Significantly, Edward's visit was to follow immediately after a visit from the French President, Fallières. The socialists promptly commenced a crusade to arouse the labour movement to an awareness of the significance of the visit, and to oppose it. MacDonald contributed perhaps his most vitriolic article ever to appear in the pages of the *Labour Leader*:

Will our people tolerate such an insult? The Tsar is a common murderer. He shoots scores of his subjects daily. The sands behind Riga are red with the blood of the best of mankind . . . To the Russian people

[140] *LL*, 7 February 1908; Tsiang, pp. 132–3.

[141] *Justice*, 22 February 1908: 'The Labour Party has no place in such a debate'; *Hansard*, IV: 184: 460–564.

[142] *LL*, 24 April 1908; *ILP Year Book*, 1909, p. 10; *ILP Annual Conference Report*, pp. 55–6.

[143] The only complaint over the Anglo-Russian agreement which I could discover in trade union publications was in A.E. Fletcher's column in the ASE *Journal*, June 1907.

our right hand of fellowship; to the Russian Czar our spittle of contempt.[144]

MacDonald appealed to every branch of the ILP to send protest resolutions to the King, Grey, and the Russian ambassador. Glasier reminded all branches of the victory in 1906 over the naval visit to Kronstadt.[145] The ILP leaders also stressed that the Reval meeting would inevitably be interpreted as an effort to isolate Germany. MacDonald complained bitterly that Grey's diplomacy was dragging Britain into a disastrous triple entente which could only arouse distrust in Germany and so endanger peace.[146] The SDP also interpreted the visit as an attempt to 'checkmate Germany', and Quelch attacked King Edward for attempting to impose his own vision of a triple entente.[147]

The socialist MPs in the Labour Party took their battle to the floor of the House of Commons. Here they chose to highlight the horrors of tsarism rather than the probability of Germany's irritation over her apparent 'encirclement', perhaps because the Liberals were more vulnerable to protests which recorded the spectacular brutalities of the tsarist regime. Hardie, Thorne, and O'Grady set down questions for Grey and Asquith, some of which were deemed 'too argumentative' to be acceptable at the table of the House.[148] On 4 June the Labour Party formally moved a reduction in Grey's salary as a protest over the Reval visit. In the debate that followed both Hardie and O'Grady took a moderate approach, perhaps in an effort to win over as many Liberals as possible. If the visit sprang simply from Edward's desire to see his nephew, as Asquith contended, then could not the visit be deprived of its state character? O'Grady was careful

---

[144] *LL*, 29 May 1908.

[145] Editorial, ibid.

[146] On the encircling of Germany, see 'The Czar of Massacres', *LL*, 5 June 1908; 'The Debate of Last Thursday', *LL*, 12 June 1908; and *LL*, 26 June 1908. Hardie took the issue onto the public platform at Bristol on 24 May; see *LL*, 29 May 1908. The *Leader* also publicized the French socialists' protests over Fallières's visit, *LL*, 3 July 1908.

[147] *Justice*, 30 May, 13 June 1908, and editorial, *Social Democrat*, June 1908, p. 256. The ILP and SDP also united in passing a protest resolution at the BNC; see BNC *mins.*, 1 June 1908.

[148] Morris, *Radicalism against War*, p. 177; *LL*, 29 May 1908.

to observe that he did not want 'to reflect upon the honour of his Majesty the King' for whose peace work he had the 'highest admiration'.[149] Hardie, using material prepared by H.N. Brailsford,[150] dwelt upon the brutalities of the tsarist regime. When he was challenged by the Speaker on his use of the word 'atrocities', he refused at first to withdraw the offensive word but then backed down.[151] This uncharacteristic moderation was to no avail, for the Commons upheld Grey's policies by a vote of 225 to fifty-nine. Even so, the vote was a qualified success for the socialists in their campaign to awaken the labour movement to the tendencies of Grey's foreign policy. Of the thirty-two Labour Party MPs at this time, twenty-five were in attendance and all of these supported the motion.[152] Several trade unions and trades councils also protested over the Reval visit.[153] The beginnings of concern were evident, but only the beginnings. Neither the TUC Parliamentary Committee nor the TUC itself, which met in September 1908, made any statement on the Government's policy toward Russia.

The campaign against the Reval visit had a curious sequel which gave further valuable publicity to the socialists' case. In July 1908 it was learned that Hardie, Grayson, and the Liberal MP Arthur Ponsonby had not received the normal invitations to the King's garden party at Windsor. It was an obvious move of petty reprisal for their opposition to the Reval visit. Hardie saw the chance for further propaganda against Edward's tendency to interfere in foreign policy, and so he requested Glasier to write a 'peppery article' for the

---

[149] *Hansard*, 4 June 1908, IV: 190: 211–14.
[150] See H.N. Brailsford to Keir Hardie, 3 June 1908, in ILP Archives, 1908/240.
[151] *Hansard*, 4 June 1908, IV: 190: 252–9.
[152] Voting figures at *Hansard*, IV: 190: 266.
[153] Aberdeen TC *mins.*, 3 June 1908. The Triennial Conference of the Dock, Wharf, Riverside and General Labourers' Union also protested against the King's visit to Reval; see *Dockers' Record*, June 1908; see also ASE *Journal*, 1908. There was a struggle in the Executive of the Railway Servants' Society in September 1908 when a bitterly anti-tsarist comment on the visit was rejected in favour of a more mild comment for inclusion in the ASRS Parliamentary Report; see EC meeting, 14–19 September 1908 in ASRS *Annual Report* 1908.

Labour Leader to get the campaign rolling again.[154] The
Parliamentary Labour Party also came to Hardie's assistance
and it was decided that the secretary should write to the
Lord Chamberlain requesting that all Labour MP's names
should be removed from the invitation lists for official functions until such time as Hardie's name was restored.[155]

Developments in Persia in 1908 and 1909 also kept the
Russian agreement and Grey's foreign policy in the public
and parliamentary eye.[156] In the Commons the Labour MPs
repeatedly cautioned Grey against conniving with Russia
at any intervention to 'restore order' in Persia.[157] MacDonald
had personal contacts with Persian socialists, and, armed
with their reports of Russian military activity, he sought to
extract promises from Grey regarding Persian independence.[158] The fall of the Shah, early in 1909, did not erase
the impression that Grey had done nothing to discourage
Russian military encroachments because of the higher priority
he placed on the 'triple entente'.

Not until the Tsar's visit to Britain in August 1909 was the
labour movement as a whole finally stirred to protest over
the direction of British policy toward Russia. At the time of
the Reval meeting the Labour Party MPs had suspected that
a return visit from the Tsar would soon be made and they
had questioned Grey on the matter.[159] When the news of an

---

[154] J. Keir Hardie to J.B. Glasier, June 1908, Glasier Papers, I. 1. 08/43. See
editorial 'The King's Prerogative', *LL*, 3 July 1908. Hardie also spoke on the
matter at Stockport on 28 June; see *LL*, 3 July 1908. Jowett also wrote a number of articles on this issue for the *Clarion* and *Bradford Daily Telegraph*; see
Brockway, *Socialism over Sixty Years*, pp. 119–21.

[155] *LL*, 17 July 1908.

[156] For example, see the *Labour Leader*'s coverage of events in Persia. 'The
Shah's Massacre', 26 June and 30 October 1908, and 15 January 1909; 'Russia,
Persia and Sir Edward Grey', 16 July 1909.

[157] Hardie questioned Grey on 8 July 1909, and O'Grady also questioned
Grey on 13 July 1909; see *Hansard*, V: 7: 1399.

[158] J. Longuet to J. Ramsay MacDonald, 1909 (?), MacDonald Papers, PRO,
30/69/19 is a letter of introduction for two Persian socialists and a plea for
MacDonald to use his influence to encourage Grey to caution Russia. See also
ISB to MacDonald (telegram) 30 April 1909, requesting the same, LP/INT/08/1/
106, and MacDonald to Grey, 1 May 1909, LP/INT/08/1/108, in which MacDonald
asks whether Russia had guaranteed not to intervene against the Constitutional
Party in Persia.

[159] *Hansard*, 16 June 1908, IV: 190: 712.

impending visit broke in June 1909, the *Labour Leader* set the tone of the socialist press by proclaiming that 'no words of condemnation can possibly be too strong for this gross outrage on public decency and national sentiment'.[160] Grey was the target of particularly bitter criticism. In a full-page open letter in the *Labour Leader*, G.H. Perris accused the Foreign Secretary of establishing a personal dictatorship at the Foreign Office, based upon 'the unspoken assumption that foreign affairs are not fit matter for public curiosity'. Perris bemoaned the 'great game of encirclement' played by Grey, and remarked that if Grey stood for anything it was 'the policy of the triple entente against the triple alliance'.[161]

The most significant aspect of the labour movement's response to the Tsar's visit was that this time the Labour Party and the trade unions showed no hesitation in unfurling their banners against 'the hanging Tsar' and Grey's 'shameful alliance with Russian despotism'. The Labour Party executive was in the forefront, and, in a rare display of socialist unity, the ILP and the SDP rallied to assist the Labour Party's protest demonstration at Trafalgar Square in late July.[162] At the demonstration Henderson joined the various socialist speakers on the plinth.[163] Many trades councils and trade unions also complied with the Labour Party's special request for resolutions against the Tsar's visit.[164] The Trade Union Congress which met in September 1909 also responded to these events. Two congresses and two years had passed since

---

[160] *LL*, 11 June 1909.

[161] 'An Open Letter to the Rt Hon. Sir Edward Grey', *LL*, 30 July 1909. See also MacDonald's speech at a public meeting in Leicester to protest over the visit, *LL*, 16 July 1909, and editorial, *Socialist Review*, August 1909.

[162] Labour Party NEC *mins.*, 18, 22, and 28 June and 7 July 1909 for details on the demonstration arrangements and co-operation of the SDP. See also BNC *mins.*, 9 July 1909, where a call was made for joint protests.

[163] Henderson also joined Hardie and Grayson in denouncing Grey for sanctioning the Tsar's visit in a foreign policy debate in the Commons on 22 July 1909; see *Hansard*, V: 8: 646, 674–9, and 725–8.

[164] Liverpool TC *mins.*, 14 July 1909; Aberdeen TC *mins.*, 7 July 1909; ASRS executive 14–19 June 1909, in ASRS *Annual Report* 1909; Boilermakers and Iron Shipbuilders *Monthly Report*, August 1909; ASE *Journal*, July and August 1909; Boot and Shoe Operatives *Monthly Report*, July 1909. One union at least did not comply; see executive meeting 5 July 1909 in Operative Bricklayers' Society, *Monthly Report*, July 1909, where it was decided to let the Labour Party's invitation to the Trafalgar Square demonstration lie on the table.

the announcement of the Anglo-Russian agreement, so it was late in the day for indignation, but the TUC now proclaimed its protest none the less:

[the TUC] protests against the British government concluding agreements without first consulting the people of this country, and quite regardless of the abhorrence felt by the British people for the blood-stained Tsardom.[165]

The socialists' efforts to persuade their moderate trade union colleagues of the dangers to Britain and to peace involved in the Liberal Government's foreign policy were now making some impact. Their critique of 'secret diplomacy' and 'entangling alliances' was formally accepted at the highest levels of the trade union movement, and these same ideas were beginning to be discussed by the trade union rank and file on the local trades councils. Clearly, by 1909 there was an increasing awareness of the problems of diplomacy and defence in trade union circles.

[165] Quoted in Tsiang, pp. 133—4. The TUC went one step further and also protested over the police's seizure of *Justice* at the Trafalgar Square demonstration; see TUC PC *mins.*, 6 September 1909. On this incident see also *LL*, 6 August 1909 and Tsuzuki, *Hyndman*, p. 198.

7

Arms Limitation and the 'German Menace', 1906–1909

Meanwhile we have been in the throes of a naval scare. Well engineered it will bring us our eight dreadnoughts.

Lord Esher, *Journal*, Vol. 2, 20 March 1909, p. 378

1. The Campaign for Arms Limitation at the Time of the Hague Peace Conference, 1906–7

The victory of the Campbell-Bannerman Government in the elections of January 1906 had given great heart to those Radicals in the Liberal Party who took seriously the inheritance of Cobden, Bright, and Gladstone and cherished the vision of peace, international arbitration, and arms limitation. The Radicals looked forward to a programme of cuts in Britain's arms spending leading up to fruitful international negotations at the Second Hague Peace Conference due in 1907.[1] No doubt they confidently expected the co-operation of the Lib-Labs and the new Labour MPs, with their strong ILP component, in realizing their vision.[2] However, as we have seen the new Labour MPs seemed somewhat divided in their attitudes to the cause of arms limitation in the first months of the new Parliament. Most seemed indifferent to the issue. When in May 1906 the Lib-Lab Henry Vivian proposed a resolution calling for the issue of arms limitation to be placed on the agenda at the coming Hague Conference, no Labour Party MP spoke in the debate.[3] Neither the *Labour Leader* nor *Justice* saw fit even to mention Vivian's

[1] On the Radicals' campaign to have the issue of arms limitation placed on the agenda of the Second Hague Peace Conference, see Morris, *Radicalism Against War*, ch. 3.

[2] Since the late 1880s the Lib-Labs had maintained a fairly consistent record of opposition to increases in military spending in the House of Commons; see Tsiang, *Labour and Empire*, pp. 156–160.

[3] *Hansard*, 9 May 1906, IV: 156: 1383–1416. The resolution was agreed to without a division.

motion, absorbed as they were in the controversies over the Education Bill, the Trades Disputes Bill, and the unemployment problem. However, the ILP's interest in arms limitation was revived in July 1906 when the Government, in fulfilment of its pre-election promises, announced reductions of £2,500,000 in the naval estimates. Speaking as Labour Party chairman in the Commons, Hardie placed his party's support behind the policy of retrenchment and observed that the reductions marked 'the turn of the tide' and offered proof to foreign nations of the sincerity of Britain's purpose.[4]

However, it was clear that the socialists themselves were still not agreed as to the utility of the middle-class peace movement or of such government-sponsored peace initiatives as the Hague Conferences. One indication of the ambivalence of the socialist movement generally toward 'bourgeois pacifism' came at the meeting of the ISB's Interparliamentary Socialist Commission held in London on 17–19 July 1906. Here a disagreement arose as to whether socialists should attend the Interparliamentary Union Peace Conference which was scheduled to meet in London the following week.[5] Eventually it was agreed that the socialist parties should not be officially represented but that individuals might still attend. When the conference opened, even the normally optimistic *Labour Leader* sounded a note of caution:

Among the delegates there were many who, while professing international friendship, which is sincere enough, maybe, as far as it goes, are pledged in their respective countries to class privileges and monopolies, hostile alike to national and international peace. Still, only good can come out of their international communion.[6]

Hyndman and his followers in the Social Democrat Party were content to sneer at the 'hypocrisy' of all middle-class peace activists. *Justice* dismissed as insincere Campbell-Bannerman's call for the coming Hague Peace Conference

[4] *Hansard*, 27 July 1906, IV: 162: 80–1. See also the approving speech by the trade unionist and Lib-Lab Fred Maddison, IV: 162: 104–6.

[5] See the speeches of Troelstra, Molkenbuhr, Vandervelde, and Vaillant in 'Compte rendu de la première session plénière de la Commission Interparliamentaire Socialiste et du Travail (CIS)', in Haupt (ed.), *Bureau Socialiste International*, pp. 226–9.

[6] 'Hail Internationalism!', *LL*, 27 July 1906.

to discuss arms limitation. It was useless to propose arms reduction, argued *Justice*, without abandoning Britain's imperial outlook and cutting free from entangling alliances.[7]

The trade unionists for their part seem to have remained largely unconcerned with the coming Hague Conference and the arms limitation debate. In contrast to the enthusiasm shown in 1898 and 1899 for the First Hague Conference, very few trades councils made any formal statement on this occasion. Perhaps the very limited achievements of the First Conference, as well as the embarrassment of the Boer War that followed so closely on its heels, had been a rather chastening experience for those union leaders who had so uncharacteristically declared their position and campaigned publicly on this 'non-trade union' issue. At the TUC in September 1906 John Ward did secure support for his resolution which endorsed international arbitration and arms limitation;[8] but the resolution meant very little, for no attempt was made after the congress to popularize the peace campaign amongst the trade unions.

Nor did the socialists use the organizational resources available to them, as they might have done, in support of the Radicals' campaign to have arms limitation discussed at The Hague. Even Hardie's attitude to the 'bourgeois pacifists' seems to have hardened in 1907. In March he remarked that some peace activists were 'strangely inconsistent' in seeking to glorify Empire-building at the same time as they talked of peace.[9] He refused to join W. T. Stead's new Peace Pilgrimage, in spite of his good relations with Stead during the Boer War. Explaining his reasons for declining Stead's invitation, Hardie complained that Stead's *Review of Reviews* had supported the 'militarism' inherent in the Haldane Territorial Army scheme, and he added that he could not accompany

---

[7] *Justice*, 28 July 1906. For *Justice*'s response to the famous article by Campbell-Bannerman in the *Nation* of 2 March 1907 see *Justice*, 9 March 1907: 'We are a very virtuous lot now our belly's full!'

[8] TUC, *Annual Report*, 1906, p. 147.

[9] Quoted in *Concord*, 7 March 1907, cited in Morris, *Radicalism Against War*, p. 110.

Stead's wealthy friends, many of whom had made their fortunes by exploiting the labouring poor.[10]

The failure of the Hague Conference (15 June—18 October, 1907) seemed to confirm the predictions of the sceptics. The Germans refused point-blank to discuss the vital question of arms limitation, and the British refused to consider the proposal to abolish the right of capture of private commerce at sea in time of war. When Edward Fry, the eighty-three-year-old leader of the British delegation, tried to save face by introducing a pious resolution that the powers declared it 'highly desirable' to continue studying the question of arms limitation,[11] the *Labour Leader* commented that a 'quiet laugh' must have passed around the chancelleries of Europe.[12] The conference was 'rank hypocrisy', declared the *Leader*.[13] In the pages of *Justice* the Hague Conference was incessantly denigrated as mere 'humbug'.[14] In fact, the hostility of the SDP was assured by one dramatic incident at the International Socialist Congress at Stuttgart in August 1907. In a speech to the Congress Quelch described the Hague Conference as a 'thieves supper', and was promptly presented with a demand for a public retraction on pain of expulsion by the Wurttemburg authorities. His carefully phrased partial retraction failed to satisfy the authorities. During an evening reception hosted by the British delegates, Quelch was served with a notice of expulsion which immediately made him a celebrity in the eyes of the International.[15]

While the British socialists might complain of the 'hypocrisy' of the middle-class peace movement and basked momentarily in the reflected notoriety of delegate Quelch, it soon became clear that not all the representatives of the British working class professed the socialists' faith in internationalism and anti-militarism. In the military expenditure debates of 1906 and 1907, a small number of Labour Party

---

[10]   F. T. Whyte, *The Life of W. T. Stead* (London, 1925), Vol. 2, p. 289.

[11]   Morris, *Radicalism Against War*, p. 119.

[12]   *LL*, 23 August 1907.

[13]   *LL*, 2 August 1907.

[14]   *Justice*, 29 June and 12 October 1907.

[15]   *Justice*, 7 September 1907. The ISB itself had also issued a formal denunciation of the Hague Conference, see 'Manifeste contre la dissolution de la deuxième Douma et contre la seconde Conference de la Paix, 21 juin 1907', in Haupt (ed.), *Bureau Socialiste International*, pp. 292—5.

MPs, chiefly those representing dockyard and arsenal constituencies, demonstrated that they were not persuaded of the need for any armaments reductions. As noted previously, seven Labour Party MPs refused to support a motion proposing reductions in the army estimates in March 1906. Similarly, in the naval estimates debates of March 1907 a small group continued to defy the Labour Party majority. J.H. Jenkins, President of the Cardiff Shipbuilding Society and Labour MP for the dockyard constituency of Chatham, declared that reductions in naval spending meant unemployment in the dockyard towns. *Hansard* records his ardent support for the 'big navy' case:

Speaking from the Labour benches he was glad to have the PM's assurance that it was the intention of the government to keep to the two power standard. He was in sympathy with the whole of the arguments from Conservative members in reference to this matter. It was not a political question.[16]

In a critical vote on 31 July 1907, three Labour MPs, Crooks, Duncan, and Jenkins, refused to support a motion to reduce the naval estimates.[17]

These three desertions were not the only disconcerting aspect of the 1907 naval estimates debates so far as the socialist MPs were concerned. Several other prominent trade unionist MPs revealed in their speeches a fundamental sympathy for 'adequate' defence spending. This was a far cry from the socialists' determination to oppose all military spending as a matter of principle. William Brace, for example leader of the South Wales Miners' Federation, supported the cause of arms reduction on this occasion; but he hastened to reassure the Commons that the labour movement was a friend of the Navy. Indeed, he declared, 'everyone in the House is a friend of the Navy'. The representatives of the labour movement were 'just as anxious' as any member, he said, to ensure that Britain's Navy was able to provide 'sure defence of our shores and our commerce'.[18]

In the military estimates debates of March 1908 there were

16 *Hansard*, 7 March 1907, IV; 170: 1052–6.
17 Voting list given at *Hansard*, IV: 179: 1047–52.
18 *Hansard*, 5 March 1907, IV; 170: 700–1.

further indications of the differences of outlook between the socialist and the trade unionist MPs on the issues of national defence. Once again there was a small number of deserters from the cause of arms limitation. On 2 March 1908, only one Labour Party MP, Jenkins, refused to support a motion in favour of general reductions in military spending.[19] In his opposition Jenkins was joined by a number of prominent trade unionist Lib-Labs and miners' MPs, a disturbing development because the miners' unions were expected to join the Labour Party within a short time.[20] Jenkins's own motive was quite plain when on 9 March, he obstinately proclaimed that he 'would never vote for a reduction of men and displace labour until this government had seen its way clear to cater for the unemployed'.[21] Here was a rallying cry likely to appeal to more Labour Party MPs, for the whole of the labour movement was engaged in a national agitation for the 'right to work' at that time.

Two problems therefore confronted the socialist leaders of the ILP who sat amongst the Labour Party MPs in the Commons. First, the speeches of their own MPs and the Lib-Labs indicated that there was a strong feeling in the labour movement that defence expenditure should be supported if a real threat to Britain's security could be demonstrated. The socialists' determination to oppose the steadily rising arms expenditure on principle, as laid down by the International, seemed to have little support. Second, some Labour Party MPs had serious objections to arms limitation on the ground that unemployment relief should precede any reduction in arms spending. A small group of Labour Party MPs felt so strongly on this issue that they were prepared to support increases in armament expenditure in the lobbies of the House of Commons.

The problem of unemployment in the war materials industries obviously weighed most heavily upon the con-

---

[19]   Voting list given at *Hansard*, IV: 185: 467–72.

[20]   Ibid. The Miners' Federation voted to join the Labour Party in October 1908, on the understanding that the miners' MPs would not be called upon to sign the Labour Party constitution until the next election; see Labour Party NEC *mins.*, 14 October 1908.

[21]   *Hansard*, IV: 185: 1215.

sciences of those Labour Party MPs who represented dockyard
and arsenal constituencies or who held office in trade unions
whose members relied upon the production of war materials
for their livelihood. J. H. Jenkins, Will Crooks, Alex Wilkie,
and Charles Duncan belonged to this group. The problem
faced by Crooks illustrates the general predicament of the
group. Crooks was elected as LRC candidate in a by-election
for Woolwich in 1903. Even at that time the socialists of the
ILP were suspicious of Crooks for failing to mention the ILP's
support of his candidature in his election address.[22] Upon
election Crooks was confronted with the problem of rising
unemployment among his constituents, for the Balfour
Government was at that time scaling down operations at
the Woolwich Arsenal following the restoration of peace in
South Africa. Crooks quickly made unemployment his first
responsibility. He was a leading light on the Woolwich Joint
Unemployed Committee,[23] he enlisted the support of the
London Trades Council in his efforts to pressure the War
Office into a revision of the steady retrenchments at the
Arsenal,[24] and in the Commons he complained that the
Arsenal's difficulties were compounded by the loss of con-
tracts to private firms.[25] The retrenchments continued under
the Liberal Government. Late in 1906 the Parliamentary
Labour Party considered the question and sent a party of
six MPs to inspect the Arsenal and report on the chances
of putting idle machinery to work upon alternative products.
The Labour Party then pressed Haldane to appoint a
Commons committee to investigate the same matters, and
eventually Haldane complied.[26] In the meantime, however,
Hardie made it quite plain that in his opinion the employment
arising from military spending was not a sufficient reason to

[22] See J. Keir Hardie to W. M. Barefoot (Secretary, Woolwich TC), 25
February 1903; Banner to J. Keir Hardie, 25 February 1903; W. M. Barefoot to
J. Keir Hardie, 26 February 1903; W. Crooks to Brownlie (secretary, Woolwich
ILP) 5 March 1903; 'How I left the ILP out of my address I don't know. I am real
sorry and have been ever since I noticed the omission'; ILP Archives 1903/20,
21, 23, and 25.

[23] *LL*, 8 December 1905.

[24] See London TC *mins.*, 13 July and 28 September 1905, 26 July and
8 November 1906, and 9 May 1907.

[25] *LL*, 7 July 1905.

[26] *LL*, 23 November and 7 December 1906.

abandon the principle of arms reduction.[27] *Justice* and the
Labour Leader sympathized with the Arsenal employees in
their plight, and called upon the Government to provide
unemployment relief. The employees at the Arsenal, however,
demanded a more immediate solution. At a mass meeting at
the Arsenal in April 1907 they called upon the Government
to place more orders with the Arsenal.[28] Crooks maintained
what pressure he could on the Government, and he questioned
Haldane repeatedly during 1907 on the rate of dismissals at
Woolwich. When he enquired as to whether the Government
could not direct more orders to the Arsenal, Haldane
explained that the dismissals 'were the outcome of general
reductions in naval and military expenditure'.[29] Such replies
were hardly calculated to endear the cause of arms limitation
to Crooks and to his like-minded colleagues. Finally, in late
July 1907, it was announced that the Government had
rejected even the suggestions of the Commons Committee for
improving the situation at Woolwich. Campbell-Bannerman
himself then turned aside Crooks's personal plea for two
hours to debate the issues in the Commons.[30] There seemed
no escape from the fact that armaments reduction under the
Liberal Government meant unemployment in selected
regions.

It should not be thought that Crooks was alone in voicing
concern on this matter. In late April 1907 Jenkins introduced
a motion into the Commons calling for new dry docks to be
built at Chatham, that is, in his own constituency.[31] Jenkins
had not consulted any of his Labour Party comrades before
introducing the motion, and he was criticized in the *Labour
Leader* for this precipitate move.[32] His haste probably
indicates the growing impatience of some Labour Party MPs
on the unemployment issue, and their dissatisfaction with the

[27] *Justice*, 4 August 1906.
[28] *Justice*, 20 April 1907.
[29] *LL*, 19 April 1907. See also *LL*, 3 May, 26 July, 2 and 23 August 1907
which contain reports of Crooks's questions in the House of Commons.
[30] *LL*, 26 July 1907.
[31] The formal motion was that Item B in the naval estimates be reduced by
£100, to protest over the need for new docks at Chatham; see *Hansard*, 25 April
1907, IV: 173: 308—10, 337.
[32] *LL*, 3 May 1907.

priority accorded to arms reduction by the Labour Party leaders.

Thus, in the first two years of the Liberal Government, the only years of cuts in armaments spending as it turned out, there were already signs of restlessness amongst the Labour Party MPs. The stature of the ILP members among the members of the Parliamentary Labour Party, however, prevented any major rebellion in the Commons. Furthermore, it seemed in early 1908 that enthusiasm for arms limitation was also beginning to dwindle on the Radical wing of the Liberal Party. On 2 March 1908 a motion in the Commons in favour of continuing cuts in military spending had failed badly, attracting the votes of only fifty-three Radical MPs,[33] a poor performance considering the fact that 136 Radicals had signed a special anti-armaments memorial to the Prime Minister in November 1907.[34] With Campbell-Bannerman's death in April 1908 and the elevation of Asquith to the Prime Ministership, the Radicals' cause received a further set-back. Thus, in the face of a general weakening of the anti-armaments forces in Parliament and a rising tide of speculation in the popular press about the threat from Germany, the Labour Party's relatively firm stand in support of arms reduction seemed unlikely to escape challenge in the immediate future.

2. *The 'German Menace' Debate of 1908*

Relations between Britain and Germany had failed to improve with the arrival of the Liberal Government at Westminster in 1906.[35] Grey and his assistants at the Foreign Office had soon displayed their concern to preserve and strengthen the Entente with France even at the cost of creating a climate of coolness in relations with Germany. Britain's support for France at the Algeciras Conference in 1906, the conclusion

[33] Howard Weinroth, 'Left-wing opposition to naval armaments in Britain before 1914', *Journal of Contemporary History*, Vol. 6, no 4 (1971), p. 107.

[34] Stephen E. Koss, *Sir John Brunner: Radical Plutocrat 1842–1919* (Cambridge, 1970), p. 217 and Appendix 1.

[35] On Anglo-German relations in the years 1906 to 1908 see D. W. Sweet, 'Great Britain and Germany, 1905–1911', in F. H. Hinsley (ed.), *British Foreign Policy Under Sir Edward Grey* (Cambridge, 1977), pp. 216–24, and Zara Steiner, *Britain and the Origins of the First World War* (London, 1977), ch. 3.

of the Anglo-Russian agreement in 1907, and the clash of interests at the Hague Conference had helped to foster a sense of rivalry and estrangement between the two powers. Grey's determination to give primacy to the French relationship was also demonstrated in minor incidents: in September 1907 he vetoed a proposed visit by the Coldstream Guards' Band to Mainz, and in late 1907 Grey sought to downgrade the importance of the Kaiser's visit to Britain by resisting the German suggestion that Bülow should accompany Wilhelm. The situation worsened early in 1908 when sections of the press sought to embarrass the Government, at the time of a Cabinet struggle over the naval estimates, by publishing sensational reports of German naval growth. In February 1908 the Kaiser's indiscreet letter to Lord Tweedmouth was misrepresented by the press as a knavish attempt by the Kaiser to influence Britain's First Lord of the Admiralty. Edward's visit to Reval in June 1908 was yet another cause of irritation, the visit being interpreted in Germany as proof of the British plot to encircle Germany. It was therefore in the context of deteriorating Anglo-German relations and increasing public awareness of the so-called 'German menace' that the leaders of British socialism clashed publicly in the summer of 1908 on the question of whether or not Germany posed an immediate threat to Britain's security.

It was the old guard of the SDP, Hyndman and Quelch, who began the quarrel. The idea of the German threat had never really been absent from the pages of *Justice* since the Moroccan crisis of 1905. Early in 1908, during the press speculation on the naval estimates, the articles of Hyndman and Quelch became more alarmist. In February, Hyndman warned that Germany's naval preparations could only mean that she was planning an attack on Britain and France, and he added that in his opinion the German socialists had been quite unable to contain the Kaiser's militarism.[36] In March, he advised socialists to scorn 'sham peace twaddle' and speak plainly of the threat from Germany. He recalled that the German naval manoeuvres of the previous summer had provided clear evidence of her aggressive intentions:

[36] *Justice*, 22 February 1908.

If an immediate raid on the British coast had been intended, the arrangements could not have been more complete. What is the use of pretending to keep all this secret when everybody who takes the slightest interest in foreign politics knows perfectly well what is going on? The German Government I say, and I speak as a Social Democrat and a man of peace, is steadily making ready for an invasion of this country, and is building a fleet strong enough to cover that critical military operation.[37]

Such statements were no different in their essentials from the alarmist material in the popular press and the conservative reviews, except for the fact that neither Hyndman nor Quelch yet suggested that Britain should respond to this threat with higher armaments spending. For the moment, both SDP leaders simply affirmed their right to warn of the danger to Britain from the 'most active reactionary force in Europe'.[38]

Then, at the end of July 1908, Hyndman contributed an article entitled 'The Coming German War against Great Britain' to the *Clarion*, and this touched off a major quarrel within the labour movement.[39] Just a few days before the appearance of Hyndman's article, the Labour Party executive had issued a statement to the press condemning the 'reckless and mischievous attempts being made by small interested sections both in Britain and Germany to persuade the peoples of the two countries that a war between them is inevitable'.[40] The title and the tone of Hyndman's article seemed to be contributing to this sense of inevitability. However, Hyndman defended his position with great determination, denying that there was any underlying jingoism in his message.[41] He pointed to his own record of opposition to the South African War as proof of his internationalism. Crucial to Hyndman's position was his argument that it would assist in containing German militarism if socialists drew attention to the threat, whereas endless peace propaganda would simply encourage the Prussian military elite to assume that Britain was weak. On 30 August 1908, in an effort to make it clear that the 'German menace' theme did not mean the abandonment

[37] *Justice*, 14 March 1908.
[38] *Justice*, 4 April 1908; see also *Justice*, 27 June 1908.
[39] Tsuzuki, *Hyndman*, p. 205; see also *Justice*, 8 August 1908.
[40] Labour Party, NEC *mins.*, 28 July 1908.
[41] *Justice*, 15 and 22 August 1908; *Social Democrat*, September 1908.

of the internationalist convictions of the SDP, the party
executive reaffirmed the party's commitment to an 'entente'
with Germany so as to end the ruinous competition in
armaments.[42]

It should be stressed that at the root of this profound
concern over the German threat lay the SDP leaders' continuing disillusionment with the German socialists. The
inability of the German socialists to contain German militarism was a recurring theme in Hydnman's and Quelch's
writings at this time. In June 1908 Quelch had complained
bitterly that the ISB was not to be convoked until later
in the year in spite of the tensions between Britain and
Germany. In explanation Quelch recalled that the Germans
had not been in favour of the creation of the ISB in the first
place and, of course, had prevented a meeting at the time of
the Moroccan crisis in 1905.[43] In August 1908 Hyndman
warned that socialists should not overestimate the strength
of the SPD. The party had only half a million members, he
argued, and 'their full support could scarcely yet be reckoned
upon if it came to actual fighting'.[44]

Just as in 1905, other prominent figures in the SDP,
including Askew, Rothstein, and Hunter Watts, sought to
challenge the 'German menace' theme pursued by the leaders
of the party. This time the critics concentrated on the tactical
error of 'German menace' propaganda as much as they
disputed the facts about Germany's particular aggressiveness.
'Do we diminish the danger of war by encouraging our own
jingoes at home?' asked Askew.[45] Rothstein and Watts argued
that it was a serious tactical error to paint Germany in the
blackest of colours at a time when the press was bellowing
for more arms.[46] It was a propaganda theme which could

[42] *Justice*, 5 September 1908; SDP *Annual Conference 1909*, p. 11.

[43] *Justice*, 20 June 1908.

[44] *Justice*, 15 August 1908. See also *Justice*, 22 and 29 August, and November
7 1908. See similar stress upon the powerlessness of the German socialists to
prevent war in Hyndman's 'The antagonism between Germany and England',
Justice, 5 September 1908, and Quelch's argument that the general strike against
war had proved impossible in 1870 in *Justice,* 3 October 1908.

[45] *Justice*, 5 September 1908.

[46] See J. Hunter Watts 'Guardians of Peace', *Justice*, 29 August 1908 and
Rothstein 'Peace or Revolution', *Justice*, 26 September 1908.

only strengthen the popular belief that war with Germany was inevitable, which in turn added to the difficulties of achieving a reconciliation with Germany.

Meanwhile the ILP leaders seized upon the outbursts in the *Clarion* and in *Justice* as an unmatched opportunity to blacken the names of their socialist rivals in the eyes of the Continental socialists. The temptation to exaggerate was overwhelming. The *Labour Leader* declared that 'no more humiliating incident has disfigured the history of our movement'.[47] Glasier, as the *Leader*'s editor, wrote promptly to Bebel, Jaurès, and Bernstein asking for their response to the 'German menace' articles. Hardie produced a venomous and over-dramatic reply to Hyndman's 'gutter press insults' and Blatchford's 'absurdities' and 'hysterics'.[48] However, Hardie's criticisms were not all froth and bubble. He discerned real dangers in his rivals' propaganda, and he warned that the belief in a 'German menace' would lead them inevitably into an alliance with the advocates of security through Dreadnoughts and conscription; and indeed, within two years Blatchford would begin to support conscription and Hyndman and Quelch would advocate increased naval spending. Hardie also stressed that the cardinal sin of Blatchford and the SDP leaders was to add to 'the fatal feeling that war was inevitable'. Other prominent Labour MPs, such as Shackleton, Snowden, and Curran, supported Hardie and publicly attacked the German 'scare'.[49] Hardie also achieved valuable publicity for his views when, at the opening ceremony of the TUC in September, Arthur Richardson MP praised Hardie for his stand against the fomenters of chauvinism.[50]

The quarrel between the SDP and the ILP became particularly heated when, in early September 1908, the SDP's lone MP, Will Thorne, announced that he would soon introduce a private member's bill to give effect to the SDP's citizen army scheme.[51] The bitter arguments over the citizen

[47] *LL*, 14 August 1908.
[48] *LL*, 14 August 1908.
[49] *LL*, 21 and 28 August 1908.
[50] *LL*, 13 September 1908.
[51] Kendall, *The Revolutionary Movement in Britain*, pp. 47–8; *Justice*, 29 August 1908.

army were now added to the furore of the 'German menace'.
The ILP was aghast at the timing of Thorne's announcement
of his forthcoming bill. The *Labour Leader* proclaimed that it
was abominable that Thorne had chosen to 'unbag his little
abortion to the public gaze' during a press scare on the threat
from Germany.[52] It seemed to the ILP that their marxist
rivals were willing to exploit the worst popular emotions,
even an anti-German panic, in order to popularize their
citizen army scheme.

Although this quarrel had lifted the reputation of the ILP
at the TUC, the ILP had failed to pick up all the plaudits
on the Continent which Glasier had hoped for when he had
written to Bernstein, Jaurès, and Bebel. On the contrary,
Glasier's attempt to enlist the aid of the Continental socialists
rebounded upon the unfortunate *Labour Leader* editor.
Bernstein, who had a low opinion of Hyndman in any case,
dutifully contributed an article regretting the 'German
menace' propaganda.[53] Jaurès was absent from Paris and
could not contribute.[54] Bebel's reply was a brief, enigmatic
letter assuring Glasier that the socialist press in Germany
was taking Hardie's side in the quarrel, and reaffirming his
personal detestation of war and his party's determination
to do all it could to prevent any war. However, on the
Hyndman—Hardie clash he added:

For myself, I would not interfere in this quarrel. I do not like any
meddling in the differences which have arisen between foreign
comrades. It might easily lead to unpleasant consequences.[55]

Bebel then went on to recommend that the Labour Party
should not proceed with a projected visit to Germany by a
group of Labour MPs, because there was no need for any
'fresh assurances' of the socialist movement's desire for
peace, and because 'it would look as if in England people
were afraid of Germany'. Glasier, anxious to muster as much
favourable Continental opinion as possible, then published

---

[52] *LL*, 4 September 1908. For *Justice*'s reply see 'The Labour Party and the
Citizen Army Bill', *Justice*, 12 September 1908.

[53] *LL*, 21 August 1908.

[54] *LL*, 28 August 1908.

[55] 'Britain and Germany: Message from August Bebel', *LL*, 28 August 1908,
and see also the editorial, 'Bebel's Message' in the same issue.

the letter, in spite of the fact that Bebel's professed unwillingness to 'meddle' in the Hyndman—Hardie quarrel implied
that the letter was a private opinion only. Bebel was greatly
offended at the publication of his letter in the *Labour
Leader*, and he wrote to Vorwärts complaining of Glasier's
discourtesy.[56]

The 'Bebel letter affair' was perhaps a storm in a teacup,
and yet the incident revealed a good deal about the inner
workings of the German and British socialist parties. First,
Bebel's attempt to discourage the British Labour MPs from
visiting Germany tended to increase suspicions that the
SPD leaders were indeed reluctant to parade their internationalism before the German public, perhaps because they
had come to fear the 'anti-patriotic' jibes of the party's
opponents. Moreover, it seemed that Bebel was trying to hide
his reluctance to participate in internationalist gestures from
his own left wing. Glasier naturally resented the imputation
that he had betrayed Bebel's trust, and he and all the ILP
leaders were left to puzzle over the sincerity of Bebel's
internationalism. Second, Hyndman and Quelch were irritated
that the German marxist, whose internationalism they
personally doubted, should have the temerity to side with
Hardie in the dispute, apparently endorsing Hardie's charge
that the two SDP leaders were merely hysterical jingoes.[57]
Finally, Bebel was annoyed that, in spite of his wishes not
to be involved, he had been cast headlong into a British
squabble. No doubt he now considered the ILP to be as
impulsive and unreliable as Hyndman's SDP.

The timing of this squabble, demonstrating the fragility
of socialist fellowship, was particularly unfortunate. For, in
the autumn of 1908, several events combined to rekindle
international tensions.

In September there was renewed tension between France
and Germany over Morocco when a dispute arose concerning
deserters from the French Foreign Legion. Then, on
6 October, the Austrian annexation of Bosnia-Herzegovina
precipitated another dangerous war scare. Suddenly the ISB

[56] *LL*, 11 September 1908; and Letter from Glasier, *LL*, 2 October 1908.

[57] 'We cannot congratulate our Comrade Bebel on his letter to the *Labour
Leader*', *Justice*, 5 September 1908.

meeting scheduled for 11 October seemed fortuitously timed, and the agenda item inserted by the French, that the ISB should consider what combined action the working class should take to prevent war, seemed uncomfortably relevant. When the ISB met in Brussels, however, it soon became clear that there was still no certainty among the delegates as to what concrete measures could be adopted. After debate it was resolved that all socialist parties should redouble their 'vigilance, activities and efforts' against war, and should, in consultation with the ISB, continue 'to search for means and practical measure which, applied in a national or international framework, can, depending on the situation and the circumstances, best prevent war and preserve peace'.[58] In this convoluted prose the ISB signalled that it was still looking for something in addition to mass demonstrations to ward off war, but that nothing could be agreed upon. Neither of the British delegates present was satisfied with this result. Glasier warned the meeting that 'such obscure and meaningless resolutions can have no influence on politics'.[59] He noted peevishly that the demonstration held at the Maison du Peuple in the evening was 'a poor affair compared with what could have been done in Manchester or Bradford'.[60] Hyndman also confessed that he was 'disappointed'. He complained that both he and Glasier had detected

an apparent lack of deep interest in the business by those around us. . . It may be that we are passing through a period of transition in the socialist movement, and that a feeling of depression as to the vastness of our task is weighing upon the men in responsible positions.[61]

The despondency Glasier and Hyndman discerned was real enough in the case of the Germans. Molkenbuhr privately confessed at that time his personal misgivings that the International was straying from its true business, the 'workers policy', and was producing 'pompous statements' on international affairs.[62]

---

[58] *Compte rendu analytique*, ISB, 11 October 1908, p. 56.
[59] Ibid.
[60] J. B. Glasier to K. B. Glasier, 11 October 1908, Glasier Papers, I.1.08/30.
[61] *Justice*, 17 October 1908; see Glasier's endorsement of Hyndman's opinion in his own report of the ISB meeting in *LL*, 23 October 1908.
[62] Haupt, *Socialism Against War*, p. 37.

A few days later Kautsky and Ledebour arrived in London to speak at an international demonstration in St James's Hall on 14 October. The demonstration was held in an atmosphere of some tension, not only because of the war scare in the Near East, but also because of the recent strife among British socialists and with the German leader Bebel on the 'German menace'. At the St James's Hall meeting, Hyndman introduced the two German speakers and he took the opportunity of explaining that his own recent stress on the danger of a coming war with Germany sprang from his determination to arouse public opinion against war. Both Ledebour and Kautsky studiously avoided controversy in their speeches. They stressed the SPD's devotion to peace, outlined their own optimism that peace could be preserved, and urged the British labour movement to continue the struggle against war. Keir Hardie then rose to formally move the motion in favour of international peace, but to the great annoyance of the SDP members present, he used the occasion to attack the concept of the citizen army.[63] Even at an internationalist demonstration the two wings of British socialism could not refrain from strife.

The following day Kautsky and Ledebour were entertained in turn by both socialist factions, the ILP and the SDP seeking to extract maximum political significance from the courtesies shown by the two hapless Germans. Yet, in spite of the effusive goodwill reported at the ILP's luncheon at the House of Commons[64] and then at the SDP's reception at the Westminster Palace Hotel,[65] any sober analysis of the events of 1908 gave little joy to those who wished to see a feeling of trust binding German and British socialists together in their common campaign against chauvinism and militarism. The pursuit of the 'German menace' theme by the British marxists had now become a bitterly divisive issue, while the ILP leaders had themselves begun to puzzle over the reliability of the German socialist leader, Bebel. Beneath the veneer of

---

[63] For the proceedings of the meeting see the acount in *Justice*, 24 October 1908.

[64] *LL*, 23 October 1908.

[65] *Justice*, 24 October 1908.

conviviality, growing personal animosities and suspicions could be discerned.

3. *The Competition for Continental Favour*

Undoubtedly though, these suspicions and animosities took a heavier toll upon the fortunes of the British marxists than the ILP. Indeed, it is very likely that the damage done to the reputation of the SDP during the 'German menace' furore had a decisive impact on the long-running competition for Continental favour between the British marxists and the supporters of the British Labour Party. For, it was at the meeting of the ISB in October 1908 that the crucial decision was taken to reaffirm the Labour Party's membership of the International, a decision taken in the face of the most vehement objections from the British Social Democrats.

The decision was, for the ILP faction, a most gratifying climax to almost a decade of constant manoeuvring for leadership of the British section. The leaders of the LRC had been aware for some years how precarious was their claim to membership of the International, bearing in mind the LRC's spirited rejection of the SDF's efforts to give the party a clear and binding socialist objective. The rules of the International allowed the admission of bodies which formally adhered to a socialist objective and of 'labour organisations [trade unions] which accept the principles of class struggle and recognise the necessity of political action (legislative and parliamentary) but do not participate directly in the political movement'.[66] The LRC was clearly not an avowedly socialist body, and it was a matter of opinion as to whether or not it accepted 'the principles of class struggle'. Ramsay MacDonald admitted as much to Hardie in June 1906, when he complained of the International's rule for admission:

It is drawn with continental methods in mind and I am not at all sure but that it excludes us, because we are not an association which adheres to the essential principles of socialism.[67]

[66] Regulations of the Congress and of the Bureau (Brussels, 1912), p. 23, LP/INT/11/1/427. This wording was decided at the Paris Congress in 1900.
[67] Ramsay MacDonald to Hardie, 18 June 1906, LPGC/5/169.

No doubt the ILP leaders' awareness of the lack of ideological rigour within the 'labour alliance', at least compared
with the Continental parties, lay behind their continuing
efforts to court the favour of their 'Continental comrades'.
Jaurès was invited to Britain in 1905, and Hardie and
MacDonald made visits to the Continent in 1906.[68] Also, on
MacDonald's suggestion, a meeting of the ISB's parliamentary
group, the CIS, was held in London in July 1906. Elaborate
preparations for the visiting delegates were made (including
the presentation of volumes from the ILP's Socialist Library
series as souvenir gifts); and, no doubt, it was realized by the
ILP leaders that the occasion was a golden opportunity to
display to the Continental socialists the new parliamentary
strength of the 'labour alliance' group and the utter weakness
of the SDP. Only by special concession was Hyndman, who
was not a Member of Parliament, permitted to observe the
deliberations of the socialist parliamentarians.[69]

And yet, in spite of their eager pursuit of better relations
with all the Continental socialists, Hardie, MacDonald, and
Glasier had made no secret of their preference for the idealist
socialism of Jaurès and the revisionism of Bernstein over the
marxist orthodoxy represented by Bebel, Kautsky, and
Guesde. Hardie, for instance, was pleased to report after his
first ISB meeting in March 1906 that 'the old bureaucratic,
dogmatic, doctrinary spirit is dying out from the socialist
movement, which is passing from the speculative into the
sphere of the practical'.[70] During the years under study,
the ILP leaders seem to have become progressively alienated
from the German socialist leaders because they personified
the much-resented dour marxism which still dominated the
ISB. Glasier's comments were perhaps the most critical in
this regard. Reviewing the ISB meeting of June 1907, Glasier
wrote of Bebel:

[68] On Jaurès invitation, which was politely declined, see ILP NAC *mins.*,
23–4 February 1905, Hardie to Jaurès, 24 February 1905 and Jaurès to Hardie,
2 March 1905, ILP Archives, 1905/20–21. MacDonald spoke at the official
banquet held by the SFI0 in Paris to celebrate their recent election victory; see
LL, 8 June 1906.

[69] Moreover the SDP seem to have been kept in the dark over the CIS
meeting; see *Justice*, 14 July 1906.

[70] *LL*, 9 March 1906.

Were he a prosecutor at a court martial he could hardly betray less rapprochement with those around him. One wonders if he has the least emotion of that personal feeling of fellowship which we rightly cultivate between high and low in our British socialist movement.[71]

The SDP leaders on the other hand, always prided themselves on their apparent acceptance on the Continent as the only reliable socialist party in Britain. Thus, the SDP's hardline critics of the 'labour alliance', after having achieved their party's withdrawal from the LRC in 1901, continually claimed the support of the Continental socialists for their own stand. In 1904, for example, Kautsky had responded to a request from Quelch and had written an article for *Justice* which rebuked the *Labour Leader*'s revisionist point of view and reaffirmed the marxist faith of the German party and the 'whole of the International Socialist movement'.[72] As late as May 1906, Huysmans still listed Hyndman's *Social Democrat* as the chief organ for the publication in Britain of the reports of the International.[73] Naturally the SDP leaders were not going to surrender their position of pre-eminence in the eyes of the European socialists without a struggle. Thus *Justice*, as well as individual SDP correspondents,[74] never lost an opportunity of pointing out to socialist leaders abroad the so-called failures of the Labour Party, and in particular the party's refusal to adopt a socialist objective.[75]

However, the SDP's proud policy of socialist purity through grand isolation was progressively undermined by several developments. First, the success of the LRC in attracting trade union support, and then its achievement of twenty-nine seats in the 1906 election, led to persistent calls within the SDP for reaffiliation with the LRC.[76] Even more important

[71] *LL*, 14 June 1907.

[72] See *Justice*, 27 February 1904. See also other requests by Quelch for articles, Quelch to Kautsky, 13 April and 19 July 1904, and 16 April 1910, IISG Kautsky Archive, D XIX, 17—19.

[73] Huysmans to Kautsky, 4 May 1906, IISG Kautsky Archive, D XIII, 218.

[74] The outstanding example is Rothstein whose letters to Kautsky were always laced with venom against the LRC and its supporters; for example, Rothstein to Kautsky, 5 August and 14 September 1903, IISG Kautsky Archive, D XIX, 580—1.

[75] *Social Democrat*, February 1907, pp. 71—2.

[76] See SDF *Annual Conference, 1905*, pp. 11—12 and SDF *Annual Conference*, 1906, p. 14, where motions to reaffiliate were lost. But note SDP *Annual Conference* 1907, p. 9, where a ban on affiliation to local LRCs by SDF branches was lost.

for the SDP's reputation abroad, the apparently unbalanced reaction of Hyndman and Quelch to the Moroccan crisis in 1905, and their preoccupation with the 'German menace' in the years that followed, damaged the standing of the two leaders most closely identified with attacks upon the Labour Party. Certainly the German socialists could not have remained unaware of these developments, for the sins of Hyndman and Quelch were privately reported to the German socialists by their critics within the SDP.[77] From as early as 1902 Max Beer, London correspondent of *Vorwärts*, began to send to Berlin favourable reports of the LRC and critical accounts of the SDP leadership.[78] No doubt it was beginning to be realized by socialists abroad that the LRC, with its twenty-nine parliamentary members, had a more valid claim than the SDP to be the real representative of advanced working-class opinion in Britain. The SDP, by contrast, seemed more and more to take on the appearance of an insignificant sect led by an ageing and unreliable clique.

The struggle for supremacy at the International reached a critical phase in 1908. As was noted previously, after the unsuccessful attempts made by the ILP to change the International's rules of admission prior to the Stuttgart Congress in 1907, it became apparent that the Labour Party would have to justify its membership on the basis of the existing regulations. In September 1907 the ILP assembled a document which summarized the history of the LRC and put forward the case for the Labour Party's admission to the International.[79] The document reiterated the familiar arguments that had been used to justify the 'labour alliance' policy. Then, in an apologetic tone, the document explained that 'Wherever slight differences exist between the English Labour Party and the Continental Socialist and working-class parties, they are owing to the special conditions of English industrial development and particularly to English trade unionism'. Thus, the document concluded, 'we ask with

[77] See for example Rothstein's denunciation of these 'very queer sort of men' in Rothstein to Kautsky, 22 November 1905, 11SG Kautsky Archive, D XIX, 587.

[78] See Beer's confession to Hardie: Beer to Hardie, 26 August 1906, ILP Archives, 1906/319.

[79] ILP Circular, 3 September 1907, LPGC/19/267; Francis Johnson to Huysmans, 3 September 1907, ILP Archives, 1907/216.

much confidence that the Bureau will finally settle that the English Labour Party and the trade unions affiliated with it are eligible to be recognised as part of the international working class movement'.

At the same time the SDP's criticism of the Labour Party continued unabated. When the annual conference of the Labour Party in January 1908 affirmed that the party's candidates must appear before their constituencies with the title 'Labour' candidate only (and not 'Labour and Socialist' candidate), *Justice* argued more and more forcefully that socialist convictions were being submerged in the 'labour alliance'. In Quelch's words

the Labour group can never become a Socialist Party. On the contrary, the stronger it becomes numerically the less socialist will it be in character. . . The non-socialists are the predominant partner. They pay the piper and it is only fair that they should call the tune, and the socialists must humbly dance to that tune, whatever it may be; and they must not dance too fast or too far.[80]

Thus it was clear that the SDP as a matter of great principle, would oppose any attempt to confirm Labour Party membership of the International. For the Hyndmanites the ISB meeting of October 1908 was virtually an international trial of the policy of the 'labour alliance' which they had so fervently opposed since leaving the LRC back in 1901. As for the Labour Party leaders, and particularly the ILP men amongst them, they were seeking the endorsement of the International for their own ideological position—a formidable victory, could it be achieved, in the small world of ILP/SDP squabbles. Recognition by the continental socialists and admission to the Bureau also involved its own satisfactions and would, of course, be of crucial importance in forwarding internationalist and anti-militarist campaigns in the labour movement. Thus it was an anxious Ramsay MacDonald who, upon learning of the coming ISB meeting, urged Hardie to make every effort to attend in order to defend 'the admission to the Congress of such non-socialist groups as our Labour Party'.[81] In the event Hardie was unavailable, and it was

[80] *Justice*, 21 March 1908.
[81] ISB *Agenda Circular*, 7 September 1908, LP/INT/08/1/56; MacDonald to

Bruce Glasier who travelled to Brussels, where he successfully put forward the Labour Party case. On the motion of Karl Kautsky the British Labour Party's right to affiliate was upheld, with the curious explanation that, although the party did not formally recognize the class war, it carried it on in practice.[82] Thus, an excited Glasier telegraphed home the news, 'Labour Party fully accepted by Bureau. Kautsky moved the resolution. Great triumph!'[83] The decision so irritated the SDP that Kautsky was still offering wordy justifications of his actions as late as 1910, by arguing that no mass socialist party was possible in Britain without a firm trade union basis.[84] It was also the case that the International could hardly exclude the only successful British working-class party simply on account of its ideological haziness, especially when it was recalled that British—German enmity was looming as a factor of vital importance in international affairs. A realistic international socialist movement could on no account afford to break its connections with the major working-class party in Britain in this increasingly dangerous international situation. The Bosnia-Herzegovina crisis had, in fact, only just begun when the ISB met to settle the matter of British affiliation. It was in this tense atmosphere that the British Labour Party, by its own admission a non-socialist party, was confirmed in its membership of the Second Socialist International.[85]

Huysmans 14 September 1908, LP/INT/08/1/60; MacDonald to Frank Smith (for Hardie) 14 September 1908, LP/INT/08/1/61. Note MacDonald's comment here, 'I would go but I am very doubtful if our Nat. Committee would select me as the SDF element is predominant, I think'.

[82] ISB, *Compte-rendu officiel*, 11 October 1908, p. 42. The proceedings are the only ISB proceedings preserved at Transport House; at LP/INT/08/1/160.

[83] Telegram, Glasier to Labour Party, 12 October 1908, LP/INT/08/1/69; see also Glasier to Katharine Glasier, 11 and 13 October 1908, Glasier Papers, I. 1. 08/30—1.

[84] Kautsky in *Socialist Review*, May 1910, pp. 223—40.

[85] For the continuing controversy on the Labour Party's affiliation see Hyndman's reaction, *Justice*, 17 October 1908; Lenin's article, *Justice*, 28 November 1908; and the major quarrel caused by Max Beer's statement in *LL*, 27 November 1908, *Justice*, 5 December 1908, and Rothstein to Kautsky, 27 May 1909, 11SG Kautsky Archive, D XIX 590. Hyndman's resentment is best captured in a letter to Kautsky in July 1909: 'I hope you are satisfied with the further progress of your protégés of the Labour Party here'. Hyndman to Kautsky, 30 July 1909, 11SG Kautsky Archive, D XIII 234.

4. *The Naval Scare of 1909*

If the decision to reconfirm Labour Party membership of the
International did reflect growing concern among Continental
socialist leaders over the British marxists' apparent unre-
liability on defence and foreign policy matters, then the
events surrounding the famous naval scare of 1909 must have
reinforced their belief that they had made the right decision
in October 1908. For again, in this spectacular public
controversy, it was the moderate socialists of the ILP and
the Labour Party who seemed best able to keep their heads.

The history of the naval scare of 1909 itself has already
been fully outlined by several writers[86] so that only a brief
summary is necessary here before exploring the role of the
labour movement during the crisis. Regarding the origins of
the scare, suffice it to say that during 1908 the Admiralty
believed it had discovered evidence that Germany was
building ships of the Dreadnought class in advance of her
published timetable. In October 1908 these rumours of
German acceleration had begun to appear in the press, adding
to the sense of panic already engendered by persistent press
speculation about German imperial pretensions, German
invasion plans and German spies in Britain. In the Cabinet
discussions of early 1909, the advocates of naval expansion
were locked in combat with the 'economists' over Britain's
response to the German acceleration. Eventually Asquith's
compromise was accepted: four Dreadnoughts to be laid
down immediately and another four if German acceleration
was proved beyond doubt. In presenting the naval estimates
to the Commons on 16 March 1909, McKenna and Asquith
spoke quite openly of their apprehension over German
naval growth, both men seeking thus to overcome the
objections of the Radicals to the increased estimates. Their
alarmist speeches had the desired effect upon the Radicals,
most of whom 'scattered like sheep'[87] and accepted the
increases. On the other hand, Asquith and McKenna had

---

[86] Oron J. Hale, *Publicity and Diplomacy, with special reference to England
and Germany, 1890–1914* (Gloucester, Mass., 1964); E. L. Woodward, *Great
Britain and the German Navy*, ch. 10.

[87] See the extract from John Ellis's diary quoted in Morris, *Radicalism
Against War*, p. 157.

underestimated the response of the Conservatives and the press reaction. A full-scale scare erupted, the theme of which was that the Liberals had been dawdling in a fool's paradise, toying with socialist pension schemes while the services were starved of funds and the nation left in mortal peril before the Prussian monster.

Even before the scare was fully developed the ILP leaders were preparing to deal with an apparent 'boom' in invasion propaganda. In early February the *Labour Leader* singled out for attack the London production of Guy du Maurier's invasion drama *An Englishman's Home*.[88] MacDonald heaped scorn on this 'nonsensical' play in his public speeches at the time, and he promised that the Labour Party would not tolerate increased expenditure to secure the nation against the 'imaginary' invasion plots dreamt up by Lord Roberts and his satellites. 'The supreme need of the moment', MacDonald pleaded, 'is to come to an understanding with Germany'.[89] The socialists' insistence that the invasion threat was a mere bogey evidently prevailed at this early stage within the Labour Party. On 16 February Arthur Henderson, now Labour Party chairman, announced that the party would oppose any increase in the naval estimates in the coming parliamentary session.[90]

However, the debates on the army estimates in early March revealed some divergent views among the Labour MPs. J. A. Seddon reiterated his support for the Territorial Army, describing it as a 'bulwark against conscription'. Seddon also spoke enthusiastically about the need for defence and proclaimed that 'notwithstanding what may be said against the old country, I think it is still the best country'.[91] G. H. Roberts obediently opposed the army estimates, but in doing so he assured the House that he recognised the need to maintain the Navy in a 'state of efficiency'.[92] These were not the speeches of men opposed to all military spending on principle. In the final vote on the army estimates on

---

[88] *LL*, 12 February 1909.
[89] See the report of MacDonald's speech at Todmorden, Yorkshire, ibid.
[90] *LL*, 19 February 1909.
[91] *Hansard*, 4 March 1909, V: 1: 1651.
[92] *Hansard*, 8 March 1909, V: 2: 103.

9 March, two Labour Party MPs and three miners' MPs once again refused to support a motion to reduce expenditure.[93]

The publication of the increased naval estimates on 12 March provoked a hostile reaction from the ILP. The *Labour Leader* condemned the Government's 'gross betrayal' of its own principles and called upon the Labour Party to oppose the estimates.[94] The speeches of Asquith and McKenna in the Commons on 16 March and the scare that followed only stiffened the ILP's resolve. MacDonald claimed that Asquith and McKenna had made a 'colossal blunder' in provoking the scare: 'It is easy to be impressive when telling a ghost story to frightened people', he remarked.[95] It was clear from the outset that not all the representatives of labour in the Commons viewed the current crisis as just another scare. The speech of John Ward, the Lib-Lab MP, on 16 March revealed just how persuasive had been the 'revelations' of Asquith and McKenna. Ward contended that the Government was 'perfectly justified' in assuming that the German naval build-up was a challenge to Britain and quite correct to take precautions.[96] This was a blow to the hopes of the ILP, coming as it did from the most prominent opponent of 'bloated armaments' within the TUC.

Nevertheless, the Labour Party MPs seemed at first to be standing firm. On 17 March MacPherson and Henderson disputed that there was any peril to Britain. MacPherson dissociated the Labour Party from Ward's remarks and boldly asserted his internationalism:

We want to say to the German workmen from our places in this House 'We fight for peace in our country—you oppose, as you did oppose in the Reichstag all these estimates, and the socialist representatives and labour representatives must oppose them in this House'.[97]

Henderson questioned the Government's data, and accused

---

[93] *Hansard*, 9 March 1909, V: 2: 258; the two Labour Party MPs were Seddon and W. T. Wilson, and the three miners' MPs were S. Walsh, J. Haslam, and W. Wadsworth.

[94] *LL*, 19 March 1909. See also the report of MacDonald's speech at Latchmere Road Baths and Glasier's speech at Briton Ferry in the same issue.

[95] Editorial notes, *Socialist Review*, April 1909, p. 83.

[96] *Hansard*, V: 2: 977—9.

[97] *Hansard*, V: 2: 1123.

the Liberals of wilting in the face of Navy League pressure. If these increases were permitted, Henderson predicted, 'we may say ta-ta to all social reform'.[98] When the vote was subsequently taken on 17 March the majority of Labour Party MPs did indeed oppose the estimates, but three supported the Government. These were Crooks, Jenkins, and Alex Wilkie, the Dundee-based Secretary of the Shipwrights' Union. This was a small rebellion certainly; but the impression of relative unity among the representatives of labour was undermined by the fact that nine of the thirteen miners' MPs also voted for the naval estimates, along with two of the best-known Lib-Labs, Ward and Steadman.[99]

Outside the House of Commons the ILP endeavoured to resist the scare, and to put its case as to the origins of the naval rivalry. Central to the ILP's argument was the claim that the current sensation was a fabricated panic designed to undermine reform. The ILP argued that the competition in armaments must be halted because it was a ruinous and unremitting rivalry which could never achieve real security for either Britain or Germany. It was far better to come to a general understanding with Germany and to throw all Britain's diplomatic skill into achieving a naval agreement. Soon after the initial naval estimates debates of 16–17 March, Hardie and MacDonald, amongst other Labour Party MPs, took this message into the provinces.[100] Speaking at Sheffield on 20 March, Hardie presented what was to become the standard ILP explanation of the German naval build up. He advised the crowd to 'look at the situation as Germany saw it'. The Germans, he claimed, were increasing their navy in response to British provocations. Chief among these, Hardie argued, had been the Government's decision to go ahead with the new naval base at Rosyth, the refusal at the Hague Conference in 1907 to discuss the abolition of the

---

[98] *Hansard*, V: 2: 1133–8.
[99] *Hansard*, V: 2: 1142.
[100] See the reports of MacDonald's speech at Leicester on 21 March, Hardie's speech at Sheffield on 20 March, S. Walsh's speech at Wigan, and Seddon's speech at Blackburn in *LL*, 26 March 1909. Also see the report of Hardie's speech at Merthyr in *LL*, 2 April 1909, and G. H. Perris, 'The Panic Passes', *LL*, 26 March 1909.

right of capture, and the venomous anti-German press campaigns of recent times.[101]

In spite of the ILP's agitation, a small number of Labour Party MPs continued to desert the party whip on naval estimates voted throughout 1909. Those MPs representing shipbuilding unions and dockyard constituencies were clearly under great strain, for a serious slump in the ship construction industry in 1908 had already brought some hardship to their constituents.[102] Some Labour MPs also approached the problems of national defence from the old-fashioned trade unionists' viewpoint which suggested that the Navy was a sacrosanct cause above the superficial criticism of party politics. Alex Wilkie, followed this line in explaining his support for the naval expenditure increases of March 1909, when he informed the Commons:

I was always more or less of the opinion that in this House we approach the question of our first line of defence on non-party lines, and from a national or imperial position. Tonight, however, I am not speaking for any party, but I am simply speaking for myself. I am, and have always been, a strong advocate of an efficient navy.[103]

Wilkie went on to attack the German naval programme as totally unnecessary and blatantly provocative. The strength of the dissenting minority within the Labour Party was shown in a Commons debate in July 1909 on a motion to reduce the shipbuilding estimates. Barnes announced that the Labour Party would support this reduction motion, and he delivered a strongly internationalist speech, praising the German socialists' anti-militarism. Perhaps for the benefit of the Labour MPs from the shipbuilding constituencies, Barnes also noted that MacDonald would shortly be joining the German socialists in a peace demonstration in the shipbuilding port of Kiel.[104] Nevertheless, when the vote was taken, eleven Labour Party MPs supported the cuts, but five,

---

[101] From a report of the speech in the *Sheffield Telegraph*, 23 March 1909, a clipping from which appears in the Sheffield TC *mins*.

[102] Weinroth, 'Left-wing opposition to naval armaments in Britain before 1914', *Journal of Contemporary History*, Vol. 6, no. 4 (1971), pp. 114–5.

[103] *Hansard*, 22 March 1909, V: 2: 1548.

[104] *Hansard*, 26 July, V: 8: 924–8.

Jenkins, Wilkie, Duncan, Bowerman, and W. T. Wilson voted against the reduction motion.[105] Three of these votes no doubt reflected concern over unemployment in shipbuilding industries. As was noted previously Jenkins and Wilkie held positions in shipbuilding unions, while Duncan represented the shipbuilding constituency of Barrow. The two remaining votes, however, indicated a widening of dissent amongst the trade unionist MPs on the arms limitation issue. Neither Bowerman nor Wilson had any direct interest in war industries: Bowerman, a leading figure on the TUC Parliamentary Committee, was secretary of the London Society of Compositors, and Wilson held a position with the Carpenters' and Joiners' Union. One of the five dissenters, Duncan, was a member of the ILP. Even the socialist tag seemed to be no guarantee against desertion from the cause of arms limitation.

This small group of Labour Party rebels was probably less disturbing to the stalwarts of the ILP than the apparent desertion of the cause of internationalism by Hyndman and Quelch at this time. On the eve of the scare *Justice* was still warning of the 'German menace' and still insisting that the true safeguard against this menace was the citizen army. At the same time Hyndman and Quelch dissociated themselves from the 'German menace' propaganda of the popular press, arguing that the transparent aim of that campaign was the heinous proposal of conscription.[106] But when Asquith and McKenna presented their evidence of accelerated German naval building, Hyndman and Quelch gloated over the fact that their 'German menace' theme had now been confirmed by the Government's own intelligence experts. 'This Liberal government of peace and retrenchment is in a perfect panic, and we once more are completely justified',[107] Quelch boasted. In his first editorial on the scare Hyndman reiterated

---

[105] Voting list at *Hansard*, V: 8: 970. See also Wilkie's speech on the motion which was devoted entirely to the issues of wages and conditions of workmen in the dockyards; *Hansard*, V: 8: 969.

[106] 'We know as well as Lord Roberts. . . that there is a serious danger of a successful German invasion. But we intend to have a thoroughly democratic Citizen Army ready for service against domestic even more than against foreign enemies', *Justice*, 6 February 1909. See also R. Edmondson, 'War Inevitable', in the same issue and 'Labour Party and Conscription', *Justice*, 6 March 1909.

[107] *Justice*, 20 March 1909.

his conviction that Germany was carefully organizing an attack on Britain. He concluded with a call for a citizen army; and, without specifically endorsing the actual naval estimates increases, he noted that 'a sufficient fleet' was also essential for Britain's defence.[108]

The naval scare of March 1909 produced an even more remarkable response from Robert Blatchford. Like *Justice*, the *Clarion* had been stressing the 'German menace' from about 1904, and Blatchford had also joined with the SDP in advocating a citizen army to improve the nation's defences.[109] Blatchford's insistence on the danger from Germany had become more extravagant and alarmist in 1908 and had attracted the criticism of the ILP.[110] During the press panic of March 1909 Blatchford's *Clarion* began to advocate increased naval spending quite openly. In a celebrated series of articles in the *Clarion* Fred Jowett challenged Blatchford's assessment of Britain's peril; but the fiery independent socialist journalist refused to revise his convictions and it was clear he had been converted to the 'big Navy' school.[111]

The extent of Blatchford's conversion was dramatically revealed late in 1909. In December, on the very eve of the general election, the *Daily Mail* suddenly produced a series of ten articles by Blatchford on the 'German menace'. According to Blatchford, the peril of a German invasion was now so extreme that nothing less than an extra £50 million for the Navy plus immediate conscription could save Britain. Blatchford's desertion to the conscriptionists was a serious blow to the advocates of peace and arms limitation in Britain. For although Blatchford no longer had any formal links with the socialists or labour movement, he still enjoyed popularity as an able propagandist for the socialist cause. Several Liberal ministers, as well as the *Labour Leader* and *Justice*, saw the need to speak out against Blatchford's articles.[112]

Why had Blatchford consented to write his alarmist articles

[108] Ibid.

[109] Thompson, *Portrait of an Englishman*, pp. 186–7.

[110] For example, see the criticism of Blatchford's 'jolly rogering' in *LL*, 4 December 1908; and Thompson, *Portrait of an Englishman*, pp. 208–11.

[111] Brockway, *Socialism over Sixty Years*, pp. 123–5.

[112] See the review of Liberal press opposition and an extract from a speech of Lloyd George's in Thompson, *Portrait of an Englishman*, pp. 215–6.

for the staunchly conservative *Daily Mail*? His letters and his memoirs give some insight into his motives. In 1908 Blatchford had informed Alec Thompson, his trusted sub-editor on the *Clarion* that:

At present I am interested chiefly in the German danger. If I can wake up the country to that I shall have done as much as any man need hope or care to do. I don't think I can do it; but I will try.[113]

In September 1909, Fenton McPherson, a former socialist and friend of Blatchford, and now the *Daily Mail*'s foreign editor, offered Blatchford the task of reporting for the *Mail* on the autumn manoeuvres of the German Army. Blatchford accepted, and his visit to Germany heightened his fears for Britain's security. He confessed, 'I would lie awake and think: my God! This horror is marching steadily upon us and our people will not believe it'.[114] Soon after his return from Germany, Blatchford rang McPherson and offered his services to the *Daily Mail* free; 'I said I did not want payment... I wanted to get the public ear'.[115] Sometime in early November his ten articles were submitted to the Mail. In seeking publication with Northcliffe's *Mail*, Blatchford must have known that his articles would be used to reinforce that paper's theme that the Liberals were foolish idealists who had abandoned the nation to the German moloch. He evidently felt so strongly on the 'German menace' issue that he was willing to see his work used to evict the Liberals from office. The strengthening of Blatchford's emotions at this time is well illustrated in a note to Thompson written the following year:

The imperial situation is very much more serious than I have said. We shall lose India, we shall lose Egypt, we shall very likely lose South Africa; we shall be lucky if we keep Australia. These things are coming. I see no sign that our people will rise to the occasion.

[113] Blatchford to A. M. Thompson, ? 1908, Blatchford Papers, Manchester.
[114] Blatchford, *My Eighty Years*, p. 222.
[115] Ibid., p. 223. It is noteworthy, however, that in Blatchford's papers there is a review of the payment received for a later series of articles from 1911. Blatchford listed his assignments for the year, including 'German menace articles', which earned him £150, and he wrote 'I should say I earned about £18 per thousand words'. By 1911, warning Britain against the German menace was evidently a lucrative assignment. See the assessment of work and pay for 1911 in Blatchford Papers, Manchester.

You see the Labour Party have become the tools of the Liberals; and the whole of the British democracy are peace-at-any-pricers.

This splits the nation into halves. Also it cuts me off from the socialist parties. I am agin 'em. They will wreck the Empire.[116]

Clearly Blatchford had abandoned the internationalist and anti-imperialist ideals of the socialist movement.

At the end of November 1909 the Lords' rejection of the budget provoked a general election. After holding Blatchford's articles for over a month, the *Daily Mail* began to publish them on 13 December.[117] Their appearance in the midst of an election may not have been in accord with Blatchford's original intentions, but he did not protest.

This was too much even for Blatchford's sympathizers in the SDP. Quelch was astonished that Blatchford had chosen to write for the 'plutocratic jingoes' of the *Daily Mail*, and he attacked Blatchford also for expressing his anxiety over the safety of 'the Empire'. While Quelch agreed that there was a real danger from Germany, he also believed that a socialist was bound to work against the armaments rivalry and the spirit of national hatred.[118] In the light of *Justice*'s own 'German menace' propaganda, Quelch's readers must have found this earnest disavowal of Blatchford somewhat unreal. *Justice*'s editor seemed to be running away from the consequences of his own paper's favourite theme. None the less, *Justice* continued to refute Blatchford;[119] and in January 1910 the SDP executive formally dissociated the party from Blatchford's point of view.[120]

The ILP, having always steadfastly opposed the idea of the 'German menace', took up the fight against Blatchford without the sense of embarrassment that must have haunted the SDP.[121] The appearance of Blatchford's articles during an election campaign also provoked the ire of the ILP. Surely

---

[116] Blatchford to A. M. Thompson, 28 November 1910, Blatchford Papers, Manchester.

[117] Thompson, *Portrait of an Englishman*, p. 215.

[118] *Justice*, 25 December 1909.

[119] *Justice*, 8 and 15 January 1910, and see also F. Colebrook, '1909—1910' in *Social Democrat*, January 1910, pp. 2—3 and editorial, *Social Democrat*, February 1910, pp. 80—1.

[120] *Justice*, 22 January 1910.

[121] *LL*, 17 December 1909.

the danger of a German invasion was 'not so very imminent'
that Blatchford could not have waited a few weeks, protested
the *Leader*. [122] Evidently the German socialists were alerted
to this latest betrayal of socialist principles on the part
of an enemy of the ILP, for Albert Sudekum, a friend of
MacDonald, contributed an article to the *Leader* lashing out
at 'Blatchford's bogie'.[123] The *Labour Leader* concluded in
January 1910 that Blatchford was in some way psycho-
logically disturbed, his outbursts against Germany being
described as a 'super-manifestation of ego-mania'.[124] For the
ILP, the *Daily Mail* articles signalled Blatchford's eclipse: he
had ceased to count. 'He has filled the enemy with glee, has
scandalised the whole movement, and has become a betrayer
of the party and a peril to the cause. . . The pity of it; the
shame of it. After eighteen years',[125] lamented the *Labour
Leader*.

[122]   Ibid.
[123]   *LL*, 31 December 1909.
[124]   *LL*, 14 January 1910.
[125]   Ibid. See also *LL*, 31 December 1909 and 21 January 1910.

8

From the 'German Menace' to the 'Big Navy': The Discrediting of the British Marxists, 1909–1914

It is certainly a fact that your attitude on the present war scare tends to ally you with the jingo scaremongers quite regardless of your sentiments on the subject.

Zelda Kahan to Henry Hyndman *Justice*, 1 May 1909

1. *The British Social-Democrats: from the 'German Menace' to the 'Big Navy'*

Throughout the controversies over the 'German Menace' during 1908 and 1909, Hyndman and Quelch had been careful never to offend against the letter of the law so far as the Second International was concerned. They had never recommended extra military spending in reply to the German military build-up, and had spoken about 'adequate' defences or the creation of a citizen army as the solutions necessary for the military problem. Furthermore, they had always insisted that they were willing to come to a special ISB meeting to discuss these issues face to face with the German socialists.

None of this had shielded Hyndman and Quelch from attack from within the SDP or from abroad. Indeed, as we have seen, their critics within the party informed the German socialists of the waywardness of the two leaders and thus encouraged German suspicions of Hyndman and Quelch. In May 1909, Rothstein, fearful that the party would soon 'go to the dogs', wrote to Kautsky pleading with him to use his influence to bring about the ISB meeting asked for by the leaders, and so 'bring Hyndman and Quelch to reason'. Rothstein explained that the situation was desperate:

Our discussions in *Justice* seem to have some effect, but utterly insufficient, and whenever Hyndman confronts the members the latter quail. The Executive, as usual, is completely under the sway of

Hyndman. . . At our last Annual Conference on Easter Day we simply were afraid to raise the question, as we felt sure that the authority which Hyndman commands will prove sufficient to inflict a crushing defeat upon us, which will make matters worse than at present.[1]

Kautsky's reply is not preserved; but, judging from a further letter from Rothstein, Kautsky explained that the Germans had grave reasons for rejecting this call for an ISB meeting.[2] Perhaps the Germans responded negatively because they were unwilling to draw attention to their contacts with the 'unreliable' British marxists and so damage their own credibility at home. Hyndman had been calling for more frequent meetings of the ISB for some years now, and had requested a special meeting to discuss the Anglo-German naval rivalry in 1908. He renewed the call for a meeting in July 1909, but majority opinion on the ISB was against increasing the frequency of meetings.[3] This continuing reluctance on the part of the Germans in particular to meet with their fellow socialists on the ISB may well have been a decisive factor in the eventual decision of Hyndman and Quelch to publicly embrace the cause of the 'big Navy' for Britain. Signs of Hyndman's change of mind could be seen during the elections in January 1910. While *Justice* was still lashing Blatchford for his *Daily Mail* articles, Hyndman invited him to chair one of his election meetings.[4] In his election address Hyndman announced that he would support the conclusion of an international agreement to stop the ruinous arms rivalry, but he added that, in the meantime, he would vote 'for a strong Navy and the formation of a citizen army'.[5] At the annual conference of the party in late March 1910 Hyndman let slip some hints of the direction his mind was taking on the issue of national defence. While proclaiming that the party's record of opposition to war, imperialism,

[1] Rothstein to Kautsky, 18 May 1909, 11SG, Kautsky Archive, D XIX 589.

[2] Rothstein to Kautsky, 27 May 1909, 11SG Kautsky Archive, D XIX 590: Rothstein wrote, 'I now understand many things which I have not understood previously—among others, the reason why you Germans have always been reluctant to have meetings of the Bureau'.

[3] *Justice*, 17 July 1909; BNC *mins.*, 9 July 1909.

[4] Letters column, *Justice*, 29 January 1910.

[5] The address is reprinted in *Justice*, 29 January 1910. See also the equivocal statements on the 1910 naval estimates, *Justice*, 26 February 1910.

and chauvinism was 'absolutely unimpeachable', Hyndman pointed out that:

> It would be madness to overlook what is going on in every country—to imagine that we have entered upon a period when imperialist aggression and military ambitions are at an end, or to flatter ourselves that the workers in any nation are sufficiently well organised to impose the maintenance of peace upon their rulers when they have determined upon making war. The tremendous competition in armaments now proceeding in every direction must convince us to the contrary, even if our own experience during the South African campaign and the plain statements of our German comrades as to their inability to control German policy were not sufficient evidence of the truth.[6]

Hyndman's reasoning now seemed to be that if the workers could not prevent war, and if socialists were right in wanting to defend the liberties of Britain, then the party must support 'the provision of an adequate navy for the defence of our commerce and coasts'.[7] In a speech to the conference, Quelch too stressed that organized socialism was not capable of resisting war effectively.[8] He explained that in a war situation, 'when people get blood-lust upon them', patriotic reflexes would override all argument. A general strike against war would never eventuate. 'I can call spirits from the vasty deep, but will they come when I do call them?' he quipped. Still, the conference concluded with the usual resolutions denouncing the proliferation in armaments and calling for an entente with Germany and a citizen army.[9]

However, the dissidents in the party remained extremely mistrustful of the two leaders. Soon after the 1910 Conference, Rothstein wrote once more to Kautsky:

> I wonder if you could find time to write a letter to Quelch—Hyndman is past cure—on the errors of his attitude. I am sure a letter from you would have more effect on him than all the swearing I am pouring out on his head every time I see or write to him.[10]

Accordingly, Kautsky submitted a brief and rather ineffective article for the May Day edition of *Justice* in which he

---

[6] *SDP Conference 1910*, pp. 5—6.
[7] Ibid., p. 6.
[8] Ibid., pp. 20—23.
[9] Ibid., pp. 23 and 25.
[10] Rothstein to Kautsky, 7 April 1910, 11SG Kautsky Archive, D XIX 596.

provided arguments against the 'big Navy' point of view. Britain could secure her food supply in time of war simply by agreeing to the abolition of the right of capture of private commerce at sea during wartime, Kautsky argued. Moreover, Germany had no desire to invade Britain, for she did not wish to be saddled with more foreign nationalities within her borders. Britain, as an island, was 'invulnerable' in any case. Finally, Kautsky declared, the German elite would never launch a war against Britain because it would be strongly opposed by the German people 'thanks to the work of enlightenment carried on by German Social Democracy'.[11] These assurances cut little ice with Hyndman and Quelch. Both men had already made quite plain their view that neither the International nor German socialism could really prevent a German attack.

Suddenly, in July 1910, first Hyndman and then Quelch announced quite openly that they supported additional naval expenditure to maintain British naval superiority. In a move designed to give maximum publicity to his views, Hyndman wrote a letter to the conservative paper, the *Morning Post*, and it appeared on 6 July 1910. Hyndman proclaimed his belief in the need for an invincible Navy to protect Britain's freedom and independence, her food supply, her right to asylum, and her power to protect the small nations of Europe from despotism.[12] To ensure that invincibility, Hyndman advised, the Government should open a £100 million loan, to be funded by a cumulative tax on all incomes over £300 a year.

This remarkable letter marked a completely new departure in SDP policy, one scarcely reconcilable with the International's insistence that socialists must oppose every penny spent on militarism. Nevertheless, in the weeks that followed, Hyndman managed to bring such leading figures on the party executive as Quelch and H. W. Lee into the 'big Navy' camp.[13] Hyndman also prepared an elegant defence of his flouting of Second International policy. Britain had no

---

[11] *Justice*, 30 April 1910.
[12] Reprinted in *Justice*, 20 August 1910.
[13] *Justice*, 23 July 1910.

significant army and relied upon her Navy as a true defence force, he argued. 'The British Navy, consequently, takes the place of a Continental citizen army', he explained.[14] Hyndman also sought to justify his position by once again pointing the finger at the ISB and the German socialists, who, he asserted, had repeatedly refused his invitations to have the matter of Anglo-German relations discussed by the Bureau.[15]

Protests from party branches against the leadership's advocacy of a 'big Navy' now multiplied.[16] A flood of letters condemning the renegade chairman from Rothstein, Askew, and others, filled the letter columns of *Justice*. Quelch replied by reprinting a *Vorwärts* article that insisted that the German naval build-up was indeed for offensive imperialist purposes.[17] Zelda Kahan, an influential German expatriate and socialist, was outraged at this: of course the Germans attacked the militarism of their own government, but British socialists 'play directly into the hands of the Jingoes by helping to throw stones at the German beast, as though England were a poor, white, innocent, wronged little lamb'. Like Kautsky, Kahan insisted that Britain's security lay not in a bigger Navy but in seeking abolition of the right of capture.[18] 'War is not a chess game', Quelch replied sourly.[19] Another prominent critic, E. C. Fairchild, noted that the Hyndman—Quelch position provided the poorest of propaganda themes which could only lead to the confusion of socialists everywhere. For a great many socialists that was the paramount consideration: the people needed 'a plain, clear policy'.[20]

One of the interesting aspects of this dispute is its timing. The controversy erupted on the eve of the International Socialist Congress at Copenhagen which was due to open at the end of August. At the beginning of the month Hyndman declared himself ready to go to Copenhagen and face criticism

[14] *Justice*, 13 August 1910.
[15] *Justice*, 30 July 1910.
[16] Kendall, *The Revolutionary Movement in Britain*, pp. 53—4. See the terms of the resolution of the Central Hackney Branch in *Justice*, 30 July 1910.
[17] *Justice*, 13 August 1910.
[18] *Justice*, 20 August 1910.
[19] Ibid.
[20] *Justice*, 27 August 1910.

on the issue; but, he added, in a confused sentence, that 'thirty years of continuous, wholly unremunerated, and to me, most costly propaganda of revolutionary Socialism have rendered it doubtful whether I shall be able to afford the time necessary for so long an absence at such an awkward period of the year'.[21] Among his critics, Askew promised Hyndman 'a more than unpleasant quarter of an hour' at Copenhagen.[22] Finally, and without any explanation, Hyndman was not included in the party of British socialists who travelled on the SS *Titania* to Copenhagen in late August. Glasier, one of the ILP leaders on board, was not slow to point to the most obvious reasons for Hyndman's absence:

Hyndman we hear is not coming. Why I don't know. But probably it is because he is rather ashamed to face the Germans after his jingo vapourings, and probably because he realises that the SDF will be there in sadly diminished force and would thus symbolise the failure of leadership.[23]

Whatever the real reason, Hyndman's failure to attend the congress is another sign that his dissillusionment with the German party leaders who dominated the International probably played a role in his crucial decision to embrace the cause of the 'big Navy'.

The first serious challenge to the dominance of Hyndman and Quelch over the SDP on these issues came at the Easter conference of the party in 1911. Zelda Kahan moved a resolution with a crucial phrase calling on the party 'to combat with utmost energy the demands for increased armaments'. After long speeches from the antagonists, Quelch moved an amendment supporting 'the maintenance of an adequate Navy and a Citizen Army' as 'the immediate objects for which we should work'.[24] The conference divided 28–28 on the Quelch amendment.[25] Later, a branch-by-branch plebiscite gave victory to Quelch by a slim margin.[26]

---

[21] *Justice*, 13 August 1910.

[22] *Justice*, 6 August 1910.

[23] J. B. Glasier to Katharine Glasier, 25 August 1910, Glasier Papers, I. 1. 10/30.

[24] *Justice*, 22 April 1911.

[25] Ibid.

[26] Kendall, *Revolutionary Movement in Britain*, p. 54.

While Hyndman and Quelch had just managed to win victory in their own party on this issue, they were steadily losing their influence among Continental socialits. Certain comments made by Hyndman at the 1911 SDP Conference concerning the German socialists' unwillingness to co-operate in the ISB's peace campaign soon attracted the German's attention. Kautsky promptly asked Huysmans to institute an investigation for the purpose of exposing Hyndman's false charge.[27] At the same time, Hyndman moved to secure his personal reputation among the Germans by sending to Kautsky a long letter explaining his position.[28] Hyndman began by asserting that he had always been on friendly terms with Kautsky 'in spite of a serious difference between us on one very important matter'—no doubt a reference to Kautsky's role in the reaffirmation of the Labour Party's membership of the ISB in 1908. He then reminded Kautsky of his impressive credentials as a pioneer of socialism in England and as a dedicated anti-imperialist. It was, therefore, 'ridiculous and impertinent for anyone, however ignorant, to speak of me as a chauvinist', Hyndman asserted. He then reaffirmed his belief in the special threat Germany posed to Europe, and again justified his support for increased naval spending by comparing the British Navy to the citizen army concept. He explained to Kautsky:

I am quite satisfied that nothing whatever is to be gained by pretending that we are living in days of peace and international concord, and I am convinced that those who advocate disarmament by one power, while another imperialist power is arming to the teeth, as Germany is, merely invite and foster war.

A few days later, after reading an attack on his position in *Neue Zeit*, a German socialist journal edited by Kautsky, Hyndman dashed off another angry letter accusing Kautsky of allowing malicious 'lies' about him to be printed in *Neue Zeit*.[29] Clearly the 'big Navy' controversy had destroyed any

[27] Haupt notes this letter from Kautsky to Huysmans, dated 15 May 1911, in the ISB Archives; see Haupt, *Socialism and the Great War*, p. 32. It is not clear whether Kautsky had received Hyndman's letter of explanation (dated 11 May 1911) when he wrote to Huysmans on 15 May.

[28] Hyndman to Kautsky, 11 May 1911, IISG Kautsky Archive, D XIII 235.

[29] Hyndman to Kautsky, 15 May 1911, IISG Kautsky Archive, D XIII 236.

sense of mutual confidence between the SDP leaders and the German socialists.[30]

2. *The British Socialist Party, the 'Big Navy', and the Last Campaign for Continental Recognition*

This coolness in relations between British and German marxists had serious consequences for the fortunes of organized political marxism in Britain. To begin with, the doubts now surrounding Hyndman did much to take the sting out of the Hyndmanites' criticisms of the Labour Party abroad. Specifically, the British marxists' smug comments regarding the lack of unity on the Parliamentary Labour Party benches on the vital armaments issue now looked rather ridiculous.[31] Even more significant though, the bitter quarrel on the 'German menace' issue served to bring into discredit, both at home and on the Continent, the new British Socialist Party (BSP), a Hyndmanite experiment in socialist unity which made quite a promising start in 1911.

The new party was born of the desire to give a fresh impetus to 'pure' socialism in Britain. After years of fruitless negotiations over schemes of fusion or federation between the ILP and the SDP, Hyndman's followers finally elected to sponsor their own socialist unity conference.[32] The special conference, which it was hoped would attract dissident ILP socialists, was eventually planned for 30 September 1911 in Caxton Hall, Salford. The SDP leaders made a great effort to advertise the conference abroad by dispatching broadsheets to the ISB and to the various European socialist parties, a standard tactic for soliciting good wishes.[33] On receiving his broadsheet, a puzzled Camille Huysmans wrote to

---

[30] As Haupt notes, the controversy was continued in the pages of *Neue Zeit*; Haupt, *Socialism and the Great War*, p. 33.

[31] See, for example, *Social Democrat*, April 1913, pp. 169–70.

[32] This followed the failure of another attempt to achieve unity in 1910. For these negotiations see ILP NAC *min.*, 13 June, 7–8 July 1910; letters from H. W. Lee and J. R. MacDonald to the ILP secretary, dated 25 and 27 July 1910 respectively, also in ILP NAC *mins.*, and ILP NAC *mins.*, 12 August 1910 and 29–30 January 1911. As always, the stumbling-block in these negotiations was the ILP's insistence that the Labour Party must be involved in the discussions.

[33] One broadsheet can be found in the files of the Dutch Socialist Party; see IISG, SDAP Archive, Z. Letters from the ILP in this file also show that the ILP solicited good wishes from abroad.

MacDonald enquiring about his attitude to the proposed unity conference.[34] MacDonald replied curtly:

I do not think there is much use in trying to bring about socialist unity behind the back of the Independent Labour Party which, like my individual self, has not been consulted on the matter.[35]

Nevertheless, the European socialists were more generous than MacDonald in their opinions. When the conference met, many messages of goodwill were read to the delegates and proudly reprinted in the conference proceedings.[36] There were greetings from the German, French, Austrian, Belgian, Dutch, Romanian, and Serbian socialists, and a long note too from Rosa Luxemburg urging the ILP and the SDP to combine so as 'to secure the necessary influence to put the policy of the Labour Party on a socialist basis'. These were impressive credentials indeed, and, on the face of it, the new British Socialist Party which emerged from the Salford conference seemed well on the way to capturing Continental recognition as the primary socialist force in Britain.[37]

At the first annual conference of the BSP the new party decided to make an all-out bid for that Continental recognition by seeking separate affiliation to the International. Hyndman explained to the conference that the Labour Party had captured the BNC, and that the BSP was, therefore, forced to seek affiliation with the ISB in its own right, and thus to establish its claim to be 'the only definite socialist organisation in this country'.[38] Hyndman was adamant that the International's acceptance of the Labour Party in 1908 must be reversed. Quelch made it clear that in seeking separate affiliation with the ISB the BSP was indeed seeking to displace the Labour Party. In October 1912, he reported proudly that, while he had represented the BSP at the recent German SPD Congress at Chemnitz, the Labour Party had failed to send a delegate. Quelch concluded:

[34]   Huysmans to MacDonald, 14 August 1911, LP/INT/11/1/329.
[35]   MacDonald to Huysmans, 16 August 1911, LP/INT/11/1/330.
[36]   See the Official Report of the Socialist Unity Conference, Caxton Hall, Salford, 30 September to 1 October 1911, pp. 29–30.
[37]   See also BSP Conference 1912, pp. 47–50.
[38]   Ibid., p. 25.

The British Labour Party, of course, is out of its element in the International. It is avowedly not a socialist organisation—indeed, it is very unfortunate for us that our German comrades. . . should have insisted upon the admission of our Labour Party to the International Congress. By doing so they fastened upon us in international matters an incubus which had already proved a troublesome enough drag upon the movement in domestic politics.[39]

Thus, Quelch explained, the BSP was to seek separate affiliation, although that would not finally bring to an end a problem 'which can only be solved by the Labour Party conforming to the rules and conditions of the congress, or leaving the International altogether'.[40]

The BSP's request for separate affiliation with the International set a difficult problem for the ISB. At first it was decided that the matter should be settled at a full Bureau meeting, and invitations were duly sent out. When the invitation to the meeting and its alarming agenda arrived at the Labour Party offices there was some panic. Jim Middleton the assistant secretary, explained to Huysmans that this was the first they had heard of the BSP's request, and he asked Huysmans to consider holding this vital meeting in London, where, clearly, the Labour Party could more easily marshal its leaders and exert pressure on the ISB.[41] The Bureau meeting was eventually held at Brussels in late October 1912 as planned. The ISB was not to be rushed into a decision on this delicate matter. Although the ISB appreciated that the Labour Party was not a committed socialist party, it was obviously reluctant to offend the largest working-class party in Britain in order to admit a minor socialist party which would in all probability fail to attract a significant following. Faced with these unpalatable alternatives, the Bureau preferred to delay a final decision on the BSP's application pending a final effort to achieve

---

[39] Editorial, *Social Democrat*, October 1912, pp. 446–7.
[40] Ibid.
[41] Middleton to Huysmans, 1 October 1912, LP/INT/11/1/184–5. See also the string of letters from Middleton to the various Labour Party chiefs in an effort to get someone of note to the Brussels meeting, LP/INT/11/1/186–93. The request for a London meeting was not acceptable.

socialist unity in Britain, guided this time by the mediation of the ISB itself.[42]

Accordingly, an informal conference of BSP, ILP, and Fabian Society delegates, presided over by Huysmans and Vandervelde, met at long last in London on 18 July 1913.[43] According to Glasier, the two ISB officers adopted 'an imperative tone' and made it quite plain that further delays in the quest for unity could not be tolerated.[44] A break-through came when the BSP delegates indicated that they would abandon their long-standing objection to affiliation with the Labour Party if their candidates could be permitted to stand at elections under a 'Labour and Socialist' title.[45] This was to surrender the claim for separate membership of the International, so naturally a fierce battle raged over this surprising development in *Justice* immediately after the preliminary conference.[46] There was a good deal of opposition to the proposed compromise, but Quelch, the man at the centre of continuing resistance, was by now a very sick man. He retired from all active work in September 1913 and died soon after. The forces favouring reaffiliation with the Labour Party were clearly gaining strength. In any case, the ISB had made it perfectly plain that its desire to see the BSP join the Labour Part was more in the nature of an instruction than a request. (In August, Quelch had complained of the ISB's 'dictum' on this matter,[47] and in September Russell Smart noted that the BSP had 'received a request from the Bureau of such a serious character that it is tantamount to a command that it should affiliate to the

---

[42] BSP Executive Report, *BSP Conference 1913*, p. 38; *LL*, 7 November 1912.

[43] For the proceedings of the meeting see *Justice*, 6 August 1913.

[44] Glasier's diary, quoted in Thompson, *Enthusiasts*, p. 195.

[45] W. C. Anderson confirmed that this was the suggestion of the BSP delegates; see his comments at an ILP—Fabian Conference at Keswick, reported in *LL*, 31 July 1913.

[46] See Quelch, 'Shall we Haul Down Our Flag?' *Justice*, 26 July 1913 and F. Gorle, 'Shall We Raise the Red Flag in the Labour Party?' in *Justice*, 2 August 1913, and the continuing correspondence on this issue in *Justice*, 9, 16 August, 20 September, and 11 October 1913.

[47] Editorial, *Social Democrat*, August 1913.

Labour Party'.[48]) The BSP delegates were clearly under some pressure, therefore, when the ISB met in London on 13 December to consider the unity proposals once more. Agreement was suddenly made easy when, to the surprise of the other traditionally reluctant ILP delegates,[49] Hardie announced that in the spirit of compromise he would support a change in the Labour Party constitution to allow the 'Labour and Socialist' title to be used in elections. The BSP executive in turn agreed to request its party members to vote in favour of affiliation with the Labour Party. Hardie, Hyndman, and Webb also agreed to attend a series of 'socialist unity demonstrations' to mobilize support for unity.[50] In February 1914, as agreed, the BSP executive issued a manifesto urging the members of the BSP to support the executive's proposal to affiliate with the Labour Party.[51] It was clear that the proud isolationist policy, the political creed of 'pure socialism', as preached by Hyndman and Quelch from 1901, was finished.

There is no doubt that the proposal to return to the Labour alliance had good support within the BSP.[52] In May 1914 the membership of the BSP finally voted in favour of reaffiliation with the Labour Party.[53] However, the turning-point in this struggle had very definitely come when the International itself refused to support the isolationist policy of the 'old guard' and virtually commanded the BSP to return to the Labour Party. As if to make the International's view

[48] *Justice*, 6 September 1913. In October, *Justice* was forced to explain that the BSP had not yet decided to join the Labour Party, and *Justice* noted that a false report on the matter 'appeared to have emanated from Brussels'; *Justice*, 11 October 1913.

[49] 'Hardie has in a sense betrayed us', Glasier observed; see Thompson, *Enthusiasts*, p. 196. See also the ILP NAC *mins.*, 12 December 1913.

[50] For the proceedings of the 13 December meeting, see *Justice*, 20 December 1913; and see Fabian Society, *Annual Report*, 1914.

[51] *Justice*, 5 February 1914; *LL*, 29 January 1914. The BSP eventually applied for reaffiliation in June 1914. Hardie urged the NEC to admit the BSP, but the NEC voted to defer the application to the next Party Conference; NEC *mins.*, 30 June 1914. Because of the outbreak of war the BSP did not finally re-enter the Labour Party until 1916. BSP delegates returned to the BNC meetings in April 1914; see BNC *mins.*, 7 April 1914.

[52] See H. W. Lee to Kautsky, no date, 1914, Kautsky Archive, IISG, DXV 358; and also articles by Lee in *Justice*, 23 April 1914 and *LL*, 30 April 1914.

[53] *Justice*, 28 May 1914; *LL*, 28 May 1914.

crystal clear, Huysmans himself had addressed the BSP conference in April 1914, just a month before the vital ballot on reaffiliation. Huysmans reminded the conference that Marx had said he preferred 'a half-socialist labouring class to a complete socialist club'.[54] A repentant Hyndman, also addressing the BSP Conference, added an historic disavowal of his old guiding ideology:

Looking back upon the past thirteen or fourteen years he regretted that they had ever come out from the Labour Party. Had they remained in it socialism would have had a stronger hold among the workers.[55]

Why had the International chosen to retain its special relationship with the British Labour Party at the expense of the BSP? Practical rather than ideological considerations were most likely of paramount importance. The International recognized that a mass working-class party such as the Labour Party had to be given precedence ahead of the tiny BSP, no matter how 'pure' its socialism. Yet, just as had been the case in 1908, it is also likely that another factor played an important role here, namely, the apparent failure of the new BSP to stand boldly and unequivocally against militarism and chauvinism. The continuing squabbles on these issues in the BSP almost certainly added to the suspicions on the Continent that the new party, dominated as it was by the 'old guard' of the SDP, was destined to be nothing more than a small socialist sect, and a somewhat unreliable member of the International. For indeed, the same controversies that had so divided the SDP had flared up in the new BSP very soon after its formation in October 1911.

The final round in this long-standing quarrel can be quickly summarized. There was some sparring in the party press late in 1911 and early in 1912, and it appeared that the anti-Hyndman forces had at last found an articulate leader in the German expatriate Zelda Kahan.[56] At the first conference of the BSP in May 1912 the Hyndman group had

[54] *Justice*, 23 April 1914.
[55] *Justice*, 16 April 1914.
[56] See for example, editorial, *Social Democrat*, December 1911, p. 169, and Kahan 'Peace and its Perils', in the same issue, continued also in *Social Democrat*, February 1912.

stood firm, and Quelch gained the support of the conference for a paper of his entitled 'Socialism and Patriotism'.[57] Even so, a major clash came when, at a meeting of the BSP executive on 14 December 1912, Kahan moved a long resolution that involved a complete repudiation of the Hyndman–Quelch position. Through the Kahan resolution, the BSP recognized that 'there is nothing to choose between German and British imperialism and aggression' and the party was called upon to dissociate itself from the 'propaganda for increased naval expenditure'. Put to the vote this time the Kahan resolution passed by four votes to three.[58]

Faced with this virtual vote of censure, Quelch and Hyndman rallied their forces. In a major statement of his position in January 1913 Quelch reasserted his conviction that Germany was the chief danger to peace.[59] When the BSP executive met again in February 1913 the two sides were locked in a conflict and finally the Kahan resolution was suspended on Hyndman's casting vote as chairman, and the issue was turned over to the coming party conference.[60] At the Easter conference of the BSP in 1913 a final set-piece clash on this issue was expected. Certainly in his writings prior to the conference Quelch showed no signs of moderating his position.[61] However, events at the conference took a surprising turn. A resolution was put forward which attempted to side-step the issues completely by declaring that in a 'party of freedom' such as the BSP members were free to hold whatever views they liked on subjects apart from socialism 'such as armaments'.[62] This rather clumsy attempt to make the armaments issue into a private matter attracted some support from those who were determined to avoid a party split at all costs, but the Kahan faction refused to

---

[57] *BSP Conference 1912*, pp. 20–2.

[58] The resolution is reprinted in the BSP Executive Report, *BSP Conference 1913*, p. 37.

[59] Quelch, 'An International Policy for Socialists', *British Socialist* (formerly *Social Democrat*), January 1913, p. 9.

[60] BSP Executive Report, *BSP Conference 1913*, p. 38.

[61] See Quelch's reply to Kahan's 'Peace and its Perils' in *British Socialist*, February 1913, and Quelch, 'Socialism and Internationalism' *British Socialist*, March 1913.

[62] *BSP Conference 1913*, pp. 16–18.

accept this face-saving compromise. In her speech, Kahan pointed to the very damaging effect Hyndman's statements had upon the reputation of the party. She conceded that Hyndman was neither an imperialist nor a jingo, 'but', she protested, 'his views on armaments made people here and abroad think that he was'. Hyndman replied in a conciliatory tone, and he noted Kahan's courteous remarks. Then, in a move that was tantamount to a complete surrender on his part, Hyndman announced that he would henceforth keep his opinions on the armaments issue to himself, 'in order to avoid any disunity in the BSP'. His offer was received with applause. Quelch, who had seemed so immovable in the weeks prior to the conference, did not speak on the issue. Quite clearly, then, Hyndman's offer to keep silence amounted to a victory for Kahan and her supporters. In an obvious demonstration of this, the conference went on to pass a new resolution congratulating the French and German socialists on their vigorous campaigns against the increase of armaments and pledging the BSP 'to pursue the same policy in Great Britain'.[63]

In this manner, after intermittent controversy within the party over the 'German menace' for almost a decade, the party dissidents had finally triumphed over the imperious Hyndman–Quelch faction. This protracted struggle, as noted previously had begun to damage Hyndman's personal relations with the German socialists from about 1910, and the reputation of the SDP had certainly suffered too. The quarrels in the new BSP in 1912 and 1913 had also erupted at the very time the ISB was wrestling with the BSP's application for separate affiliation. Undoubtedly, then, the spectacle of still further squabbles over armaments in the BSP had weakened the party's chances of making good its claim for membership of the International in its own right.

It is important to see through the welter of rhetoric in this debate to the real issues at stake. It was always easy for Rothstein, Kahan, and their supporters to cry 'jingo!' and just as easy for Hyndman and Quelch to retort 'bourgeois pacifist!', but neither label accurately described the two

---

[63] Ibid., p. 18. The former resolution was withdrawn.

competing points of view. Certainly Hyndman harboured some long-standing personal grievances against the German socialists, and he and Quelch were suspicious of the Germans' evident reluctance to be active in the ISB in support of peace, but these suspicions hardly amounted to anti-German chauvinism. The insistence of Hyndman and Quelch upon an adequate British Navy was logically reconcilable with the International's acceptance of every nation's right to wage a defensive war. Conversely, the International's own dictum directing socialists to oppose each and every item of military expenditure was, if sheer logic was the only guide, inconsistent with the obvious need to maintain a military capacity to wage a successful defensive war. Indeed, that was exactly the point at issue—was sheer logic to be the only guide in this matter, or was the propaganda impact of socialist policy to be considered too? Here the International insisted that the spectacle of socialists pleading for 'adequate' defences, however logical, was poor propaganda in a crusade for peace. Hyndman and Quelch adhered to a very different assessment of the propaganda needs of the situation. They believed that ceaseless propaganda in favour of arms limitation for Britain would only encourage the predatory Prussian élite to wage a war of aggression. The debate, therefore, was not really one between loyal international socialists and wayward marxists who had been seduced by jingoism. It was a debate over tactics, involving different assessments of the propaganda impact of certain positions.

Yet the logic of the arguments of Hyndman and Quelch, and their quite genuine devotion to the ideals of internationalism, were really beside the point. For the fact remained that their advocacy of increased armaments for Britain went against the contemporary socialist consensus, and, in that sense, the two veteran marxists did irreparable damage to the cause of British marxism. Largely through the actions of Hyndman and Quelch, the British Socialist Party failed to contribute to the campaign against militarism and failed to win the confidence of the International.

9

Doubting One's Comrades: British and German Socialist Internationalism under Strain, 1909–1911

Prejudice is still very strong in these quarters.

Eduard Bernstein to Ramsay MacDonald, 8 October 1912.
MacDonald Papers, PRO, 30/69/3A/61

1. *The Labour Party and the Search for Continental Goodwill, 1909–11*

As the quarrels within the British SDP over the 'German menace' became more serious during 1909 and 1910, it had not escaped the attention of the ILP and Labour Party leaders that here lay a perfect opportunity to capitalize on the discredit of the Hyndmanites and advance their own cause within the International. In the rivalry for Continental approval, the moderate British socialists believed that they now held a decisive advantage over their marxist rivals. The ISB's acceptance of the Labour Party in October 1908 had been an encouraging indication of this. Therefore, during the period 1909 to 1911 the leaders of the ILP and the Labour Party made a determined effort to consolidate their victory of 1908, squeeze out their troublesome marxist rivals and present themselves as the only trustworthy socialist leaders in Britain. As explained in the previous chapter, the ISB's decision in 1913 to reject the Hyndmanite's claim for separate affiliation to the International indicated that victory had gone, in the last analysis, to the moderate British socialists. However, while the war was eventually won it should not be imagined that the moderate socialists were easily victorious in every skirmish. To the contrary, over the period 1909 to 1911, the moderates found it extremely difficult to overcome the lingering prejudices against them among their Continental colleagues. In particular, the British Labour Party bosses failed to establish close and friendly relations with the German socialists.

This persistence of cool relations arose principally from the great ideological distance which separated the two parties, notwithstanding the alleged tendency toward moderation in the SPD. The Labour Party, without a socialist basis and too often appearing as the ally of the Liberal Government, was a natural target for criticism from the German socialist press. The German leadership, under scrutiny from its own left-wing, was inclined to be wary of showing too close a kinship with its reformist British counterpart. But, in their efforts to be even-handed in all dealings with the British socialists, the Germans risked antagonizing both the 'labour alliance' group and Hydman's SDP. For its part, the Labour Party remained suspicious of the Germans' continuing contacts with the Hyndman group.

Relations had also suffered in 1909 when a serious quarrel erupted over a visit to Germany by a Labour Party delegation.[1] The story of the goodwill visit that turned sour reveals how precarious was the supposed spirit of mutual trust between the two parties. The origins of the quarrel can be traced back to October 1908, when, during the Kautsky—Ledebour visit to London, Hardie asked the SPD visitors to arrange for an invitation for a return visit to Germany to be extended to the Labour Party. However, on 5 November, the Germans advised Hardie that they preferred to issue a general invitation to all the parties affiliated to the BNC, since it was that body which had invited Kautsky and Ledebour to London.[2] The Germans, to cover themselves, then informed the BNC of this correspondence with Hardie.[3] A general invitation was obviously distasteful to the Labour Party leaders as it would mean that they would have to travel to Germany in company with Hyndman's SDP delegates. Irritated perhaps by the Germans' unwillingness to invite the Labour Party in its own right, the Labour Party leaders decided on a bold strategy to side-step the general invitation. Thus, on 23 February 1909 the Labour Party majority on

---

[1] The best source on this incident is the statement by *Vorwärts* at the end of the affair, reprinted in *Justice*, 19 June 1909.

[2] Ibid.

[3] The Germans did so because Hardie made no reply to their letter of 5 November; *Vorwärts* statement, ibid.

the BNC arranged for the secretary to inform the Germans that, although the official invitation to the BNC would be considered, a group of Labour Party parliamentarians would be visiting Germany independently.[4] On 9 March, Albert Sudekum informed the SPD that he had learned through a private letter from MacDonald that the Labour Party had refused to accept the general invitation addressed to the BNC.[5]

How was this rather devious plan devised? With the full support of the ILP Administrative Council, MacDonald had at first asked his friend Sudekum to have the German invitation altered. When Sudekum explained that the SPD executive were 'connected with Hyndman' and would not alter the invitation, MacDonald decided to make alternative arrangements for a Labour Party visit. Thus, when the BNC met on 2 April, the Labour Party majority brazenly explained that they were quite unable to accept the Germans' general invitation to the BNC and it was formally rejected. Late in April the Germans informed MacDonald that they were still willing to greet the Labour Party delegation; but MacDonald replied that the Labour Party had now made alternative arrangements through an international travelling club.[6]

All seemed to be going well until the delegation arrived in Berlin. Here, the German–English Conciliation Committee, which included several political enemies of the SPD, sought to take charge of the English visitors. The SPD were furious at this turn of events. MacDonald pleaded ignorance of the Berlin arrangements, and he insisted that the Labour Party had made its separate arrangements only because Bebel had seemed so unwilling to welcome the delegation when he had written to Glasier in August 1908.[7] *Justice*, naturally,

---

[4] BNC *mins.*, 19 February 1909; *Vorwärts* statement, *Justice*, 19 June 1909.

[5] *Vorwärts* statement, *Justice*, 19 June 1909.

[6] ILP NAC *mins.*, 21 January 1909; see Sudekum to MacDonald, 12 March 1909, in MacDonald Papers, PRO/30/69/5/19; BNC *mins.*, 2 April 1909. According to G. N. Barnes, the 'Travel Club of Walworth' arranged the details of the visit and they had passed on an invitation from the 'German–English Conciliation Committee' to the Labour Party inviting the visiting delegates to a reception in Berlin; *LL*, 11 June 1909.

[7] *Vorwärts* statement, *Justice*, 19 June 1909. See Barnes's letter to *LL*, 11 June 1909. See MacDonald's letters in *LL*, 18 and 25 June 1909; and Glasier to MacDonald, 13 June 1909, MacDonald Papers, PRO/30/69/5/19.

gloated over the incident and, predictably, reminded the Germans of their folly in admitting the Labour Party to the International in 1908.[8] In the end the whole affair was smoothed over, and yet the embarrassing quarrel in Berlin had served to underline the instinctive distrust between the British and German parties.

In spite of this public clash, and the consistently negative reports on the Labour Party flowing back to Berlin from German expatriate socialists in Britain,[9] the Germans endeavoured to preserve their policy of impartiality in all dealings with the divided British socialists. The policy was genuinely held; for instance, when approached by Hyndman's SDP for a loan to establish a socialist daily in Britain, Kautsky explained that the ILP would have to be involved in the venture before any German party funds could be provided.[10] But such gestures of neutrality bought little goodwill from the Labour Party leaders. New quarrels across the North Sea soon blossomed, frequently concerning the intensely critical coverage of the Labour Party's parliamentary performance in the German socialist press. MacDonald was particularly irritated by the 'tissues of nonsense' written by J. Köttgen, the official SPD correspondent in Britain, and a heated exchange took place with Kautsky on the issue.[11]

The high-pitched indignation of the Labour Party leaders suggested a certain unrealistic hypersensitivity on their part. For in 1909 and 1910 ideological heart-searching and consequent factionalism within the Labour Party were particularly intense, and it was impossible to hide their existence from the enquiring gaze of the Continental socialist press. After the election of Victor Grayson as a 'clean socialist' in the Colne Valley by-election of 1907, the murmurs of dissatisfaction over the policy compromise and equivocations

[8] *Justice*, 19 June 1909. See also *Social Democrat*, June 1909, p. 266, and the SDP Executive Report, *SDP Conference 1910*, p. 30.
[9] Rothstein to Kautsky, 13 December 1909, IISG Kautsky Archive, D XIX 591. Rothstein to Kautsky, day and month not indicated, 1910, IISG Kautsky Archive, D XIX 593.
[10] Quelch to Kautsky, 21 May 1910, IISG Kautsky Archive, D XIX 20; Quelch to Kautsky, 27 May 1910, IISG Kautsky Archive, D XIX 21.
[11] MacDonald to Kautsky, 7 June 1910, IISG Kautsky Archive, D XIV 301.

within the 'labour alliance' had become more insistent.[12] The dramatic resignations of Hardie, Glasier, MacDonald, and Snowden from the ILP Administrative Council in April 1909, when the ILP Conference appeared to have sided with Grayson, did not silence the critics.[13] When the elections of January 1910 resulted in a much reduced Liberal majority, the Labour Party's freedom of action in the House of Commons was virtually wiped out. As a result, the debate within the ILP became more bitter, with mounting criticism of the lack of independence now exhibited by the Labour Party in order to sustain the Liberal Government in office.[14]

Hyndman had not been slow in seizing the opportunity presented by the Labour Party's parliamentary predicament and the consequent in-fighting to impugn its reputation on the Continent. Shortly after the elections of January 1910 Hyndman appealed to his Continental colleagues to observe the Labour Party's virtual alliance with the Liberals, and he again argued that the International should reverse its decision of 1908 to admit the Labour Party. He recalled that the Continental socialists had set aside all his warnings about the Labour Party's evasion of socialist principles:

and now we have been proved right and our Continental authorities on socialism in England have been shown to be utterly wrong. All that we predicted has taken place. . . [The Labour Party] has become virtually an integral portion of the Liberal Party.

Now we do sincerely hope that this will serve as a lesson to our able but ill-informed socialist friends of the great European centres when they are dealing in future with English affairs.[15]

The jostling between the Labour Party and the SDP for the prize of Continental favour was clearly becoming more energetic during 1910. The Labour Party leaders certainly had no intention of surrendering the foothold they had

[12] On the Grayson episode see ILP NAC *mins.*, 15–16 February, 29–30 March, and 5–6 July 1907; and the coverage of his election in *LL*, 19 and 26 July 1907.
[13] See K. O. Morgan, *Keir Hardie*, p. 226–7; Marquand, *MacDonald*, pp. 113–15; and Thompson, *The Enthusiasts*, pp. 156–8.
[14] *ILP Conference 1910*, pp. 52–4. See the 'Green Manifesto' affair also in ILP NAC *mins.*, 12 August 1910, and 'Report from Head Office', 2 November 1910 in ILP NAC *mins.*
[15] *Justice*, 5 February 1910.

gained in the International in 1908. Indeed, Hardie seemed determined to suppress the voice of Hyndman's group in the International entirely if he could. At a Labour Party NEC meeting in June 1910, Hardie moved that the NEC should try to secure the abolition of the present BNC 'in order that the Labour Party should become the national body affiliated with the International Bureau'. This extreme proposal, a barefaced attempt to wipe out the representation of Hyndman's group, was not supported, the NEC preferring the more cautious approach of raising the matter of the BNC structure at the coming Copenhagen Congress.[16] But at Copenhagen a more straightforward tactic was tried. Realizing that for the first time the ILP—Labour group was represented in greater strength than the SDP, the moderates attempted to use their majority to seize the two British seats on the ISB and thus eliminate Hyndman's influence at one stroke. Only a last minute technicality interrupted this plan and SDP representation was preserved in the person of Quelch.[17]

This did not bring to an end the moderates' efforts to weaken the voice of the SDP in the International. During 1911 the Labour Party leaders attempted a more daring step. This was the take-over of the BNC itself, a move which would have given the Labour Party effective control over all official British contacts with the International. At the January 1911 Conference of the Labour Party, Robinson and MacDonald presented a report complaining that too few trade unions were represented at International Congresses and upon the BNC itself. With a view to strengthening the internationalism of the trade unions, as well as increasing the preponderance of the Labour Party over the SDP, they urged that every trade union affiliated with the Labour Party should be eligible for representation upon the BNC. The report contained a candid admission of the reasoning behind the suggested change:

The labour movement in this country has for too long been maligned and misrepresented by certain small outside sections which, neverthe-

---

[16] Labour Party NEC *mins.*, 30 June 1910.
[17] *Justice*, 3 and 10 September 1910, and *LL*, 16 September 1910. On this incident see also correspondence between Huysmans and MacDonald, *LL*, 14 and 21 October and 11 November 1910.

less, unfortunately have the ear of the Continental and American socialist and working class press.[18]

In response, the Labour Party executive soon produced a set of proposals for the BNC designed to remedy this defect.[19] The most important change proposed was that the Labour Party secretary should by right assume the secretaryship of the BNC.

When the BNC met on 17 February 1911 to decide upon a new constitution, the committee first considered a proposal to divide the positions on the BNC according to the formula of five to the Labour Party and unions, two each to the SDP and ILP and one to the Fabians. Then Hardie, characteristically the loner, countered with a more radical proposal. He suggested that only the Labour Party and the SDP should compose the BNC, a scheme which would, on balance, have improved the Labour Party's direct control over the BNC. Hardie's suggestion was not supported, but it had revealed his intentions quite clearly. Next the secretaryship issue was considered. Here the Labour Party's proposition that the post of BNC secretary should by right belong to the Labour Party secretary was lost.[20] Even so, MacDonald was elected BNC secretary. This meant that, although the Labour Party's right to the secretaryship was not accepted, the post was won for the time being.

Some confusion evidently surrounded these events. For in March, MacDonald requested the former BNC secretary, W. S. Sanders, to call the BNC together again to clarify the secretaryship issue. A rather peevish MacDonald explained his purpose to Sanders:

It is a great pity that you were misled to begin with, as I made it perfectly clear at the Executive meeting here [the NEC] that I would not possibly take the secretaryship, but that what was needed was a linking up of the two bodies.[21]

Accordingly, MacDonald reported to the Labour Party

[18] Labour Party, *Annual Conference Report, 1911*, p. 15.
[19] Labour Party, NEC *mins.*, 30 January 1911.
[20] BNC *mins.*, 17 February 1911.
[21] See the exchange of letters between MacDonald and Sanders, 21 and 22 March 1911; LP/INT/11/1/446–7.

executive in April that he had declined the secretaryship of the BNC as he had been elected to it 'individually, and not as secretary of the Labour Party'.[22] The Labour Party had some obvious advantages in this complex struggle: it was a simple matter for the executive to request Hardie, who was conveniently chairman of the BNC, to support MacDonald's call for a special meeting of the BNC to resolve the secretaryship issue.[23]

The showdown on this issue came just a week later, on 4 May 1911. At a rather poorly attended meeting of the BNC,[24] with only one SDP delegate present, the Labour Party's right to the secretaryship was accepted by three votes to two. F. H. Gorle, the astounded SDP delegate, reported later that MacDonald had told him that he was 'anxious to stop certain attacks on members of the Labour Party by some journalists and correspondents of the Continental and American Socialist Press'.[25] Later in May, MacDonald reported triumphantly to the Labour Party executive that the party offices in Victoria Street were now the official headquarters of the British section of the International.[26]

2. *The Weakening of the Labour Party's Anti-Armaments Position, 1910—11*

The struggles within the BNC certainly testify to the determination of the Labour Party leaders to improve the reputation of their party in the eyes of Continental socialists and, if possible, to silence the British marxists altogether. However, the attacks of the foreign socialist press on the equivocations of the Labour Party seemed not to diminish, much to MacDonald's displeasure. The ideological inadequacies of the Labour Party certainly explain a good deal of the continuing suspicion of the party in Continental socialist circles. But another important factor in explaining Labour's failure to capitalize on the discrediting of

[22] Labour Party NEC *mins.*, 26 April 1911.
[23] Ibid.
[24] Eight members were present, compared with fifteen at the February meeting; BNC *mins.*, 4 May 1911.
[25] *Justice*, 13 May 1911; and see also *Justice*, 27 May 1911.
[26] Labour Party NEC *mins.*, 25 May 1911.

Hyndman's SDP was the obvious difficulty the Labour Party itself faced in ensuring unity on the crucial issue of arms reduction. In spite of the efforts of the ILP faction, a determined minority of Labour Party MPs, now strengthened by the admission of the miners' MPs, refused to accept the policy of the leadership on this issue. Moreover, some of those Labour MPs who obeyed the whip and loyally voted against armament increases were quick to insist that they were none the less in favour of an 'adequate' Navy. Such statements were irreconcilable with the policy of the International, so proudly maintained by the German socialists, that *all* military expenditure should be opposed by socialists in Parliament.

The inability of the Labour Party to comply with the strict letter of the International's ruling in this regard was dramatically revealed during the army estimates debate in March 1910. MacDonald proposed a resolution seeking to ensure that employees of the War Office enjoyed conditions at least as good as those employed by private contractors and local authorities. However, when it became clear that the Conservatives would support MacDonald's resolution in an effort to defeat the Government, the Labour Party MPs were forced to abstain from supporting their own resolution, some actually voting against it.[27] This indignity served to reinforce upon the Labour MPs the stark truth that, since the elections of January 1910 had abolished the Liberals' safe majority, the cost of keeping the Liberals in office was a severe curtailment of the Labour Party's freedom of action in Parliament. The possibility of the Conservatives combining with the Labour Party in opposition to armaments was, admittedly, very remote; but the fear of 'turning out the government' was yet another reason for some Labour MPs refusing to oppose the Government's military expenditure.

None the less, the leaders of the Labour Party were determined to oppose the new naval increases announced in March 1910.[28] The *Labour Leader* sought to inspire the Labour MPs to reject the new increases by arguing that the scare of 1909

---

[27] *Hansard*, 8 March 1910, V: 14: 1317.
[28] See Hardie's remarks, *LL*, 25 February 1910.

should have taught everyone a lesson. There was also a hint of a threat in Perris's remarks in the *Leader*:

I repeat that a Labour Party which will stand this [increase] will stand anything. . . No Labour man who gives it his support will deserve to receive the renewed mandate of a labouring constituency.[29]

When the £40 million naval estimates for 1910 were presented to the Commons there came a series of powerful speeches against them from the Labour Party benches. Barnes and Henry Twist, the new trade unionist MP from Wigan, denounced the Government for sabotaging social reform in order to feed the 'imperial vanity'.[30] Snowden refused to accept any delay in social reform so that military spending targets could be met. He warned:

I will not betray the poor in order that the property of the rich might be protected. If there is to be money for Dreadnoughts there shall be money for the unemployed, or we shall make every hall in this country ring with our condemnation of the government.[31]

He ended his speech with the proud boast that the peace of Europe was safeguarded by the thirteen million men in Europe 'enrolled under the red flag of socialism'.[32] Yet, in the vote that followed, it was clear that not all the Labour Party MPs were enrolled under Snowden's red flag. Of the forty Labour MPs seventeen were absent, fifteen voted against the increases in naval spending, while eight MPs rebelled against the leadership and voted for the increases. It was the worst desertion from the ranks to that date. The list of deserters even included one ILP member, J. A. Seddon, and one member of the socialist-dominated BNC, namely John Hodge.[33]

The speeches of the moderate Labour MPs in the 1910 military estimates debates gave some indications of the feelings within the Labour Party that led to these desertions.

---

[29] G. H. Perris, 'The Cost of Provocation—Labour's Reply to the Navy Estimates', *LL*, 18 March 1910.
[30] *Hansard*, 14 March 1910, V: 15: 69—81; *Hansard*, 15 March 1910, V: 15: 228—34.
[31] *Hansard*, 15 March 1910, V: 15: 307.
[32] Ibid. See also Snowden's speech at Ipswich on 20 March, in *LL*, 25 March 1910.
[33] *Hansard*, 15 March 1910, V: 15: 315—18.

For instance, G. H. Roberts, who in fact opposed the increases in naval spending, declared that opposition members were quite wrong if they imagined that the Labour Party was opposed to an efficient navy. He explained that Labour was agreed that the Navy must be strong enough to defend the nation:

We look upon the Navy as a force of national insurance, and the real difference between us is that we on these benches say that every pound spent in insurance premium beyond what is actually necessary is a waste of national resources.[34]

According to Roberts, then, most labour MPs did not vote against naval expenditure out of any sense of loyalty to the International's policy of parliamentary opposition to all military expenditure. J. A. Seddon's explanation of his decision to support the increases in naval spending also affords an insight into the sentiments of rank-and-file labour supporters. Seddon maintained that he had supported the increases in order to give the working people a shock. He argued that:

Our difficulty is patent to every labour candidate. Declaim against war and the crowd will cheer. Place reduction of armaments in your election address, the same crowd will reject you.

Give them a rude shock. . . estimates that will stagger humanity. If this fails, I see nothing but a bloody armageddon.[35]

Seddon's opinions, dubious as they may be in terms of logic, certainly do betray the Labour MPs sensitivity to the apparent lack of enthusiasm for arms reduction in the constituencies. The members from dockyard towns were, of course, particularly sensitive to that lack of enthusiasm. 'They are only human',[36] commented Barnes. Fear of unemployment, arising from armaments reductions, was now sufficiently widespread that even at the ILP Conference in late March 1910 there were some objections raised to the long-standing policy of opposition to military expenditure, objections

[34] *Hansard*, 16 March 1910, V: 15: 445–6. See also Roberts's speech on the army estimates where he made similar comments; *Hansard*, 8 March 1910, V: 14: 1399–1404.
[35] *LL*, 8 April 1910.
[36] Ibid.

which the *Labour Leader* unsympathetically dismissed as 'More Dreadnought patriotics'.[37]

It is also important to note that many Labour MPs clearly felt 'out of their depth' on defence and foreign policy matters. There was even a tendency to defer to the opinions of 'experts' on such matters and to suggest that defence was somehow above party. Henry Twist had acknowledged during the 1910 naval estimates debate that he had no 'expert knowledge' on the subject, nor 'the same knowledge of details which a naval officer speaking as a member of this House can claim'.[38] G. H. Roberts had been exceedingly deferential during the same debate:

I find it to be extremely difficult to understand the policy of the nation and what standard of naval efficiency should be adjusted to that policy. I agree with all Hon. Members that questions like the Navy ought to be lifted far above the sphere of party, and I can assure the most anxious Hon. Members on the other side of the House that we who are called socialists or labour men are desirous to get to understand what is best in the interests of the nation from the standpoint of its security and its safeguarding.[39]

Old trade union approaches to problems of national defence had clearly not vanished from the political outlook of the new Labour MPs.

The predicament of the Labour Party leadership on the armaments issue was compounded by the fact that, although there was little risk to the Government in the Labour MPs opposing military expenditure at the estimates stage, the life of the Government did depend upon the Labour MPs supporting the budget as a whole in the final stage. Thus, the Labour Party had come to support the Government's entire budget, including the military expenditure provisions. At the International Congress at Copenhagen, therefore, it was not only the group of deserters on the arms issue who came under attack but the whole of the Labour Party. Ledebour, the German left-wing socialist, accused the British Labour MPs of keeping the Liberals in office in spite of the massive increases in military expenditure. This was a humiliating

[37] *LL*, 1 April 1910.
[38] *Hansard*, 15 March 1910, V: 15: 228.
[39] *Hansard*, 15 March 1910, V: 15: 446.

dressing-down at the very moment when the Labour Party leaders had hoped that their star was rising and that of the 'socialist jingo' Hyndman was falling.[40]

Even before Copenhagen the ILP had decided on a major initiative of its own—a sustained propaganda campaign for arms reduction in the coming autumn. No doubt the ILP hoped to exert pressure on the recalcitrant Labour Party MPs on this issue as much as they hoped to bring militarism to the attention of the British public. The 'autumn campaign' was planned in detail by the ILP chairman, W. C. Anderson; and the National Peace Council and the Society of Friends co-operated by sending free literature for distribution.[41] The heart of the campaign was a continuing series of public meetings addressed by the most well-known ILP leaders. Hardie and MacDonald in particular threw themselves unstintingly into the campaign, speaking in the major towns and cities of Britain constantly throughout October 1910.[42] The crowds present at these meetings were enjoined to pass a resolution condemning the armaments burden and the threat of compulsory military service and urging the workers to take 'organized action' with their comrades in Germany to defeat the 'scare-mongers and war-makers'.[43] From all accounts the campaign went well. However, it was symptomatic of the unrest in the ILP at the time that some branches complained about the party's obsession with a basically 'Liberal' concern.[44]

The climax of the 'autumn campaign' was a great international meeting on 10 December at the Albert Hall in London, an ambitious project which strained the finances of the ILP. Vandervelde, Jaurès, and Molkenbuhr attended, and elaborate preparations were made to provide an inspiring evening. The Woolwich Pioneer Labour Choir set the scene with songs from *Judas Maccabaeus*, including 'We will never bow down'. The tone of the speeches that followed was

---

[40] *ISC Proceedings 1910*, pp. 186–99.
[41] ILP NAC *mins.*, 12 August 1910; *LL*, 21 October 1910.
[42] See MacDonald's press cuttings, MacDonald Papers, PRO/30/69/5/85.
[43] ILP NAC *mins.*, 9 September 1910.
[44] *Mins.* of ILP Divisional Council 6, 19 November 1910, LSE Herbert Burrows Collection; see also *LL*, 28 October 1910.

radical, with Hardie, Vandervelde, and Jaurès mentioning the general strike as a means of preventing war. Jaurès exclaimed that 'the long-enduring proletariat are tired of being the straw with which the middle-class, the militarist, and the rich light the flame of their glory'.[45] The next evening a crowd of six thousand at St George's Hall, Bradford, listened as Jaurès, Vandervelde, and Molkenbuhr repeated their speeches. As a comment on the meetings, it may be noted that Mills, editor of the *Labour Leader*, was drawn, like so many of the ILP leaders, to Jaurès's style and somewhat disappointed by the German-speaking Molkenbuhr. 'If Jaurès typified feelings, Molkenbuhr stood for facts', Mills observed kindly.[46]

The autumn campaign coincided with an attempt on the part of the ILP to put pressure on the Labour Party to declare a firm policy on arms reduction and so curb the rebel MPs. In April 1910, the ILP Administrative Council had suggested that the Labour Party should hold a special conference on armaments, and Lansbury and Anderson were sent as a deputation to put the ILP's view on the matter at the next meeting of the Labour Party executive.[47] However, when the executive met in June to consider the proposal, 'next business' was successfully moved and, in a humiliating incident, the ILP deputation was turned away.[48] Obviously there was some resentment building up against the ILP's passionate commitment to the cause of arms limitation. Undeterred, the ILP Administrative Council, meeting in July 1910, decided to approach the Labour Party once again.[49] This time the ILP was successful; and Glasier was given the task of drawing up a resolution for a special conference on arms limitation to be held immediately before the regular Labour Party Annual Conference scheduled to meet in Leicester in January 1911.[50]

[45] *LL*, 16 December 1910; and see J. B. Glasier to Lizzie Glasier, 12 December 1910, Glasier Papers, I. 1. 10/12.
[46] *LL*, 16 December 1910.
[47] ILP NAC *mins.*, 21–2 April 1910.
[48] Labour Party NEC *mins.*, 30 June 1910.
[49] ILP NAC *mins.*, 7–8 July 1910.
[50] J. B. Glasier to Francis Johnson, 30 October 1910, Glasier Papers, I. 1. 1910/63.

The special conference on 'Disarmament and the present International Situation' duly gathered on 31 January 1911.[51] MacDonald opened the proceedings with a powerful speech attacking the Government's anti-German foreign policy and its boundless faith in security through ever-increasing armaments. There was 'extraordinary enthusiasm' when he called upon the humble men of the party to realize their sublime duty to proclaim 'that blessed day when the sword shall be finally sheathed'. M. Camelinat, a French socialist veteran, then delivered greetings from the French socialists. It was significant perhaps that no representative from the German party was present, much to MacDonald's disappointment. The Conference was then urged to endorse a general resolution which denounced the 'armaments burden' and compulsory military service, recommended the international arbitration of disputes, and again urged the workers to take 'organised action' with their comrades in Germany and elsewhere to ensure peace. Egerton Wake from the shipbuilding area of Barrow-in-Furness immediately moved an amendment that:

before demanding the reduction of armaments, the Labour Party should secure the passage of the Right-to-Work bill, which would safeguard workers in arsenal and dockyard towns against the misery of unemployment.[52]

Wake pointed out that over 120,000 skilled workers were directly employed in the manufacture of armaments and he insisted that the Labour Party could not ignore the employment consequence of arms reduction.[53] W. C. Anderson and Henderson both argued against the amendment, and explained that it would be foolish to tie the hands of the Labour Party on the issue of armaments while it awaited the outcome of the Right-to-Work campaign. In the final vote, the rhetoric of MacDonald, Clynes, and G. H. Roberts prevailed and the amendment was defeated by a large majority. In a series of further votes the conference endorsed the abolition of

[51] The proceedings are reported in *LL*, 3 February 1911.
[52] Ibid.
[53] Much the same concern for the employment consequences of arms limitation was voiced at the Women's Labour League Conference held at the same time; see the proceedings ibid.

the right of capture and the Copenhagen Congress's policies of peace propaganda, parliamentary ratification of treaties, and the conclusion of an international convention to limit armaments. Only the proposed inquiry into a general strike was defeated. Overall, the policies of the ILP had triumphed, and the Labour Party's deserters on the armaments issue had been censured. Officially now, Labour MPs who supported increases in armaments spending were flouting the will of the Annual Conference.

The acid test of the ILP's success, however, would be seen in the response of the Labour MPs to the military estimates debate in the coming parliamentary session. When the Labour Party executive drew up its list of bills and motions for the coming session the resolution of the Leicester conference on militarism was placed first.[54] MacDonald, now the new chairman of the Labour Party, announced in February that the party would 'strenuously oppose' both arms increases and the Government's provocative foreign policy.[55] The ILP Administrative Council rallied to the cause, and issued a manifesto on 13 March which reviewed the scare of 1909 and urged all democrats in Parliament to stand firm against the Government's latest increases.[56] On the same day, however, these hopes were shattered. Two Radicals, Murray MacDonald and Arthur Ponsonby, introduced a motion in the Commons calling for a diminution in arms spending. In the vote only twenty-one of a possible forty-one Labour MPs[57] supported the reductionist motion. Eighteen Labour MPs were absent, and there were two rebels, Charles Duncan, the member for Barrow, and W. T. Wilson, the member for Westhoughton. The number of deserters had declined compared to the eight who had rebelled in March 1910; but now almost half the Labour MPs had failed to vote at all.[58] The *Labour Leader* was aghast at this 'grave dereliction of duty' and promised to print all future division

---

[54] Labour Party NEC *mins.*, 6 February 1911.

[55] Interview in *LL*, 17 February 1911.

[56] Reported to the ILP NAC on 14 March 1911, ILP NAC *mins.* For the text, see *LL*, 17 March 1911.

[57] *Hansard*, V: 22: 1995–2000.

[58] John Hodge was in Australia at this time, so there were forty-one Labour Party MPs able to vote in the House of Commons.

lists to keep pressure on the malcontents. As for Duncan and Wilson, the *Leader* announced gravely that these two were in 'direct defiance of the imperative mandate of the party conference' and had shown 'high treason to the cause'.[59]

There were more disappointments to come. On 16 March the Labour Party introduced its own amendment contending that 'the increasing expenditure on the Navy is not justified by foreign events, and is a menace to peace and to national security'. This time twenty-nine Labour MPs, including the rather indecisive W. T. Wilson, voted for the motion; but Duncan refused to abandon his stand and cast his vote against his own party's amendment to the naval estimates.[60] This was certainly something of a recovery from the sad lack of attendance at the vote on the MacDonald–Ponsonby amendment. However, on 20 March the strength of the dissenters within the Labour Party group was once more dramatically revealed. On a motion introduced by the Radical David Mason to reduce the personnel of the Navy by 1,000 men, as a protest against 'bloated armaments', only seventeen Labour MPs voted in favour, eighteen were absent, and this time the number of deserters who opposed the motion climbed to six.[61] The vote was final proof that less than half the Labour Party's MPs could be relied upon in the House to support proposals to reduce armaments, in spite of all the efforts to the ILP, in spite of the influence exerted by the leadership, and in defiance of the Labour Party Conference.

In the wake of the vote of 20 March a battle raged in the *Labour Leader* on the question of arms limitation and unemployment. Councillor Wake defended Charles Duncan's voting behaviour and insisted that the right to work must be achieved *before* cuts in arms spending could be supported.[62] When the issue came up at the ILP Conference in late April the majority reaffirmed the view that the pursuit of arms limitation must take priority.[63]

[59] *LL*, 17 March 1911.
[60] *Hansard*, 16 March 1911, V: 22: 2483 and 2558.
[61] *Hansard*, 20 March 1911, V: 23: 165–8.
[62] *LL*, 14 April 1911.
[63] *LL*, 28 April 1911.

The ILP had preserved its record but the Labour Party's reputation had suffered a grievous blow. The *Labour Leader*'s German correspondent, J. W. Schwarz, made no attempt to hide the disappointment felt in German socialist circles. The vote of 20 March, he noted 'justified much of the criticism of the Labour Party by the German socialist press'. Schwarz reminded his readers in Britain that many SPD Reichstag members represented arms manufacturing towns, and, he boasted, 'not one of them has ever voted, nor indeed has any other socialist Reichstag member, for bloated armaments and against his principles'.[64] The German socialists certainly had cause now to doubt their British comrades.

Why had the ILP and Labour Party leaders failed to hold the party to the cause of arms limitation? The answer to this question is of course bound up with the power over public opinion wielded by the press and the various lobbies and leagues committed to the militarist, imperialist, and ultra-nationalist point of view. Undoubtedly the problem of unemployment in dockyard and arsenal towns also contributed to the desertions. The root of the problem for the Labour Party leaders was to be found in their failure to persuade the party that the issue was indeed important enough to 'make every hall in this country ring with our condemnation of this government'—to borrow Snowden's words. After the election of December 1910 the Labour Party was in practice committed to the preservation of the Government until the Parliament Bill became law. Once that had happened, arguments multiplied in the party as to what causes were so dear to the labour movement that they might justify the threat of turning out the Liberals. Womens' suffrage? The right to work? Or opposition to militarism? As chairman of the Labour Party, MacDonald declared in March 1911 that for him the issue of militarism was an exceptional question, even taking precedence over the Parliament Bill. Referring to the 1911 military estimates, he warned that

Parliament Bill or no Parliament Bill, our desire to support the government can never make it possible for us to accept such estimates. The

[64] *LL*, 7 April 1911.

most precious peace asset is the friendship of the working classes,
L'Internationale.[65]

However, the votes recorded in the Commons in March 1911
demonstrated that MacDonald and the other socialists of the
Labour Party had manifestly failed to persuade their trade
union comrades of the priority of the struggle against
militarism.

3. *The Second Moroccan Crisis, 1911: Doubts Laid Bare*

Not many months were to pass before the international
situation seemed suddenly full of danger once again, providing
a sharp reminder to the British socialists and trade unionists
that the controversies over armaments and war were not
based upon idle speculations. From the dispatch of the
German cruiser *Panther* to Agadir on 1 July until a compromise settlement was concluded between France and
Germany in November 1911, the Moroccan crisis occupied
the centre stage in European diplomacy. It was a time for
socialists to parade their faith in the international solidarity
of labour against the schemes of the war-makers. The French
and German socialists organized a series of mass rallies against
war, and the socialist press in both countries printed each
other's denunciations of imperialism.[66] In Britain, a rally at
Trafalgar Square on 13 August, which had been organized
months before in order to welcome a visiting group of French
trade unionists, was turned into a peace demonstration.[67]
However, behind the public face of a united and confident
anti-war campaign, a bitter quarrel developed once again over
the apparent reluctance of the SPD to co-operate fully with
the International.

In the early stages of the crisis its seriousness was difficult
to weigh. There were signs of confidence even among the
socialists. Jaurès did not postpone his planned visit to South
America, and he departed from Lisbon on 24 July, although

---

[65] *LL*, 31 March 1911.

[66] The German and French socialists' anti-war rallies were held intermittently
throughout July, August, and September; see Haupt, *Socialism against War*,
pp. 46–8, and Drachkovitch, *Les Socialismes Francais et Allemand et le Probleme
de la Guerre*, pp. 146–7.

[67] Labour Party NEC *mins.*, 26 April 1911; and see the resolution presented
at the demonstration in the Labour Party archives, at LP/INT/11/1/368.

with 'considerable hesitation'.[68] However, the dangers of the situation did impress the SFIO executive. In response to its suggestion, the ISB secretary Huysmans wrote on 6 July to the various national sections asking whether a meeting of the ISB should be called.[69] MacDonald, Hardie, and Quelch all replied that they were in favour of a meeting.[70] However, just as in 1905, both Molkenbuhr and Bebel advised against a meeting, Bebel remarking that it would be better to wait and 'economise our shot a little'. No doubt to the surprise of most sections,[71] the ISB executive announced on 14 July that it agreed with Bebel in delaying a meeting. With engaging honesty, the ISB included with this announcement copies of the entire correspondence on the issue, thus revealing that German opinion alone had prevailed.

The failure of the ISB to call a meeting on the crisis was clearly a disappointment for British socialists. At first MacDonald appeared to accept the situation, and he explained to the readers of the *Socialist Review* that the Germans were trying to play down the crisis so as not to facilitate their Government's drumbeating over 'patriotic issues' so close to the coming January 1912 German elections.[72] *Justice*, however, was extremely critical. Noting that it was the duty of the ISB to call a meeting when any national section requested it, *Justice* attacked the abandonment of the proposed meeting 'at the instance of our German comrades'. It recalled bitterly that the Germans 'have always set their faces against any such meetings'.[73] This attack on the SPD added to the quarrels in *Justice* over the 'German menace' which had, naturally, been revived in the course of the crisis.[74]

---

[68] Goldberg, *Jaurès*, p. 421.

[69] Huysmans to MacDonald, 6 July 1911, LP/INT/11/1/325.

[70] Middleton (for MacDonald) to Huysmans, 8 July 1911, LP/INT/11/1/326. The ISB circular reproducing the entire correspondence on this issue is in the Labour Party Archives, LP/INT/11/1/137.

[71] MacDonald had already written to other members of the BNC announcing that an ISB meeting would be called shortly, see LP/INT/11/1/430.

[72] *Socialist Review*, August 1911.

[73] 'The Lost Opportunity', *Justice*, 22 July 1911.

[74] See 'The Prowl of the Panther', *Justice*, 8 July 1911, and for criticisms of this article see the letters of Rothstein and W. P. Coates, and Quelch's reply, in *Justice*, 15 July 1911. See also, *Social Democrat*, August 1911.

On 21 July the crisis over Morocco suddenly became very grave when, at the Mansion House, Lloyd George delivered a speech which was interpreted everywhere as an unequivocal warning to Germany. The British Labour Party now decided to force the issue of ISB action. On 26 July, in an unprecedented step, the Labour Party executive decided to request an immediate meeting of the ISB.[75] On the same day the British SDP made a similar request.[76] However, once again Bebel, supported by the Austrians, advised against a meeting, and the ISB executive again bowed to Bebel's advice.[77]

In the meantime, MacDonald, still waiting for a reply to his second effort to rouse the ISB to action, used the opportunity of a major debate in the Commons on 27 July to declare the attitude of the Labour Party to the crisis. He criticized Lloyd George's Mansion House speech which, he claimed, had needlessly inflamed opinion at home and abroad. The Moroccan affair should be settled, he advised, at the Hague Court. In the manner of so many socialist anti-war speeches, MacDonald threatened the rulers of Europe, in unspecific terms, with the power of labour:

The House knows perfectly well the forces, the organizations, the movements in Europe with which we are associated. The House knows perfectly well that so long as there is a Labour party in Germany, in France, or in England, those parties will cooperate together to the very last moment to seek peace.[78]

Like Hardie, MacDonald was willing to build up the 'threat value' of organized labour on the side of peace.

The failure of the second attempt to gain a meeting of the ISB was difficult enough to swallow; but when Köttgen, London correspondent of *Vorwärts*, attacked MacDonald's speech in the Commons as being too patriotic, this was too much for the Labour Party chairman. In an outburst against the SPD in the *Socialist Review*, MacDonald revealed that he too had his doubts about the sincerity of the Germans' internationalism:

[75] Labour Party NEC *mins.*, 26 July 1911.
[76] *Justice*, 29 July 1911.
[77] Haupt, *Socialism and the Great War*, pp. 45–6.
[78] *Hansard*, V: 28: 1830–1.

No national section of socialists is less entitled to object to Mr MacDonald's words than the German. At International Congress after International Congress they have objected to active measures being taken against militarism, and in the present crisis they have taken no part in putting difficulties in the way of Wilhelmstrasse.[79]

MacDonald hastened to assure his readers that he did not blame the Germans, who must judge their own situation; but in the face of Köttgen's criticism 'we must remind our German comrades of their own position'. He then returned to the attack:

If we had been certain that the German Social Democracy would have laid down its tools and left its workshops when it became certain that war would have been declared, the Chairman of the Labour Party would have had a simple task to perform. It would have been to announce that in both countries a paralysing strike would be declared. But until that, or something like it, can be done, an international crisis may find us in a deplorably weak position.[80]

These accusations, that the International without a general strike policy was 'deplorably weak' and that the German socialists were to blame for the lack of such determined policies, were most serious; and they indicated a very real decline in trust between MacDonald and the German socialists.

An exchange of letters between MacDonald and Bernstein later in 1911 is revealing in this respect. In November 1911, only two months before the national elections, the SPD faced a major foreign policy debate in the Reichstag over Morocco. In Germany it was widely believed that, during the recent crisis, Britain had encouraged French belligerence. In an effort to prepare Bebel for this debate, Bernstein sought to obtain from MacDonald information concerning contacts between the German ambassador and the British Foreign Office. Bernstein confided to MacDonald:

Bebel is not so strong on the matter as he in my opinion ought to be. But we are on good terms, and I do my best to dispel wrong impressions which sometimes influence him. If he only knew more English.[81]

---

[79] *Socialist Review*, September 1911.
[80] Ibid.
[81] Bernstein to MacDonald, 4 November 1911, MacDonald Papers, PRO/30/69/6/14.

In his reply, MacDonald admitted that, despite what he said in public, in private he was confident about the role of the Foreign Office on this occasion. He assured Bernstein that the Foreign Office had been urging a peaceful settlement upon the French and he put the blame for the friction in London squarely on the shoulders of the German ambassador. MacDonald even used the terms 'us' and 'we' when speaking of the British Government.[82] Bernstein replied the day after Bebel's speech in the Reichstag on foreign policy. He informed MacDonald that:

Bebel. . . is I am glad to say much sounder on the subject than was to be expected from his Jena speech, and has said yesterday some very good things about Great Britain.[83]

After the experiences of 1911, British socialists would need stronger assurances than this of the good faith of their German comrades.

In the main the publications of both the British and German socialists still stressed the idea that the representatives of the working people joined their hands across the sea, shrugged off the enmity assumed by their governments, and rejoiced in the knowledge that their socialist solidarity could preserve peace. However, a more realistic measure of the quality of the relations between the British Labour Party and the SPD in this period can be seen in the fact that the Labour Party never saw fit to sponsor an official fraternal delegate to the SPD's annual congresses right up to 1914. And, a year after the Moroccan crisis Bernstein commiserated with MacDonald that still too little was known about the Labour Party in German socialist circles. 'But I am too busy to write much about it, and the *Vorwärts* would in most cases not even print it. Prejudice is still very strong in these quarters', he concluded.[84]

---

[82] MacDonald to Bernstein, 13 (?) November 1911, 11SG, Bernstein Archive, D 438. The date of this letter or of Bernstein's reply (see next footnote) would appear to be mistaken.

[83] Bernstein to MacDonald, 12 (?) November 1911, MacDonald Papers, PRO/30/69/6/14. On Bebel's speech at the Jena Congress of September 1911, see Schorske, *German Social Democracy*, p. 201.

[84] Bernstein to MacDonald, 8 October 1912, MacDonald Papers, PRO/30/69/3A/61.

10

The Pretence of Power:
Keir Hardie and the Plan for a Strike
against War, 1910–1914

The working class of the two nations will take the issues of war
and peace out of the hands of bankrupt statesmen, and, instead
of shooting each other in a quarrel which is not theirs, will join
hands and hearts, and upon a given day make war forever
impossible by means—if nothing else suffices— of the weapon of
the general strike.

> Keir Hardie, Trafalgar Square, 24 August 1913, *Labour
> Leader,* 28 August 1913

1. *A New Understanding of the Anti-War Strike*

In spite of the private reservations that were held within
Labour Party circles concerning the sincerity of the German
socialists' internationalism, in the period 1910 to 1914 Keir
Hardie became a determined advocate of a bold new plan
to prevent war, a plan which required absolute trust between
the socialist parties of Europe if it was to work—a plan for a
simultaneous anti-war strike. The origin of Hardie's interest
in the proposal for a strike to prevent war is not certain. No
doubt the idea appealed to Hardie because it touched his own
deep conviction that the struggle of the working-class movement was an international struggle. In the late 1880s Hardie
had professed a strong interest in working-class internationalism and he had been in Paris in 1889 when the
Second International was founded.[1] He did not attend
the International Congresses in Brussels in 1891 or in Zurich
in 1893, but undoubtedly he was aware of the discussions
on the general strike against war that took place on both
occasions. As noted previously, it was early in 1896, in the
immediate aftermath of the Jameson Raid, that Hardie first

---

[1] On the development of Hardie's internationalism, see Morgan, *Keir Hardie*,
p. 179, and for a more critical account of Hardie's views in the 1880s, see Fred
Reid, *Keir Hardie: The Making of a Socialist* (London, 1978), pp. 121–2.

endorsed the concept of a strike against war.[2] When the International Congress met in London in 1896 Hardie also defended the Dutch delegate Nieuwenhuis who was at that time the most well-known proponent of the anti-war strike.[3] At the ILP Conference the following year, Hardie declared his faith in the power of international socialism, and of German socialism in particular, to dissuade the militarist monarchies of Europe from unleashing war.[4] Little was heard of the anti-war strike proposal in ILP circles again until 1905 when Glasier, perhaps inspired by revolutionary general strikes in Russia, began to explore the idea of a strike to prevent war in the *Labour Leader*.[5] On the eve of attending his first meeting of the ISB in March 1906, Hardie also suggested that the Russian workers' general strikes had shown the power which the working class possessed to prevent war.[6] No doubt Hardie's interest in this question was further stimulated at the ISB meeting in Brussels, where the Bureau debated the still rather vague proposals of Vaillant and Jaurès that the ISB should examine what measures socialists could take to prevent war.[7] Some indication of an emerging interest within the ILP on this issue was given in April 1907 when the ILP Conference called on the ISB to redouble its internationalist work so that the socialist parties of Europe would be prepared to resist a war crisis.[8] By 1907, therefore, the idea of an anti-war strike had been floated several times by the leaders, but there had been no serious or systematic dicussion of the concept.

For this reason, the ILP delegates to the International Congress at Stuttgart in August 1907 were somewhat unprepared for the intense debate that took place. Nevertheless, the debates at Stuttgart and the advocacy of the anti-war

[2] *LL*, 11 January 1896. See also Chapter 3.

[3] Morgan, *Keir Hardie*, p. 88.

[4] *ILP Conference 1897*, p. 15.

[5] 'Socialism and War', *LL*, 3 March 1905.

[6] 'No Militarism!', *LL*, 9 March 1906.

[7] See 'Circulaire transmettant une proposition Vaillant sur les mesures à prendre pour conjurer la guerre', and 'Proposition du Parti socialiste SFIO' and Compte rendu de la septième réunion plénière du BSI' in Haupt (ed.), *Bureau Socialiste International*, Vol. 1, 1900–7, pp. 175, 183, and 197–207.

[8] Haupt, *Socialism and the Great War*, p. 20; *LL*, 5 April 1907.

strike by the colourful French delegate Hervé appear to have given a fresh impetus to the discussion of anti-militarism among British socialists.[9] Thus, at the Labour Party Co-ference in January 1908, the ILP moved an internationalist resolution which, in addition to the usual professions of faith in peace, urged the conference to consider 'the question of formulating a policy of international action in the event of immediate danger or actual occurrence of war'.[10] This was the first indication that the ILP was seriously considering some form of action to physically prevent the outbreak of war.

Hardie had missed the vital discussions at Stuttgart and the Labour Conference of 1908 because of his sudden illness in May 1907 and his decision to take a recuperative world tour. Even so, on his return to Britain in April 1908 he was soon in touch with the mood of the ILP on the question of action to prevent war. During the naval scare of 1909, Hardie indicated to one ILP branch that, 'if the worst comes to the worst', he was prepared to advocate a strike in the war materials industries in order to prevent war.[11] It is possible that Hardie was encouraged to consider seriously the idea of a general strike against war at that time also because of the intense concern over the 'German menace' shown by Blatchford, Hyndman, and Quelch, a concern which seemed to be founded upon the argument that international socialism was quite incapable of preventing war. Perhaps Hardie appreciated that more socialists would desert the cause of internationalism and arms limitation unless the socialist leadership could devise some viable scheme to contain the forces making for aggressive war. A commitment to engage in an international general strike when war threatened would certainly reassure the working-class movement in Britain and in every other land that it was safe to continue the campaign against militarism. Whatever the reason, by 1910 Hardie was suggesting that the international working-

[9] For example, see Russell Smart 'In the Military Commission at Stuttgart', *LL*, 6 September 1907, where he comments favourably on Hervé.
[10] Labour Party, *Annual Conference Report*, 1908, p. 81.
[11] See Hardie's speech to the Newcastle branch of the ILP in *LL*, 9 April 1909.

class parties were 'heralds of the day' when the people would be in a position to enforce peace against the will of the war-mongering kings, aristocrats, and diplomats.[12] It remained to devise a scheme of international working-class action to enforce the people's peace.

There is some evidence to suggest that by 1910 some British socialists were increasingly dissatisfied with the vague understandings that had been reached at the International Congress at Stuttgart for working-class agitation to forestall war. One indication of this dissatisfaction could be seen at the Labour Party Conference in 1910. A delegate from the Carpenters' Union proposed that the Labour Party executive should take steps to initiate 'an international committee' drawn from all the European Labour parties in order to decide upon united action 'at the least sign of war'.[13] Months later the Labour executive dismissed this demand, on the ground that the proposal was covered already by the existence of the ISB.[14] In theory this was perfectly true, but the conference resolution was an unmistakable indication that either the International was not well known, or its current arrangements to meet the crisis of war were not highly regarded. Similarly, the debate on militarism at the ILP Conference in March revealed something of this same deter-mination to adopt more specific plans for the preservation of peace than had emerged at Stuttgart in 1907. A resolution introduced by George Lansbury called upon the coming Copenhagen International Congress to make the problem of militarism its first business, and 'to formulate a practical and effective scheme of international action on the part of the workers for the preservation of peace, and to secure a concerted preventive policy by the Labour and Socialist parties in each country in the event of war being declared'.[15] Lansbury's motion did not mention the general strike itself, merely the need to clarify a viable anti-war policy; but some prominent people within the party were showing a genuine interest in the idea. Earlier in March 1910, J. A. Seddon had

[12] *LL*, 11 February 1910.
[13] Labour Party, *Annual Conference Report*, 1910, p. 94.
[14] Labour Party, NEC *mins.*, 30 June 1910.
[15] ILP, *Annual Conference*, 1910, pp. 66–7.

warned the House of Commons that in many countries the idea of enforcing peace through a 'cessation of production' was being considered.[16] Furthermore, in April 1910 Gustave Hervé's classic anti-patriotic work *Leur Patrie* was published in Britain, and Harry Snell gave the book a favourable review in the *Labour Leader*.[17] ILP members were certainly sympathetic toward Hervé's point of view, and this was made clear at the 1910 ILP Conference with the passing of a resolution expressing indignation at Hervé's recent imprisonment.[18] There were signs, therefore, of a growing conviction among British socialists that the moderate and generalized anti-war position determined by the International at Stuttgart was not really adequate.

Those within the ILP who favoured the general strike as an anti-war weapon made a determined effort to win over the party to their view in May 1910. On 24 May the ILP head office issued a report containing two resolutions on militarism and war, as well as supporting arguments, which the ILP proposed to submit to the forthcoming Copenhagen Congress.[19] The second of the two resolutions called on the workers of all civilized countries 'to lay down their tools on the first rumour of war'. The authorship of this unsigned head office report is difficult to establish. It is unlikely that Hardie wrote the report, for he had resigned from the ILP Administrative Council back in April 1909 over the Grayson Affair.[20] Although he had been appointed by the Administrative Council as an official ILP delegate to Copenhagen in April 1910,[21] it seems unlikely that he would have written a report emanating from head office while still declining to serve on the Administrative Council. The April 1910 meeting of the ILP Administrative Council had also appointed Anderson and Lansbury to a special subcommittee to try to arrange the conference on armaments which Lansbury had proposed in his resolution at the recent ILP Conference.[22]

[16] *Hansard*, 9 March 1910, V: 14: 1547.
[17] *LL*, 1 April 1910.
[18] Ibid.
[19] 'Report from Head Office', dated 24 May 1910, pasted in ILP NAC *mins*.
[20] K. O. Morgan, *Keir Hardie*, p. 228.
[21] ILP NAC *mins.*, 21–2 April 1910.
[22] IBid.

It is possible, then, that Lansbury and Anderson undertook the task to which Lansbury had referred in that same resolution, namely, that of defining a 'practical and effective scheme' for the prevention of war to be considered by the International at Copenhagen. It should be stressed, however, that the ILP Administrative Council minutes do not make clear who exactly was reponsible for drawing up resolutions for submission to Copenhagen.

The question of authorship of the 24 May 1910 head office report is important, for it was the first definite proposal within the ILP in favour of a general strike as a weapon against war. Moreover, it offered an entirely new concept of an anti-war strike, one which was carefully framed to avoid the obvious shortcomings of the traditional proposal. In the discussions within the International in the 1890s and again in the writings of Hervé, the general strike against war had always been assumed to mean a strike in reply to a declaration of war, a strike which would interrupt mobilization by preventing the provisioning of troops and impeding their movement toward the frontiers of the belligerent countries. Critics of this plan had always insisted that a general strike after a declaration of war would prove impossible to organize because of the ineluctable tide of patriotic emotion amongst the people and the probability of swift and draconian coercion of all strike organizers by the government. The ILP report acknowledged these difficulties, and, in place of the 'reply to war' strike, it suggested the initiation of a strike in the crisis period prior to any outbreak. The aim in this case would be to demonstrate massive public objection to any aggressive war, and, consequently, governments would be encouraged to abandon war and choose negotations instead. The actual resolution proposed in the report for Copenhagen urged the coming congress to consider 'the advisability of recommending the workers of all civilised countries to lay down their tools on the first rumour of war, especially the workers in the carrying and kindered trades'. The report then acknowledged that 'it is a fatal policy to remain quiet until war has broken out' and foreshadowed that the British labour movement would soon attempt to organize their various trade unions and Labour organizations in such a manner as 'to secure their taking such action *previous* to a threatened war as will paralyse the carrying and other agencies'. The writers of the report next sought to counter the long-standing objection to the plan based on the argument that well-disciplined strikes against war in one country would simply deliver it up to a more reactionary power. Since it would be imperative for any international strikes to begin simultaneously, the report requested the ISB to leave aside one full day at Copenhagen so that such simultaneous and international strikes could be planned. Finally, the report offered some reassurance to the Germans, whose hestitation on this issue was well known. In deference to their fears, the proposed resolution included the now familiar concession that the congress would be 'leaving to each nation to choose its own best methods for giving effect to this resolution'.

One other aspect of the report is worth stressing. Several times in the course of the argument in support of the anti-war strike, the tremendous propaganda value of such an idea was emphasized. Where the ruling classes were concerned, it was argued that 'if the governing classes once recognise that the workers are in earnest they will find some other means of settling international disputes than those of war'. The report also appealed to the forthcoming congress to 'determine not to separate until we have registered our determination to take jointly such action as will compel our governments to listen'. Through the use of these arguments the report laid great stress on the persuasive impact of the socialists' commitment to an anti-war strike. It is possible too that the framers of the report were not deeply concerned with the practicalities of implementing a general strike against war. The real aim appears to have been simply to secure the inclusion of the general strike proposal in the International's official policy because of the propaganda value of that commitment, even if it was largely a matter of bluff. This may explain the trouble taken to answer the usual objections that had been raised to the idea in the past. The report concluded with the plea:

Remember action in this matter really means no action. We ask you to urge your comrades to simply lay down their tools, refuse to work, refuse to carry armaments or handle explosives and the whole dread business will be at an end.

There is some doubt, therefore, whether the advocates of an anti-war general strike within the ILP genuinely believed in the measure as a practical weapon. Rather, they believed in the strike as a spectre worth summoning forth in order to scare the ruling elites into the paths of peace.

In any case, these particular resolutions and arguments were doomed for the dustbin, at least in the short term. Glasier challenged the head office report and submitted a resolution in which the commitment to strike action in a crisis was deleted and replaced with a simple commitment to 'a vigorous anti-war campaign with the object of promoting concerted action by the working class'.[23] In explaining the change, Glasier argued that an anti-war strike was not realizable. 'The idea of the workers ceasing work in the event of war is really a very doubtful one: it is much better not to fix down the method at the present stage of discussion'.[24] Glasier had quite overlooked not only the arguments raised in the first report concerning strikes prior to war, but also the argument concerning the propaganda or 'scare' value of the proposal. Nevertheless, when the Administrative Council members were consulted on the matter it was Glasier's resolution that was preferred, and so it went forward to Copenhagen as the official ILP recommendation.[25]

Keir Hardie's position at this stage is uncertain. He was soon to champion the cause of the general strike against war at Copenhagen, yet neither his speeches in the Commons on the military estimates in March nor his writings at this time make mention of the idea. In late July 1910, Hardie mentioned, during the course of a review of the existing international tension, that it was the duty of German and British socialists 'to find means for combining their forces, so as to make war between their country and ours

---

[23] 'Head Office Report', dated 28 May 1910, pasted in ILP NAC *mins*. See also Glasier to Francis Johnson, 27 May 1910, Glasier Papers, I. 1. 1910/59.

[24] 'Head Office Report', dated 28 May 1910, ibid.

[25] *Bulletin Périodique du Bureau Socialiste International*, no. 3, in IISG, SDAP file, no. 4471. The decision to forward Glasier's resolution was not unanimous. Leonard Hall wrote to Johnson: 'I consider the resolution already agreed on much the best—far more practical and definite and understandable than Mr Glasier's amendment', Hall to Francis Johnson, 30 May 1910, ILP Archives, 1910/228.

impossible'.[26] Apart from this, his writings give no hint of any sudden determination to commit the International to the anti-war strike. Hardie may, however, have made contact with Vaillant prior to the Copenhagen Congress: and it is very likely that Hardie would readily have sympathized with the ageing Blanquist's dissatisfaction over the International's policy on war as it had been determined at Stuttgart. This contact may have occurred at the ISB meeting in November 1909 which both men attended,[27] or, as is more likely, during a brief visit to France made by Hardie in May 1910 for the Pleasant Sunday Afternoon Brotherhood. Certainly on this latter trip Hardie met several SFIO deputies and, therefore, had an opportunity to reacquaint himself with the long-standing support for the anti-war strike in France, support coming from the highest levels of the SFIO and the CGT.[28] However, the evidence is not complete on this point, and it may be that Hardie first decided to join Vaillant in proposing the famous general strike amendment at the Copenhagen Congress only after informal discussions with Vaillant during the course of the congress.

2. *The International Socialist Congress at Copenhagen, 1910: Decision Delayed*

When the International Congress opened at Copenhagen in late August 1910 the Commission on Anti-Militarism attracted the leading lights of European socialism, such as Vaillant, Ledebour, Hardie, and Glasier. After an initial discussion, a small subcommittee was formed to draw up a composite resolution, Hardie remaining as the sole British delegate on this subcommittee.[29] It was here that the famous paragraph was proposed in the name of Hardie and Vaillant. It read:

Among the means to be used in order to prevent and hinder war, the Congress considers as particularly efficacious the general strike, especially in the industries that supply war with its implements (arms

---

[26] *LL*, 22 July 1910.

[27] *Bulletin Périodique du Bureau Socialiste International*, no. 2

[28] The visit to France is described in *LL*, 3 June 1910.

[29] J. B. Glasier to Katharine Glasier, 30 August 1910, Glasier Papers, I. 1. 10/32.

and ammunition, transport etc.) as well as the propaganda and popular action in their most active forms.[30]

Ledebour, the SPD representative on the subcommittee, refused to accept this paragraph in the composite resolution and also opposed its being referred to the Bureau for investigation. This left no alternative but to present the Hardie—Vaillant proposal in the full congress as an amendment to the Commission's resolution.[31]

On 1 September, when the congress met in full assembly, Ledebour presented the first resolution which was in essence a reaffirmation of the Stuttgart position.[32] This urged the working-class parties to do 'all they can to prevent war'. As at Stuttgart, the anti-war strike was not mentioned. The Hardie—Vaillant amendment was then discussed. Ledebour opposed the amendment on the grounds that such a specific commitment to treasonable action could lead to the suppression of the German socialist and labour movement.[33] Moreover, he argued, the strike proposal was not realizable in all countries and thus should not form part of an International Congress resolution. Then Ledebour attacked the British delegation, questioning its right to propose such a measure on the strength of its own poor anti-militarist record. After all, he claimed, the SDP, and Quelch in particular, had actually supported the British Navy's right of capture; and the British Labour Party had supported the last budget with all its military expenses. Revealing his own suspicions regarding the British commitment to the general strike idea, Ledebour went on:

You, MacDonald and your party are practical politicians—so practical that you lose sight of principles. By what right do you take it upon yourselves to commit other people to the general strike against war when you do not in your country take up the same anti-militarist position as the socialist party in all other countries? So long as you vote

[30] *Huitième Congrès Socialiste International, Copenhagen, 1910* (cited hereafter as *ISC Proceedings, 1910*), p. 202.

[31] Hardie referred to this resistance on Ledebour's part in his speech to the Congress, *ISC Proceedings, 1910*, p. 203.

[32] For the complete resolution, see ibid., pp. 472–3.

[33] Ibid., pp. 186–99.

the budget, and thereby the arming of the British soldiery, you cannot come to us with more far-reaching proposals.[34]

The following afternoon Hardie presented his case in favour of the amendment.[35] First, he defended the British Labour Party from Ledebour's charge of insincerity by explaining that voting for the budget was not a question of principle but simply one of tactics. Willingly he dissociated himself and the Labour Party from Quelch and the SDP group whom Ledebour had also criticized. The Labour Party, Hardie proclaimed, would most certainly agitate for the abolition of the right of capture at sea. Hardie then moved on to his main business, the general strike amendment, and explained Vaillant's and his own purpose in putting forward this proposal:

[We] did not wish to impose upon the party in all countries the obligation of calling a general strike against war in all cases. [We] simply wished to point out to the working class of all countries that by the organization of their economic power they were strong enough to make war impossible.[36]

In these words, Hardie hinted, in the same way as the ILP report of May 1910 had done, that the real purpose of the anti-war strike proposal was to provide propaganda rather than to impose an obligation to strike upon all the European socialist parties. Hardie continued:

If they educated the working class to agitate, by every means, in parliament and in the workshop, against militarism, they might be assured that their appeal would be listened to when they called upon the workers to act.[37]

Finally, Hardie pleaded with the congress not to reject this motion as that would be rejecting the only possible action whereby war could be prevented. Then, to the surprise perhaps of Quelch who was always sceptical of the strike idea, the next British delegate to speak, J. Jones, announced the support of the British SDP for the proposal, 'because whatever the differences there might be between us and the

---

[34] English translation from the report in *Justice*, 10 September 1910.
[35] *ISC Proceedings, 1910*, p. 203.
[36] *Justice*, 10 September 1910.
[37] Ibid.

Labour Party, we were determined to do all in our power to prevent war'.[38] At the end of the debate Vaillant added his respected voice to those supporting the amendment.[39]

At length, Vandervelde, the ISB chairman, announced that the Germans had softened their stand and were now agreeable to the compromise originally suggested in the Commission, namely, that the proposal should be remitted to the ISB for investigation. A report would be ready for the next International Congress which was scheduled to meet in Vienna in 1913. Hardie and Vaillant accepted this compromise, and so a final decision on the anti-war strike was postponed.[40] The Ledebour resolution was then accepted in its original form, that is, without any specific mention of the general strike.

What, then, had the congress revealed? In the first place, it was clear that the Germans were quite hostile to the anti-war strike proposal and sensitive also to criticism of their stand. The SPD obviously resented that such a radical suggestion as an anti-war strike should come from the British Labour Party. After all, only two years before, the Germans had agreed to support the membership of the British Labour Party in the International as a special case, in spite of the party's moderation. In addition, the notorious stand of Hyndman and Quelch on the naval issue had damaged the credibility of British socialists in general. Why, the Germans asked, should they commit themselves to a proposal that was probably not viable in Britain or France, and involved grave risks of suppression for the movement inside Germany? In the end, the only advance made at Copenhagen in the International's strategy for the prevention of war was the agreement that in a war crisis situation, where any delay might be tragic, the ISB executive should call an immediate meeting of the Bureau upon receipt of a request from any one section of the International.[41] The granting of this minor initiative to the ISB executive reveals how closely guarded

---

[38] Ibid.

[39] *ISC Proceedings, 1910*, pp. 202–3.

[40] Describing these events, Glasier remarked that 'the Germans capitulated': J. B. Glasier to Katharine Glasier, 2 September 1910, Glasier Papers, I. 1. 10/34. See also *LL*, 9 September 1910, and *ISC Proceedings 1910*, p. 475.

[41] *ISC Proceedings, 1910*, pp. 212–3.

were the powers that devolved on the Bureau; the national interests of each section of the International were certainly paramount.

After the Copenhagen Congress Hardie, with Jaurès, attended a peace demonstration at Frankfurt and then made a fraternal visit to the SPD Congress at Magdeburg before returning to Britain.[42] On his arrival home Hardie immediately threw himself into the ILP's 'Autumn Campaign' against armaments. His speeches during the campaign reveal that his visit to the Continent had given a fresh impetus to his internationalism. In place of the more generalized professions of faith in international working-class solidarity as the chief safeguard of peace, Hardie now laid stress upon the anti-war strike. His argument in favour of the general strike had become very similar to the argument outlined in the ILP head office report of May 1910. In a speech at Birmingham on 18 October, Hardie argued that socialists must agree in advance that 'if ever war should come within the range of possibility' a conference of the workers of the nations in danger of conflict would be held and threats of a general strike should then be made. Hardie continued:

It was too late to begin to take action when the war fever had maddened the blood of the people, but if the warmongers in Germany and in this country knew beforehand that the working class of the two countries had come to an understanding, and would stand by it, the influence of that knowledge upon their counsels would be such as to compel them to submit to arbitration the points which would otherwise have been submitted to war.[43]

At Dundee, on 27 October, Hardie argued along similar lines:

If war was threatened the duty was incumbent on the working class to strike, stop work, stop supplies, stop the railways and shipping, and cease making the guns and materials of war. If they did that they would soon end war; the very threat of the possibility of such a strike would make statesmen pause before sanctioning its outbreak. (Cheers.)[44]

Two points should be stressed here. First, Hardie was now

---

[42] *LL*, 16 September 1910; J. B. Glasier to Katharine Glasier, 7 September 1910, Glasier Papers, I. 1. 10/35.

[43] *LL*, 28 October 1910.

[44] *LL*, 4 November 1910.

suggesting that the anti-war strike should be organized prior to the outbreak of war, that is, during the period of imminent danger of war. Second, quite apart from the practicalities of organizing a strike to prevent war, Hardie was arguing that the real value of commitment to such an idea was the potent educative effect it would have upon the governing élites of Europe.

It should not be thought that Hardie was alone in seeking to popularize the concept of an anti-war strike. In the *Socialist Review* MacDonald was also examining the idea with a favourable eye. After the French railway strike in October 1910, MacDonald announced that the events in France had shown clearly that a general strike against war would soon be practicable.[45] The *Labour Leader* also lent its support to this view, by commenting that the paralysis of the French railway network during the strike 'demonstrates how war may be averted by working class solidarity'.[46] However, the official resolution which was presented to the meetings held during the 'Autumn Campaign' was drawn up by Glasier,[47] and it revealed his continuing hesitation regarding the anti-war strike. The resolution returned to the more generalized language of the past and urged the British people 'to take such common action with their fellow workers in Germany and other lands as will defeat the purposes of panic-makers and scaremongers'.[48] The speakers at the international meeting at the Albert Hall on 10 December, 1910, which closed the 'Autumn Campaign', were not so reluctant to mention the general strike plan. Hardie reminded the audience of the decision made at Copenhagen to inquire into the viability of the anti-war strike. Vandervelde revealed his support for the idea, and he urged the transport workers to prepare to strike whenever there was the threat of an aggressive war. Jaurès too commented that the time had arrived for the people to 'compel' peace. Significantly,

---

[45] Editorial notes, *Socialist Review*, November 1910.
[46] *LL*, 21 October 1910.
[47] J. B. Glasier to W. C. Anderson, 26 September 1910, Glasier Papers, I. 1. 10/3.
[48] ILP NAC *mins.*, 9 September 1910 (resolution pasted in after this meeting).

Molkenbuhr, the secretary of the SPD, made no mention of the general strike plan in his speech.[49]

Just one week later the ISB began the inquiry into the anti-war strike as had been agreed upon at Copenhagen. A special ISB circular was issued reminding all member organizations of the Hardie-Vaillant proposal and requesting them to contact their trade unions, sound out their opinions of the proposal, and report back to the ISB 'as soon as possible'.[50] The general strike inquiry had begun.

3. *The Inquiry into the Anti-War Strike: from the Copenhagen Congress to the Basle Congress of November 1912*

As a member of the International the Labour Party had, of course, received the ISB circular of 15 December 1910 initiating the inquiry into the anti-war strike. Immediately this was known Hardie began to exert pressure in support of the inquiry. In early January 1911, he contacted the ILP chairman, W. C. Anderson, informing him that he no longer wished to move Glasier's generalized anti-armaments resolution at the coming special Disarmament Conference of the Labour Party. Instead, he wished to propose an addendum endorsing the ISB's inquiry into the general strike.[51] Opposition to Hardie's proposal emerged even before the conference opened. Arthur Henderson, apparently unwilling to be associated with a strike resolution in any form, announced his refusal to move the Glasier motion because of Hardie's intention to move the anti-war strike addendum.[52] A struggle on the issue was to be expected, therefore, when the Disarmament Conference opened at Leicester on 31 January 1911. Hardie sought to reassure the delegates that all that was asked of them was a simple endorsement of the inquiry, not an endorsement of the general strike itself. None the less, he defended the idea.

[49] For the proceedings of the demonstration, see *LL*, 16 December 1910.
[50] ISB Circular, 15 December 1910, Labour Party letter files, LP/INT/11/1/172/1.
[51] 'Head Office Report', dated 13 January 1911, in ILP NAC *mins*.
[52] Marquand, *MacDonald*, pp. 165–6.

You have the power to prevent the war. Where do the soldiers that fight come from? They are your sons. And does not the material for the war come from your hands? If war were threatened between Germany and ourselves, why should not an international conference be held between the workers of this country, and Germany, and France, and Italy, and every civilised power, and determine that the day war was declared they would stop preparing any materials until war came to an end. Is not that worthy of enquiry?[53]

Glasier supported Hardie, indicating that he no longer held, or was no longer proclaiming, the reservations he had expressed in May 1910. Other speakers clearly had deep reservations. As expected, Henderson moved the deletion of the clause in Hardie's addendum which referred to the general strike inquiry. To take up the issue of an anti-war strike, Henderson argued, would distract attention from parliamentary action as the chief means of achieving reform. After a keen debate Henderson's motion was passed narrowly by 125 votes to 119.[54] This must have been a severe disappointment for Hardie. The Labour Party executive had only just received the ISB's request for a sounding out of opinion, and now the annual conference had refused this inquiry. As Brockway lamented, it was 'a very discouraging opening to this investigation'.[55] In deference to the conference nothing could be done inside the Labour Party for twelve months at least.

Nevertheless, Hardie's enthusiasm for the concept of an anti-war strike was not diminished by the defeat at Leicester. In his public speeches he continued to summon up a vision of peace preserved by means of the very threat of a general strike. Speaking in the Commons on the naval estimates on 13 March 1911, he simply ignored the recent decision at Leicester and reminded the House of the Socialists' plan to investigate the viability of a general strike to prevent war.[56] In a speech at Manchester on 26 March he also outlined the anti-war strike plan.[57] Through Hardie's personal prodding the ILP Administrative Council also accepted for the coming

---

[53] *LL*, 3 February, 1911.
[54] Ibid.
[55] *LL*, 10 February 1911.
[56] *Hansard*, 13 March 1911, V: 22: 1929.
[57] *LL*, 31 March 1911.

ILP Conference in April the entire Copenhagen resolution, including the reference to the general strike enquiry.[58] At the conference itself a further resolution was also passed declaring the ILP's faith in the strike as an anti-war weapon and instructing the party to report in this sense in reply to the ISB's formal inquiry.[59] This marked the success of Hardie and his supporters in converting the ILP to the anti-war strike plan in less than a year. In June there came another test of the new policy, at the more 'respectable' and sedate National Peace Congress at Edinburgh. With ILP Administrative Council backing, Hardie moved an addendum to the anti-armaments resolution which urged the working-class organizations to arrange strike action to avert war. However, he decided to withdraw the addendum on the understanding that member organizations should consider it before next year's Peace Congress.[60] Hardie did not confine this propaganda for the anti-war strike to conference halls; in the summer he took it to the streets. At the peace demonstration in Trafalgar Square on 13 August, during the Moroccan crisis, Hardie demanded that 'the English workers must hold themselves prepared so that if the order for war and the murder of brothers went out, not a soldier or a cannon should be transported by steamer or railway'.[61] It is noteworthy that, in these various speeches during 1911, the strike Hardie envisaged was sometimes to break out when war threatened and sometimes on 'the day war is declared'. Sometimes he described the anti-war strike as a general one; but, following Snell's insistence at the ILP Conference in April 1911 that a strike by the transport workers would suffice, Hardie seems to have reduced his claim similarly to a transport workers' strike. The details, therefore, do not seem as yet to have become clear in Hardie's mind. In his speeches he never failed to mention the comforting thought that even the threat of a general strike could dissuade the militarists from an impulsive warlike action. It is likely, then, that for Hardie

[58] 'Head Office Circular', 22 February 1911, ILP NAC *mins.*
[59] *LL*, 28 April 1911.
[60] *LL*, 23 June 1911. See also ILP NAC *mins.*, 14–15 June 1911, and *Herald of Peace*, September 1911.
[61] *LL*, 18 August 1911.

the propaganda value of such an idea, quite apart from the details of its implementation, was always uppermost in his mind.

When the next Labour Party Conference gathered in Birmingham in late January 1912 the prospects for an acceptance of Hardie's anti-war strike plan were perhaps a little stronger. Not only had Hardie himself been supporting the plan for over a year now, but the great labour unrest of 1911 had created a climate within the party more conducive to Hardie's radical style. The presence, for the first time, of a German socialist fraternal delegate at the conference in the person of Molkenbuhr, who was uncharacteristically ebullient following the SPD's triumphs at the polls in the previous week, added to the internationalist spirit of the conference. It was most helpful to Hardie's cause also that the conference chairman, Ben Turner, who had opposed Hardie in 1911, declared himself to be a convert to the anti-war strike plan in his opening address.[62] The ILP had prepared its tactics carefully.[63] When the conference turned to the subject of militarism, Glasier first introduced a generalized motion condemning war, the arms burden and the threat of conscription. When this was safely passed Glasier moved a second resolution:

This Conference expresses its approval of the proposal to investigate and report on whether and how far a stoppage of work either partial or general, in countries about to engage in war would be effective in preventing an outbreak of hostilities; commends the whole subject to the consideration of every section of the movement; and asks the Executive to take such action as may be necessary to secure a full report for next year's conference.[64]

Careful planning and Hardie's own propaganda now reaped their reward: the resolution passed easily by 1,323 votes to 155. The *Labour Leader* was jubilant. In its view the sacrifice that might be required in prosecuting a strike against war was

---

[62] *LL*, 26 January 1912.

[63] The resolution had been formulated by the NAC in October 1911: see ILP 'Report from Head Office', dated 26 October 1911, in ILP NAC *mins.* The *Labour Leader* also maintains that the more general resolution was proposed first for fear of opposition to the general strike proposal, see *LL*, 2 February 1912.

[64] *LL*, 2 February 1912.

[65] Ibid.

nothing compared with the carnage that might be averted. The *Leader* also pointed out that the recent industrial unrest had shown clearly that British workers did have the power to organize a strike of sufficient dimensions to prevent war.[65] Like Hardie, the *Leader* did not fail to mention that perhaps 'the mere threat of a strike' might be sufficient to encourage arbitration of a dispute.[66]

The Labour Party executive, meeting on 13 February 1912, immediately referred the general strike inquiry to the BNC, and set up its own subcommittee to await a report from the BNC.[67] The very next day, the BNC, with Hardie as chairman, in turn decided to draft a series of questions on the anti-war strike plan for submission to the trade unions.[68] It was not until early August 1912 that the BNC's circular regarding the anti-war strike was finally dispatched to the trade unions and societies affiliated to the BNC and the Labour Party.[69] The most noteworthy feature of the circular was its repeated insistence that the real value of the unionists' agreement on the anti-war strike plan would be found in its tremendous propaganda impact. The gist of the argument put forward in the circular was that if the unions committed themselves to ceasing work in order to preserve the peace, the ordinary political struggle against war would be given such 'a tremendous backing' and the governing classes would be so fearful of 'the possibility' of a strike on the eve of war, that the peace would never be violated. Consequently, the question of actually staging an anti-war strike would never arise. The trade unions were assured that the plan was a supplement to political action and not an alternative. After this reassuring explanation the trade unions and councils were asked to poll their members on the following question:

Are you in favour of the organized working class movements of all countries being asked to come to a mutual agreement whereby in the event of war being threatened between any two or more countries

[66] Ibid.
[67] Labour Party, NEC *mins.*, 13 February 1912. The subcommittee consisted of Hardie, Pease, Roberts, and Henderson.
[68] BNC *mins.*, 14 February 1912.
[69] BNC *mins.*, 26 July 1912; *LL*, 15 August 1912, has the full text of the letter to the trade unions.

the workers of those countries would hold themselves prepared to try to prevent it by a mutual and simultaneous stoppage of work in the countries affected? [70]

The phrasing of the question again suggests the essentially propagandist purpose of the BNC inquiry for the unions were not being asked to commit themselves to an anti-war strike at this stage, but simply to declare themselves in favour of all working-class movements 'being asked to come to a mutual agreement'. The implication was that the actual negotiations would follow in the future, perhaps at Vienna in 1913. A response to the circular, and other suggestions on the plan, were expected by 30 September 1912, just two months hence.

In the interim, both MacDonald's *Socialist Review* and the *Labour Leader* commended the anti-war strike plan.[71] Hardie also kept his colleague Vaillant informed regarding the inquiry, and he sent him a copy of the BNC circular in August 1912. Vaillant assured Hardie that the SFIO would arrange a 'similar consultation' with the CGT, but he reminded Hardie, the CGT were not affiliated to the ISB. He advised Hardie to send copies of the circular to all national sections of the socialist movement.[72] Hardie was certainly already doing his best to popularize the concept; and even when he visited America in late August 1912 he talked enthusiastically about the prospects of organizing a strike against war in Britain and Germany.[73]

The trade unions, however, were slow to reply to the BNC circular. When the BNC met on 9 October the replies so far were of such an 'incomplete character' that further consideration was postponed.[74] The ISB also was finding it difficult to elicit responses from its member bodies on the Hardie—Vaillant amendment. In June 1912, eighteen months after the original request for information issued in December 1910, the ISB sent out another circular reminding all national

[70] *LL*, 15 August 1912.
[71] See E. W. D. 'Armaments: Their Purpose not National', in *Socialist Review*, October 1912, pp. 116—17; *LL*, 15 August 1912.
[72] Vaillant to Hardie, 12 August 1912, ILP Archive, 1912/125.
[73] *LL*, 5 September 1912.
[74] BNC *mins.*, 9 October 1912.

sections of their duty to consult with their trade unions on the anti-war strike issue.[75] The ISB circular complained that only four sections, the French, Armenians, Danes, and Finns, had so far replied.[76]

Suddenly the outbreak of war in the Balkans in October 1912 breathed new life into the International's campaign against war. The ISB met in Brussels on 28–9 October to consider the crisis in the Balkans; and, because Hardie was still in America, Glasier took his place as British representative.[76] A committee was quickly appointed to draft a manifesto urging the socialists of all European countries to hold massive demonstrations to oppose any extension of the Balkans conflict. The ISB then turned to consider another problem which was, indirectly, to be of great importance in the history of the anti-war strike inquiry namely, the question of postponing the International Socialist Congress scheduled for 1913 in Vienna. The suggestion of postponement had first been made in August 1912 by the Dutch who had pointed out that the year 1914, the fiftieth anniversary of the First International and the twenty-fifth anniversary of the Second International, would provide marvellous opportunities for propaganda.[77] The French and the British had rejected this proposal,[78] but the Germans and a small majority of national sections had agreed. Vaillant had protested angrily to Huysmans in September that it was vital, in the light of the growing danger to peace, for the International to settle as soon as possible what steps the workers should take to preserve peace.[79] When the matter was debated afresh at Brussels on 28 October the British delegates in particular stood out strongly for 1913. Vandervelde eventually intervened with a compromise proposal, first suggested by Jaurès, that a special extraordinary Congress should be held in December to protest against the Balkan

[75] ISB Circular, no. 11, June 1912, LP/INT/11/1/172/1.
[76] *LL*, 31 October 1912.
[77] ISB Circular, no. 19, 7 September 1912, LP/INT/11/1/182.
[78] See A. Henderson to Huysmans, 12 September 1912, LP/INT/11/1/183, and BNC *mins.*, 9 October 1912 where the Dutch proposal was rejected by five votes to one. There is also a strong statement against postponement in *Justice*, 5 October 1912.
[79] Haupt, *Socialism and the Great War*, p. 76.

War, and then the ordinary congress scheduled for Vienna could be delayed until 1914. At the root of the quarrel on postponement lay the now long-standing suspicions on the part of the French and British that their German comrades were seeking to evade their responsibilities to the International. As Glasier confided to his wife Katharine:

The decision to hold a special anti-war Congress in December looks better on paper than its results will, I fear, justify. The German side approved it in order to get the next general Congress postponed till 1914, the French because Jaurès is honestly so warmly in favour of arousing anti-war feeling in all lands.[80]

The real significance of this decision to postpone the 1913 Vienna Congress to 1914 was that a final settlement of the anti-war strike issue would also have to be delayed. Clearly the extraordinary congress could not determine the matter, for the inquiries in the various nations were still proceeding slowly. So, for another twelve months at least, the general strike against war would have to remain in the realm of speculation and without the formal backing of the International. This was indeed a fateful decision. For the outbreak of war in August 1914 was to crush the International just a month before the scheduled Vienna Congress.

As arranged at Brussels, the member parties of the International organized a series of massive demonstrations during November 1912 in order to mobilize public opinion against any spread of the war in the Balkans. The largest demonstrations were planned to take place simultaneously in all the major European capitals on Sunday 17 November.[81] The Labour Party co-operated with this plan, and J. O'Grady attended the demonstration in Berlin and MacDonald spoke in Paris.[82] A demonstration was also held at the Kingsway Opera House in London, where Hardie, Anseele the Belgian socialist, Dr Ludwig Frank, Jean Longuet, and the Greek socialist Drakhoules, denounced the Balkan War before a small audience of about 1,000 people. Hardie and Anseele

[80] J. B. Glasier to Katharine Glasier, 29 October 1912, Glasier Papers, I. 1. 12/13.
[81] Telegram, Huysmans to Henderson, 6 November 1912, LP/INT/11/1/398; BNC *mins.*, 8 November 1912.
[82] *LL*, 21 November 1912; *Daily News* clipping, LP/INT/11/1/106.

did not let the opportunity slip to advocate the anti-war strike. Hardie promised that:

Someday the workers of the world would meet simultaneously to flash to each other the message that on the rising of the sun on the morrow the international revolutionist anti-war strike would begin to end war once and forever (cheers). That day was coming and could not be long delayed.[83]

However, as Hardie indicated, that day had not yet come. Certainly the crowds in Britain at the demonstrations of November 1912 were not very gratifying. Indeed, they looked quite insignificant beside the huge demonstrations in Paris and Berlin. Although the capacity of the Kingsway Opera House was only 1,000 people, the BNC still incurred a loss of £140 on the meeting.[84] A similar meeting in Leeds turned out to be a 'fiasco' according to the chairman of the Leeds ILP.[85]

The extraordinary congress of the International was now fixed to open in the cathedral at Basle on 24 November 1912. On the previous day the ISB met and a special commision of five was appointed to draft an anti-war resolution which could be agreed upon unanimously by all parties.[86] At this meeting, for which no complete record exists, it seems likely that Hardie made common cause with Vaillant and Jaurès, and possibly Luxemburg also, in urging the necessity of listing the anti-war strike as one of the viable means of enforcing the will of the people for peace. In the end, however, Hardie agreed once more to back down on this issue so that the forces of socialism could present a united front to the governments of Europe. The manifesto presented the next day to the delegates in Basle cathedral therefore made no special recommendations regarding the means to be used to prevent war.[87] The workers were urged to 'use every

---

[83] *Morning Post* clipping, 18 November 1912, LP/INT/11/1/105.

[84] Financial details, see J. S. Middleton to BNC Affiliates, LP/INT/11/1/30 and BNC *mins.*, 16 April 1913.

[85] W. H. Milnes to J. S. Middleton, November 1912, LP/INT/11/1/251.

[86] Haupt, *Socialism and the Great War*, pp. 88–9.

[87] *Compte Rendu Analytique du Congrès Socialiste International, Basle, 1912,* issued as *Bulletin Périodique du Bureau Socialiste International,* no. 10 (cited hereafter as *ISC Proceedings, 1912*), pp. 9–12. (The pagination is that of the *Bulletin.*)

means' to show the governments their resolve to keep the peace, and to 'raise unanimous protests in every parliament, in demonstrations and massed action'. Again, the anti-war strike was not specifically mentioned. Instead, the real theme of the manifesto was its warning to the governments of Europe that massive social unrest and even revolution would surely come in the wake of the disaster of a European war.[88] These more generalized threats took the place of the specific commitment to the anti-war strike which Hardie and the French leaders in particular would have preferred. As Hardie explained:

> It was the duty of everyone with any sense of responsibility to secure unanimity, good feeling and fellowship throughout the entire movement. The one object of the Congress was to make the voice of organized labour heard and felt in all its strength and power in protest against war and aggression, and that nothing should be allowed to be said or done which would detract from the effect of the great gathering, or lead to unseemly wrangles or disputation over details. The situation was too serious for that.[89]

The anti-war strike was not mentioned in the Basle manifesto, but neither was it ruled out. Accordingly, Hardie felt himself free to advocate it in his speech to the assembled delegates on the opening day of the congress. Speaking from the pulpit of the cathedral, Hardie proclaimed:

> If diplomacy takes advantage of the Balkan question in order to kindle a world war, democracy has a sacred duty to employ all the means at its disposal to prevent war. If political action is not sufficient I hope that the working class will have no fear in using the second great weapon. The economic weapon, the international revolutionary anti-war strike.[90]

At the end of the Congress the *Labour Leader* again took up the issue. Under the bold heading 'Prepare to Strike Against War', the *Leader* expressed the ILP's disappointment that no real progress in anti-war plans had been made at Basle.[91] At the same time it agreed with Hardie's argument that the compromises were necessary to preserve unity. The defeat of

88   Ibid., pp. 11–12.
89   *LL*, 5 December 1912.
90   *ISC Proceedings, 1912*, p. 5.
91   *LL*, 28 November 1912.

a general strike amendment would have been disastrous because this would have been an incitement to reckless militarists everywhere. It was far better to keep campaigning in support of the anti-war strike proposal and have the matter settled at Vienna in 1914, counselled the *Leader*: 'The heather smoulders and in the distance can be heared the oncoming wind which shall fan it into flame'.[92]

By no means then was the anti-war strike proposal dead because of the further compromise made at Basle in November 1912. Hardie and the ILP still supported the concept of an anti-war strike and sought to win over the trade unions to the plan. However, the composition of the British delegation at the Basle Congress was itself an indication of how great would be the task of awakening a strong internationalist fervour among British trade unions, for only one of the thirteen British delegates at Basle was a formal union representative.[93]

4. *The Trade Unions and the Anti-War Strike Inquiry, 1912–14*

It was always perfectly clear to Hardie, and to all the socialists of the International, that the policy of an anti-war strike amongst the socialist and Labour parties had no credibility unless the trade unions were fully in agreement. Accordingly, both the ISB and the BNC inquiries on the anti-war strike were addressed principally to the trade unions and sought to elicit their opinions on the strike plan. The BNC's inquiry, undertaken in August 1912, had been held over in October 1912 because of the poor number of responses. Similarly, in January 1913, the ILP was forced to drop the anti-war strike proposal which it had planned to introduce at the Labour Party Conference, again because many of the trade unions had not yet replied to the BNC's original circular.[94] Quelch,

---

[92] Ibid.

[93] Tom Griffiths from the Steel Smelters' Union; *ISC Proceedings, 1912*, p. 16. MacDonald had twisted the rules even to get this single union delegate. He had written to the Dockers', Steel Smelters', and Gasworkers' Unions explaining that those unions 'formerly affiliated' to the BNC should send a delegate (MacDonald to Tillett, Hodge, and Thorne, 11 November 1912, LP/INT/11/1/114–16).

[94] *LL*, 6 February 1913.

for one, was quick to see in this record of delay evidence of the apathy of the British trade unionists on the issue. 'We knew that the matter would not interest the trade unionists as a whole and we were right', Quelch boasted.[95] Certainly the slow rate of the replies seems to indicate that the idea of a general strike had no mass of enthusiastic supporters within the British trade unions. The story, however, is not as simple as that. There was a core of supporters within the union movement and they did make progress during 1913 until, in September, the TUC initiated its own inquiry into the viability of a strike against war.

The beginnings of a trade union interest in the idea could be seen at the TUC in 1911 when, during discussion on a motion expressing solidarity with the peace demonstrations taking place in Germany, Thomas Burt, the miners' MP, declared himself to be in favour of the concept of a military strike to prevent war.[96] When the BNC's circular was issued in August 1912 the positive replies of some trades councils also indicated an interest in the idea, at least among those delegates of trade unions willing to attend the local trades councils. There is no exact information on how many trades councils declared either for or against the anti-war strike. However, at least six passed resolutions in favour of the idea in response to the BNC's circular in the latter months of 1912. These included the trades councils at Bradford, Manchester, Blackpool, Sheffield, Huddersfield, and Belfast.[97] Feeling on the issue at some trades councils seems to have been quite determined. The Sheffield Trades Council passed a motion in favour of the plan by fifty-one votes to three. However, the dissenting delegates warned of the 'inherent jingoism of the Britisher' and predicted that 'come another war and all questions of a strike would

---

[95] Editorial notes, *Social Democrat*, April 1913, p. 170.

[96] TUC, *Annual Report 1911*, pp. 231–2.

[97] Alan Clinton, *The Trade Union Rank and File*, p. 207, lists Belfast, Blackpool, and Sheffield. My own research shows that Bradford, Huddersfield, and Manchester also passed resolutions in favour of the anti-war strike. See Huddersfield TC *mins.*, 28 August 1912; E and R. Flow, *To Make that Future Now* (Manchester TC), p. 67; Mary Ashraf, *One Hundred Years 1872–1972* (Bradford TC), p. 91. See also Blackpool TC, *Diamond Jubilee History* (1951), p. 23 and Belfast and District Trade Union Council 1881–1951, *A Short History*, p. 14.

disappear from the workers' minds and give place to the jingo sentiment'.[98] It is noteworthy too that during the long debate in the council, the International itself was not mentioned once. One major trades council which did reply negatively to the BNC circular was the London Trades Council. The Council executive pointed out that it had no power to take a ballot of its members on the matter of strikes, that being the province of the individual unions.[99] It is possible that Quelch, who was chairman of the London Trades Council at that time, brought his influence to bear against the BNC plan. Apart from the London result, surviving records indicate that there was indeed some sympathy for the idea of an anti-war strike among certain large and important trades councils.

The other centre of support for the concept was the Miners' Federation. A close friend of Keir Hardie, Robert Smillie, had become president of the International Miners' Federation (IMF) in 1912, and during 1912 and 1913 Smillie did his best to commit the Federation to the anti-war strike plan. The French miners' delegates had declared their support for the idea of a strike against war as early as the IMF Congress in 1910.[100] However, the German delegates were always insistent that the IMF should not discuss such political questions because this would furnish the German police authorities with a pretext for declaring their union a political organization, which would in turn give rise to certain disabilities such as a prohibition on enrolling workers under eighteen years of age.[101] At first, the other national sections of the IMF complied with the German's requests in this regard; but by 1913 some resentment against the German's reservations was evident and Smillie, as IMF president, openly advocated the anti-war strike and a special IMF conference to consider simultaneous action if ever war

[98] Sheffield TC *mins.*, 24 September 1912.
[99] London TC *mins.*, 29 August 1912.
[100] 'Proceedings of IMF Congress 1910', p. 51, in MFGB *Proceedings*, 1910. (Speech of M. Cordier.)
[101] 'Proceedings of the International Committee of the IMF, 4 May 1912', pp. 22–3, in MFGB *Proceedings* 1912. See also the German delegate Sasche's response in which he restated the German's reasons for requesting that there be no discussion of anti-war measures, p. 11; in MFGB *Proceedings*, 1912.

looked imminent.[102] In their hearts, however, Smillie and the other leaders of the IMF must have known that the chances of an anti-war strike were in any case very slim. For in March 1913, the IMF and the British mining and transport unions had discovered that they were virtually powerless to organize an effective boycott of coal supplies to Belgium in support of the general strike which was planned to take place there in April in favour of franchise reform.[103] The incident was no doubt a sobering experience for Smillie and his comrades. The deficiencies of international trade union organization prevented efforts to halt the movement of coal across national frontiers in time of peace. How much more difficult it would be for the same trade unions to prevent the movement of men and materials across frontiers in time of war!

Nor were the miners the only British trade unionists to show an interest in the plan to use trade union power to enforce peace. At the annual conference of the National Transport Workers' Federation on 6 June 1913, a resolution against war was passed recommending 'a general stoppage of work among all transport workers who are engaged in the transportation of troops and munitions of war' in order to prevent war. The resolution also instructed the General Council of the union to 'take the necessary steps to make this resolution operative'. Ben Tillett, Jack Jones, and the young Ernest Bevin spoke strongly in support of the plan, and the resolution was passed without a single dissenting vote. However, James Sexton, the Liverpool Dockers' leader, was not speaking for himself alone when he expressed his doubts that the rank and file of the Continental trade unions, especially the workers in nationalized railways, would have the capacity to organize an effective strike against war.[104]

---

[102] See speech of M. Lamedin (France), ibid., p. 11, and Smillie's speech to the American Federation of Labour, in *LL*, 5 December 1912. On the French resentment against the Germans' position see 'Proceedings of IMF Congress, 1913', pp. 10–15, in MFGB *Proceedings* 1913.

[103] For the failure of attempts to assist the Belgians see 'Proceedings of the International Committee of the IMF, 1 March 1913' and 'Special Conference of the MFGB, 27–28 March 1913', in MFGB *Proceedings*, 1913; and TUC PC *mins.*, 9 April 1913.

[104] National Transport Workers' Federation, *Proceedings of the Annual General Meeting*, 6 June 1913, pp. 31–5.

The clearest sign of growing interest in the anti-war strike plan within the British trade unions came at the Trade Union Congress at Manchester in September 1913. The presence of Karl Legien and Leon Jouhaux, for the first time, as fraternal delegates from Germany and France, helped foster an internationalist spirit on this occasion that was unique among pre-war congresses; and even the opening speech by Dean Welldon, a Manchester clergyman, touched upon the duty of labour to end war between nations.[105] In place of the traditional resolution in favour of peace there was, first, a demand for a Royal Commission into the activities of armament firms. Then, F. Sanderson from the Liverpool Dockers moved:

That this Congress strongly condemns any action likely to lead to war between nations and pledges itself to do everything possible to make war impossible; and, further, instructs the Parliamentary Committee to confer with the British Miners' Federation, the National Transport Workers' Federation, and the National Union of Railwaymen with a view to opening negotiations with foreign trade unions for the purpose of making agreements and treaties as to common international action in the event of war being forced upon us.[106]

Speaking in support of his motion, Sanderson remarked upon the presence of Legien and Jouhaux as real evidence of the comradeship that existed among Europe's workers. 'And yet, if we leave it to peace conferences or to Parliament some of us will be dead and in our graves before effective steps will be taken to stop war', declared Sanderson, expressing the wish of a great many workers no doubt to do something tangible to bring the forces of labour into account on the side of peace. The motion passed without dissent.[107] The apparent conversion of the whole of the TUC to the idea of 'common international action' against war no doubt gave great encouragement to Hardie and all the supporters of the anti-war strike. However, it is important to note that the TUC decision was only an endorsement of further negotiations toward common action. No commitment to a general strike was implied. Yet, Hardie's own BNC circular of August

[105] *LL*, 11 September 1913.
[106] TUC, *Annual Report*, 1913, p. 339.
[107] Ibid.

1912 had sought nothing further than this endorsement of negotiations; and so Hardie could be well satisfied with this turn of events within the TUC. Thus, following the TUC's decision in September, Hardie returned to the advocacy of an anti-war strike with renewed vigour.[108]

When the ISB met in London on 14 December 1913 to consider the agenda for the coming Vienna Congress, Hardie was naturally appointed, along with Haase, Jaurès, and the Dutch socialist Vliegen, to the commission on 'Imperialism and Arbitration'. Hardie and his colleagues were requested to draw up reports on the whole subject of war and imperialism in time for the Vienna Congress which was now fixed, on Vaillant's suggestion, for the 3 August 1914, exactly fifty years after the foundation of the First International. At the ISB meeting Hardie also gave notice of a motion which he intended to move, in the name of the ILP, at Vienna. The motion noted the growing strength of internationalist feeling amongst trade unionists and called upon the ISB to

arrange for a series of conferences and demonstrations in the capital cities of Europe to consider how best peace may be maintained by the combined action of the nations, and a beginning made in the creation of the United States of Europe.[109]

This notice of motion for the forthcoming Vienna Congress gives a very important insight into Hardie's thinking at this time. It would appear that he envisaged a formal adoption of the Hardie–Vaillant amendment at Vienna, and not a binding commitment. For, clearly, this additional motion indicates that Hardie wanted a continuing series of debates and demonstrations on the problem of how to preserve peace. Vienna, therefore, was to be a further stage in the propaganda campaign in support of the anti-war strike. In Hardie's mind, the anti-war strike was not going to be

---

[108] For example, Hardie's speeches at Edinburgh (reported in *LL*, 27 November 1913), Clydebank (*LL*, 27 November 1913), Bethseda (*LL*, 11 December 1913), Worthington (*LL*, 18 December 1913); and also Brockway's confident prediction that the new trade union 'triple alliance' would assist the strike plan, *LL*, 16 October 1913.

[109] The proceedings are in *Supplément au Bulletin Périodique du Bureau Socialiste International*, no. 11, p. 3.

imposed upon reluctant parties at Vienna. He did not wish to 'win' in that sense. A further indication of his own uncertainty at this stage was given when he announced his foreshadowed motion for Vienna in the *Labour Leader* at the end of December 1913. Hardie openly requested assistance:

I shall be glad to hear from comrades who have any suggestions to make for dealing with any phase of this great subject of militarism and imperialism. A hint on some aspect which might otherwise be overlooked, or some reference to some book or document, is often very valuable.[110]

Unfortunately, Hardie's final opinions on the subject are not known. He did report his findings on the subject of 'imperialism and arbitration', and also the results of the general strike inquiry in Britain, to the BNC on 17 July 1914.[111] The BNC, in turn, decided that Hardie should report these findings to the Vienna Congress; but the minutes give no indication as to what these findings were. Apparently Hardie had promised to send his report to Brussels after this BNC meeting; but as Georges Haupt, the historian of the ISB who has studied its archives, comments, 'it seems that this document never reached its destination'.[112] Similarly the TUC's own inquiry into the viability of 'international action' against war was cut short by the crisis of August 1914. The TUC Parliamentary Committee agreed on 24 February 1914 to contact the Railway unions, miners' unions, and the Transport Workers' Federation as requested by the 1913 TUC resolution to ask 'for their observations'.[113] However, by the time of the outbreak of war no replies had been received by the Parliamentary Committee. In any case the speed of the crisis in August swept all before it. The crucial point to note is that the world conflagration erupted whilst Hardie and his comrades were just beginning to build support for the idea of an anti-war strike, and long before the strike had been accepted either by British workers or the International itself as settled policy. The strike plan in Britain did

[110] *LL*, 24 December 1913.
[111] BNC *mins.*, 17 July 1914.
[112] Haupt, *Socialism and the Great War*, p. 157.
[113] TUC PC *mins.*, 24 February 1914.

not evaporate before the fire of patriotism. When the war began no specific strike plan existed, just a threatening vision of a future weapon.

5. *The Anti-War Strike as 'Bluff and Bluster'*

It is sometimes suggested that, in advocating an anti-war strike, such socialists as Hardie, Vaillant, and Jaurès revealed only how complete was their own self-deception and how blind to the realities of the situation they had become.[114] According to this view Hardie and his comrades were victims of their own optimistic dreams, men who grossly over-estimated their own influence and were foolish enough to believe that the workers would shrug off the patriotic yoke and down tools to stop war. In the light of the rush to war in 1914 it is easy to denounce these socialists as deluded dreamers. However, this simplistic assessment of Hardie and his comrades misunderstands the logic of their case.

First, Hardie and the other leaders of the International were well aware of the numerical weakness of their own parties and had no illusions about the true dimensions of the power at their disposal. Second, it was a realistic assessment of this weakness which had led the International to reject the general strike against war in 1907, and to focus instead on a more generalized policy of threatening European governments by mustering the numbers that were available into mass anti-war demonstrations. Third, Hardie, Vaillant, and Jaurès accepted this emphasis on the 'propaganda of threat' by mass demonstrations, believing that governments would not choose war if public opinion was not in support of an aggressive policy. They accepted, therefore, that their chief task was to evoke public manifestations of opposition to war, and to raise the spectre of a possible revolt. It was in this special sense of adding to the 'propaganda of threat' that Hardie, Vaillant, and Jaurès returned to the advocacy of a revised anti-war strike proposal, revised in that it was now presented as a strike prior to an outbreak of war, designed to force disputing governments to arbitration. This was certainly

---

[114] See, for example, Gerhart Niemeyer, 'The Second International: 1889–1914', in Milorad M. Drachkovitch (ed.), *The Revolutionary Internationals 1864–1943* (Stanford, 1966).

an improved proposal; but the crucial point to note is that the details of its implementation were not the primary consideration. The real purpose of the inclusion of the anti-war strike policy in the International's formal resolutions was simply to add to the 'pretence of power'. It was the propaganda impact of such an inclusion that fascinated Hardie and his French comrades.

It is perfectly clear that Hardie and the other leaders of the International were under no illusions as to the true dimensions of the organized working-class movement. Naturally they did not proclaim to the world their own weakness; but, when their guards were down, they made candid admissions of their limited influence amongst the working classes. Those who sat amongst the forty MPs on the Labour Party benches in the House of Commons, a House numbering over 650 members, could not come away with anything other than a sense of the power still exerted by the established parties over the British people. Hardie admitted as much when he replied to a suffragette interjector at a meeting in Manchester in 1913:

The trouble is that you are up against the same thing as we are. You have not the women of the nation behind you any more than we have the workman behind us. Shout less and work more.[115]

Sometimes the task of converting the masses seemed too overwhelming and the progress too slow, so that occasionally even the socialist press fell to railing against the apathy and stubbornness of the working people, and especially their indifference toward foreign affairs.[116] These complaints in the socialist press were certainly not the work of labour leaders with an inflated sense of their own influence.

The British socialist leaders were also under no illusions as to the real power exercised by the Continental parties of the International. Although the ILP and Labour Party leaders quite naturally stressed in public the dimensions and great prestige of the German SPD, they did not suggest that their German comrades wielded a preponderant influence in the

---

[115] *Daily Citizen*, 24 March 1913.
[116] For example, D. F. Griffiths, 'The Real Enemy', *Socialist Review*, August 1912; editorial notes, *Socialist Review*, July 1913, pp. 329–30.

Kaiser's Germany. During the Moroccan crisis of 1911, MacDonald declared in the Commons:

We know the gravity of the situation. We know that those who work with us upon the Continent cannot control Continental national policies. But we also know this, that it may be very useful for rulers of all the countries to know that there is a strong organization that will stand for peace through fair weather and foul.[117]

Liberals and Conservatives were fond of underlining the fact that the German socialists did not yet control German policy. During the naval estimates debates in 1909, L. G. Chiozza Money, a Radical MP and friend of the Labour Party, reminded the Labour MPs that:

the Socialist Party in Germany, if it counts for a great deal in numbers and for a great deal in the life of the people, is not in charge of the German Government, and it is in spite of the existence of that great Socialist party that the Germans are now building Dreadnoughts.[118]

Even more sobering in 1910 was the speech of one Unionist who ridiculed the anti-war strike as an absurd contention 'because leading socialists in Germany have distinctly said that they are quite incapable of preventing war'.[119] MacDonald certainly realized that the International could provide no guarantees of peace. In 1912 he noted that it was 'doubtful' whether the Congress at Basle could decide upon any action which could offer effective resistance to war. 'The call of battle', he wrote, 'is still the most irresistible and intoxicating of all political appeals'.[120]

Keir Hardie in particular was not blind to the immense practical difficulties in the path of the International in resisting war, and especially the difficulties surrounding the general strike plan. Indeed, judging from Hardie's writings during the labour unrest, when the use of troops to quell strikes became frequent, it seems likely that Hardie realized that a general strike against war would almost certainly fail. In May 1912, he wrote in the *Socialist Review* cautioning the railway unions against a national strike contemplated for

---

[117] *Hansard*, 27 July 1911, V. 28: 1830.
[118] *Hansard*, 29 March 1909, V: 3: 102.
[119] *Hansard*, 11 March 1910, V: 14: 1848.
[120] Editorial Notes, *Socialist Review*, December 1912, pp. 244–5.

the coming summer. He noted that the Government, the companies, and the Army were 'ready to cope with it'. Hardie explained that increasing numbers of soldiers were being trained for the railways:

They are being specifically trained and equipped, and wherever possible given actual experience of the working of railways so as to be ready to take charge of trains at any moment. On one section of one of our principal railways I know for a fact that twenty of these men are being employed in learning how to operate the signal boxes. In addition to that, armour protected engines and vans are being contructed ostensibly for war purposes, but actually for home use. . . Within a week therefore of a general railway strike breaking out, the Army, and possibly the Reserve Forces would again be mobilized to protect the lines. A limited train service would be run partly by blackleg labour and partly by the military. Every train would carry its escort of armed men.[121]

In a speech at Merthyr in June 1913, Hardie repeated his accusation that the Government was training soldiers to 'blackleg' in the event of another railway strike.[122] Although these warnings of the futility of a general railway strike were not directed against the anti-war strike as such, it seems clear that Hardie appreciated that the practical difficulties of staging an effective railway strike in a war emergency would be colossal. His precise reasoning with regard to the anti-war strike is unknown; but it seems likely that Hardie did not really believe that his anti-war strike plan could stop war by creating physical barriers to military manpower deployment. What then was his purpose in supporting the anti-war strike from 1910 to 1914, and what were the motives of his French colleagues, Jaurès and Vaillant?

To answer this question one must first appreciate the extent to which the International had come to rely on the persuasive force of public opinion, in terms of its 'threat value' to the European governments, as the chief weapon in the struggle to maintain peace. At the Stuttgart Congress in 1907, the International had finally rejected the vision of a general strike *after* the declaration of war as a means of preventing mobilization and enforcing peace. The consensus at Stuttgart was that this would be 'heroic folly', for it was

---

[121] Hardie, 'The Lessons of the Strike', *Socialist Review*, May 1912, p. 211.
[122] *LL*, 3 July 1913.

'too late' to counter war once the fury was unleashed. Instead, the International pledged itself to incessant anti-militarist propaganda to create a public opinion so strong that governments would not dare to flout the will of the people. Accordingly, the Stuttgart resolution itself provided a long list of the internationalist demonstrations of the workers which showed their 'absolute determination' to maintain peace; and the resolution promised even stiffer resistance to war 'when public opinion is influenced to a greater degree than at present'.[123] The guiding principle of the International's peace strategy from Stuttgart to Sarajevo was well expressed by the SPD Executive in 1911:

> It will be too late to resist once war has broken out. What is vital is to avoid a spirit of belligerence spreading among the masses, because modern war can hardly happen without the agreement of the masses, and if it does happen the rulers have everything to fear from its deadly consequences.[124]

There is a great deal of evidence to show that the British and French leaders of the International, as well as the German leaders, accepted this argument that governments would not contemplate war if a strong anti-war feeling amongst their own people had been unmistakably demonstrated to them. This was the whole point behind the massive demonstrations, the International's ceaseless collection of details of anti-war activity, the simultaneous resolutions in the various parliaments, and the ceaseless search for fresh propaganda devices. It was the search for 'the force of propaganda' which motivated the Dutch to suggest postponing the Vienna Congress from 1913 to 1914, so as to publicize the anniversaries of the First and Second Internationals.[125] Vaillant certainly accepted the theory that the European governments must be threatened by mass demonstrations and incessant propaganda in order to ensure peace. In February 1913 he explained his position to Huysmans:

---

[123]   From the English translation of the Stuttgart Resolution given in Walling (ed.), *Socialists and the War*, p. 49.
[124]   Quoted in Haupt, *Socialism and the Great War*, p. 40.
[125]   ISB Circular, no. 19, 7 September 1912, LP/INT/11/1/182.

Given that the most important factor in the struggle for peace is a pacifist orientation of public opinion. . . it is important that our propaganda against war and for peace does not diminish, and that the anti-war and anti-militarist campaign is always placed on the agenda of all demonstrations and rallies for whichever reason they are held, in all countries, in yours, ours and everywhere else. Only by these means can further and perhaps imminent threats be banished.[126]

Jaurès also believed that the governments of Europe needed to feel threatened by the sight of vast numbers of potentially 'disloyal' citizens who would openly voice their opposition to war. At the ISB meeting in October 1912, Jaurès declared that:

The socialist bureau must organize immediate, impassioned and effective international action to oppose any possible spread of war, action that will unite the whole thinking proletariat, and rouse it into making a unanimous protest, an unambiguous protest.[127]

The ISB manifesto of October 1912, the Basle Congress, and the mass demonstrations in all the European capitals in November against any extension of the Balkan conflict, marked the high point of the International's propaganda of threat and bluster.

A secondary aim in this programme of mass demonstration by the socialists was undoubtedly to reassure the workers of every land that their anti-war feeling was paralleled by their comrades abroad. Thus Glasier suggested in October 1912 that there should be an ongoing series of mass demonstrations with an interchange of speakers from the various European nations.[128] The French socialists too hoped that the mass demonstrations for peace in Germany would reassure their own followers. In early 1913, Jean Longuet, the editor of *L'Humanité*, was therefore commissioned to write a pamphlet on the SPD's struggle against war in reply to Charles Andler who had cast doubt on the willingness of the SPD to resist war. Longuet's purpose in writing the pamphlet was made perfectly clear to Kautsky:

Now I would like to publish at the first page of my pamphlet the photo of a typical Berlin meeting against war, and the included reproduction I

---

[126] Quoted in Haupt, *Socialism and the Great War*, p. 100.
[127] Quoted ibid., p. 80.
[128] Glasier to Henderson, 19 October 1912, LP/INT/11/1/455.

found a year ago in the *Chicago Magazine* is much more lively and
convincing than the other photos... where you do not see this extraordinary view of those thousands of hands uplifted.[129]

Jaurès also continually stressed in public his faith in the SPD.
As he explained in 1913, 'There is no power, however intoxi-
cated with its divine right, that can afford to ignore the
clearly expressed determination of four million human beings
united in the socialist party and fight for democracy and
peace'.[130]

An awareness of these principles which underlay the
International's peace strategy assists in reaching an understanding of the real motives behind the renewed advocacy
of the anti-war strike by Hardie, Jaurès, and Vaillant in the
period after Stuttgart. It was not a reversion to Hervéism, nor
was it an attempt to replace the basic strategy. On the
contrary, the anti-war strike agitation was an effort to
supplement the theory of threatening propaganda and
demonstrations. The evidence indicates that Hardie, Jaurès,
and Vaillant appreciated the unlikelihood of their forces
ever organizing an anti-war strike, and also that these three
socialists accepted the basic strategy of threat and bluster.
The anti-war strike, therefore, was not proposed because
Hardie, Vaillant, and Jaurès really believed it was a viable
weapon at the time. Rather, they campaigned to place the
anti-war strike among the International's policy resolutions
primarily because they wished to achieve the propaganda
impact of such a commitment. Even if the anti-war strike was
simply mentioned as one possible means of preventing war,
it would add to the 'threat value' of the international
working-class movement; and it would reassure the movement in each nation that the comrades abroad were indeed
in earnest in straining every nerve to prevent war.

In Hardie's writings and speeches on the anti-war strike
there were many indications that, above all, he looked to the
anti-war strike agitation as a means of frightening the ruling
élite into caution. In his speech to the Copenhagen Congress

---

[129]   Jean Longuet to Karl Kautsky, 19 February 1913; 11SG, Kautsky Archive,
DXVI 96.
[130]   Quoted in Haupt, *Socialism and the Great War*, pp. 110—11.

in 1910, when he first presented his famous amendment, Hardie declared:

We must give the workers a great lead. He did not expect that the workers were at present ready to strike against war. But they never would be ready to do so unless we helped to educate them by pointing out to them their duty.[131]

From the outset the issue in Hardie's mind was not so much whether a strike in the present circumstances was feasible or not. The prime necessity was to give the workers 'a lead'. In his speeches during the 'Autumn Campaign' against armaments Hardie stressed that fear of even the 'possibility' of a strike would be enough to dissuade European governments from war.[132] The propaganda impact of a commitment to an anti-war strike by the International clearly fascinated Hardie. Moreover, the idea was in the air in pacifist circles in Britain. Among others, Maurice Hewlett had outlined this argument in the *Labour Leader* in July 1910:

Undoubtedly its [organized labour's] greatest, most terrible, most dangerous weapon will be the general strike. So dangerous is it that I think the mere threat of it (backed by knowledge of the reality behind the threat) will be enough to frighten the financiers, who are nowadays the real war-makers.[133]

Hardie spoke in this vein quite frequently after 1910. It has already been noted above that the key document of the anti-war strike inquiry in Britain, the BNC circular of August 1912, drawn up by the BNC under Hardie's chairmanship, referred three times to the educative and persuasive impact of an anti-war strike policy. At the London peace demonstration of 17 November 1912, during the Balkan crisis, Hardie noted that 'already the very existence of the propaganda of the anti-war strike is having an immense moral effect upon the governments'.[134] In a special May Day message, which appeared in the *Labour Leader* in 1913 and again in 1914, he argued in favour of the anti-war strike from the same propagandist point of view;

[131] Glasier's report of Hardie's speech in *LL*, 9 September 1910.
[132] *LL*, 28 October and 4 November 1910.
[133] 'The Work of the Peace Societies', *LL*, 22 July 1910.
[134] *LL*, 21 November 1912.

if the rulers know that the workers will not fight each other no war will ever be declared. That much is obvious, and a consideration of that fact is an additional argument for the anti-war strike propaganda. It brings the question before the workers in a concrete form which they can understand. It shows the need for a more cordial and intimate international relationship, so that prompt action could be taken should the occasion ever arise. That of itself would have an educational value of a far-reaching kind, and would strengthen the wholesome fear of socialism which already disturbs the chancelleries of Europe.[135]

Similarly there is good evidence to show that Jaurès and Vaillant were keen to see the anti-war strike policy appear among the International's policy resolutions, not because they had a full-blooded commitment to use it to prevent war, but because they believed its appearance in the International's resolutions on war would frighten the governments. As early as 1907 Jaurès had privately revealed his motives in this regard, according to Bernstein's recollection of a private conversation with Jaurès in a park in Stuttgart during an interlude in the International Congress of 1907:

Jaurès was trying to win me over to his viewpoint on the general strike. All my objections concerned its impracticality, but he kept coming back to the *moral* effect of such a commitment.[136]

It is likely, then, that Jaurès did not dispute that a successful anti-war strike was improbable; but, like Hardie, he focused his attention on the propaganda advantages. This interpretation of Jaurès motives accords with his strong insistence on the importance of a propaganda of optimism to break down the sense of war being inevitable.[137] Vaillant also showed great interest in the effective prosecution of the International's propaganda against war, and it is likely that he too was very aware that the anti-war strike policy had great propaganda value. He was certainly most insistent to Hardie in 1912 that if the British unions favoured an anti-war strike they should 'tell their decision'.[138] Vaillant's speech at the Basle Congress also showed his determination

---

[135]   Hardie, 'Socialism as a World Force', in *LL*, 1 May 1913 and *LL*, 30 April 1914.
[136]   Quoted in Goldberg, *Jaurès*, p. 383.
[137]   See ibid., p. 305.
[138]   Quoted in Morgan, *Keir Hardie*, p. 261.

to advocate the anti-war strike during this most spectacular of the International's peace demonstrations. He explained that the strike had been omitted from the congress manifesto in order to achieve perfect unity; but, he reminded the delegates, it was not rejected. He then proceeded to review the power of the general strike as it had been manifested in the Russian Revolution.[139]

For Hardie, Jaurès, and Vaillant the anti-war strike was largely a matter of bluff. Even so, it is important to note that both Hardie and Jaurès did take the trouble to reshape the details of their planned anti-war strike so that it appeared as a more viable proposition than the traditional Hervéist 'reply to war' strike. As noted above, Hardie and his colleagues in the ILP usually emphasized that the strike they envisaged would come into force 'when war threatened' in order to force the governments in dispute to submit their quarrel to international arbitration. Hervé himself assisted in this remodelling of the traditional proposal. When he was released from prison in July 1912 he declared himself a convert to a more moderate socialism;[140] and one of the many subjects upon which his opinions had changed was that of the anti-war strike. In August 1912, soon after the launching of the BNC inquiry into the strike, the *Leader* published an important article by Hervé on the question.[141] He argued that the Hardie–Vaillant plan would surely fail should war be declared, because the railwaymen and munitions workers would be mobilized and placed under military law, especially in France and Germany. Before the outbreak of war, however, the danger of court martial would be less and the wave of nationalism might not yet have struck the population. There were difficulties in motivating the workers; but certainly, he concluded, the best chance for an effective anti-war strike existed before any shots were fired. Vaillant, who vacillated in his thinking on the matter, seemed at one stage to be drawn to the older slogan of 'insurrection rather than war'.

[139] *ISC Proceedings, 1912*, p. 15.
[140] J. D. Ellis, 'French Socialist and Syndicalist Approaches to Peace, 1904–1914' (unpublished thesis), p. 161.
[141] Hervé, 'A Strike Against War: Declare it Before Shots are Fired!', in *LL*, 29 August 1912.

Jaurès, by contrast, held to this new view of the anti-war strike, perhaps discerning in it an element of moderation which might appeal to the Germans at the coming Vienna Congress. Thus, at the special SFIO Congress held in mid-July 1914 to discuss the coming Vienna Congress, Jaurès championed the cause of an anti-war general strike 'to force upon the governments the international arbitration of the dispute'.[142] He carefully explained that the strike he envisaged would take place 'in the period of preparation for war, in the period of press agitation'. He specifically ruled out any such action after war had begun. Like Hardie, Jaurès acknowledged the weakness of the socialists' forces but stressed the moral impact of adopting the strike policy:

> We are told not to use big words. Certainly we shall not. We know that at the present time, in Europe, no national section of the working class can give a guarantee to that of other countries that it will join in the common action. And I confess that we French especially, who have not been able up to the present to create a great economic organization of the proletariat, must not use big words. We do not demand that a pledge should be given to strike. We must make the proletariat conscious of what the world expects from it, and if we fill it with the idea that its mission is to give peace to the world, we shall make it capable of accomplishing this ideal. (Thunderous applause.)[143]

To sum up, the socialists of the International who advocated the general strike against war were not blind or unrealistic optimists. The fact that strikes against war never materialized in the crisis of August 1914 does not prove their self-delusion. To see the socialists as self-deluded men is to misunderstand the reasoning behind their advocacy of an anti-war strike policy. From the evidence it is clear that Hardie and his two closest French colleagues understood that it was highly unlikely that the present forces of the International would be able to organize a strike against war. In their view, that was not a sufficient reason to disown the plan and lose the tremendous 'threat value' which even a formal commitment to an anti-war strike would bring. Hardie, Vaillant, and Jaurès believed above all that the

---

[142] Jaurès's speech is given in Walling (ed.), *The Socialists and the War*, pp. 55–7.

[143] Ibid., p. 56.

inclusion of the anti-war strike in the International's policy resolutions would enhance the 'pretence of power' possessed by the International. From their point of view, the debate with the Germans over the anti-war strike should not have been an argument about practicalities but an argument about propaganda. Essentially they believed that it was good propaganda to threaten the ruling class, to offer guidance to the people, and to keep the anti-war strike before the masses in an effort to create the determined majorities against war which they knew did not yet exist. The anti-war strike was a matter of bluff and bluster, a matter of assuming even the pretence of an ultimate power to prevent war. Perhaps Bernstein realized the truth of this in 1917, when, recalling his conversation with Jaurès in 1907 and his own practical objections to the anti-war strike, he commented, 'Sometimes our lack of imagination can lead us to serious mistakes'.[144]

[144] Quoted in Goldberg, *Jaurès*, p. 383.

11

Cause without Followers:
The Last Campaigns against Militarism,
1911–1914

> This system [of armaments competition] is a system of progress
> down and down in obedience to a momentum that somebody
> must stop somehow... We are not avoiding war by what we are
> doing. It is bound to come. We are not going to go on year after
> year building, building, building, increasing our Estimates by
> millions and millions every year. Neither Germany or ourselves
> can stand this.
>
> J. Ramsay MacDonald, 22 July, 1912, *Hansard*, V: 41:
> 876–7

The mixed success experienced by Hardie in his advocacy
of an anti-war strike appears not to have dampened his
enthusiasm or the determination of the small group of
activists around him to press on with a broad peace agitation.
However, perhaps these careworn campaigners did come to
appreciate during the years 1911 to 1914 that, for many
of their followers, the danger of a future war was too vague
a threat to be considered the burning issue of the moment.
For, notwithstanding the foreign crisis of the Balkan Wars
of 1912–13, these years saw considerable social and political
upheaval in Britain, and it was only natural that much of the
interest and energy of the labour movement was absorbed
in such domestic issues as national insurance, the struggle
with the House of Lords, the suffragette crisis, the 'Labour
Unrest', and Ireland. While these domestic difficulties were
always accorded the prominence they deserved, at the same
time the ILP activists and their contacts within the Labour
Party drummed away steadily in their effort to alert the
labour movement to the less readily discernible dangers in
the international situation. Some lessons appear to have
been drawn from the anti-armaments campaign of 1910–11,
which, as noted previously, had been disappointing in some
respects, in particular, the lack of impact which it had made

within the Parliamentary Labour Party. In an effort to improve upon the experience of 1910–11, several new propaganda themes emerged.

1. *Foreign Policy and Armaments: the Labour Party Divided 1911–13*

The first of these new themes was a special concentration upon the vital question of the management of British foreign policy by Sir Edward Grey, which, it was alleged, had locked Britain into the rivalries of Europe and had spurred on the armaments competition. In the aftermath of the Moroccan crisis of the summer of 1911, the question of Grey's foreign policy was attracting a good deal of critical interest from concerned Radicals in the Commons.[1] The Labour Party was at that time preoccupied with the sudden upsurge in industrial unrest and the Parliamentary Party was embroiled in an internal wrangle over the Government's new Insurance Bill. Nevertheless, during November 1911, the *Labour Leader* attempted to bring to prominence the issues of British foreign policy, in particular Britain's response to events in Persia and to the recent Italian invasion of Tripoli. In early November the *Leader* denounced the Government's failure to condemn the invasion of Tripoli, and called upon the socialist and labour movement to strive against the system of secret diplomacy that produced such immoral equivocations.[2] In the following weeks the *Leader* lashed out in passionate tones against Grey, the 'Arch Tory', for his failure to support Persian independence against the threat of Russian intervention. The *Leader* complained that Grey had assumed the dictatorial powers of a 'Caesar' in foreign policy, and that his secret diplomacy had saddled the nation with 'crippling and compromising alliances'.[3]

Feeling was running high, therefore, when on 27 November the Commons debated the Government's foreign policy. Grey defended his actions in the crisis of the preceding summer, and asserted that he had never consented to 'a single secret article of any kind' in any international agreement. According

---

[1] See Morris, *Radicalism Against War*, pp. 251–72.
[2] *LL*, 10 November 1911.
[3] *LL*, 24 November 1911.

to Grey, Britain's 'friendship' with France and Russia was an aid to the maintenance of peace in Europe. Grey argued that both France and Russia were constrained to pursue genuinely peaceful foreign policies by the knowledge that Britain would never agree to intervene in a European conflict on their behalf if that conflict arose from their aggression.[4] In reply to Grey, MacDonald delivered a respectful but strongly critical speech. He questioned Grey's allegiance to the concept of continuity in foreign policy, and accused Grey of betraying the Liberal tradition. He denounced the alliance with Russia and insisted that Grey had surrendered the fate of Persia to a merciless Tsar in order to preserve the alliance. The need of the hour, he proclaimed once more, was a determination to reach a cordial understanding with Germany so that arms limitation could follow.[5] There was no hint in MacDonald's speech of anything other than pride in the German socialists, whose work for peace in Germany he praised.[6] Hardie also attacked Grey for not actively seeking friendship with Germany. Grey's policy toward Persia, India, and Egypt, Hardie argued, ignored the needs of the people and aimed rather at 'the protection of profits and dividends'. In spite of Grey's assurances, Hardie insisted that secret diplomacy was a major problem; and he reminded the House of the many occasions when the Foreign Secretary refused to answer questions on foreign policy because of 'the delicate stage of diplomatic negotiations'.[7] The following day, Charles Duncan, one of the leading rebel Labour MPs on the armaments issue, also attacked Grey's policies and spoke of the need for Anglo-German reconciliation.[8] Evidently, the Labour MPs were more united on this issue than upon the vexed question of cuts in arms spending.

While many of the Radical MPs and newspapers were satisfied with Grey's defence of his administration,[9] the

---

[4] *Hansard*, 27 November 1911, V: 32: 57—9.

[5] Ibid., V: 32: 74—8. MacDonald had made similar points in his speech in the debate on the Address, *Hansard*, 6 February 1911, V: 21: 99—101.

[6] Ibid., V: 32: 75; and see also the review of German anti-war demonstrations, in *LL*, 17 November 1911.

[7] *Hansard*, V: 32: 130—2.

[8] Ibid., 28 November 1911, V: 32: 2661.

[9] Morris, *Radicalism Against War*, p. 278.

ILP was not so easily disarmed. In the week immediately following the Commons debate, the *Labour Leader* announced boldly on its front page that 'the immediate necessity can be summed up in one phrase—Sir Edward Grey Must Go'. The *Leader* condemned Grey outright for undertaking a systematic and prejudiced campaign to hinder German expansion while encouraging the equally despicable expansionist pretensions of France and Russia, thus alienating Germany irrevocably. The *Leader* asked why there were no Mansion House speeches of indignation over Italian massacres in Tripoli and Russian aggression in Persia?[10] A week later the *Labour Leader* focused even more closely upon Grey as the chief stumbling-block in the path of reconciliation with Germany:

No sincere reformer must rest content until Sir Edward Grey has been deposed. There is only one possible result of our present foreign policy and that is—war. Unless Sir Edward Grey goes Europe will, within a few short months, be the scene of a conflict, the effects of which we shrink from depicting.[11]

No doubt to the satisfaction of the Labour Party chiefs, the Parliamentary Labour Party seemed quite united in criticizing Grey's management of Britain's foreign policy. As chairman of the Parliamentary Party, MacDonald was, therefore, encouraged to pursue this theme. It was through his efforts that, in mid-December 1911, the entire membership of the Parliamentary Labour Party signed a memorial of greetings to the German socialists reaffirming the desire of the working people of Britain to live in peace with the German working people, and placing the blame for the 'present unfortunate estrangement' between the two nations squarely at the feet of 'political and economic interests'.[12] It is likely that the memorial was also an attempt to paper over the mutual suspicions that had been generated by the German socialists' hesitations at the time of the Moroccan crisis on the one hand, and by the Labour Party's failure to stand united against arms spending on the other. Certainly the Labour Party's message showed some sensitivity on this

[10] *LL*, 1 December 1911.
[11] *LL*, 8 December 1911.
[12] *LL*, 22 December 1911.

point, for it made no reference at all to the contentious issue of armaments reduction but was confined entirely to lamentations over the state of Anglo-German relations. Bebel's reply was full of goodwill, but he did not sidestep the armaments issue. On behalf of the SPD he assured the Labour Party of his party's determination to use 'every effort' to ensure the peaceful settlement of any international disputes: 'Above all, we shall consider it our first duty to oppose strongly the competition in naval and military armaments'.[13] For the Germans it seemed that the Labour Party's record on the armaments issue was still the real test of the sincerity of the party's internationalism.

A number of factors combined in the new year to intensify the concern felt within the Labour Party over Sir Edward Grey's control of foreign policy. First, the worsening of the situation in Persia, and in particular Russia's success in achieving the expulsion of the pro-Persian financial adviser Morgan Shuster, led to renewed criticism of Britain's agreements with Russia. Of course, the Russian connection had already proved to be the one element in British foreign policy capable of rousing widespread indignation across the labour movement. Second, the spectacular victories of the German socialists in the elections of January 1912 seemed to give the lie to the vision of Germany as a nation where Prussian militarism was supreme. The fear of Germany, which was presumed to lie at the heart of Grey's foreign policy, seemed to have been unmasked as a mere bogey.

The Labour Party Conference that was scheduled to meet in late January 1912 was the appropriate forum in which to focus the attention of the labour movement upon the alleged evils of Grey's foreign policy. Accordingly the ILP submitted four resolutions to the conference: one denounced militarism, another attacked Sir Edward Grey's 'anti-German' foreign policy and his connivance with Russian aggression in Persia, a third repudiated secret diplomacy, and finally there was a resolution expressing approval of the enquiry into a general strike against war.[14] The Labour Party itself needed no real

[13] Ibid. See also J. Middleton to Huysmans, 1 January 1912, LP/INT/11/1/ 365, and a reprint of the exchange of greetings in *Bulletin Périodique de Bureau Socialiste International*, no. 8, pp. 6–7.

[14] ILP NAC *mins.*, 22–3 January 1912; *LL*, 2 February 1912.

prodding on these matters. Herman Molkenbuhr was invited
by the Labour Party executive to attend the conference
and his effective speech ('more French than German in its
emotion', observed the *Leader*)[15] served to reinforce the
importance of the German socialists' recent election victories
in the minds of the delegates. From the floor of the conference a resolution on behalf of the Portsmouth Trades
Council, calling upon all labour organizations to disavow
hostility toward Germany and send fraternal greetings, won
unanimous support.[16] The ILP's several resolutions were
also enthusiastically accepted. However, a reference to the
'growing burden of armaments' in Glasier's resolution on war
and militarism was challenged once more by Councillor
E. Wake from Barrow-in-Furness. His insistence that measures
to relieve unemployment must be enacted prior to armaments
reductions was countered in turn by George Barnes who
argued that the general interests of all workers in disarmament
must take procedence over those of the shipbuilding section
of the working people. Glasier's resolution was carried
with unanimity.[17] It seemed the high-water mark of internationalism in the Labour Party, and a demonstration also of
the influence of the ILP.

No doubt MacDonald waited expectantly to see the performance of his Labour Party MPs in the military estimates
debates of the new session. In the March number of the
Socialist Review, he reminded his readers that Molkenbuhr's
visit to the party conference in January had symbolized
the fact that the four and a quarter million votes cast for the
German socialists were 'pledges of friendship and peace to
the British people'.[18] On the eve of the parliamentary session,
the *Labour Leader* expressed its hope that this time 'the
Labour ranks should remain alert and unbroken'.[19] On
18 March, Winston Churchill, the recently appointed First
Lord of the Admiralty, announced the new naval estimates.
Britain would maintain a sixty per cent superiority in
Dreadnoughts, not the 'two keels to one' margin pressed for

[15] *LL*, 2 February 1912.
[16] Ibid.
[17] Ibid.
[18] Editorial notes, *Socialist Review*, March 1912, p. 7.
[19] *LL*, 16 February 1912.

by some journalists, notably W. T. Stead. Moreover, Churchill declared, Britain would not increase the pace of its building unless the new German naval law announced increases. The Radicals seemed satisfied with these proposals, and it was even agreed not to move the usual motion for reductions. Thus, the Labour Party was virtually alone in criticizing the new estimates. Nevertheless, Hardie spoke strongly, describing Churchill's 'naval holiday' as woefully inadequate. What was required, he claimed, was a more daring initiative, such as a one-year total suspension in the Dreadnought programme, so as to achieve an 'instantaneous effect' in Germany. Once again, Hardie pledged the Labour Party to continuing co-operation with the German socialists to safeguard the peace.[20] However, since there was neither a reduction motion nor a division on the 1912 naval estimates, it was not possible to determine how many Labour MPs agreed with Hardie.

In May 1912 attention suddenly shifted back to the thorny naval spending question when Churchill announced that, owing to the provisions of the new German naval law, he would soon be introducing supplementary naval estimates. The 'naval holiday' had lasted barely two months. This announcement evidently inflamed the passions of some of the ILP's parliamentary representatives. When, on 22 July 1912, Churchill rose to present the increases to the Commons, he was immediately cut short by J. O'Grady, an ILP member, who defied the chairman's cautions and repeatedly insisted that the House had no business discussing navies in the face of unemployment and while, in the East End of London' 'the lives of children are being blotted out as if they were of no more importance in God's creation than flies'.[21] After parliamentary decorum was restored, Churchill announced the construction of a further four capital ships over the next five years, thereby lifting the total to twenty-one.[22] Churchill's speech was littered with comparisons of British and German

---

[20] *Hansard*, 18 March 1912, V: 35: 1586−9. Wilkie also spoke on 18 March but confined his remarks to the rates of pay for shipwrights; *Hansard*, V: 35: 1653−4.

[21] *Hansard*, 22 July 1912, V: 41: 835−7.

[22] Ibid., V: 41: 837; Woodward, *Great Britain and the Germany Navy*, p. 378.

naval strength, and French Mediterranean squadrons were quite openly counted as part of the British force. MacDonald replied for Labour.[23] Clearly his task was to persuade the former deserters in his own party, as much as anyone else in the House, that the increases were unnecessary. He began by casting doubt on the 'experts' whose advice on German 'acceleration' in 1909 had proved to be so alarmist. The real origins of the new German naval law, MacDonald argued, were the provocative foreign policies of the British Government, as displayed in the blustering speeches made at the time of the Moroccan crisis and in Churchill's own speech in Glasgow in February 1912 when he had described the German naval fleet as a luxury. Churchill's latest oratory would only worsen the situation, MacDonald claimed. He warned prophetically that

The German situation has always been created by speeches such as we have had tonight, and then made worse by shipbuilding, and then made still worse by speeches following the shipbuilding programme. . . . This system is a system of progress down and down in obedience to a momentum that somebody must stop somehow and at sometime. Otherwise we are going to have war whether we like it or not.[24]

Finally, he proudly declared that the MPs of the Labour Party would reject the increases and stand loyally with their socialist comrades in Germany.

However, Alex Wilkie, the next Labour MP to speak, approached the subject with far less determination. He dutifully but briefly condemned naval scares and the cost of armaments, and then quickly shifted the focus of his speech to the less controversial subject of dockyard wages, until recalled by the chairman.[25] His reluctance to address the real issue was an ominous sign. When the Commons divided on the new increases, Wilkie and four other Labour MPs, Crooks, Duncan, J. Haslam, and J. Wadsworth, deserted MacDonald and voted with the Government.[26] Two days

---

[23] *Hansard*, V: 41: 872–8.
[24] Ibid., V: 41: 876–7.
[25] Ibid., V: 41: 922; Wilkie concluded: 'I want to say that I have never changed my opinion either on the platform or anywhere else, for I have always been in favour of an efficient navy and efficient defence'.
[26] Ibid., V: 41: 945–8.

later came an even more serious reversal for MacDonald and his ILP supporters. On a motion to reduce the shipbuilding vote, introduced by the Radical David Mason, twelve Labour MPs loyally supported the cause of armaments reduction but the number of deserters now climbed to eight. The list included not only the usual representatives of the arsenal and shipbuilding towns, namely Crooks, Duncan, and Wilkie, but also four from the miners' group, Hall, Harvey, Walsh, and Wadsworth, plus the independently minded Bowerman, and, worst of all, the Chief Labour Whip, G. H. Roberts.[27] In that same week the review of the battle fleet at the Spithead was held. The *Labour Leader* observed that the Dreadnoughts looked 'like cruel monsters of the deep moved by the lust for blood'.[28] Clearly not all the Labour Party MPs were in agreement with this colourful verdict. A significant minority of them still regarded the absolute superiority of the fleet as so essential that they had defied their own party's policy in the full glare of the House of Commons.

MacDonald's response was to gather the majority about him once more in the pursuit of Anglo-German friendship and a new foreign policy. The *Leader* lent its support to the campaign against Grey by highlighting developments in Persia, particularly during the Balmoral Conference in September.[29] In that same month MacDonald led a Labour Party delegation, including Arthur Henderson and Ben Turner as well as ILP MPs, on a goodwill visit to Switzerland and Germany. Fortunately the tour was free of the mis-understandings and public bickering which marked the 1909 venture. The delegation visited both Munich and Stuttgart and on each occasion was welcomed by the Bürgermeister and given a reception in the Town Hall.[30] Interestingly enough, the reports in the *Labour Leader* make no reference

---

[27] Ibid., 24 July 1912, V: 41: 1307. Barnes spoke in favour of Mason's motion (V: 41: 1256—65); but Wilkie again spoke on dockyard wages and conditions (V: 41: 1270—7).

[28] *LL*, 1 August 1912.

[29] See in particular Brockway's series 'The Story of Persia', in *LL*, 29 August—15 September 1912, and *LL*, 26 September and 10 October 1912. See also MacDonald's editorial notes, *Socialist Review*, October 1912 and W. Albery, 'Persia and Our Foreign Policy', *Socialist Review*, November 1912, pp. 177—94.

[30] *LL*, 26 September 1912.

to any representatives of the SPD being present at these gatherings. In addition, although the German Socialist Congress at Chemnitz coincided with the visit of the British delegation to Germany, no member of that delegation presented fraternal greetings to the congress. Quelch attended it on behalf of the BSP, but there was no official Labour Party delegate. Aware of the bad impression that was being given, Bernstein complained to MacDonald that no one from the Labour Party had been appointed to attend this important congress.[31] Perhaps the rancour of 1909 and 1911 had not yet been forgiven. Nevertheless, in public both the Labour Party and the SPD maintained the appearance of working-class camaraderie. In October 1912, in response to a suggestion made by the BNC, the Labour Party and the German socialists issued another joint manifesto, this time decrying the tension between the two countries.[32] The manifesto proclaimed that the working people of Britain and Germany had no quarrel and stood 'most determinedly' against all those who would incite war. No doubt it was disappointing to the Labour Party leaders that, in order to meet the needs of propaganda, they had to bend the truth in the document regarding their party's parliamentary performance. For the manifesto began with the bold declaration that both the SPD and the Labour Party had fought against and voted against the latest round of armament increases.[33] Fact had given way to half-truth.

The war in the Near East, which began in October 1912, served to intensify fears in radical, socialist, and labour circles that Britain could soon be drawn into a European war through secret commitments to France or even expectations that Grey might have raised in France. The redistribution of the fleet as announced by Churchill in May, involving some withdrawals from the Mediterranean to bolster the home waters defences, now gave the appearance of a naval arrangement with France which assumed an alliance in wartime.

In a speech at Preston in early November, Hardie

---

[31] Bernstein to MacDonald, 8 October 1912, MacDonald Papers, PRO/30/69/3A/61.
[32] BNC *mins.*, 26 July and 9 October 1912; text of the manifesto, *LL*, 17 October 1912.
[33] *LL*, 17 October 1912.

catalogued the 'blunders' of British foreign policy. Why was it that Britain was now in danger of being drawn into a European conflict, he asked? Hardie stressed that it was Grey's determination to preserve the exclusive interests of British financiers in Egypt which had led to Britain's foolish support for French claims in Morocco in 1905, an action which had in turn transformed the Entente of 1904, into an anti-German alliance. The same determination to safeguard business interests in Persia lay at the root of the alliance with Russia in 1907. It was through these commitments that Britain was 'almost certain' to be involved in war in Europe, Hardie protested.[34] The *Labour Leader* kept hammering away at these themes. Great prominence was also given to the demonstrations against the war in the Balkans arranged by the Continental socialist parties and co-ordinated by the ISB. The BNC's own 'Hands Off the Balkans' demonstration at the Kingsway Opera House on 17 November also stimulated interest in the issue. Hardie, the Belgian socialist Anseele, Jean Longuet, and the German revisionist Dr Ludwig Frank, addressed the crowd. There was enthusiasm when toward the end of his speech Frank broke into English to declare

The working classes desire the spread not of cartridges, but of ideas; not of death and sickness, but of life and the ennobling of life. We regard ourselves no longer as Germans, or French, or English but as citizens of the United States of Europe. In the name of the German Social Democracy, I bring you this message, that we desire nothing more fervently than to work together with our English comrades, and that each one of the four million votes cast for the German Social Democracy is a vote for friendship with England. We are the guards of peace.[35]

This was the vision of the socialist leaders. What further need had the working classes of Churchill's Dreadnoughts and Grey's entangling alliances when their German socialist comrades offered such guarantees against German militarism?

Yet the question remained: did the Labour Party share that vision? In January 1913 the Labour Party Conference politely passed an ILP resolution condemning militarism. In addition, the conference took steps to tighten party dis-

---

[34] *LL*, 14 November 1912.
[35] *LL*, 21 November 1912.

cipline by accepting that 'violations of the constitution' and
'acts of disloyalty calculated to injure the effectiveness of
the party' should involve penalties. However, it was clear that
the new stress on party discipline was directed not so much
at those MPs who repeatedly refused to support arms
reduction (which was not an element of the constitution) but
rather at those rebel MPs who appeared on Liberal Party
platforms.[36] Again, the most reliable indication of the
firmness of the Labour Party's devotion to internationalism
would come in the naval estimates debates due in March
1913.

On the eve of these debates, the armaments competition
on the Continent took a sudden and decisive turn for the
worse. From Berlin came an announcement of major increases
in military spending, including a twenty per cent increase
in the manpower of the Army.[37] The French responded with
promises to lift their own spending and a proposal to lengthen
military service to three years.[38] In an important editorial
on the armament crisis on 6 March, the *Labour Leader* called
upon the Labour Party to vote not only against the British
Government's naval estimates, but to 'vote unitedly against
the Budget'.[39] This was an action which the Labour Party
had never taken. The *Leader* repeated its advice in clear
unequivocal terms the following week. 'A bold stand' was
needed according to the *Leader*.[40] However, this extreme
view was clearly not that of the majority of the ILP. At the
ILP Conference on 24 and 25 March, Fred Jowett's proposal
that the Labour Party should be instructed to vote on each
issue in Parliament 'on its merits', that is, ignoring the
possibility of a defeat of the Government, was rejected.
Significantly, the resolution against armaments, presented as
the last business of the conference, did not include any call
to the Labour Party to vote against the budget.[41]

When the estimates were finally presented to the Commons

[36] *LL*, 6 February 1913.
[37] See V. R. Berghahn, *Germany and the Approach to War in 1914* (London,
1973), ch. 7.
[38] Weber, *The National Revival in France*, pp. 110–15.
[39] *LL*, 6 March 1913.
[40] *LL*, 14 March 1913.
[41] *LL*, 27 March 1913.

in late March 1913, Hardie and Barnes spoke strongly against them. Hardie made his mark by re-emphasizing the First Lord's own admission that shipbuilding delays had resulted from the number of foreign orders occupying British yards. Such was the strength of capitalistic 'patriotism', declared Hardie.[42] However, once again in the lobbies there was bitter disappointment for the Labour Party leadership. Only sixteen Labour MPs voted in favour of a motion to reduce the estimates, four voted against, and twenty-one were absent.[43] It was a bitter blow. In a letter to the *Labour Leader*, J. T. Walton Newbold, a young Quaker at Manchester University at that time and later the first communist MP, blamed in part the peremptory manner in which the subject had been handled at the recent ILP Conference:

I do not think that there went out to the nation from our midst any resounding message, such as the times require. Two speeches at the tail end of the gathering and a unanimous vote give the press some reason to regard it as a pious expression of opinion.[44]

Ramsay MacDonald also regretted that his old comrades in the ILP had given only ten minutes to 'perhaps the most important of all questions at present demanding the attention of the people'.[45] It may be that Hardie, who had indeed surprised his colleagues at the recent ILP Conference by offering just two sentences in support of the anti-armaments resolution, was simply dispirited over the endless effort to curb the small group of Labour Party rebels on the armaments issue. Whatever the reason, the performance of the Labour Party MPs in the vote on the naval estimates in March 1913 provided fresh evidence of the limited impact of the ILP's campaign. Even the heightened emphasis on the mistakes of Britain's foreign policy had not succeeded in instilling a passionate opposition to militarism amongst the majority of the Labour Party MPs.

[42] *LL*, 3 April 1913.
[43] Division List, *Hansard*, 28 March 1913, V: 50: 2055—8.
[44] *LL*, 3 April 1913.
[45] Editorial notes, *Socialist Review*, May 1913, p. 170.

2. *The Campaign Against the 'War Trust' and Conscription, 1913–14*

At the ILP Conference of 1913 Keir Hardie was returned to the position of chairman of the ILP. At the end of March, immediately after the disappointment of the Labour Party's half-hearted opposition to the latest naval estimates, the new ILP chairman addressed a special 'Pastoral Letter' to the faithful of the ILP. He called for a mighty effort to double the party membership in the next twelve months and for a new crusade against 'Landlordism, Capitalism, Militarism, the unholy trinity' so that the party could face its coming-of-age in 1914 with renewed hope.[46] For the next twelve months the ILP did indeed stand virtually alone in a sustained campaign against militarism and war.

The major theme of the ILP's anti-militarist propaganda was influenced at the outset by events in Germany in April 1913. In a sensational sequel to the recent announcements of major increases in military spending, Karl Leibknecht revealed to the Reichstag evidence of corrupt practices which involved Krupp's, newspaper journalists in France, and even the German War Office. The details of a conspiracy to boost German armaments orders to the benefit of German arms firms were skilfully exposed.[47] The *Daily Citizen* as well as the *Labour Leader* gave detailed reports of these exposures and both papers hinted at the activities of 'armour-plate patriots' in Britain.[48] In late April the ILP Administrative Council, full of admiration, telegraphed its congratulations to the German socialists and its special thanks to Liebknecht.[49] The impact of the sensational disclosure on public debate was not lost upon the young Fenner Brockway, who was confirmed in his new position as editor of the *Labour Leader* at the same meeting of the ILP Administrative Council. Brockway was determined to make a campaign against the 'war trust' his first task. This involved shifting attention away from the sheer costs of armaments and on to the structure

---

[46] *LL*, 3 April 1913.
[47] For a reprint of Liebknecht's speech of 18 April 1913, see *Peace Movement*, vol. 2, no. 5, 15 May 1913.
[48] *Daily Citizen*, 22 and 25 April, 16 and 26 May 1913; *LL*, 24 April 1913.
[49] ILP NAC *mins.*, 24–5 April 1913.

of the armaments industries, in order to emphasize the excellent profits that were being made and to suggest that the advocates of ever-higher military spending were seeking personal gain. Brockway soon discovered that Walton Newbold was only too willing to co-operate in this task by providing his own continuing research upon the patterns of ownership and contracting with British armaments firms.[50]

A major series on the 'war trust scandal' began in the *Labour Leader* on 22 May 1913. Pages of the most complex details were published in support of a series of allegations: first, that the degree of concentration of ownership among armaments firms constituted an 'armaments ring'; second, that through the ring, British firms assisted in the manufacture of arms in countries allied to Germany, especially in Italy; third, that the Liberal Government had starved the state shipyards and boosted the order books of private contractors; and, finally, that certain politicians and ex-servicemen, who were most active in campaigning for higher military spending, stood to gain directly from 'bloated armaments' through their directorships or shareholdings in armaments firms. On 5 June Newbold produced his work on patterns of share ownership, which revealed that German and British banks, army officers, politicians, and churchmen held large packets of shares in major armaments firms, such as the Nobel Dynamite Trust. One week later, under a wishful front-page heading of 'Worse Than the Marconi Scandal', the *Leader* provided an even more detailed list of shareholding patterns, showing the interests of British MPs, Cabinet Ministers, bishops, bankers, peers, military officers, and members of the National Service League in armament firms.[51] The most charitable view was that the proponents of militarism were unflinching in their determination to risk their own capital in support of their cause. The *Leader* was angry, but not surprised, that the big dailies of the British

---

[50] Walton Newbold had first drawn attention to the 'arms trust' in *LL*, 23 February 1912. For a critique of the attacks on the armaments firms made by Newbold and others see Clive Trebilcock 'Radicalism and the Armament Trust', in A. J. A. Morris (ed.), *Edwardian Radicalism, 1900–1914* (London, 1974).

[51] *LL*, 12 June 1913; see further disclosures *LL*, 24 and 31 July 1913.

press chose to ignore its revelations.[52] In the meantime, however, the facts outlined by Newbold had been raised in the Commons. On 2 June, Frank Goldstone, an ILP member and National Union of Teachers' official, requested Churchill to provide the House with the Admiralty's official list of war materials contractors; he also asked whether any of these firms had shareholding connections with firms that were building warships for foreign navies. Churchill dodged the question, replying that it was 'contrary to the practice of the Admiralty to make known the names of firms on its contractors' lists' and that he had 'no precise information' on the interests of British armament firms in foreign companies.[53] Asquith later denied all knowledge of any 'revelations' and turned aside suggestions that there was a need for an inquiry. ILP delegates at the National Peace Congress in Leeds on 10 June also did their best to draw attention to Newbold's carefully documented articles. Glasier and Anderson successfully guided through the congress a resolution directing attention to the 'vast financial interests behind militarism'.[54] MacDonald likewise was unwilling to see the issue die. During the course of a major speech in the Commons on 17 July, in reply to Churchill, MacDonald attacked those British firms who would build ships for Britain's supposed enemies and then 'incite us to build other ships to blow the first lot into smithereens'.[55]

In the meantime the ILP had also been admiring and applauding the propaganda campaigns mounted by the French and German socialists against the sudden worsening of the armaments rivalry on the Continent. The attendance of the French and German socialists at the Rapprochement Conference in Berne in May 1913 attracted particularly favourable attention in the British labour and socialist press.[56] Perhaps in imitation of the drive against militarism mounted by the Continential socialist parties, the ILP Administrative Council decided in late July to initiate

[52] *LL*, 29 May 1913.
[53] *Hansard*, 2 June 1913, V: 53: 563–4.
[54] *LL*, 12 June 1913.
[55] *Hansard*, V: 55: 1503–13.
[56] *Daily Citizen*, 12 May 1913; editorial notes, *Socialist Review*, April and June 1913.

another 'autumn campaign' to combat the menace of conscription.[57] The choice of theme was not an idle one, for the National Service League had displayed renewed energy during 1913. In January 1913 the governing committee of the League had decided upon a drive for labour support.[58] Early in the year also Glasier had faced National Service League speakers in public debates.[59] In the Commons in April, Hardie and G. H. Roberts had spoken up boldly against an abortive private members' bill to make service in the Territorials compulsory.[60] The 'autumn campaign' on the theme 'No Conscription' finally began in mid-November 1913 and for the next month scores of public meetings were held featuring the leading ILP MPs and also Oscar Peterson, a visiting member of the SPD.[61] The official resolution put to these meetings declared strong opposition to the National Service League's agitation and called upon the organized workers and the Parliamentary Labour Party 'to resist, by every means in their power' the threat of conscription and the massive arms expenditure.[62] The campaign ended with another international meeting at the Kingsway Hall on 13 December, held under the auspices of the BNC. Members of the ISB, who had been meeting in London that same day in the negotiations over socialist unity in Britain, provided a strong group of platform speakers which included Jaurès, Molkenbuhr, and Vandervelde.[63] Jaurès dwelt upon the awesome costs of armaments and called for a three-way *rapprochement* to unite Britain, Germany, and France, and so make war impossible. Anatole France, a late inclusion in the list of speakers, warned the meeting that it was not war itself but the endless preparation for war which provided the ruling élites with political and economic advantage. Molkenbuhr took up a favourite theme of the German

[57] ILP NAC *mins.*, 28–9 July 1913.
[58] James, *Lord Roberts*, p. 459.
[59] *LL*, 3 April 1913.
[60] *Hansard*, 11 April 1913, V: 51: 1592.
[61] On the campaign see Snowden, *An Autobiography*, vol. 1, p. 244.
[62] *LL*, 20 November 1913.
[63] The meeting had been planned long in advance; see BNC *mins.*, 16 July 1913 and ILP NAC *mins.*, 28–9 July 1913. For the proceedings of the meeting, see *LL*, 18 December 1913 and *Justice*, 20 December 1913.

socialists, assuring the audience of his party's role as a guardian of peace. From amongst the speakers, as always, Jaurès 'torrential vigour' was singled out for special praise in the British socialist press, and, significantly enough, the 'Marseillaise' was chosen to close the meeting.[64] With the end of the 'No Conscription' campaign, so too ended the last public anti-war campaign mounted by the labour movement prior to the outbreak of the Great War.

One final task remained, however, the conversion of the recalcitrant minority within the Parliamentary Labour Party to the cause of arms limitation. As early as December 1913 the ILP leaders turned their attention to the forthcoming 1914 military estimates debates. Brockway urged the Labour Party to reject further increases in naval spending, even if it meant turning out the Government.[65] Snowden too pleaded with the Labour Party to oppose the entire budget, not just the naval estimates. He put his case quite bluntly:

In past years the Labour Party has not offered that determined and united opposition to naval expenditure which it was its duty to do in view of its principles and its position in the internationalist socialist movement. There is nothing in the record of the Labour Party more regrettable than the fact that some of its members of parliament have always voted for every increase in the Army and Navy votes which the government has proposed.[66]

Labour MPs representing arsenal and dockyard towns, Snowden advised, should note that German socialists in the same positions 'do not sacrifice their socialist principles in order to keep their seats'.[67] In early January 1914 W. C. Anderson, a former chairman of the ILP, also stressed the crucial importance of the struggle against armaments.[68] Clearly the coming Labour Party Conference and the 1914 naval estimates debates were shaping up once more as major tests of strength on the armaments issue. In late January 1914 two ILP members on the Labour Party executive, W. C. Anderson and J. R. Clynes, persuaded the executive to

[64] *Justice*, 20 December 1913.
[65] Brockway, speaking at Urmston, reported in *LL*, 4 December 1913.
[66] Editorial, *LL*, 11 December 1913.
[67] Ibid.
[68] Editorial, *LL*, 8 January 1914.

accept an 'emergency resolution' on naval armaments for the impending Labour Party Conference. The terms of the resolution were:

That this Conference strongly condemns the enormous, ruinous, and unnecessary growth in naval expenditure which in the present year is likely to exceed £50,000,000; and believing that armaments are governed by policy, declares that as a first step towards a better understanding this country should abandon its policy of maintaining the right of capture of private property at sea in time of war, and should press by every means in its power for a peace federation including Britain, Germany, and France.[69]

The wording of the resolution was stronger than on former occasions, and the specific objection to naval estimates in excess of £50,000,000, as well as the proposed abolition of the right of capture, would seem to have invited criticism. However, when the resolution was presented to the Labour Party Conference at the end of January 1914 it was passed unanimously after speeches in support from Clynes, Anderson, and Katharine Glasier.[70] The group of MPs who supported the 'big navy' evidently chose not to challenge the majority of the conference, perhaps because they realized that the resolution could not curb their freedom of action to vote for the military estimates. Brockway voiced his own disappointment over the almost perfunctory treatment of the ILP's resolution:

The situation called for more than that. The country is on the eve of a great crisis, and speech should have followed speech in denunciation of the Liberal policy. Instead the very unanimity of the Conference led to a short and undemonstrative discussion.[71]

The priorities of the Labour Party in the new session became clear in the amendments to the address that were submitted by the Labour Party. These amendments regretted the failure of the King's Speech to mention measures to mitigate accidents in railways and mines, to establish votes for women, to set up an inquiry into the recent industrial violence in Dublin, or to extend special aid to local education authorities. There were no complaints regarding the

[69] Labour Party NEC *mins.*, 24 and 28 January 1914.
[70] *LL*, 5 February 1914.
[71] Ibid.

Government's failure to limit arms spending or support the abolition of the right of capture.[72] None the less, MacDonald spoke out strongly against armaments when, on 2 March 1914, Churchill presented supplementary naval estimates in order to cover the additional shipbuilding expenditure which had followed the embarrassing withdrawal of the Canadians' 'gift' of a Dreadnought in 1913. MacDonald accused Churchill of callous disregard for Parliament in spending beyond the original estimates and then expecting additional sums to cover these excesses. Then, widening the debate, MacDonald outlined to the House the nefarious plotting of the 'arms rings' which, he asserted, were the real cause behind the sudden increase in armaments rivalry across Europe. A Parliamentary Committee was required, argued MacDonald, to analyse and prepare naval estimates.[73] In spite of the determined tone of the Labour Party chairman's speech, the vote on a motion to reduce the supplementary estimates by £100 split the Labour MPs yet again, twenty-one supporting MacDonald and a rebel group of five deserters refusing to join the protest against 'bloated armaments'.[74]

When Churchill presented the main naval estimates to the Commons on 17 March, his figures revealed a rise of £5,240,700 on the previous year, thus bringing the total to £51,500,000.[75] This time it was Snowden who undertook to deliver the major speech against the estimates, and in preparation for the debate he consulted with Walton Newbold.[76] On 18 March Snowden rose to speak against the naval estimates and delivered what must have been the swan-song of the ILP's own distinctive brand of anti-militarism, drawing inspiration as it did from pacifism, socialism, and primitive Christianity. According to Brockway, Snowden spoke for more than an hour 'unassailed by dissent and unassisted by cheers, listened to indeed in an utter silence more significant than the wildest applause'.[77] The inter-

---

[72] *LL*, 12 February 1914; *Hansard*, V: 58: 429 and 974.
[73] *Hansard*, 2 March 1914, V: 59: 109—17.
[74] Ibid., 191—4. The five Labour MPs who voted against the reduction motion were Abraham, Crooks, Wilkie, Johnson, and Duncan.
[75] *Hansard*, 17 March 1914, V: 59: 1896.
[76] Snowden, *An Autobiography*, vol. 1, pp. 248—51.
[77] *LL*, 26 March 1914.

connections between the various armaments firms, and the patterns of private shareholding in those firms, were outlined to the Commons. Snowden alleged that these facts revealed a giant armaments ring at work, the purpose of which was to inflate armaments spending across Europe. The loudest proponents of militarism, the journalists, and the members of the various military lobbies and leagues, were frequently found to be shareholders in the armaments ring, he claimed. In fact, Snowden charged, the Opposition benches were so thick with shareholders in the armaments firms that a stone cast amongst them could not fail to hit one or more of them. Snowden next detailed the attempts of various war material manufacturers to enlist naval officers and civil servants into their employment so as to increase the firms' influences upon the services and the departments of state.[78] At the end of the speech 'came applause, so long continued as to constitute almost an encore'.[79] Unfortunately, so far as the cause of the ILP was concerned, the Curragh Incident in the same week quite overshadowed the speech and reduced the possible press coverage. The Labour Party immediately announced that Snowden's speech would be issued as a penny pamphlet by the National Labour Press, and soon afterwards it did indeed appear under the title *Dreadnoughts and Dividends*. Yet, in a sense, this was all to no avail. For Snowden's speech, valuable a piece of propaganda as it was, had failed in its principal purpose, namely, to inspire the Labour Party to a full-blooded opposition to the massive new naval estimates. On 23 March, just five days after Snowden's speech, the ranks of the Labour Party were broken yet again on a motion protesting against the huge growth in naval spending. Only twenty-one Labour Party MPs supported the motion, two opposed it, and the remainder did not register a vote.[80] In these, the last military expenditure debates before the Great War, the combined forces of the Labour Party and the Radicals could raise only thirty-five MPs willing to protest against the

---

[78] *Hansard*, 18 March 1914, V: 59: 2126—48.

[79] *LL*, 26 March 1914.

[80] *Hansard*, 23 March 1914, V: 60: 141—14. Two Labour MPs, Crooks and Duncan, voted against the protest motion.

doctrine of security through ever more extensive armed preparedness, a number that seemed insignificant beside the formidable consensus in support of that alluring idea. In spite of the long campaigns, the internationalist gestures, the party resolutions and the speechmaking by the socialists within the Parliamentary Labour Party, at the end of the day only half of the Labour MPs seemed to accept the seriousness of the struggle against militarism.

12

The Last Days of Peace, 1914

> The International Socialist parties must go some way yet in per-
> fecting their organisation before they have established finally the
> conditions of the world's peace, and before that is done the
> Chancelleries of Europe may precipitate war.
>
> J. Ramsay MacDonald, *Socialist Review*, August 1911

The first six months of 1914 seemed by comparison with the
turmoil surrounding the Balkan Wars in 1912 and 1913 a
period of reduced international tension. There was no longer
an obvious sense of urgency in socialist circles surrounding
the discussion of the dangers of war. The success of the SFIO
in the elections of May 1914 was a welcome sign of a possible
strengthening of the will of the French people to keep the
peace in Europe.[1] The *Labour Leader* noted with pride that
this 'boom in socialism' in France was in line with the German
socialist victories in 1912, all of which buttressed the forces
guarding the European peace.[2] In this confident atmosphere
the ILP maintained its propaganda against Grey's foreign
policy and against the 'armaments ring', but there was no
sustained campaign.[3] The issue of the anti-war strike, which
was expected to be resolved at the International Congress in
Vienna, was not forgotten either. At the National Peace
Congress in Liverpool in June, Harry Dubery and Katharine
Glasier introduced an ILP motion that the workers should
take 'organized action' with their fellows in France, Germany,
and other lands to arrive at 'an understanding to secure
international peace'.[4] The trade unions also continued to
manifest their internationalism, sometimes a newly found
internationalism, by inviting fraternal delegates from the
Continent to join them in the round of summer congresses.

---

[1] On the elections see Weber, *National Revival in France*, p. 138.
[2] *LL*, 28 May 1914.
[3] See *LL*, 8, 22, 29 January, and 16 July 1914; Labour Party NEC *mins.*,
17 March 1914.
[4] *LL*, 18 June 1914.

The TUC Parliamentary Committee dispatched invitations to the Germans and the French to send fraternal delegates to the forthcoming Trade Union Congress.[5] When the International Textile Workers' Federation met at Blackpool in June, Germans, Belgians, and British sang the 'Internationale' and 'The Red Flag'.[6] The London Trades Council, the Bookbinders' Union, the General Federation of Trade Unions, and several other unions also invited German and French delegates to join them in their conferences during the summer months.[7]

Even the assassination of Archduke Francis Ferdinand and his wife on 28 June did not disturb the belief in the basic stability of the international scene. W. C. Anderson, now chairman of the Labour Party, condemned the assassination and saw some danger in the possibility that Austria–Hungary might choose to use the murders in Sarajevo as a pretext for 'picking a quarrel' with Serbia. 'This is a dangerous game to play, for the moment the peace is broken the big powers will be drawn in',[8] Anderson warned: but there was not as yet any general expectation of this. The socialists planned confidently for the Vienna Congress in September, and on 17 July the BNC even decided to offer London as the site for the next International Congress due in 1917.[9] Snowden, who left Britain for a world tour in mid-July, recalled later that at the time 'the international situation was considered to be more satisfactory than it had been for years'.[10] When in mid-July the ILP Administrative Council met to consider subjects for the coming 'autumn campaign', the anti-militarist subjects of the past years were notably absent from the list under consideration.[11]

Both the ILP and the BSP also sent fraternal delegates to the SFIO's election celebrations and to the special congress

[5] TUP PC *mins.*, 16 June and 8 July 1914.

[6] *LL*, 11 June 1914.

[7] London TC *mins.*, 30 July 1914; *LL*, 9 July 1914; Clement J. Bundock, *The Story of the National Union of Printing, Bookbinding and Paper Workers* (Oxford, 1959), p. 97.

[8] *LL*, 9 July 1914.

[9] BNC *mins.*, 17 July 1914.

[10] P. Snowden, *An Autobiography*, vol. 1, p. 320.

[11] ILP NAC *mins.*, 14–15 July 1914.

which the French socialists had called for 14—16 July for the purpose of debating the agenda items for the Vienna Congress. The Labour Party sent fraternal greetings but decided against sending a delegate, thus providing something of an indication, even at this late stage, of the lower priority the Labour Party accorded international contacts compared with the attitudes of the socialist societies.[12] Hardie was unable to accept an invitation to attend owing to previous engagements,[13] and so Glasier attended the demonstrations and the congress in his place as ILP delegate. In his account of the congress Glasier gave no indication of any personal discussions with the French leaders on the anti-war strike proposal. That subject was to come up at Vienna; and he confessed that he understood 'very imperfectly' the great debate on this issue in the French Congress.[14] The BSP delegates, by contrast, appear to have taken a close interest in the debate. A. S. Headingley reported cynically that the anti-war strike proposal was really 'a sop thrown out to quieten a brood of half-fledged revolutionists'; and he reiterated the view so often espoused by the late Harry Quelch that the plan was quite impractical. He did note Jaurès's new stress upon a pre-war strike to force the arbitration of disputes, but observed that if Jaurès and Hardie were really in earnest about this they should have been championing a general strike in Austria—Hungary and Serbia immediately following the Sarajevo incident. Similarly, Headingley argued, in order to prevent the extension of the conflict, general strikes should now be beginning in Germany, France, and Russia. Finally, Headingley claimed that Hardie ought 'at this very moment to be at the head of a great British general strike'.[15] According to the Hardie—Jaurès plan of an international and simultaneous general strike to force arbitration of a dispute, Headingley was theoretically quite correct in asserting that general strikes should have been organized soon after the assassinations in Sarajevo, or

---

[12] Labour Party NEC *mins.*, 30 June 1914.
[13] Hardie to M. Camelinat, July 1914, in *Bulletin of the Society for the Study of Labour History*, no. 25, pp. 39—40.
[14] *LL*, 23 July 1914.
[15] *Justice*, 30 July 1914.

at the latest after the presentation of the Austrian ultimatum. However, this was to overlook the fact that the International had not yet agreed to such a plan; that agreement was to be one of the tasks of the Vienna Congress. Even had the socialists made a solid commitment to such action, the 'prior to war' strike plan still had one major flaw which even Hervé had recognized as early as 1912. In his words

the great obstacle to this preventive general strike is that the peoples never believe the peril imminent, and that to obtain a general throwing down of tools it is necessary that every man shall feel the imminence of the butchery, shall feel it on his track like the breath of a monster.[16]

Certainly this sense of imminent war was not produced by the assassinations in late June. In addition, Hardie, Jaurès, and Vaillant were well aware that, as yet, the German socialists had not relaxed their determined opposition to the proposed anti-war strike. Until the matter could be resolved at Vienna the simultaneous and international character of the anti-war strike could not be guaranteed. Thus, in July 1914, even the chief promoters of the anti-war strike recognized that their idea was still in the pre-planning stage.

The Austrian ultimatum to Serbia on 23 July demolished expectations of continuing calm on the international scene. The socialist leaders gradually became aware of the seriousness of the crisis only after the shock of the ultimatum. Huysmans decided soon after learning of this new development to transfer the coming International Congress from Vienna to Berne and to call for a meeting of the ISB in Brussels for Wednesday 29 July.[17] Kautsky's comments are most revealing at this time in relation to the anti-war strike. He too realized that, according to the plan proposed by Hardie and Jaurès, this was the precise moment for an anti-war strike in Austria; but he acknowledged that the weakness of peace opinion in the Austrian working class made such a demonstration impossible. As he wrote to Victor Adler on 25 July:

This state of affairs probably means the end of the Keir Hardie—Vaillant amendment. Now would really be the moment for an anti-war

---

[16] *LL*, 29 August 1912.
[17] Haupt, *Socialism and the Great War*, pp. 186–7.

protest in Austria with a mass strike. But there is not the slightest sign of any protest campaign by the masses. [18]

In Kautsky's view, then, it was the basic patriotism of the Austrian working class that prevented any more determined a stand than propaganda, speech-making, and demonstrations at the moment of crisis.

The Continental socialists were apparently still optimistic that, even if war broke out in the Balkans, the war could be localized, as it had been in 1912 and 1913. [19] Certainly, in the week leading up to the ISB meeting on 29 July, the socialist leaders did not act as if the danger of world war was imminent. In order to have a clear picture of the point of view of those caught up in the crisis, it is useful to recall the timing of events during the Balkan crisis two years earlier. Fighting had begun in the Balkans in early October 1912, and it was not until 28 October that the ISB met. Even then, the ISB decided that its major initiative, the special Basle Congress to protest against any extension of the conflict, should be held some time before the last week in December. [20] The socialist leaders, therefore, were used to long-drawn-out periods of crisis. As can be seen from the correspondence of the leaders, there was no feeling of impending doom in the immediate aftermath of the Austrian ultimatum. Jean Longuet, editor of *L'Humanité* wrote to Kautsky on 26 July and admitted that the situation was 'grave', but promised confidently that he would see Kautsky at the coming congress in Vienna or Berne in any case. [21]

The feeling in Britain was similar, In an article, probably written about 27 July, W. C. Anderson remarked that 'despite all signs to the contrary, there will, I believe, be no war. Nothing, at any rate, in the nature of an extended warfare'. [22] Similarly, on 29 July, Ben Tillett wrote to Herman Jochade, still president of the International Transport Federation, a perfectly innocuous letter about trade union fund-raising

[18] Quoted, ibid., p. 189.
[19] Ibid., pp. 190–4.
[20] *Bulletin Périodique du Bureau Socialiste International*, no. 9.
[21] Longuet to Kautsky, 26 July 1914, 11SG Kautsky Archive, D XVI/100.
[22] *LL*, 30 July 1914.

in Germany and ignoring the foreign crisis altogether.[23] In general, there was virtually no discussion within the British trade unions up to the end of July of the crisis in the Balkans. The TUC Parliamentary Committee was not called together to consider a trade union response, and the Committee did not finally meet until 12 August.[24] The surviving trades council records do not show a single case of a council being called together in these last days of July to formulate a response to the crisis. Those trades councils which did hold their ordinary meetings during these critical days do not seem to have been possessed by any great sense of urgency. When the Leeds Trades Council met on the evening of 29 July, there was apparently no discussion of the developing danger abroad.[25] On 30 July the executive of the London Trades Council met and decided to send its chairman and secretary to Victoria Station the following day to welcome three visiting comrades from the Berlin Trades Council. The executive also decided to draft a resolution to be sent to Grey 'protesting against the prospect of this country being dragged into a European war'. It was then resolved that 'should the occasion require it the executive were to be called together'. This last decision reveals that even at that late stage the London Trades Council executive foresaw that they would need to meet again in the future only if a serious crisis threatened. The imminence of war was clearly not appreciated on 30 July.[26] Similarly the executive of the Liverpool LRC met on 31 July in ordinary session and proceeded to discuss quite normal business items, such as the coming municipal elections. The last item in the minutes reads: 'The Chairman was deputed to represent the LRC at a stop-the-war meeting next week'.[27] There was apparently no discussion of the crisis itself. It is unlikely that the executive in this case imagined that the war in question would be, by the following week, a great European war involving Britain. It is also indicative of

[23] Tillett to Jochade, 29 July 1914, ITF Correspondence, Dock, Wharf, Riverside, and General Labourers' Union file, MRC.
[24] TUC PC *mins.*, 12 August 1914.
[25] Leeds TC *mins.*, 29 July 1914.
[26] London TC *mins.*, 30 July 1914.
[27] Liverpool LRC *mins.*, 31 July 1914.

the lack of a sense of crisis that such a leading trade union journal as the *Railway Review* made no mention of the Balkan troubles at all or of any danger of war in its issue of 31 July.[28]

When the ISB meeting opened at the Maison du Peuple on Wednesday morning, 29 July, the three British delegates, Hardie, Glasier, and Dan Irving from the BSP were naturally as concerned as their Continental counterparts about the Balkan situation, but no one believed that an escalation of the conflict into a European war was likely.[29] The records of the last meeting of the ISB show that the Continental leaders were confident that the Austro-Serbian war would be contained.[30] The various interventions in the debate by Hardie and Glasier show that they in particular were expecting a protracted period of dangerous international tension and did not fear any imminent widening of the Balkan conflict. Thus, when the ISB considered a proposal to advance the date of the Vienna Congress and change the venue to Paris, the British delegates objected. The proposal seemed, from their point of view, an over-reaction which would rob the coming congress of its formal power by transforming it into another Basle demonstration. No doubt Hardie's suspicions were aroused when the German delegate Haase suggested that any such congress must avoid 'all disputed questions, for example, that of the general strike in case of war'.[31] Glasier objected to the change of date and argued that fewer British trade union delegates could attend an earlier congress.[32] Hardie's protest was an emphatic affirmation of his own confidence regarding the international situation:

If the only argument in favour of advancing the date of the Congress is to hold an anti-war demonstration I cannot support the proposal. This is not a sufficient reason. We must keep the agenda. The items on it are of lasting interest whereas the war may pass.[33]

[28] *Railway Review*, 31 July 1914.
[29] See Glasier's article, *LL*, 6 August 1914.
[30] Haupt, *Socialism and the Great War*. Haupt's appendix contains the full text of the official record of this last ISB meeting.
[31] Official Record, ISB, 29 July 1914, in Haupt, ibid., p. 256.
[32] Ibid., p. 256.
[33] Ibid., p. 257.

Earlier in the meeting Hardie had suggested London as an alternative venue for the congress,[34] perhaps because a show of British strength at the congress would assist the victory of his anti-war strike plane. Glasier and Hardie saw no immediate need to rush forward the congress, particularly if that would mean yet another delay in the settlement of the anti-war strike question. Glasier and Hardie were satisfied, therefore, when it was finally decided that the agenda for the congress would not be altered, except for the insertion of 'War and the proletariat' as the primary item. The date was, however, advanced to 9 August, and the venue altered to Paris.[35]

Apart from taking this decision there was little the ISB could do. Those delegates from the seat of conflict, Victor Adler and Nemec, a Bohemian delegate, reported gloomily that their parties were powerless against the tide of patriotism and the threat of government coercion. A general strike was quite unthinkable; and Adler reported that even anti-war demonstrations involved risk to one's life.[36] At the moment of crisis, then, it was the pressure of pro-war opinion at home, and not any chauvinist tendency on the part of the leadership, that prevented any decisive action. The masses of the Austro-Hungarian Empire were simply not at the disposal of the socialist leaders. Impulsively, Glasier attacked the Austrians for not doing their duty; but he later confided to his diary that he had been 'rather unjust'.[37] At this critical moment, therefore, Hardie and Glasier conceded that the initiation of an anti-war strike was not possible. Their efforts in this, the last ISB meeting, were directed to ensuring the viability of the coming International Congress as a full congress with full powers, and ensuring that the anti-war strike was not removed from the agenda. In order to achieve these aims, Hardie and Glasier were opposed to any attempt to rush the congress forward, and they evidently expected that the original date of 23 August would cause no difficulty. Jaurès and Vaillant supported their British comrades arguments, and they insisted in particular that the coming

---

[34] Ibid., p. 255.
[35] Ibid., p. 259.
[36] Ibid., pp. 251–3.
[37] Ibid., p. 256; Laurence Thompson, *The Enthusiasts*, p. 202.

congress must discuss the anti-war strike proposal.[38] Both the British and the French socialists, therefore, were content to wait for the decision of the Paris Congress; neither delegation dared to suggest that now was the time for the ISB to make definite plans for the immediate implementation of a strike against war. All the socialist leaders seemed quite satisfied when, in its final resolution to be issued after the meeting, the ISB simply renewed its plea to all the member parties to stage mass demonstrations, and nothing more, in response to the Balkan crisis.

The extreme gravity of the crisis was still hidden from the ISB leaders. Hardie did not even stay for the reconvening of the ISB on the morning of the 30th July.[39] Glasier, who did stay on, explained confidently that:

People in Britain at present were not seriously concerned with the consequences of the Austro-Serbian war. It was true that they felt the economic repercussions of the Balkan War, but they did not think that they would be affected by the present war. The British wanted peace. The whole of the Cabinet wanted peace.[40]

Similarly, the French and German delegates assured one another that, to the best of their knowledge, their respective Governments were honestly seeking peace.[41] On the face of it, then, there was good reason to expect a localization of the conflict. Jaurès advised Vandervelde, 'This is going to be another Agadir, we shall have ups and downs. But this crisis will be resolved like the others'.[42] In this confident mood the ISB delegates dispersed to their respective countries.

The next morning, Friday 31 July, the BNC under Hardie's chairmanship and including Glasier, Hyndman, and Henderson met at the House of Commons.[43] The atmosphere must still have been relatively calm, in spite of the news of partial

---

[38]   Official Record ISB, 29 July 1914, in Haupt, *Socialism and the Great War*, p. 257 and 258–9.

[39]   Glasier maintained that Hardie was 'rather huffed' at the lack of attention paid to him on the previous day; quoted in K. O. Morgan, *Keir Hardie*, p. 264; Thompson, *The Enthusiasts*, p. 203.

[40]   Official Record, ISB, 30 July 1914, in Haupt, *Socialism and the Great War*, p. 263.

[41]   Ibid., p. 206 and note 27.

[42]   Ibid., p. 204.

[43]   BNC *mins.*, 31 July 1914.

Russian mobilization on the previous day, for the BNC agreed to renew its protest over the decision to advance the date of the International Congress. It was also decided to hold a peace demonstration in London 'at the earliest and most convenient date possible'. Later that same day the BNC reconvened, perhaps now with the knowledge that German mobilization was a distinct possibility. At this second meeting it was decided to accept arrangements which Lansbury, no longer a Labour MP but a member of the Daily Herald League, had made to hold a peace demonstration in Trafalgar Square on the next Sunday, 2 August. MacDonald produced a resolution which he had drafted for the Trafalgar Square demonstration. It catalogued the strongest arguments that could be used against British involvement in the now threatening European war. First, such involvement would be the tragic result of 'secret alliances and understandings'; second, the rendering of assistance to Russia would be 'offensive to the political traditions of this country and dangerous to Europe'; and third, the people of Britain had no direct or indirect interest in the Austro-Serbian quarrel. Finally, in line with the ISB's request, the resolution urged the workers to hold massive demonstrations against war, and it called upon the British Government to 'rigidly decline to engage in war'. At the end of the meeting Hardie and Hyndman undertook to draft a manifesto in the name of the BNC, and it was also decided to insert advertisements announcing the Trafalgar Square demonstration in seven major London newspapers. Only then, on 31 July, was the gravity of the situation facing the major powers appreciated by the socialist and labour leaders. For the first time since the opening of the crisis Glasier recorded in his diary, 'Outlook suddenly very grave'.[44]

The next morning, Saturday 1 August, came news of the assassination of Jaurès in Paris the previous evening. This event seems to have brought home to the British socialist leaders the terrible fact that Europe stood on the brink of an awesome conflagration, and at the same time it struck a great blow at their sincere hopes that the European socialist

[44] Thompson, *The Enthusiasts*, p. 203.

and labour movement might just have the strength and influence necessary to preserve the peace. Glasier confessed to his sister on that day that the European situation was 'appalling':

The news of the last few days is unspeakably dreadful. The assassination of Jaurès has quite stunned me. It is just two days since he bid us all a cheery good-bye at Brussels. One has no words to express the horror of the calamity of his death in the midst of the appalling situation of Europe.[45]

Glasier's words reveal also his sense of shock at the speed of events now overtaking the entire socialist movement. That same day, 1 August, news arrived of German and French mobilization. The British leaders had barely two days in which to try to co-ordinate the mass meetings then being organized in the major centres for the following Sunday, 2 August, in order to protest against the prospect of British involvement in the war. The BNC manifesto, drafted by Hardie and Hyndman, was now issued. The tone was unmistakably one of great urgency. The manifesto's chief purpose was to urge massive demonstrations by organized labour against British intervention. The argument was straightforward: any intervention would be based upon spurious and secret alliances, and such intervention would be in support of Russian despotism. The stress upon Russia was very clearly an appeal to the most popular internationalist feelings of the trade union movement. The manifesto was a clarion call to action:

Hold vast demonstrations in London and in every industrial centre. Compel those of the governing class and their Press who are eager to commit you to co-operate with Russian despotism, to keep silence, respect the decision of the overwhelming majority of the people, who will have neither part nor lot in such infamy. The success of Russia at the present time would be a curse to the world. There is no time to lose.[46]

The rush of events can be clearly appreciated if again it is recalled that in the Balkans crisis of 1912 the ISB manifesto calling for mass protests against war was issued on 29 October

---

[45] Glasier to Lizzie Glasier, 1 August 1914, Glasier Papers, I. 1. 14/4.
[46] Typed copy pasted in BNC *mins.*, 31 July 1914.

and the massive demonstrations in response were eventually held in the European capitals on 17 November. This time the war-makers were to tolerate no delay.

On the day of the BNC meeting, 31 July, Francis Johnson, the ILP secretary, had telegraphed fifty of the larger ILP branches recommending that they devote their normal Sunday meetings to the war crisis, and that they should organize demonstrations.[47] The Scottish Divisional Council of the ILP, led by James Maxton and William Stewart, also contacted the Scottish branches urging the holding of peace demonstrations.[48] As a result a number of ILP branches joined with their local Labour Party and BSP branches in staging protests on Sunday evening, 2 August. Reports of these gatherings show that at least sixteen of them were genuine public meetings held in public places, such as market-places, town halls, squares, or central parks.[49] The feeling within the country at that time was said to have been 'grave', with little evident enthusiasm for war.[50] So it is likely that these protest meetings were as successful and as undisturbed as the *Leader* claimed. It is noteworthy too that in several towns, such as York, Oldham, Blackburn, and Northampton, the ILP branches that met on Sunday 2 August laid plans for their major anti-war demonstrations to be held later in the coming week. Evidently there were few who suspected Britain would be at war by Tuesday, 4 August.

The major Sunday demonstration was that held by the BNC at Trafalgar Square. The crowd, generally regarded as the largest to have filled the square for many years,[51] was addressed from three platforms by prominent figures from the socialist societies, the trade unions, and the Labour Party. The speakers included Hardie, Henderson, Lansbury,

[47] *LL*, 6 August 1914.
[48] Ibid.
[49] Reports given in *LL*, 6 August 1914, show that such protest meetings were held in Manchester, Leicester, Huddersfield, Glasgow, Newcastle, Oldham, Ipswich, Norwich, Chester, Rochdale, Northampton, Keighley, Birmingham, Bingley, Great Yarmouth, Exeter, and Hyde. The *Leader* also claimed that large meetings were held at Newport, Sunderland, York, Swadlincote, Clitheroe, and Great Harwood, but as the specific venues in these cases are not given it is difficult to determine whether these were genuine public meetings.
[50] R. C. K. Ensor, *Modern England, 1870–1914*, p. 495.
[51] *Manchester Guardian* report, quoted in *LL*, 6 August 1914.

Hyndman, Thorne, Marion Phillips, Cunninghame Graham, Margaret Bondfield, and Robert Williams. Hardie began his speech[52] in a melancholy tone which perhaps revealed the extent to which his confidence had been sapped by the news from Paris:

> Our hearts today are sorrowful for the loss of our great comrade, Jaurès. His silver voice is now stilled and the great white fire of his moral enthusiasm quenched forever.

Hardie then pleaded eloquently for British neutrality, and argued that secret treaties and understandings could not bind the people, especially when intervention in the war would be on the side of Russia. Hardie's words made it clear that he already anticipated the basic argument that Sir Edward Grey would use in the Commons the following day, namely, that Britain was morally bound to stand by certain understandings made with France. Hardie rejected this reasoning out of hand, and laid stress on the Russian connection rather than the commitments that may have been given to France:

> We are told there are international treaties which compel us to take part. Who made those treaties? The people had no voice in them.
>
> Are we going to allow Courts and the ruling classes to make treaties leading into war without our having a word to say?
>
> We should not be in this position but for our alliance with Russia.
>
> Friends and comrades, this very square has rung with denunciations of Russian atrocities. Surely if there is one country under the sun which we ought to have no agreement with, it is the foul government of anti-democratic Russia. . .
>
> Italy is as much involved by treaty as we are, and yet Italy has decided to stand neutral. Why cannot Great Britain do the same?[53]

Finally, Hardie asked the crowd, 'What can we do?' He provided two answers to his own question. First, the people must 'say to our government and to our King that we, the working classes of England will not have war'. In these words Hardie made his call for continuing demonstrations. Second, at the end of his speech, he explained that the workers could organize to stop war. 'They could stop it by the international

---

[52] The account of Hardie's speech is based upon *LL*, 6 August 1914, and the *Daily Citizen* report given in Emrys Hughes, *Keir Hardie*, pp. 226–7.
[53] Ibid.

anti-war strike'. Bearing in mind the evidence presented previously as to Hardie's knowledge of the still inadequate strength of the trade unions on this point, his reference to the anti-war strike at this moment would appear to have been the last gasp of his rhetoric of bluff.

Witnesses to the demonstration have reported that the mood of the meeting was one of resignation rather than of gathering power. George Wardle, Labour MP and editor of the *Railway Review*, recalled in an article written soon after attending the demonstration that

> there was an uneasy feeling, which I could not help perceiving, that the issue did not rest with us or even with the government. We may protest against the inevitability of this or that as we like, but there are moments when, strive as we may, the feeling of helpless drifting is uppermost, and that, in my opinion, was the prevailing mood of the crowd in Trafalgar Square on Sunday.
>
> It is not easy to forget that in Berlin on the previous Sunday the crowds who had demonstrated against war were larger and even more unanimous than was the case in Trafalgar Square. Yet before the week was out, Germany had not only mobilized her forces but actually declared war against Russia.[54]

Wardle was probably correct about the sense of powerlessness. The newspapers of that morning were already announcing the news that France and Germany had mobilized. The forces of labour in Britain had time for only one day of protest. On 1 August, MacDonald, sensing the national mood, had laughed at the suggestion of the Liberal Chief Whip, Percy Illingworth, that a war would be unpopular.[55] Evidently, MacDonald already acknowledged that the impulse of the people, in spite of all the efforts of the last ten years, was not to resist war. On 2 August MacDonald missed the Trafalgar Square demonstration as he was at Downing Street, waiting in Illingworth's room at No. 12 for news of the Cabinet meetings. There he learned of several threatened cabinet resignations.[56] On his way to Downing Street MacDonald had met John Morley, the prominent anti-war Radical, in the street. Morley assured him of his personal opposition to war

---

[54] *Railway Review*, 7 August 1914.
[55] Ramsay MacDonald, Diary, entry dated 23 September 1914. (PRO).
[56] Ibid.

but agreed with MacDonald that a war against Germany 'would be the most popular war the country had ever fought'.[57] That evening MacDonald dined at Sir George Riddell's house with Masterman, Simon, and Lloyd George. He discovered that the radical Charles Masterman was a 'jingo', that Simon was 'broken', and from Lloyd George's conversation he gathered 'that excuses were being searched for'. In his diary MacDonald noted, 'I walked home through the park feeling that a great break [had] now come'.[58] By 2 August, therefore, MacDonald believed that public opinion would favour war and that the Liberal Cabinet was most unlikely to resist it.

The following afternoon, Monday 3 August, attention focused upon the Commons where Grey outlined the policy of the government. In Grey's view there was a moral obligation to defend France, and it was in Britain's interest to safeguard Belgium's independence.[59] A special meeting of the Parliamentary Labour Party earlier that day[60] had agreed with MacDonald's proposal that he should reply to Grey and outline the Labour Party's unequivocal opposition to Britain's involvement in the European War. When the time for the Labour Party chairman came to speak he was faced with open hostility from many MPs. As a result, the speech was brief and the argument hesitant.[61] MacDonald began diffidently, noting that he would have 'preferred to remain silent this afternoon', and conceding 'the moving character' of Grey's appeal. He then questioned the necessity of British involvement on the grounds of the nation's honour, the moral obligation to France, or the need to defend Belgium. He denied that the nation's honour was involved; and he noted that the statesmen of the past had appealed to the nation's honour in waging war in the Crimea and South Africa. MacDonald refused to acknowledge that the issue of Belgian independence provided a possible *casus belli*:

If the Right Honourable Gentlemen could come to us and tell us that

[57] Elton, *MacDonald*, pp. 242–4.
[58] MacDonald, Diary, entry dated 23 September 1914 (PRO).
[59] *Hansard*, 3 August 1914, V: 65: 1809–27.
[60] MacDonald to Henderson, 21 August 1914, MacDonald Papers, PRO 5/98.
[61] *Hansard*, 3 August 1914; V: 65: 1832–4.

a small European nationality like Belgium is in danger, and could assure us he is going to confine the conflict to that question, then we would support him. What is the use of talking about coming to the aid of Belgium, when, as a matter of fact, you are engaging in a whole European war which is not going to leave the map of Europe in the position it is in now.

Then MacDonald turned to the one point which perhaps might still have had a little sway with the public, that is, the strange prospect of Britain fighting as comrade-in-arms with tsarist Russia. Grey had wisely ignored this; but MacDonald seized upon it:

The Right Honourable Gentleman said nothing about Russia. We want to know about that. We want to try to find out what is going to happen, when it is all over, to the power of Russia in Europe, and we are not going to go blindly into this conflict without having some sort of a rough idea as to what is going to happen.

Finally, MacDonald cast doubt on the idea that France was in mortal peril; and he asserted that no state of friendship between two nations ever carried with it the obligation for either nation to go to war on the side of the other. This short speech was not designed, however, to win over the House of Commons. It was merely a postscript in protest, for Grey's words had obviously carried the majority of the Commons with him.[62]

On the morning of 4 August German troops invaded Belgium, and in the afternoon Asquith announced to the Commons that Britain had delivered an ultimatum to Germany demanding the withdrawal of her troops. At 11 p.m. on 4 August the ultimatum expired and Britain was at war.

At first the Labour Party appeared to be girding itself to stand firm against the tide of public opinion. On the morning of Wednesday, 5 August, the Labour Party executive met in the party's Victoria Street offices and set up a small subcommittee, consisting of Anderson, MacDonald, Roberts, and Hodge, to draft appropriate resolutions.[63] These were presented when the executive reconvened at the House of Commons at 2 p.m. that afternoon. By eight votes to four the

[62] Morris, *Radicalism Against War*, p. 417.
[63] Labour Party NEC *mins.*, 5 August 1914.

executive confirmed the subcommittee's three resolutions, which in essence restated the position MacDonald had taken in the Commons on 3 August. The resolutions blamed the war upon secret diplomacy, and attacked Grey's policy of 'understandings' with Russia and France and more especially Grey's entanglements with France. The resolutions laid down that it was the duty of the labour movement to seek peace at the earliest possible moment.[64] That same afternoon a 'War Emergency Conference' of over a hundred delegates from socialist, co-operative, trade union, the women's organizations convened at the House of Commons to consider the war crisis and certain recommendations from the Labour Party executive concerning war relief.[65] It was at this conference that the first real cracks in the united front began to appear. The meeting decided to consider first of all, the recommendations on war relief. In Glasier's words, it was 'ominous that Hyndman hastily endorsed the suggestion that the first thing to be considered should be means of relief'.[66] The conference put forward a series of suggestions regarding food prices, citizens' committees, unemployment, school meals, and the milk supply. What clearly concerned Glasier was the apparent acceptance of the war as a *fait accompli*, and the directing of the movement's whole attention towards various measures to ensure equity in the nation's assumption of the burdens of war. When it appeared that the conference would not discuss the wider issues at all, Glasier, Herbert Burrows, and Cunninghame Graham protested; but the majority, including Hyndman, voted to adjourn.[67]

In the evening of 5 August the Parliamentary Labour Party met to consider its attitude to the Government's request for a war credit of £100 million.[68] MacDonald, no doubt aware of the shifting mood among his followers, suggested that the party should simply abstain on the vote and that he, as

[64] Ibid.

[65] Ibid.

[66] Glasier's Diary, quoted in Thompson, *The Enthusiasts*, p. 205.

[67] Ibid.

[68] In his letter to Henderson of 21 August 1914 MacDonald says this meeting was on the Thursday (PRO 5/98). But in the editorial notes of the *Socialist Review*, October 1914 and in *LL*, 13 August 1914, the date of the Parliamentary Labour Party meeting is given as the evening of Wednesday 5 August.

chairman, should in his speech to the Commons that evening read the text of the resolutions decided upon by the party executive during its afternoon meeting.[68] However, a majority of the Labour MPs were in favour of the party supporting the war credit outright. As MacDonald recalled the situation later:

When I left the party to come to its own decision without any expression of opinion from me, it not only took the view that we should vote for the credit of £100,000,000 (I thought we should not oppose it) but that we should not take that last opportunity of reiterating our position...
In this silence I could not acquiesce.[70]

On this specific issue MacDonald then resigned his chairmanship of the Parliamentary Labour Party. A few days later the breach widened when the Labour MPs agreed to support the Liberal and Conservative parties in setting in train a joint recruiting campaign. Only four members of the parliamentary group, MacDonald, Hardie, Jowett, and Richardson, all ILP members, refused to identify themselves with the Government's campaign.[71] The ILP Administrative Council quickly endorsed MacDonald's action and also refused to participate in the Government's recruiting campaign.[72] After fifteen years in the 'labour alliance' the socialists of the ILP were forced to recognize that, on the most crucial issue of the age, the Great War, their own socialist faith still left a great gulf between them and their non-socialist trade union comrades in the Labour Party.

How had the trade unions themselves reacted during these last days of peace? In most cases there had been insufficient time to mobilize a protest before war was declared. The very speed of the crisis cut short the efforts of many trades councils to organize protests. The Birmingham Trades Council secretary had only just called an executive meeting to arrange a stop-the-war demonstration; but, to use his own words, 'immediately afterwards, however, Britain was involved'.[73] Similarly, the Edinburgh Trades Council met on 4 August

[69] Editorial notes, *Socialist Review*, October 1914, pp. 315–6.
[70] MacDonald to Henderson, 21 August 1914, MacDonald Papers PRO 5/98.
[71] Editorial notes, *Socialist Review*, October 1914, p. 316.
[72] ILP NAC *mins.*, 31 August 1914.
[73] Birmingham TC *mins.*, 5 August 1914.

and decided to join the local ILP in an anti-war demonstration the following night; but again, within hours, Britain's involvement in the war was an accomplished fact.[74] The Aberdeen Trades Council did not meet until 5 August, and then proceeded with plans for an anti-war demonstration on the following Sunday in spite of the declaration of war.[75] The Glasgow Trades Council also met on 5 August and, in a vote which indicated the deep division within the trade union movement, the delegates voted forty-six to thirty-five to be represented at an ILP demonstration to be held on Glasgow Green on the coming Sunday to 'express its regret at the outbreak of war'.[76] Some individual unions who happened to be in conference during these crucial days in early August also protested about the prospect of war. On 3 August the Electrical Trades Union entered an emphatic protest against any British involvement.[77] The Bookbinders' Union, meeting in Manchester with fraternal German delegates attending for the very first time, also passed a resolution advocating strict neutrality on Britain's part.[78] These were chance protests. There was simply no time for the trades councils or unions to organize a unified protest throughout the country. Most trades councils met soon after the outbreak of war and discussions centred on the recommendations passed by the 5 August War Emergency Conference with the aim of mitigating the hardships that were expected to follow during the war. Within the first few weeks of the war most councils declared their support for the Labour Party's attitude toward recruiting, and they accepted the war in a mood of genuine reluctance and resignation.[79] The Oldham Trades Council's

[74] Edinburgh TC *mins.*, 4 August 1914.

[75] Aberdeen TC *mins.*, 5 August 1914.

[76] Glasgow TC *mins.*, 5 August 1914.

[77] *The Story of the Electrical Trades Union* (Foreword by W. C. Stevens) (Bromley, n.d.), p. 85; and *LL*, 6 August 1914.

[78] Clement J. Bundock, *The Story of the National Union of Printing, Bookbinding and Paper Workers* (Oxford, 1959), p. 97.

[79] For example, Birmingham TC *mins.*, 5 and 16 August 1914; Huddersfield TC *mins.*, 19 August 1914; Sheffield TC *mins.*, 18 August and 22 September 1914; Nottingham TC *mins.*, 6 August 1914; Camberwell TC *Annual Report* 1914, Aylesbury and District TC, *Silver Jubilee 1911–1936*, records an August decision to set up a distress committee; Liverpool TC *Annual Report*, 1914–15; Aberdeen TC *mins.*, 12 August 1914; Glasgow TC *mins.*, 12 August 1914.

Annual Report of 1914 reflects the common view; the war was

> a war which every sensible person regrets. . . We do not believe in war, and whilst we are working for the victory of our forces and allies it is only because we believe that any other result would be disastrous to our nation, to our love of liberty, and to everything we hold dear. The question of the causes of war may be left for the present.[80]

The TUC Parliamentary Committee, the highest trade union body in the kingdom, seems to have allowed the crisis to pass by without a protest. The committee met on 9 July and did not meet again until 12 August, and even then the purpose of the meeting was to arrange the postponement of the Portsmouth TUC and to discuss the health insurance contributions of soldiers.[81] Only in September did the committee finally issue a manifesto on the war, heartily endorsing the Labour Party's support of recruiting and its refusal to agree to conscription.[82] By October the committee had adopted the language of the majority of the war's supporters in urging state provision for the dependents of those 'who are sacrificing their whole means of life to defend the honour and safety of *our Empire*'.[83] On 2 October, C. W. Bowerman, the committee secretary, used Grey's arguments in replying to Samuel Gompers's enquiries concerning Britain's policy. Britain was, in his view

> fighting to maintain its honour and its pledges to preserve the independence and integrity of a small but gallant nation which has been overrun by a mighty military power, despite the fact that that power had solemnly undertaken the same obligation, but found it convenient to dishonour its own signature.[84]

There was one notable exception to the mood of quiet resignation which prevailed thoughout most of the trade union movement during the rush to war in July and August

---

[80] Oldham TC *Annual Report*, 1914.

[81] TUC PC *mins.*, 12 August 1914.

[82] Ibid., 3 September 1914; text of the manifesto in TUC PC, *Quarterly Report*, December 1914, pp. 37–8.

[83] Italics mine. TUC PC *mins.*, 8 October 1914.

[84] C. W. Bowerman to Samuel Gompers, 2 October 1914, reproduced in TUC PC *Quarterly Report*, December 1914.

1914. This was the South Wales Miners' Federation.[85] The Admiralty, which relied heavily on South Wales steaming coal, requested the Federation on Saturday, 1 August, to agree to forgo the two bank holidays scheduled for the coming week in order to ensure a plentiful coal supply for the Navy in the looming war. The Federation executive met that same day and passed a militant resolution spurning the Admiralty request and strongly opposing the suggestion that Britain might be involved in the Austro-Serbian conflict. Moreover, the Federation set in train the procedure Smillie had suggested at International Miners' Federation congresses in 1912 and 1913:

we think the moment opportune for the miners of Europe to make an endeavour to enforce their views upon the governments implicated in the conflict and the pending complications, and to this end the General Secretary shall at once get into communication with the President and Secretary of the International Miners' organization, requesting that an international conference of miners shall immediately be convened to consider the attitude to be adopted by the affiliated miners during the present crisis.[86]

It was a brave affirmation of the internationalist vision; but the time for organizing conferences had already passed, if indeed there had ever been such a time during this swiftest of crises. The International itself had abandoned its plans for the Paris Congress on that same day, 1 August.[87] Churchill renewed his plea to the South Wales Miners' Federation on 3 August; but by a vote of twelve to six the executive stood by its previous defiant resolution. Three days later all had changed. The Federation granted the Admiralty's request for an extra hour on the day by eighteen votes to one, with only the syndicalist Noah Ablett still resisting.[88]

The individual unions could do little but accept the inevitable. Many union journals lamented the war, but most union executives turned without protest to the discussion of

---

    [85] The following is based upon Ness Edwards, *History of the South Wales Miners' Federation* (London, 1938), pp. 78–9; and R. Page Arnot, *South Wales Miners: A History of the South Wales Miners' Federation, 1914–1926*, pp. 1–7.

    [86] Ness Edwards, *History*, pp. 78–9.

    [87] ISB Circular, dated 1 August 1914, 11SG, SDAP file, item 4473.

    [88] R. Page Arnot, *South Wales Miners*, pp. 6–7.

measures to alleviate distress.[89] The war was accepted as a practical reality and the causes of it all had become irrelevant. The *Postmen's Gazette*, for example, announced that 'It would be idle to discuss now the pros and cons connected with our entering the business, and it is difficult to see what other position the government could take up'.[90] In the *Dockers' Record* Ben Tillett simply announced that, though the workers were guiltless in the making of the war, 'this is neither a period for regrets or whining, but it is a time for action all around'.[91] The executive of the Amalgamated Society of Engineers expressed its regret at the war but did not protest or criticize.[92] The Stonemasons' Society similarly regretted the 'horrible business' of war, but like many unions it looked to the future for deliverance from war and disparaged any concern with the past causes.[93] The Derbyshire Miners' Association Council was also typical in anticipating some future good arising from the war:

This council regrets the necessity of our intervention as a nation in this great European war, but hopes for the success of the British armies and those of our allies, and that the ultimate end may be a world's lasting peace and goodwill amongst men and nations.[94]

The Durham Colliery Mechanics hoped too that 'the very horrors of war may prove the deathblow to war in the future'.[95] The Boot and Shoe Operatives' *Monthly Journal* was more militant than most, recalling the 'German comrades of whom we are now thinking, and whom we have met' and denying that they could have desired war.[96] In short, few unions were alerted quickly enough to the seriousness of the

[89] For example, see the proceedings of the executive committee of the NUR for 13–15 August 1914 in NUR, *Annual Report*, 1914; and the proceedings of the executive committee of the MFGB Proceedings volume for 1914.

[90] From a collection of postal union reactions to the war, in *Postmen's Gazette*, 25 September 1914; see also article by G. H. Stuart, secretary of the Postmen's Federation, in *Postmen's Gazette*, 22 August 1914.

[91] Article dated 12 August 1914 in *Dockers' Record*, August 1914.

[92] Executive Council of ASE proceedings, in *ASE Journal*, August 1914.

[93] Operative Stonemasons' Society, *Monthly Journal*, 5 August 1914.

[94] Quoted in J. E. Williams, *The Derbyshire Miners* (Derby, 1962), p. 524.

[95] General Secretary's report, September 1914, quoted in W. S. Hall, *A Historical Survey of the Durham Colliery Mechanics' Association*.

[96] National Union of Boot and Shoe Operatives, *Monthly Journal*, August 1914.

crisis to enter any protest before fighting began. Once faced with the fact of war, most accepted it in tones of genuine sadness and turned to the task of surviving the struggle. In practice, that meant assisting British arms. It is worth stressing that, although there was little appeal to socialist internationalism and little criticism of the Government in trade union circles during these first days and weeks of war, one would search in vain amongst trade union records to find any overt enthusiasm for the war itself.[97]

---

[97] Revolutionary reactions were equally rare. Robert Williams, secretary of the National Transport Workers' Federation was one unionist who did respond with vehemence. He wrote to Ramsay MacDonald that he would rather 'blaze away at the enemies I know inside my own country' than murder his comrades abroad; Williams to MacDonald, 6 August 1914, MacDonald Papers, PRO 5/98.

13

Conclusion

We are told that International Socialism is dead, that all our hopes and ideals are wrecked by the fire and pestilence of European war. It is not true. Out of the darkness and depth we hail our working class comrades of every land. Across the roar of the guns we send sympathy and greeting to the German Socialists.

ILP Christmas Card 1914, 11SG Kautsky Archive, DX 334

When Keir Hardie addressed the crowd at the hastily organized anti-war demonstration in Trafalgar Square on the afternoon of Sunday, 2 August 1914, in many ways the setting of the demonstration symbolized the awesome power of the institutions and ideas that Hardie and his followers were attempting to challenge. The square itself honoured one of Britain's most glorious victories at sea, and there could be no doubt that most Britons still place their faith in the naval superiority displayed at Trafalgar to safeguard the security of their homeland. Towering above Hardie and the few rain-soaked banners of the trade unions stood Nelson, the hero of Trafalgar, and the grandeur of his memorial provided but one example of the cult of public veneration of Britain's military and imperial heroes which had been so assiduously fostered during the nineteenth century. As Hardie spoke from the plinth of Nelson's Column, he was flanked by the massive bronze lions, the ubiquitous patriotic image of the nation's supposedly indomitable power. Behind Hardie, inscribed at the base of the column, was Nelson's historic signal to the fleet: 'England expects that every man will do his duty'. This famous message was known to every Briton, and few in the square could have doubted the loyalty of the vast majority of the British people to this alluringly simple conception of patriotic duty. Here, in Trafalgar Square, surrounded by symbols of imperialism and sea power, Hardie sought to throw his slender weight into the balance in favour of peace.

The setting itself then serves to underline how immense had been the task faced by the labour and socialist peace movement over the previous twenty-five years in Britain. Two aspects of this need to be appreciated. In the first place, the peace campaign was seeking to defy a group of profoundly powerful ideas about patriotism and Empire, a set of beliefs which had gained such wide acceptance across the boundaries of class and religion that they could be deemed the fundamentals of a kind of civic faith. This bundle of ideas ranged from complex social darwinist philosophies to simple ideas about loyalty, heroism, and self-sacrifice, and even to that simplest idea of all, that defeat was the only thing worse than war. In the second place, the peace campaigners, with their meagre resources, were locked in a decidedly unequal contest for the hearts and minds of the British people. They found themselves pitted against a whole range of organized opinion-makers, with abundant resources and technologies on hand, who ceaselessly propagated ultra-patriotic, imperialist, and militarist values. The means by which these values were so successfully promoted among the people included the pro-imperialist 'adventure' genre in children's literature, the new boys' and girls' weeklies, school textbooks, the military-oriented youth movements, the spate of futuristic 'invasion scare' novels and plays, the new sensationalist popular press, the various military and imperial lobbies and leagues, military pageants and street displays, and the all-pervasive military and imperial themes in everyday advertising and public memorials. Of course it is true that the forces of the labour movement had to challenge much the same structures of ideological domination in pursuit of their ordinary domestic goals. But, when it came to the issues of Dreadnoughts and diplomacy, labour's peace activists had not only to contend with the political power of the establishment but also with the widespread conviction—even in labour's own ranks—that such issues were above and beyond party political disputes, and thus surrounded with an aura of patriotic bipartisanship that precluded criticism.

There can be no questioning that, by 1914, only a small minority of the British people had been reached by the propaganda of internationalism and anti-imperialism. The labour and socialist movement could claim the allegiance of a determined minority of the people only; and, with its limited resources, the movement could not hope to effect any swift erosion of the tremendous power exerted by the established élites over public opinion. Thus, in attempting an assessment of the British labour movement's peace campaign and its apparent powerlessness to influence events in August 1914, explanations must not be sought solely in terms of the mistakes, equivocations, or weaknesses of those leaders who organized the peace campaign. There were indeed inadequacies in the peace campaign, but they were not decisive. Above all, the labour movement simply lost the contest for the hearts and minds of the people, and indeed, even for the hearts and minds of many of its own people.

Considering the overwhelming strength of the forces propagating ideas that could only encourage an acceptance of war among the British people, the 'patriotic' reaction of most Britons to the crisis of August 1914 was not unexpected. And there can be little doubt that the working class in the main supported the war and considered the British cause noble and just. Certainly, Hardie and MacDonald realized that they had aroused widespread public hostility, including working-class hostility, in opposing Britain's decision to enter the war. During the first weeks of the war Hardie was shouted down by 'the mining folk' at a meeting at Aberdare in his constituency.[1] MacDonald decided that, for his own safety, he should not attempt to address any public meetings.[2] In September 1914 the railway companies were sufficiently concerned about the great tide of enlistments from amongst

---

[1] See Emrys Hughes's personal recollections of this meeting and the extracts from the *Aberdare Leader* in Hughes, *Keir Hardie*, pp. 229–31.

[2] A. H. Reynolds to MacDonald, 14 September 1914, MacDonald Papers, PRO/30/69/5/98: 'There is no doubt that your action has made you very unpopular for the present', commented Reynolds in advising MacDonald against public meetings in Leicester. Another friend, William Leach, had advised MacDonald that he was 'risking the fate of Jaurès'; see Leach to MacDonald, 14 August 1914, MacDonald Papers, PRO/30/69/5/24. In September 1914 MacDonald informed J. Simons, an American socialist, that 'Feeling here is of course very bad. . . I doubt if at the present moment it would be possible for me to address a public meeting in the country'; MacDonald to Simons, September 1914, MacDonald Papers, PRO/30/69/5/98.

railway workers to request special intervention by the Government to prevent futher spontaneous volunteering.[3] The British working class, therefore, would appear to have been as deeply stirred by the patriotic emotions of August 1914 as the men from the middle and upper classes.

The power of the patriotic ideal in August 1914 is clearly the decisive factor in explaining the reaction of the British working class to the crisis. However, one must also concede that the peace campaign mounted by the labour movement had suffered from certain weaknesses, and, in order to fill out any explanation of the victory of war over peace in August 1914, these weaknesses need to be examined and accounted for. Four specific problems stand out most prominently: first, a lack of involvement in the peace campaign on the part of the trade union movement; second, the emergence of differences of opinion within the movement itself over arms limitation; third, the failure to achieve close rapport with the German socialists; and fourth, the movement's inability to devise a plan to mobilize its forces *quickly* to protest against an imminent war.

The most crucial of these weaknesses was certainly the lack of involvement in the peace campaign on the part of the trade unions. Throughout this study the differences between the socialists and the trade unionists in their approaches to the general problems of peace and war have been stressed. It was not that the socialists and trade unionists quarrelled over these issues; rather, it was simply that the trade unionists took only a passing interest in them and found themselves quite unable to empathise with the passionate anti-militarism of the socialists. In spite of the influence exercised by the socialists of the ILP within the Labour Party, they failed to instil a detestation of militarism amongst the great mass of the trade unionists. Looking back over the pre-war campaign, Ramsay MacDonald observed that:

Our feebleness consisted in the fact that Great Britain was asleep in foreign affairs. Our insular position has had the effect of cutting us off from Continental affairs. Our people are indifferent to Foreign Office transactions. . . The result has been that we never have been able to get up popular interest in foreign policies, and when the war broke out the

[3] P. S. Bagwell, *The Railwaymen* (London, 1963), chapter on First World War.

minds of our people were quite unprepared to consider why we were involved.[4]

How is this record of indifference to be explained? No doubt MacDonald was correct in referring to Britain's geographical insularity as a fundamental factor. In addition, as noted previously, the growing awareness that Britain's industrial and commercial might was under serious challenge from foreign competitors from the 1890s onward, an awareness reflected even in trade union journals, provided an inhospitable atmosphere for the growth of internationalist sentiment among British workers. Also, as we have seen, the socialists' decision not to seek active participation on the part of the union movement and the LRC in the campaign against the Boer War probably set a poor precedent for the later campaigns. The unionists were used to seeing and quite ready to accept the socialists making the running on the issues of peace and war. In the years that followed, only on rare occasions, such as at the time of the Tsar's visit to Britain in 1909, did the leaders of the Labour Party take full advantage of the party's close links with the unions to invite the various trades councils and unions to undertake agitation. Perhaps this was because the Labour Party leaders had learned to recognize the limits of the trade unions' interests, as displayed at the time of the agitation over the Haldane army reforms when the union movement had reacted without any enthusiasm to the socialists' warnings of imminent conscription. Nevertheless, it is true to say that on both sides there was some tacit acceptance of the idea that the issues of peace and war were more the business of the socialist politicians than the practically minded trade unionists. Finally, the gradual estrangement of the British trade unions from the Second International also contributed to the insularity of the unions. It is true that among British trade unions there had long been a measure of suspicion regarding the fiery marxist demagogues on the Continent. For instance, at the first ILP Conference in 1893, even Ben Tillett, who was by no means a moderate trade unionist, gave full expression to these doubts:

[4] MacDonald to H. W. Laidler, 3 November 1914, MacDonald Papers, PRO/30/69/5/24.

With his experience of unions he was glad to say that if there were fifty such red revolutionary parties as there were in Germany, he would sooner have the solid, matter-of-fact, fighting trades unionism of England than all the hare-brained chatterers and magpies of Continental revolutionists.[5]

However, in spite of these very English prejudices against 'gesticulating foreigners', it was the International itself that was most responsible for the continuing alienation of the British trade unions from that organization. As we have seen, the new rules of admission created at the Paris Congress in 1900 and the campaign against revisionism which reached its climax at the Amsterdam Congress in 1904 seemed to signify that only marxist socialists were welcome at the congresses of the International. In Britain the marxists of the SDF did their best to reinforce this impression, and they protested loudly against even the Labour Party's right to membership of the ISB. At one point Quelch observed that the Labour Party's claim to be represented at the International was as silly as 'the National Secular Society to claim to be represented at a Church Congress'.[6] In the face of this kind of derision, the trade unionists' dwindling interest in the International was no surprise. The socialists of the ILP tried hard to reverse this process, even suggesting an alteration to the rules of admission so as to encourage British trade union membership, but without success.

The lack of trade union interest and involvement in the International, and in particular the decision of the TUC Parliamentary Committee in 1905 to have nothing to do with the BNC, deprived the British connection with the International of credibility and strength. The existence of the BNC, and the British representation at the periodic ISB meetings and International Congresses, still provided the appearance of a consultative machinery binding together the British working class and the Socialist International. However, without the active support of the trade unions in this process, the sentiment of socialist solidarity that was so often invoked was sentiment without power. The International required much more than the mere appearance of

---

[5] *ILP Annual Conference*, 1893, p. 3.
[6] *Justice*, 19 October 1907.

socialist solidarity if it was to make good its claim to be the guardian of peace.

The second important weakness in the labour movement's peace campaign was the emergence of serious differences of opinion within the movement on several important aspects of the campaign, most notably, on the issue of arms limitation. The most obvious and embarrassing sign of the divisions within the labour movement on this issue was the persistent rebellion of a number of Labour Party MPs during the military estimates debates. As this study has shown, when naval expenditure was voted upon in the House of Commons each year between 1906 and 1914, on no single occasion did the ranks of the Labour Party remain unbroken. A small number of Labour Party MPs steadfastly refused to support amendments calling for reductions in arms spending so long as the urgent problems of unemployment were ignored by the Government. As the Labour Party leaders hastened to point out, the number of Labour Party MPs demonstrably defying the party's official view on arms limitation was very small. Nevertheless, this claim was balanced by the fact that the number of absentees from the Labour Party benches during these divisions on armaments expenditure was always very high.

The quarrels within the socialist camp also added to the difficulties of the labour movement as a whole in presenting a confident and united face on these issues. The attitudes of Hyndman and Quelch on the 'German menace', their conversion to the 'big Navy' viewpoint in 1910, and also Blatchford's spectacular descent into the most exaggerated invasion scare rhetoric in his celebrated articles in the *Daily Mail* in December 1909, did much to undermine the credibility of the socialists' leadership in the peace campaign. With such well-known socialists as Hyndman and Blatchford proclaiming their belief in the 'German menace' and openly discarding any faith in the ability of German socialism to contain the imminent threat, it was made doubly difficult for the socialists of the ILP and Hyndman's opponents in the SDP to foster, even amongst their own people, an unquestioning faith in working-class solidarity above and beyond nationalist loyalties.

The significance of these differences of opinion within the

labour movement should not be exaggerated. In the first place, the trade unions' different attitudes to the issues of peace and war were not manifest in any open breach with the Labour Party or the socialists of the ILP. The trade unions simply allowed the campaigns against war and armaments to pass them by. Similarly, the defections from the Labour Party benches in the House of Commons on military expenditure did not lead to serious public quarrels. These defections were easily dismissed as being only minor rebellions which could be explained in terms of the special circumstances in certain constituencies. The Labour Party Conference could always be relied upon to restore the impression that the party was firmly on the side of peace and arms limitation. The discussion created by Hyndman, Quelch, and Blatchford was certainly more public in nature. Even so, because of their estrangement from both the Labour Party and the union movement, none of these socialists could pretend to speak from a position of authority. The various quarrels, therefore, did not seriously compromise the position of the labour movement as a whole. As long as neither the leaders of the Labour Party nor the leaders of the TUC were ever seen to repudiate their fundamental faith in international reconciliation and arms limitation, the labour movement retained its anti-war image in the eyes of the British public. Privately, however, the quarrels and defections, and especially the trade unions' tendency to shy away from the anti-war campaign, must have sapped the confidence of those socialists who hoped to dissipate the great cloud of indifference and mobilize the whole of the labour movement in a genuine mass campaign against the danger of war. How could they do it if even their own parliamentary colleagues and Britain's own marxist luminaries were unconvinced?

A third weakness for the labour movement in waging its peace campaign was the difficulty experienced in establishing good relations with the German socialists. The socialists of the ILP, and Labour speakers in general, were always keen to emphasize the power of German socialism and its ability to safeguard the peace in Europe.[7] After the SPD's election

---

[7] For a typical statement see *LL*, 15 December 1911.

victories in January 1912 the ILP urged the British people to trust the German socialists to contain militarism in Germany.[8] While British Labour Party leaders sounded extremely confident on this matter in public, in private they harboured certain doubts about their German comrades. As this study has shown, the trade unionists and the ILP socialists always found it difficult to overcome the ideological differences between themselves and the marxist leaders of the SPD. Mutual suspicions developed, and these occasionally blossomed into serious quarrels, as in the case of the badly mismanaged Labour Party delegation's visit to Germany in 1909. In addition to the tension over ideology, the German socialists' reluctance to agree to the calling together of the ISB during the Moroccan crisis of 1905 and 1911 disturbed the confidence of the British socialist leaders in the legendary internationalism of the SPD. The attitude of the Germans also caused Hardie difficulties in his advocacy of an anti-war strike in the period 1910 to 1914. He always found his arguments undermined by the fact that the Germans had already made clear their opposition to any anti-war strike commitment. He could assure his critics in Britain that the SPD was a powerful and anti-militarist force in Germany; but he was never able to say that the German socialists were in favour of the anti-war strike proposal.[9] As we have seen, the evidence on British participation in international trade unionism indicates that some tension with the Germans developed here also. In this atmosphere of mutual suspicion

[8] See editorial, *LL*, 12 January 1912 and *Socialist Review*, March 1912, pp. 11–12. See also Hardie's statement during the debate on the National Service (Territorial Forces) Bill in April 1913: 'We think of the 4,500,000 of socialist voters in Germany, every man of whom is opposed to militarism and jingoism'; *Hansard*, V: 51: 1592.

[9] There are some signs of Hardie's impatience with the German socialists on account of their opposition to the general strike and their growing moderation after 1910. In a series of articles on revisionism in Germany in the *Labour Leader* in 1910 Hardie noted that reformism had become 'the accepted policy' of the SPD and he claimed that the British Labour Party was a more generally proletarian party than the SPD, for 'many of the votes cast for Social Democrat candidates in Germany at present are simply those of discontented Liberals'; *LL*, 21 October 1910. After attending the SPD Congress in September 1913 he expressed his surprise at the moderation of the SPD's response to Rosa Luxemburg's suggestion of using the general strike to achieve franchise reform; *LL*, 18 September 1913.

it was difficult for the leaders of the labour and socialist movement in both countries to reassure their peoples that chauvinism could find no foothold with the working people and that German and British working-class organizations were united by bonds of mutual trust. In their hearts the leaders of the organized working-class movements on both sides of the North Sea knew that the trust existing between the two movements was, in reality, rather fragile.[10]

On both sides this particular problem produced real anxieties of profound intensity. The expected course for socialists to follow in both nations was for them to criticize the war-mongering and aggressive designs of their own government while trying to see the 'enemy' in the best possible light, thus playing down the danger from abroad and preaching reconciliation. The supposed devilish expansionism of the foreign enemy could then be exposed as a mere bogey. However, the logical impossibility of socialists in both Britain and Germany maintaining these positions was obvious. Socialists in Britain could always attack the British Government's naval build-up as an unnecessary and inexcusable provocation to Germany, but, at the same time, the German socialists were condemning their Government's naval plans as aggressive and expansionist and excusing the British naval build-up as a regrettable response. Accordingly, socialist parliamentarians in Britain were sometimes harangued by Conservative speakers gleefully citing long quotations from German socialists about the diabolical plans of the German Government for naval supremacy and world domination. Conversely, conservative Germans could point to British socialists' condemnations of British armaments and foreign policies to justify German armament responses. Worse still, in the traditional situation of diplomatic secrecy and stage-managed releases of information at moments of international crisis, both German and British socialists often found themselves fumbling about in the dark quite genuinely unaware of which government was being aggressive and which conciliatory. Thus we find Bernstein writing to MacDonald

[10] See George Lansbury, *My Life* (London, 1928), p. 206, where he notes that, in 1914, there was amongst some members of the Labour Party a 'personal hatred' of some leading figures in the SPD.

on Bebel's behalf in an attempt to discover exactly what did happen between Grey and the German ambassador in London during the Moroccan crisis of 1911! Bebel in particular appears to have suffered tremendous anxieties over the correctness of the socialists' course. Firmly convinced that the deepening domestic crisis inside Germany would prompt her rulers to attempt a major European war, Bebel gradually came to the view that, most probably, it was only the likelihood of British intervention on behalf of France and Russia which limited the aggressions of the Prussian ruling circle. In this sense he began to see that the campaigns of his socialist colleagues in Britain against entangling alliances and British naval expansion were far more likely to invite war than to avert it, were those campaigns ever to succeed. British neutrality, the British socialists' aim, was Bebel's (and Hyndman's) nightmare.[11] And, as Fritz Fischer's work makes clear, Bebel was quite correct in his estimate that Germany's rulers were earnestly in quest of British neutrality so as to facilitate European war. In such a situation of confusions and inconsistencies, inadequate information and misleading information, public confidence but private doubt, it is hardly surprising that socialists on either side of the North Sea found each other equivocal, hesitant, and, at times, downright evasive.

Finally, the history of the last days of peace in Britain underlines how devastating to the socialists' peace plans was the speed of the crisis in August 1914. The search for 'secret chauvinists' and 'naïve dreamers' has tended to obscure the crucial importance of this factor in the collapse of the International. As was stressed previously, the International's strategy rested on mass demonstrations during a protracted crisis so as to forestall any premature mobilization or declaration of war. In rejecting the schemes of Nieuwenhuis and then Hervé, the International had long abandoned any thought of action after the outbreak of war. As was noted above, the new emphasis placed by Hardie and Jaurès on an anti-war strike prior to any outbreak of conflict marked their acceptance of this position. It was crucial therefore, to

[11] See R. J. Crampton, 'August Bebel and the British Foreign Office', *History*, Vol. 58 (June 1973).

organize a massive series of demonstrations quickly, and certainly before mobilization. Previous experience had shown that the socialists were unable to make arrangements for continuing demonstrations on a mass scale in anything less than two to three weeks. When the European rulers brought about a major war in the space of a single weekend, the International's strategy became a dead letter almost overnight. In an impatient moment during the ISB meeting on 29 July, Vandervelde had revealed his worries in this regard by commenting, 'If it would take the powers as long to organize the war as it takes us to organize the war on war we could sleep in peace'.[12] Certainly, none of the socialists at the last ISB meeting suspected that a European war was imminent, but it does not follow that 'they had been more deceived than the rest of the world'.[13] As Robert Smillie, miners' leader and a foremost ILP member, colourfully explained in mid-August:

With a speed unknown in the past history of the world the war dogs were let loose, and within a few days the fiat had gone forth, and five front rank nations were at war. So rapidly did events follow each other that all the forces which usually make for peace were paralysed. The socialist and trade union movements in the various countries did not even have time to protest by demonstrations against the iniquity of the threatened holocaust, until declarations of war were being hurled from capital to capital, and the war drums were throbbing and the battle flags were being unfurled.[14]

To dwell upon the inadequacies of the anti-war agitation would give an unbalanced picture. What then were the achievements of the agitation? It is easy to be cynical, for any minor successes were, of course, quite overshadowed by the spectacular failure of the peace campaign to achieve its most cherished purpose, the avoidance of a great European war. Moreover, it is difficult to find any definite evidence to suggest that the British Government of the day ever reversed its policies with regard to foreign policy or defence matters because of the peace agitation of the labour

[12] 'Official Record of the ISB session held at Brussels on 29–30 July 1914', in Haupt, *Socialism and the Great War*, p. 257.
[13] Ibid., p. 215.
[14] *LL*, 20 August 1914.

movement. The crusade against the Boer War between 1899 and 1902 cannot be said to have caused any change in the Government's inflexible determination to see the conflict through to a successful military conclusion. The Labour Party MPs in the Commons did give assistance to the Radicals in their anti-armaments agitation between 1906 and 1914, and thus they increased the pressure on the Government with regard to this issue; but, once again, it is impossible to quantify any moderating influence on the Government's armaments programme. Similarly, the labour movement's various campaigns against militarism in the years 1906 to 1914 had no discernible effect on government policies: the Government persisted with the Haldane army reforms in 1907 without any regard to the Labour Party's opposition; and the pro-Russian and pro-French direction of foreign policy under Sir Edward Grey was maintained without any significant deviation. While government ministers seemed, therefore, to continue the broad thrust of their policies quite undeterred by the agitation of the labour movement or their own party's Radicals, there was some impact on the fringes of government policy. For instance, the Government seemed to shy away from the introduction of rifle-training in schools in 1907 following the protests of the vigilant Radical and Labour Party MPs. Similarly, the Russian Government's decision to cancel the proposed visit of British warships to the Baltic in 1906 probably resulted from the opposition voiced by Grey's critics in the House of Commons, including the Labour MPs Hardie and O'Grady. More generally, the sporadic protests of the labour movement and the presence of Labour MPs in the Commons added to the significance of the 'economist' wing of the Liberal Party which, notwithstanding its declining strength, could not be ignored by the Government.

By far the most important issue here is whether or not the labour movement's constant proclamations against war and militarism had some small sobering effect on those who guided the nation's foreign and defence policies during the various crises of the two pre-war decades. Were doubts about the people's supposedly uncritical loyalty created in the minds of those who had the power to choose between peace and war? In other words, did the campaign in any way 'keep the peace'? Unfortunately, it is impossible to find hard evidence on this intriguing problem. The most that can be said is that the possibility of some moderating influence cannot be ruled out. Certainly Sir Edward Grey was constantly aware of his critics' charge that he was provocatively anti-German and he acknowledged that this did affect his conduct of foreign policy.[15] MacDonald did his best to convince those in power of the importance of this issue. According to MacDonald, he refused a personal invitation to join the Liberal Cabinet in 1914 in a deal which would have brought the Labour Party into a formal alliance with the Liberals, and he gave as one important reason for his refusal his opposition to Grey.[16] From his perspective, Grey could hardly ignore the opinions of those like MacDonald who claimed to represent working-class opinion, for Grey had always acknowledged that British Governments could not contemplate intervention in any European dispute unless 'public opinion' supported such a move.[17] Of course, it was open to Grey to make his own estimate of how accurately MacDonald's opinions reflected those of the ordinary working man, and no doubt Grey and his com-

[15] Grey, *Twenty Five Years*, Vol. 1, p. 225.

[16] MacDonald to E. D. Morel, 24 September 1914, Morel Papers, F 8, LSE. Evidence shows that MacDonald was involved in negotiations with the Liberals over a possible alliance on several occasions between 1910 and 1914; see MacDonald Papers, PRO, notes for 22 October 1911, 8/3, Josiah Wedgwood to J. R. M., 12 June 1913, 5/23, Lloyd George to JRM, 3 March 1914, 5/24 and summary of the issue in Marquand, *MacDonald*, pp. 142–3 and 159–61. The Liberals' offers in 1914 probably included the promise of a Cabinet post for MacDonald. In the light of MacDonald's unwavering criticism of Grey's foreign policy in the House, and in the press from 1907 onwards, there seems no reason to doubt MacDonald's claim that, in the 1914 negotiations, he cited his opposition to 'Grey's policy' as one of the 'many obstacles' to his joining a Liberal Cabinet. Of course, this is not to claim that the negotiations foundered on this specific issue. More than likely the sensitivity of the ILP to the 'independence' of the Labour Party was an important consideration. Nevertheless, it seems perfectly plausible that, in the negotiations, MacDonald did draw to the Liberals' attention his own deeply felt opposition to Grey's direction of foreign policy, as he claimed in his letter to Morel.

[17] *Hansard*, 27 November 1911, V: 32: 58–9: 'No British government could embark upon a war without public opinion behind it... support we would give France and Russia would depend entirely on the feeling of parliament and public feeling'.

panions were comforted by the thought that MacDonald and other internationalists like him were exceptional in the labour movement. Still, in assessing 'public opinion', the Government had to take account of the apparent radicalism of large numbers of trade unionists in the period 1911 to 1913. Certainly we know that Asquith and Lloyd George, and perhaps the King also, were most perturbed by the coincidence of the railway strike in August 1911 with the Moroccan crisis.[18] Moreover, it seems that Lloyd George's insistence that the railway stoppage might render Britain incapable of military response to the crisis may have proved the decisive argument in his successful negotiations with the railway companies to settle the dispute.[19] It seems likely also that the Government's determination to use troops and police against the strikers, 'all the forces of the Crown' in Asquith's phrase, was linked with this sense of alarm over the paralysis of the nation's transport at a time of military emergency.[20] It is significant too that the Government's first determined moves against anti-militarism came soon after, early in 1912, with the prosecution of Tom Mann and Guy Bowman over their *Don't Shoot* pamphlet, an attempt to undermine the discipline of soldiers engaged in putting down industrial unrest.[21] If Keir Hardie was correct in his information in 1912 that the Government was organizing for the training of soldiers to run the railways, then clearly the threat of the anti-war strike was being viewed by the Government with serious concern. There is good evidence to show that the German and French Governments took seriously enough the warnings of working-class action against war in their countries to use police spies to monitor carefully the attitude of the labour movement on this question.[22] It is possible that the British Government took a similar interest in the attitudes of the British labour movement on the issues of peace and war, although no police records

[18]   Roy Jenkins, *Asquith* (London, 1969), pp. 233–5.
[19]   Peter Rowland, *Lloyd George* (London, 1975), p. 253
[20]   Jenkins, *Asquith*, p. 234.
[21]   Bob Holton, *British Syndicalism 1900–1914* (London, 1976), p. 115.
[22]   Georges Haupt notes the activity of police spies in the SPD and the SFIO; see his *Socialism and the Great War*, pp. 237 and 242.

apparently exist.[23] What is clear is that many of those established figures most closely connected with the campaigns to inculcate ultra-patriotism, militarism, love of Empire, and fear of Germany, men like Lord Roberts, Lord Esher, Lord Meath, Baden-Powell, and Lord Northcliffe, quite openly proclaimed their intention that their message should serve as an antidote to the pernicious influence of socialism in Britain.[24] Obviously then there was an awareness of the labour movement's internationalist campaign in high places. Whether this agitation had any impact in moderating 'hawkish' attitudes, however, is impossible to ascertain.

The most important effects of the pre-war peace campaign were only to be realized in the future. Only the supremely tragic experiences of the war itself were sufficient to create the widespread support for internationalist idealism within the labour movement which all the anti-war rhetoric of Hardie and his supporters in the Edwardian years had failed to create. But their efforts were not negligible on that account. For it was the participation in the extended pre-war crusade against Grey's foreign policy and the spiral of armaments which gave to some of the leading British socialists of the inter-war years an unshakeable faith in the correctness of their own internationalist outlook. Such figures as MacDonald, Lansbury, Jowett, Snowden, and Herbert Morrison firmly believed that they had seen the danger of war before 1914, had warned in vain against the policies that produced it, and they now felt completely justified by events. These were the leaders who helped to keep alive the ideals of internationalism amidst the traumas of public censure during the Great War, and, at the war's end, they set about making those ideals the guiding principles of the move-

[23] Bob Holton, *British Syndicalism 1900–1914* (London, 1976) has used police reports to the Home Office to uncover the Government's concern over the activities of syndicalists. It is not, therefore, inconceivable that the police also kept watch over the ILP and the SDF and reported to the Government on their anti-militarist activities, especially after 1910 when Hardie became a strong advocate of the anti-war strike. However, in response to my inquiries, the Assistant Departmental Records Officer at New Scotland Yard has assured me that no police files exist on the ILP, SDF, or leading individuals in the peace campaign.
[24] D. J. Newton, 'The Promotion of Militarism and the Origins of the First World War: Some Evidence from Britain', *Teaching History*, January 1982.

ment as a whole. Although the Labour Party failed to make a determined stand against the Versailles Treaty, by the mid 1920s the internationalist outlook had become the conventional wisdom of the British labour movement. In the foreign policy of the first Labour Government of 1924, firmly controlled by Ramsay MacDonald as Prime Minister and Foreign Secretary, one could trace the same faith in international reconciliation as had been proclaimed by the ILP in the Edwardian period.[25] Even Keir Hardie's 'weapon of the future', the anti-war strike, had a brief moment of glory. In August 1920 the Labour Party and the trade union leaders acted together to warn the Government that any attempt to intervene militarily in the war between Poland and the Soviet Union would be met by a general strike. The threat was seriously meant and may have proved decisive in preventing British involvement in the war.[26] In this incident, just five years after Keir Hardie's death, the leaders of the British labour movement, union leaders as well as party leaders, were united in their determination to enforce peace and were making specific preparations for a general strike to do it. Thus, the most important effect of the pre-war peace campaign was to implant powerful internationalist instincts within the labour tradition: a belief in the brotherhood of working peoples, a determination to seek reconciliation with presumed enemies, a suspicion of entanglement through alliance systems, an awareness that the appeal to simplistic patriotism can be a snare, a distrust of those sabre-rattlers who seek to use international tension as a means of forging social control at home, suspicion of the élitist military spirit that seeks to extinguish the conscience of the soldier, and a sense of deep resentment over the enormous sums that are spent in perfecting the means of destroying life. These guiding instincts, which can be seen in the policies of the Labour Party even into the 1980s, still reflect the work of the Edwardian socialists.

---

[25] David Marquand, *Ramsay MacDonald*, ch. 15.
[26] Rowland, *Lloyd George*, p. 526.

Select Bibliography

I. ARCHIVAL SOURCES

Note on archives. The so-called Huysmans Archives, the archives used by Professor Georges Haupt in his *Socialism and the Great War* (Oxford, 1972), are now housed at the Archief en Museum voor het Vlaams Cultuurleven, Antwerp. Unfortunately, access to these archives is not granted.

At the International Institute for Social History (IISG), Amsterdam:
> Karl Kautsky Archive
> August Bebel Archive
> Eduard Bernstein Archive
> Jules Guesde Archive
> Kleine Korrespondenz (mainly letters to Bruno Karpeles)
> SDAP (Dutch Labour Party) Archives

At Transport House, Smith Square, London:
> Minutes of the National Executive Committee of the Labour Party (including LRC Executive Committee minutes, 1900–6)
> Minutes of the British National Committee (British Section of the International) 1905–14
> Labour Party: General Correspondence, 1906–7
> Labour Party: Subject Files, Vol. 1: International Socialist Bureau 1908–9, and 1911–14

At the London School of Economics:
> Minutes of the National Administrative Council of the Independent Labour Party
> Herbert Burrows Collection
> Minutes of the National Peace Council, 1908–14

At Congress House:
> Minutes of the Parliamentary Committee of the Trade Union Congress

At Modern Records Centre, University of Warwick:
> International Transport-Workers' Federation: Correspondence 1903–14
> Minutes of the Political Committee of the London Society of Compositors, 1909–14

At the National Library of Scotland, Edinburgh:
> Minutes of the Parliamentary Committee of the Scottish Trade Union Congress

At Aberdeen University Library, King's College, Aberdeen:
> Minutes of the Aberdeen Trades Council

At Birmingham Municipal Library:
Minutes of the Birmingham Trades Council

At the National Library of Scotland, Edinburgh:
Minutes of the Edinburgh Trades Council

At the Mitchell Library, Glasgow:
Minutes of the Glasgow Trades Council

At the Huddersfield Public Library:
Minutes of the Huddersfield Trades Council

At the Leeds Central Archives:
Minutes of the Leeds Trades Council

At the Nottingham University Library:
Minutes of the Nottingham Trades Council

At the Sheffield Central Library:
Minutes of the Sheffield Trades and Labour Council

On Microfilm:
Archives of the Independent Labour Party: Francis Johnson Correspondence, 1896–1908 (published by Harvester Microfilm, 1980)
Minutes of the London Trades Council

II. PRIVATE PAPERS

At the Public Record Office:
James Ramsay MacDonald Papers

At the Sydney Jones Library, Liverpool:
James Bruce Glasier Papers

At the Central Library, Manchester:
Robert Blatchford Papers

At the London School of Economics:
George Lansbury Papers
Herbert Bryan Papers
E. D. Morel Papers

III. PRINTED DOCUMENTARY SOURCES AND UNION JOURNALS

Congrès International Ouvrier Socialiste tenu à Bruxelles du 16 au 23 Août 1891 (Bruxelles, 1893); now published with associated documents as Volume 8 of *Histoire de la IIe Internationale* (Geneva, 1977)

Protokoll des Internationalen Sozealistischen Arbeiterkongress, Zurich, vom 6. bis 12. August 1893 (Zurich, 1894); now published with associated documents as Vol. 9 of *Histoire de la IIe Internationale* (Geneva, 1977)

International Socialist Workers' and Trade Union Congress, London 1896: Report of Proceedings (London, n.d.)

Sixième Congrès Socialiste International, tenu à Amsterdam du 14 au 20 Août 1904: Compte Rendu Analytique (Bruxelles, 1904)

Septième Congrès Socialiste International, tenu à Stuttgart du 18 au 24 Août 1907: Compte Rendu Analytique (Bruxelles, 1908)

Proposals and Drafts of Resolutions submitted to the International Socialist Congress of Stuttgart, 18–24 August 1907 (Brussels, 1908)

Huitième Congrès Socialiste International, tenu à Copenhague du 28 Août au 3 Septembre, 1910: Compte Rendu Analytique (Gand, 1911)

Congrès Socialiste International Extraordinaire, tenu à Basle, les 24 et 25 Novembre 1912, published as *Bulletin Périodique du Bureau Socialiste International*, no. 10 (Bruxelles, 1912)

Bulletin Périodique du Bureau Socialiste International, 1909–13, now published as Vol. 23 of *Histoire de la II*e *Internationale* (Geneva, 1979)

On Microfilm:
    Labour Party, *Reports of the Annual Conference*
    Independent Labour Party, *Annual Conference Reports*

At the Marx Memorial Library, Clerkenwell
    Social Democratic Federation (Party) *Annual Conference Reports*
    British Socialist Party, *Annual Conference Reports*

At the British Library
    Trade Union Congress, *Reports of the Annual Congress*

At Congress House:
    International Metal Workers' Federation, *Reports of the Annual Congress*, 1896, 1900, 1904, 1907, 1910, 1913
    International Transport Federation, *Reports of the Annual Congress*, 1908 and 1910
    TUC Parliamentary Committee, *Quarterly Reports*

At the Modern Records Centre, University of Warwick:
    Amalgamated Society of Carpenters and Joiners, *General Council Minutes*
    Amalgamated Society of Railway Servants, *Reports and Proceedings*
    ——, *Executive Committee Decisions*
    British Steel Smelters, *Monthly Reports*
    Dock, Wharf, Riverside and General Workers' Union, *Annual Reports*
    ——, *Dockers' Record*
    Friendly Society of Iron Moulders/Iron Founders, *Executive Committee Minutes*
    ——, *Annual Reports*
    ——, *Centenary Souvenir*, 1909
    London Society of Compositors, *Executive Minutes*
    ——, *Annual Reports*
    ——, *Trade Reports*
    National Transport Workers' Federation, *Annual and Special Council Meetings: Printed Reports*

National Union of Teachers, *Conference Agenda and Minutes*
Operative Bricklayers' Society, *Minutes of Proceedings* of the *Annual Moveable General Council*
Operative Stonemasons' Society, *Journal*
The Workers' Union, *Annual Reports*

At the London School of Economics:
Amalgamated Society of Engineers, *Journal*
National Union of Boot and Shoe Operatives, *Monthly Journal*
Amalgamated Society of Carpenters and Joiners, *Monthly Journal*

At the National Union of Mineworkers, St. James's House, Sheffield:
Miners' Federation of Great Britain, *Annual Proceedings* (each volume includes Executive Committee Minutes, Reports of the Annual Conference, and Reports of the International Miners' Federation)

At the National Union of Railwaymen, 'Unity House':
Railway Review

At the National Union of Teachers, 'Hamilton House':
Annual Reports
The Schoolmaster

At the Union of Post Office Workers, 'U. P. W. House':
The Post
Postmen's Gazette
Postal Clerks' Herald

Annual Reports of Trades Councils:

At Congress House:

The following Annual Reports of trades councils:
Accrington 1905; Barnsley 1907; Bath 1906; Battersea 1905; Birkenhead 1909; Bolton 1892, 1893, 1897, 1914; Bradford 1911, 1912, 1914—16; Bury 1906; Camberwell 1914; Carlisle 1905, 1907, 1910, and 1914; Chatham 1908—9; Chester 1908—9; Chorley 1911; Coventry 1913; Crewe 1906; Croydon 1903—5; Doncaster 1906; Exeter 1905—6; Gorton 1906; Grimsby 1905—6; Huddersfield 1911—16; Hyde 1905; Kettering 1906, 1909; Leicester 1892, 1893, 1896, 1898, and *Year Books* 1910—14; Liverpool 1902, 1904—5, 1910, 1914; Mexborough 1905; Northampton 1900—14; Oldham 1904, 1906, 1914; Portsmouth 1912, 1914; Radcliffe 1906, 1908—9; Reading 1909; Retford 1912; Rochdale 1907; Rotherham 1906, 1914; Shoreditch 1907; Southampton 1906—7; Southport 1905, 1906; Sunderland 1909; Warrington 1902, 1904; Wolverhampton, *Year Book* 1913; Woolwich 1914.

At the London School of Economics:

The following Annual Reports of trades councils:
Ashton-under-Lyne 1890—1, 1899, 1902, 1903, 1905; Barrow-in-Furness 1894—6, 1897—8, 1900—2; Birmingham 1899, 1901, 1907, 1909, 1913—14; Blackburn 1891—2, 1896—8, 1904—5; Bolton 1892, 1893, 1895—7; Bradford, *Year Books*, 1899, 1901—2, 1905,

1908, 1914; Bury 1891, 1893–4, 1899; Cardiff 1886–92; Chorley 1903–5; Coventry 1890–1; 1893–4, 1913; Darwen 1894, 1896, 1898–9, 1903–4; Deptford 1900, 1902, 1912; Derby 1891, 1892, 1896–9, 1901–6; Dundee 1890, 1891, 1893–7, 1900–1, 1904; Exeter 1890–4; Fulham 1902–4; Glasgow 1889–2, 1894–1901, 1903–5; Greenock 1894–6, 1899; Grimsby 1899; Haslington 1896, 1898–1901, 1903–4; Huddersfield 1890, 1904–5; Hull 1890–2, 1900; Leeds 1899, 1900, 1904–6, 1908–9; Leicester 1891, 1893–4, 1896, 1898–9; Liverpool 1891–6, 1899, 1901–6; London 1890–4, 1896–1902, 1904–5; Newcastle-on-Tyne 1889–90, 1897–8, 1900–1, 1902–3; Northampton 1900, 1902, 1903–4; Nottingham 1891–3, 1895–7, 1898–1901, 1903–5, 1914; Sheffield 1890–2, 1894–7, 1903–4; Southampton 1894, 1902, 1907; Stockton 1893, 1895, 1897, 1903, 1913; Sunderland 1890–2, 1903–4; Warrington 1889–94.

Collections of Documents

Ensor, R. C. K. (ed.), *Modern Socialism* (London, 1907)

Grunberg, Carl (ed.), *Die Internationale und der Weltkrieg* (Leipzig, 1916), now published within Vol. 3 of *Histoire de la IIe Internationale* (Geneva, 1976)

Haupt, Georges (ed.), *Bureau Socialiste International: Comptes Rendus des Réunions, Manifestes et Circulaires, Vol. 1, 1900–1907* (Paris, 1969)

Haupt, Georges (ed.), *Correspondance entre Lenine et Camille Huysmans, 1905–1914* (Paris, 1963)

Schroeder, Wilhelm, *Hanbuch der Sozialdemokratischen Parteitage von 1863 bis 1909*, 2 vols. (Munchen, 1910)

Walling, William English (ed.), *The Socialists and the War* (New York, 1915)

IV. NEWSPAPERS AND JOURNALS

The Daily Citizen
Fabian News
Herald of Peace
ILP News
Justice
The Labour Leader
The Social Democrat (from 1912, *The British Socialist*)
The Socialist Review

V. OFFICIAL PUBLICATIONS

Hansard, *Parliamentary Debates*, Fourth and Fifth Series

Index